# Still Ramblin'

# Still Ramblin'

## THE LIFE AND TIMES
## OF JIM BEATTY

To Jim Buckman
Thanks for being my
friend for 50 years!
Best Regards,
Jim Beatty
12/17/17

*Jim Beatty*

ISBN: 1542448972
ISBN 13: 9781542448970

# Contents

$\backsim$

# Dedication

*The true hero of this book is my wife, Pauline, whose unconditional love and support for 54 of the 83 years this book covers, has helped guide me through this sometimes complicated but wonderful musical journey.*

*On our hundreds of performances and tours, Pauline made all the travel arrangements, including airplane, train and bus transportation coast to coast in the United States and countries all over the world. In all these years we never were late or missed an engagement and when we arrived for an event I could tell the fans were happy to see that Pauline was with me. It's impossible for me to list all her behind the scene duties, all I can say is that she was on call 24/7. Wild Bill Davison's wife, Anne, was in the same situation as Pauline and she often said: "No greater fan or critic hath a musician than his wife" And that's the truth!*

*After finishing this musical tale you are about to read I think you will agree with me, that above anyone else, Pauline deserves the "Congressional Medal of Honor." Thank you Pauline! You are my "stranger no more".*

# Prologue

HEY JIM! YOU OUGHT TO write a book! I can't count the many times I heard that said to me over the years. I never gave such a thing serious thoughts because I was so damn busy traveling the world playing my music and of course adding more adventures and stories to the ones I had already been telling. And for some reason or another the stories kept adding up. Some of them were hilarious and some bizarre, but most of them were interesting to whoever was listening.

After setting aside the urgings to put my tales on paper, that all changed on July 4th of 2014 when my wife, Pauline, and I attended a neighborhood Fourth of July party. It was an annual party where all the neighbors showed up with delicious dishes and a bottle or two of red or white wine. This affair was hosted by Jody Carson and John Klatt, who lived in the neighborhood. All the homes in our neighborhood were old because it was deemed an historic neighborhood and the homes had to be preserved as they were built. If you did build a new home it had to look dated, at least from the outside. It was always a fun party when John had his barbecue grill going for anyone who wanted to bring their favorite meats to be cooked. John also saved his Christmas tree and set it ablaze when it turned dark, a beautiful sight, even though it just lasted a few seconds. One year I think John might have got into the wine a little more than usual and he had a bigger fire in the barbecue than he did with the blazing Christmas tree.

Over a glass of wine, I struck up a conversation with a familiar face in the neighborhood by the name of Mike Bays. Mike and his wife, Diane, lived just a few blocks away from us in a rather large house to accommodate their four children. Mike was a retired executive of the Portland VA Hospital but started another career cooking ribs at different events around the area, and believe me those ribs were to die for as they fell right off the bone.

So with the background of the aromas of steaks, chops, burgers and hot dogs cooking away, Mike Bays and I started talking. He was the kind of guy I liked to have a conversation with because he not only was a good talker but was an equally good listener. So, oblivious to all the neighbors around us we just kept chatting until John's Christmas tree was ablaze and the fireworks started exploding over the Willamette River.

I found through our conversation that Mike and I had something in common and that was we were both veterans of the United States Army. However, after listening to his experiences during the Vietnam War I was almost embarrassed to go into my peace time adventures between the Korean War and Vietnam. Mike listened with interest when I told him about my crazy times with the Army Band, breaking out in hysterical laughter. I filled him in about my times in New York City hanging out with the jazz greats and in later years being close to royalty, celebrities and important political personalities. Mike's ears really perked up when I told him that I had a spiritual encounter on my last tour of Wales. I had given up talking about this meeting with the Holy Spirit because of all the puzzled looks of disbelief that I received from friends and relatives after telling them my story. And I understand, because I was never a church-goer and went through various periods of being an atheist, agnostic and true believer, depending on the situation. The big reaction to my spiritual story was...Oh Boy Jim! What were you drinking! But that wasn't the case at all because my encounter with the Holy Spirit was at 12 o'clock noon on a beautiful sunny day on the coast of Wales.

After the fireworks were over and the food and wine was devoured Pauline and I took the short walk home accompanied by the Bays. It was then that Mike said – Jim - have you ever thought of writing a book? I told him that it had crossed my mind now and then but it never happened. Mike said he thought I had a story to tell and that he was willing to help me get started on what was to become a huge project. We agreed to meet over coffee and donuts every Monday morning at 11 a.m. at the local Starbucks, which we have been doing ever since.

So then I had to figure out how I was going to approach my story. I didn't have a clue about writing, but Mike said that he would help me get started, so no worries there. Do I talk about what I can remember of my early childhood? My grandmother's house? The rather boring Swedish side of my family with their shots of whiskey and beer chasers, and the British side of my family drinking more of the same? Do I talk about all the drinking that went on when I was young? And later, what about the gamblers and racketeers that I became involved with - do I talk about them? Yes, I guess I do talk about where I came from, where I went and every step of the way.

What was to be very helpful for me in writing this book is the fact that I had hundreds of old photos of my childhood that were passed down to me from my mother and after I started playing music professionally I made it a point to save news stories of my concerts and club dates, along with all of my recordings. In addition to all this I had photos of all my bands through the years along with other bands that I played with as a side man. I knew this was going to be very helpful in helping me putting the pieces together of some eighty years of my life.

I've never studied religion and to be honest, I know very little about it. But I do know now that there is a God because He made himself known to me on that beautiful sunny afternoon in Wales. And I'm in no position to preach to you or anyone else. However, looking back at events before my Wales experience there was a pattern in my life that put me in places that added up to one big wonderful jigsaw puzzle that I could never have figured out by myself. And because of events that happened following Wales, I know that at least in my case, God had a purpose in my life and everything I did was not by accident. I went where I went because that is where God placed me, and in my mind there's no question about it. Think about it. I have two sons, Jame and Bob, grandchildren Brittany, Reagan, Alec, Keira and Laura, along with great grandson Jameson. None of those wonderful people would be here had I not been in Nassau, Bahamas in the winter of 1962 to meet my future wife Pauline.

When I say that I know very little about religion I'm certainly not proud of it, because when I step out the front door of my house I can't help but be amazed at all the beautiful surroundings I'm a part of. It is springtime now and the blossoms are bursting from the trees and the flowers are springing up along with Pauline's dreaded dandelions. All the different birds are helping themselves to the seeds that we put out for them, along with a sweet drink for the hummingbirds. Everything you look at is God's handiwork, and for many years I just took it for granted. I think we all have to stop and smell the roses.

Religion doesn't enter my story until much later in the book, so for now I will concentrate on the many years of events before that. I should warn you that you are going to see a part of Jim Beatty that I'm certainly not proud of, but it is part of my life and I'm going to write about it along with the good parts. You are going to meet some fantastic musicians along the way, some great and some not so great. Most of them are wonderful souls but you will also hear about a few of the jerks as well. It's an interesting musical journey around the world playing my favorite music - New Orleans jazz. There's only one way to start this adventure and that's from the beginning - so away we go.

CHAPTER 1

# Early Life

MY LIFE BEGAN ON JUNE 9th, 1934 in Jamestown, New York, where I
joined my parents, Percy Beatty (a clarinet and saxophone player) and my
mother, Alice, a secretary at the local Ford dealership. However, our little
trio of a family did not last very long. Mom and dad were divorced when
I was just three years old. The court awarded my mother three dollars per
week for child support, which my father never paid, although he did try to
make up for it in his later years. It was in the middle of the depression, and
my dad being a musician - a difficult profession even in the best of times,
could not take me...nor could my mother, as she made very little money
as well. So, what to do with little Jimmy? Over the river and through the
woods to grandmother's house I went.

My grandmother's home was on 18 Grandin Street, in a nice section
of Jamestown. She was not all that well and I believe that was the reason
that my Aunt Hildur was living there to help her out when needed. Aunt
Hildur's teenage daughter, Lois, lived there as well. My grandmother's
name was Anna Palm and my grandfather was Oscar Palm. My grandfather passed away in 1932, two years before I was born. He was Overseer of
the Poor, which would be the equivalent of the head of the welfare department now. Because of his job he was called Poor Palm.

When my grandmother, aunt, Lois and I were in the house, Swedish
was mostly spoken. My name was *Yimmy*. My grandmother had the one

and only bedroom downstairs and the rest of us were upstairs. The upstairs was very hot in the summer and very cold in winter. Occasionally at night while I was in bed there were figures roaming around the upstairs bedrooms. I thought they were ghosts and Lois and I would just lie there very still. Now I figure that they were burglars. What they were looking for I'll never know, as there was not much of anything in that house of value to my knowledge. My uncles came by one day and nailed all the windows shut and that was the end of that.

We had an ice box that was in a non-heated room off the living room, probably an add-on because I could look out into it through the living room window. Electric refrigerators were very uncommon in those days and most people depended on ice boxes to keep things like milk and perishable foods for several days. Depending on the time of the year, summer or winter, the iceman had to deliver accordingly. During the bitterly cold Western New York winter nights, ice blocks came from frozen Chautauqua Lake and in the summer from the ice factory. The iceman would come around in a big white truck that was insulated to keep the ice cold so it wouldn't melt during his deliveries. He carried the block of ice in to the box with a pair of large tongs. The ice would melt into a large tray on the bottom of the box and would be emptied when needed. The milkman was also an important part of our day. He delivered our milk and left it in a box on the front porch. His delivery truck was also insulated, of course, to keep the milk and cream cool. If you didn't go out and get the milk in time, it would freeze in the winter and spoil in the summer. One drawback about our little ice box room was that it attracted large rats trying to figure out how to get in and steal the food. That never worked. So between the rats, iceman, milkman and mailman, I had some very exciting days.

During my long stay at my grandmother's house I was very fortunate to have many loving Swedish aunts, uncles and cousins, who must have felt sorry for me. They would often stop by and pick me up and take me to their house for lunch or dinner or to some other event. My mother now had a Ford that must have come with her job at the Ford dealership, and she often stopped to see me. One day when I was about five she dropped by the house to take me for a ride and I discovered I had a sense of humor that sometimes could be good and funny and sometimes not. I must have gotten into the car first because I went around and locked all the doors from the inside. I locked myself in and my mother out and it caused quite a commotion. I remember one of my uncles coming over to the house to coax me out. I thought it was funny, but I don't think I was too popular that day. It's strange but I remember that day as if it were yesterday. Still no sign of my father; maybe I thought there was no such thing for me.

When it was time for me to start kindergarten my mother came and took me to Charles Street Grade School for the first day. It was a two-story brick building with two front doors, one for boys and the other for girls. The building had a full basement that doubled as a gymnasium and assembly area. I remember being a little frightened after leading such a sheltered life with the three ladies that I had been growing up with. Every school day my Aunt Hildur packed me a lunch and I took the short walk to school by myself. After our class had lunch we each had our own rug that we laid down on the floor and took a nap for about half an hour.

On March 2ⁿᵈ, 1940 my mother married Laurian (Lanky) Nelson, who was a well-known and well-liked salesman in the Jamestown area. They rented an apartment, 68 Barrett Avenue, not too far from the Charles Street School and my grandmother's house. I now had a real mother and father. Things were looking up.

My grandparents, Oscar and Anna Palm, originally from Sweden, had eight children. My mother, Alice, the youngest, was born in 1907 and had five sisters: Hildur, Rose, Svea, Gladys, Ella, and two brothers, Oscar and Eric. All the sisters and brothers were married and had children. So I had plenty of aunts, uncles and cousins and as I grew up we became very close. My Uncle Oscar and Uncle Eric went to work for the Jamestown Post Office and ended up with very good jobs there. In fact, Uncle Oscar became postmaster in later years.

The sisters and brothers were very close and got together often with their families for lots of good Swedish food and drink. They called it a smorgasbord. During the Christmas holidays the get-togethers were very festive. Lots of whiskey and beer and the killer homemade Swedish brew called *glogg*. It was made with port wine, brandy, lots of different spices, and served warm. It was customary during the Christmas holidays for the milkman, iceman, mailman and whoever else to drop in for a warm glass of *glogg*. They did this at all the Swedish homes on their routes, so you can imagine the shape they were in at the end of the day. I remember our mailman, Mr. Beebe, one Christmas staggering down the street trying to deliver the mail to the right houses. It was hysterical. The holiday table was loaded with different kinds of food. One of my favorite was *korv*, a Swedish meat or potato sausage. There was also lots of pickled herring and *sylta*, or as we call it, head cheese. There was also liverwurst, Swedish meatballs, lingonberry sauce and hardtack, or cracker bread. There was one Swedish dish that I always managed to avoid. It was called *lutefisk*. *Lutefisk* was lye-soaked cod, served in a cream sauce over mashed potatoes. Absolutely ghastly. My favorite Swedish food is *korv* and I still eat it to this day, if I can find it.

I ended up with one more set of Swedish relatives when my mother remarried. My stepdad had a sister and brother-in-law, Lil and Otto. They never seemed to warm up to me or I to them. The only reason I liked going over to their house was that uncle Otto always drove a new Desoto automobile, and I spent my time at their house looking at the car. The Desoto was made by Chrysler Corporation and was in-between a Chrysler and a

Dodge. Chrysler quit making the De Soto in 1951. Lil and Otto would often take my stepdad, mom and little sister Linda out for dinner, and I would be left at home. I guess they figured I wasn't really a member of the family because I was just a stepchild and just half-Swedish. I always felt left out, because going out for dinner in those days was a very big treat.

Getting used to my new life was rather strange to me. I was living with my mother, who I had only seen occasionally, and a stepfather who was a complete stranger to me. He was good-looking, about 34 years old, tall, lanky (hence his nickname), had dark, receding hair and a moustache. Because he was a clothing salesman at the time he was always immaculately dressed. It was agreed that I would address him as "Pop." Now I know what foster children must feel like when they move in to a new home.

So for the first time that I could remember there was a male figure in the house and I knew that he really wasn't my father. I felt uncomfortable when he told me to do things like, "Eat your vegetables," or "It's time for bed!" I knew I would have to get used to this because it was my new life and family, but I had a strange feeling that he married my mother and I was just part of the deal. However, as time went on we warmed up to each other and I grew to like him and I know that he did me as well. My mother was still working as a secretary at the Ford dealership and she always dressed nicely, was of medium height, attractive looking with dark hair. When she came home from work she always found time to fix a wonderful meal for us all.

The new apartment that I was living in with my mom and pop seemed quite luxurious for me compared to my grandmother's house, and in my new digs I had my very own bedroom. I had a picture of President Roosevelt that I brought with me from my grandmother's home and that was the first thing I put up on my wall. I grew up with President Roosevelt and believe I thought of him as a father figure. That picture followed me with all our moves for years to come. You don't see a picture of a president in homes anymore, but back when I was young it was common to see President Roosevelt's picture in homes and businesses around Jamestown.

Another thing that impressed me was that we had a radio, something that before I had only heard in my mother's Ford. To me, this was really a luxury and I sat in front of it every night after dinner as we listened to our favorite programs. I found that I really enjoyed comedians, like Jack Benny, Red Skelton, Bob Hope, and Abbott and Costello. I also enjoyed shows such as: *It pays to be Ignorant, Blondie, The Great Gildersleeve, Fibber McGee and Molly,* and *Amos and Andy.* There were also a few spook shows that scared the hell out of me, like *The Shadow, Inner Sanctum* (which began with a squeaky door), *Suspense Theatre* and *Lights Out.* And it is in this house that I accomplished a major feat: I learned how to tie my shoes. Things were moving along.

I was in this house when World War II was declared after the bombing of Pearl Harbor by the Japanese. Shortly after that Hitler's Germany declared war on the United States. I remember it being a gloomy time because everyone was worried about what was in store for them in the future. There became a scarcity of certain foods along with cigarette and gasoline rationing. The automobile companies also quit making new cars and switched to the war production of tanks, heavy duty army vehicles and jeeps. I remember a little song people started to sing: "There's a Ford in your future, there's a Ford in your past, but the Ford in your future, it had better last!"

It was mid-1942 and I was starting to get pretty well-adjusted to a new family life. The war was going full steam and I was taught that people like Hitler, Mussolini, and Tojo were our enemies and bad men. Because of the war, new car production came to a halt and my mother lost her job at the local Ford dealership because there were no cars to sell. Consequently, she lost her company car and we became carless. That was okay because it was an easy walk to downtown Jamestown for work and it was hard to get gas anyway.

My mother and stepdad informed me that we were moving to a new home. I was told that soon there would be a new baby in the family and that we needed a new house with more room. We moved to 131 Sampson Street, just a few blocks and an easy walk from where we lived on Barrett Avenue and a short walk to the Charles Street School. My mother was expecting the baby in the first part of 1943, and although she lost her job at the Ford dealership she quickly found another position in a local Jamestown bank as a secretary.

Our new home on Sampson Street was quite large with a nice living room, dining room, and kitchen downstairs, and two bedrooms and a bathroom on the second floor. Once again I had my own bedroom and it was even bigger than the one I just left. The house had a nice front yard and backyard along with a large garage, but of course no car. My Aunt Rose and Uncle Charlie Ball lived directly across the street and my Aunt Gladys and Uncle Ray Otander lived one block over on Colfax Avenue. Their son, Johnny, had enlisted in the Navy and was off fighting for his country.

When I moved into my new bedroom the first thing I did was to hang up my picture of President Roosevelt. My mother, on the other hand, always had a picture of Jesus that she put up above her bed. Although she wasn't outwardly very religious, she said her prayers without fail every night. I soon found out that my family went to church mostly on Easter Sunday and Christmas. My Swedish grandparents attended services every week though as my grandfather was a politician and an elected official as Overseer of the Poor in Jamestown. They were members of the First Covenant Church, as was my mother at the time. My father and my British relatives were members of the Church of England and in Jamestown that was St. James Episcopal Church. My aunt Lizzie told me that my dad went to church there as a child and during a big horse manure fight with a friend (yes, horse manure) of his after church he hit an Episcopal priest by mistake. That ended his church goings and the closest I ever saw him come to a church was a drive-by.

**Percy and Alice Beatty**              **Jim and his first Ford**
**with baby Jim**

**Jim fetching water**     **Sister Linda, Mom and Pop**

## CHAPTER 2

# Meeting My Dad

It was at the Sampson Street address in 1942 that my father showed up for the first time at the house on a Sunday at noon to pick me up and spend the afternoon with me. He didn't come to the door but honked his horn in front of the house. I'll never forget that first Sunday, as he had a beat-up old Chevrolet made in the early to mid-30s. The passenger doors were tied together by a rope and I had to enter the car on the driver's side. So off I went on an adventure with someone I really didn't know – again. He took me to 11 Shaw Avenue, a house across town that was owned by his brothers, Bill and Jim Beatty. My dad's sister Lizzie Hollings lived in an upstairs apartment with her husband, Walker. Aunt Lizzie and Uncle Walker's daughter, Ruby, and son-in-law Hibby Ogren, lived in another small apartment upstairs. It was a full house, but it seemed to work. My uncle Bill came over to the United States first. It was a family of four brothers, Bill, Jim, Harry and my father Percy, along with two sisters, Lizzie and Ada.

The Beatty's were from Wakefield, Yorkshire, England. After Uncle Bill arrived in the U.S. he got a good job at the Jamestown Worsted Wool Mills. The machinery there was made in England, and many of the skilled operators came from that country. The mill employed thousands in the Jamestown area until the depression hit in the early 30's, but the plant survived until the mid-40s. Uncle Bill brought the rest of the family over one by one, as he could afford it. He bought a house in Jamestown, 11

Shaw Avenue, and that was the Beatty home for as long as I can remember. My dad, Percy, was born in 1901 and Uncle Bill brought him over to the United States in 1910. During the First World War my dad tried to join the US Army but they knew he was under age. So, he went and joined the British Army through Canada. He was stationed in France until the war was over and he came back home to Jamestown, full of lice.

My Uncle Jim was dying of cancer when I first met him and he passed away soon after. After Uncle Jim died, Uncle Bill slept in the downstairs bedroom just off the living room. He was a ragtime piano player and had an old upright piano in his bedroom. The piano was terribly out of tune and he was constantly trying to tune it, only making it worse. But boy could he play those ragtime tunes and I asked him to play for me every time I was there. Sunday afternoon dinners were always the traditional British roast beef and Yorkshire pudding. I must admit I still like this dish and it is my signature meal if we have company and I'm doing the cooking. My Uncle Bill insisted on having it every day of the week, which I don't think is a bad idea. Aunt Lizzie carved up the Yorkshire pudding and it was put on a plate that was passed around the table. Uncle Bill was the last one to get the plate and he glared at everyone as they took their share of the Yorkshire. You wanted to make sure that there was plenty left for him by the time the plate got to him.

I soon found out that everyone ate except my dad. He just sat at the table with his whiskey shots and beer chasers. Aunt Lizzie's husband, Uncle Walker, was a real character. He had false teeth that did not fit properly and when he talked the upper teeth kept banging down to his lower teeth. He just kept on pushing them back up. Why he didn't buy some glue I'll never know, but maybe they didn't have it in those days. He also was a big smoker, but instead of using an ashtray he flicked his ashes in the cuff of his pants. Amazingly, his pants never caught fire. One thing I did notice about the Beatty clan was they were small in stature. I don't think my dad was more than 5'6" or so and the rest of the family was about the same or even smaller. My dad, however, did have one hell of a big beer gut.

Christmas day with the Beatty clan on 11 Shaw Avenue was much the same as our regular Sunday brunches. Roast beef and Yorkshire pudding was always the featured food on the menu. The only thing different on Christmas Day was Aunt Lizzie started dinner with singing, "We Wish You a Merry Christmas," and then she would bring out a flaming plum pudding soaked with 151 proof rum blazing with fire. The plum pudding was accompanied by a sweet hard sauce. Everyone pushed the plum pudding aside and ate the hard sauce. I swear that Aunt Lizzie took all the leftover plum pudding, glued it together and served it the next Christmas. My dad, true to form, would not eat but instead would sit there drinking his whiskey and beer. On Christmas day the usual rotgut booze was not served but the good whiskey was put out, like Seagram's Seven or Canadian Club. There was a small Christmas tree in the living room with the usual cartons of cigarettes wrapped up beautifully for the men and always two or three toys or games for me. When I started smoking, I got in on the cartons of cigarettes as well. And we can't forget gifts for the women. That was easy because all the guys bought them cheap perfume and boy did the room smell when they opened their gifts.

So that was about it for Christmas with the Beatty's. My dad would drive me directly home because all the bars were closed on Christmas Day. And that used to be quite an exciting ride home because he had more to drink than usual. After it was over I went home and had Christmas with my mom, pop and sister Linda, born in 1943. Most of the time we would have family over for Christmas dinner or we would go to one of my mother's sisters or brothers house. It was always a fun Christmas party with them, as well. The Swedish side of the family were lots of fun but were not the characters that the Beatty's were. Don't get me wrong, my Swedish side of the family did their share of drinking over the holidays as well, but the food was much different. At any rate it was a day that I looked forward to every year.

Sundays with my father was now a weekly event and he had a routine that never changed. He would pick me up at my mother's house promptly at noon, the passenger side doors were still tied together with rope and so I entered the car on the driver's side. We then would drive to downtown Jamestown and stop across the street from a mysterious, rundown office building next to an empty lot full of junk cars. One of the cars was an old Packard limousine that I used to admire every week, and I think that became my first fascination with big, luxury automobiles. My father would leave me in the car and go upstairs to the office building and after a short while would return with his booty. It was a black market operation where he could get all kinds of food and gasoline rationing stamps along with hard to get items from cigarettes to nylons.

With the black-market items safely locked in the trunk of the car we headed for the Beatty household on 11 Shaw Avenue. Shaw Avenue was on a hill and my dad's old Chevy had one hell of a time making it up to the top of the hill where the Beatty house was situated. We always walked in through the kitchen door where Uncle Bill was sitting at the table with a bottle of whiskey and shot glasses, waiting for us. We sat down with Uncle Bill and talked about local barroom gossip and the war, while Aunt Lizzie was busily preparing the roast beef and Yorkshire pudding. Aunt Lizzie may have been short but she was big busted and obviously the boss of the family, because when she gave her brothers hell, they listened and came to attention. Aunt Lizzie evidently had a heart attack at one time and her doctor told her to have a shot of whiskey every day. She downed her shot of whiskey without a chaser and this was the cue for everyone to sit down at the dining room table, where places were set for everyone except my father, who sat with us but wouldn't eat.

As usual the Yorkshire pudding was passed around with Uncle Bill getting the plate last. The roast beef was cooked to perfection with lots of fat, which I loved. My dad would be sitting with his cigarettes, ashtray, whiskey bottle, shot glass and bottle of beer for his chaser. After having a few drinks he would usually try to start an argument, just for the hell of it. Following dinner, Aunt Lizzie would always have a nice dessert for me, usually a chocolate cake with ice cream and chocolate sauce. As soon as I was finished with my dessert my father would announce that it was time to go and we said our goodbyes until the next Sunday.

My father would then take me downtown to the Roosevelt Theater to watch a movie. He would take me into the theater and sit with me for two or three minutes and then he left, telling me that he would be back shortly. What he did was to check what time the movie would finish and then would go to the bar next door and drink until it was time for the movie to end and come back and pick me up. The movies in those days started out with the news, mostly about the war in Europe and Japan. Following the news there would always be a serial feature shown before the main movie. The serial left you sitting at the end of your chair when it ended. You had to come back the next week to see how the hero got out of the mess he was in. It was usually a Western featuring famous cowboys of the time like Tom Mix or Hop- along Cassidy, or an outer space flick with Buck Rogers, which was all about rockets and outer space that was really out of sight in those days. Towards the end of the main feature my father would magically appear in the seat next to me and act like he enjoyed the entire show just as much as I did.

Following the movie my dad would take me to one of his favorite bars to show me off to his friends. Everybody fell all over me and bought me Coca-Cola's and any kind of sweet I wanted. I noticed several of my father's friends in the bars were very well-dressed gentleman. I later found out they were bookies and part of Jamestown's underworld of that time. My dad, it seems, was a sports fan and loved to gamble on the games. After he had his fill of whiskey he took me home and I would not see him again until the following Sunday at noon.

My father never formally became an American citizen and when the war broke out he became very close to being deported back to Britain because there were many Nazi sympathizers in the US who would have loved to see Hitler invade the UK and so the U.S. government was anxious about those kinds of people. Evidently my dad was told that if he had a job in a defense plant the FBI would leave him alone and let him stay in the United States. He got a job at the MRC Ball Bearing Company making ball bearings for the war effort and my father was safe from deportation. It became such a good job that he kept it until he retired, although he continued to play his clarinet and alto saxophone on weekends.

One Sunday, near my eighth birthday, my dad picked me up at the usual time and to my surprise the rope holding the passenger doors together was gone and the doors were fixed. With my dad's new job at MRC he probably had enough money to get his car repaired, including new synthetic rubber retread tires. Because of the war you could no longer buy real rubber tires and the retreads had to do. I actually entered through the passenger side of the car and I could tell that my dad was proud of his achievement.

Once I got in his car he handed me a little black case and said "happy birthday." The case was unwrapped and had no card and when I opened it, to my surprise, there was a clarinet staring me in the face. Who would've thought at that time that this gift would end up taking me to every major city in the United States and Canada and around the world? Not to mention, concerts, radio and television and hundreds of recordings. I was so happy with my new clarinet; it was just like getting one million dollars.

My dad never showed me anything about how to play the clarinet nor did he ever offer. I have no explanation for this except he might have thought himself as a bad teacher and also he played the old style Elbert system clarinet that was different fingering than the Boehm system clarinet that he gave me. But it wasn't *that* different and he could have taught me if he had wanted to. As luck would have it there was a clarinet teacher living right next door to us on Sampson Street named Dominic Petello, and I started lessons with him immediately. I'll never forget that he was dumbfounded that I knew nothing about getting a sound out of the clarinet considering that my father was a popular clarinetist around Jamestown, so we started from scratch. I remember my dad telling me that when I learned how to play the song "Clarinet Polka," he would give me $100. After many lessons I was able to play it, but I never received my money. Many years went by and I was playing in a nightclub in Portland Oregon, when a guy from Texas came up to me and said, "I'll give you $100 to play the 'Clarinet Polka.'" I played it for him and got my reward after all.

Unfortunately, Dominic Petello didn't teach out of his home but had a room in a downtown Jamestown office building where he saw his students. That meant it was quite a hike for me every week for my lesson. But for a young lad it wasn't that big a deal to walk into town, except on those cold snowy winter days when it wasn't much fun. After a number of lessons, things were starting to sound halfway decent and I was on my way to being a clarinetist.

CHAPTER 3

# World War Two

ON JANUARY 30TH, 1943, MY stepdad woke me up in the middle of the night to tell me that I had a new baby sister and her name was Linda. I would no longer be alone and I thought it would be fun to have a sister to hang out with. The next day, January 31st, General Field Marshal Paulus surrendered his German 6th Army to the Russians. That was the beginning of the end for Nazi Germany in World War II.

Pop was an air raid warden during our time at the rented house on Sampson Street. Looking back, it was quite funny to see him rushing out of the house when the air raid sirens blew. He had a white steel helmet, similar to the style of helmets that the soldiers wore during the First World War. He also had an air raid warden armband and a bucket of water with a hand pump and hose on it to put out fires. We took the air raids very seriously and when the sirens went off I was scared to death. We survived those air raids and as far as I can remember the Germans or the Japanese never bombed Jamestown, New York.

During the war, schoolchildren had the opportunity to buy war bonds. Once a week I took ten cents to school and bought a war bond stamp which was then pasted in a little book. When the book was full you could trade it in for a war bond or simply cash it in for its value and a little interest. I traded it in for cash every time, as I guess we needed the money. Charles Street School was always having a fundraiser for the war effort and it was during one of these fundraisers that I had my first encounter with the Jamestown Police Department. The school was having a drive to collect metal to be melted down for the war effort to make tanks, airplanes and that sort of thing. My Uncle Ray had been in the trucking business and he had a lot of old tools in his garage that were used for working on his trucks. He had heavy wrenches and pliers that he gave me to take to school for the collection. I loaded them in my wagon and took them to school and I was real proud of myself because I brought in more than anybody. Unfortunately, the school officials couldn't believe that anyone would give this to me and they called the police, who began to give me the third degree as to where I had gotten them. I suppose that after an investigation and a few phone calls they realized that I had obtained the tools on the up and up, and they let me go. This was not a good feeling for me because the word traveled through the school that I might be a thief, but I always figured that even if it was true, it was for our men in uniform.

It was while I was in grade school that I started sneaking cigarettes. I had a pack hidden in our garage on Sampson Street and me and a school buddy of mine, Gary Schwartz, would sit in the garage and puff away. We usually stole the cigarettes out of packs lying around the house and nobody missed them. My mother didn't smoke but I bet she might have smelled it on me. If she did she never said anything. Pop smoked cigarettes and pipes and I loved the aroma of the different kinds of pipe tobacco he used.

My early interests in music were probably the Western vocal stars. I had a cowboy outfit including a toy pistol that I put on and pretended to be a real gunslinger as I listened to Gene Autry singing, "Back In The Saddle Again." There was also a group called the Sons of the Pioneers that I enjoyed very much, along with Roy Rogers and his horse, Trigger. The big bands were the rage during the war and I wish I had a dollar for every time I heard Glenn Miller and his band play "In the Mood." Miller joined the service during the war and had a band that played for the troops. He disappeared when his plane was lost over the coast of England. Many years later I knew and played with his brother, Herb, who spent a great deal of time looking for his brother's plane. There were many other big bands, of course. Benny Goodman, Woody Herman, Russ Morgan, Les Brown, just to name a few. There were great singers during that period, like Bing Crosby, Frank Sinatra, and Kay Starr. In the jazz world there were people like Ella Fitzgerald and Billie Holiday, along with such great jazz artists as Louis Armstrong, Sidney Bechet, Wild Bill Davison and Eddie Condon.

There was also a comedy band called Spike Jones and the City Slickers. This band was hilarious by their wild renditions of popular tunes of the day. During the course of a tune you would hear gun shots, cannons blasting, horn-tooting and sirens blaring. They would play such tunes as the "William Tell Overture" and a popular WWII hit called, "In the Fuhrer's Face." I got such a kick out of this band that I decided to do a pantomime while playing the record. I recruited a new school chum of mine, Dan Weinstein, to be my partner and we did our show along with the Spike Jones records as they came out. We became quite a hit with our show and I think with that I got the showbiz bug. Dan Weinstein and I would also try our hand at being juvenile delinquents, but that's another story.

With my Spike Jones show going so well, I decided to join the drama club in junior high school. As it turned out, I had a talent for acting and became a part of all the major plays that the students produced at school. So at that time, music played a secondary role in my life. However, a good share of the musical stars that I listened to on the radio at the time would become friends of mine and in many cases we would end up playing music together.

My Dad was full of surprises, especially after giving me my clarinet. One Sunday he asked me if I would like a bunny rabbit. Of course. What kid would turn down a pet? After our traditional Sunday luncheon at the Beatty household and a couple of stops to his favorite bars, we drove to a house in Jamestown where a drinking buddy of his, John Jacobson, lived and had rabbits for sale. John Jacobson's two young boys were raising rabbits and had a few little bunnies that they were selling. The two boys were John Jr. and Jim Jacobson, and they would become an important part of my life in a few short years, once I got to junior high school. My dad bought me a rabbit with a cage and dropped me off at my house. He must have gotten permission from my mother to get the rabbit because she acted very pleased that I had it. That rabbit grew up to be a big one but then did not live too long, probably because I really didn't know how to take care of it or maybe it just died of boredom.

My Mom and Pop told me that we would be moving to a new house, 117 William Street, across town and closer to downtown Jamestown. I wasn't too happy about that because I had a few friends that I played with in the neighborhood and if my family was moving I had to go along with them. This would be my fourth move starting with my grandmother's house, Barrett Ave., Sampson Street, and now William Street. We never bought a house and always rented. I suppose it was due to the fact that Pop was a clothing salesman and never seemed to hold a steady job for long and moved from one store to another, and my mother, being a bank secretary, wasn't exactly in the high income bracket. Pop was also becoming a big drinker and that took a lot of our money.

Pop also had a furniture rearrangement fetish. He was constantly re-arranging the furniture in the living room. Nothing seemed to please him and he moved the sofa from one side of the living room to the other and his chair would be here and then there, along with a coffee table that was shuffled all over the room. Sometimes I would walk into the house and think I was at the wrong place because everything was different. This went on in every rented house we lived in.

There was a loose board in the upstairs hallway that I used to pry open and hide special treasures of mine and then slide back into its place. I can't remember what I had there now, but I've often thought it would be fun to go back to that old house and pry open that board and reclaim my hidden valuables. The house still sits there to this day, exactly the way we left it, badly in need of a new paint job.

I had lots of school friends in that Sampson Street neighborhood and I lost track of most of them. One old friend, in particular, went on to be very well known and a popular Jamestown personality. He was always interested in baseball and for years became extremely active in the Jamestown baseball scene. When you think of Russ Dietrich, referred to as Jamestown's "Mr. Baseball," you think of all his work with the youth and the Babe Ruth Amateur Baseball League throughout the years..

Jamestown's Municipal Stadium was built in 1941 and in 1997, in honor of Russ for all his work promoting the sport locally, it was renamed Russell E. Dietrich, Jr. Park. Russ became the host President of the Jamestown Babe Ruth World Series Committee and also a member of the National Board of Directors for Babe Ruth, Inc. Over the years when I played in Jamestown, Russ usually came by to listen to the music and say hello. Whenever I get a chance to go to a high school reunion I always see Russ there and we talk about old times on Sampson Street

When we moved to William Street I was just finishing up grade school and ready to go to junior high school. Like all the other houses we lived in it was rented and I really didn't see any improvement, if any, from the house we had just moved out of. Maybe the rent was cheaper? It had two floors and we lived on the bottom floor with a basement and a nice elderly couple lived above us. We had a living room, dining room, kitchen, bathroom and two bedrooms, plus a sun porch off the kitchen which led to a side door. We had a nice large lawn with a storage shed in the back. The house also had a full cellar with a laundry room, coal furnace and a large coal bin to hopefully get us through the winter months. When we ordered our coal a large coal truck would pull up to the side of the house with a coal chute that led to an open cellar window above the coal bin. It was always a fun time when the coal truck arrived to watch the rear end of the truck tip up and the coal pouring into the cellar. Ironically, guess who was in charge of keeping the furnace going? It was my mother. I don't know how she managed, but the house was always warm and comfortable all winter long. And those New York winters used to be horrific.

When we first moved, my sister and I shared a bedroom, but as I was getting older my parents decided I needed my own bedroom. Maybe they thought that I was getting near puberty and I'd soon find out that some body parts had other functions other than emptying my bladder. They fixed the bedroom situation by curtaining off part of the dining room and then I had a bedroom to myself.

There was one problem with this: I just had a curtain separating me from the rest of the house so I could hear everything that was going on all the time. This was especially troublesome on the weekends when my parents would often have house parties that would go well into the night. It was especially bad when my pop and my uncles decided that they were talented barbershop quartet entertainers. Believe me, it was not easy to listen to this and to this day I cringe when I hear the words "barbershop quartet." I also came to see the huge amount of alcohol consumption by my parents and relatives, not to mention all their friends. I remember this bothered me and sometimes frightened me as now and then the party would end up with an argument about some stupid thing or another. My stepdad and uncles were lightweight drinkers and they got dumb real fast.

My stepdad's drinking turned our life at home into a nightmare, and as the years went on his drinking reputation was so bad that all he could get for work was going house to house as a Fuller Brush salesman. It's too bad because he was a good-looking guy with a great personality and very well-liked by everyone. He dressed just like he was out of the latest men's fashion magazines and was a salesman at the best men's stores in Jamestown. He worked in all of them, but because of his drinking problem he went from one job to another. One job he got always amused me to this day. It was an exciting day at home when he announced that he had been made assistant manager of the new Adam Hat Store in Jamestown. But the funny part of it was the Adam Hat Store only had two employees, the manager and the assistant manager.

I also hated to see the women get drunk and still do to this day. And when I say drunk I mean falling-down drunk. The only exception to this was my mom's sister, Aunt Gladys. Give her a few drinks and she turned in to a Can-Can dancer, which I thought was quite hilarious with the bumps and the grinds. So here I was in my curtained off bedroom and with all that entertainment going on, why would I need a TV? Not to mention all the adult talk I heard.

Although we were winning the war, rationing was still on and things were hard to get, such as butter, so we used a substitute called margarine or oleo. It looked like a big hunk of soft white plastic and came with a packet of yellow powder. You mixed it up with the yellow powder, and you had butter, or at least something that looked like it. Nylon stockings for women were also out of the question, except on the black market. They were used for parachute production. So the ladies, including my mother, painted their legs to look like they were wearing nylons. They had a very small brush with which the girls painted a seam on the back of their legs. This process was quite a production and time-consuming.

President Franklin D Roosevelt was the only president I knew as he was elected for the first time in 1933. I thought the world of the president, just like the father I never had. The only enemy I knew was Adolf Hitler, and he came to power in 1934, the year I was born. Strangely enough, I was fascinated with *de Fuhrer* and even did an imitation of him for our friends and relatives. That was the beginning of my interest in acting. As far as my fascination with Hitler and his army, I think it was the uniforms and pageantry at their parades and rallies that I saw in the newsreels when I went to the movies. That was another unique thing. In those days when you went to see a movie you always got caught up on the news because they had about a fifteen minute recap of the events happening around the world. It really wasn't until after the war when the rest of the world found out the horrible things Hitler had done during his years in power.

There was a park close to the house and I used to go there often. That's where I met and became friends with German prisoners of war. There was a manpower shortage in the United States as so many of our men were off fighting a war in Europe and against the Japanese. So, German prisoners that spoke English were sent over to the States to perform various jobs, such as landscaping, in various parks around the United States. The prisoners were not guarded too much, as they were happy to be out of the war and getting three square meals a day. They were always happy to see me show up at the park and I'm sure a few of them had children themselves back in Germany about my age. They gave me a few medals that they had been awarded during the war and that's how I started my World War II memorabilia collection that I have to this day. Years later I added to it while playing concerts in Germany. Little did I know then that I would end up with many German friends and even a German movie made about me.

With our move to William Street I was looking forward to junior high school and the band there. I had been taking clarinet lessons for a while now and was getting along quite well on my music reading skills. It was questionable, however, whether I would be going to junior high school that year because of my poor performance in grade school. I attribute this to my mixed-up family life. Although I did get a lot of love from various members of my family and my mother, I still wasn't like the other kids that had regular homes to go to every night with a mother and father. Looking back, I think I became a big daydreamer, psychologically putting myself in a happy and comfortable situation. Therefore, when the teacher was teaching I was in a world of my own, oblivious to what was going on. Fortunately, the powers that be decided to give me a chance and promoted me to attend Lincoln Junior High school on trial.

President Roosevelt died from a stroke on April 12, 1945. It was hard to believe that anyone could possibly take his place. The enemies that I grew up to know were Adolf Hitler from Germany, Mussolini from Italy and Hirohito from Japan. Mussolini was executed by his own people April 28, 1945, and the war with Italy was soon over. Hitler committed suicide in his bunker in Berlin on April 30, 1945. Germany surrendered on May 7, 1945, and the long war in Europe was over. There was a huge victory celebration in Jamestown and in cities all over the United States. Horns were honking, sirens were screeching, and people were partying on the streets all over the city. It had been a long war in Europe with lots of lives lost and people were ready to get back to peacetime just as soon as we were finished with the Japanese. And that didn't take long. On August 6, 1945, a B-29 Super fortress named the *Enola Gay* flew over Hiroshima, Japan, and dropped the first atomic bomb. Then on August 9 another, more powerful atomic bomb was dropped on Nagasaki, Japan. Both of those cities were devastated along with their inhabitants. The Japanese knew then that they could not continue the war and Emperor Hirohito surrendered the Japanese forces on August 14. Finally it was all over and another large celebration was had that equaled the end of the war in Europe.

So now after the long war was over everyone looked forward to getting back to normal and happy times. I had a nice home now, a baby sister, and was getting to know my stepdad better. My father was on his usual schedule of picking me up every Sunday for roast beef and Yorkshire pudding at Aunt Lizzie's and the rest of the Beatty family and then the movie and bar routine with my dad. After he dropped me at home I wouldn't see him for another week.

There was a brief period in my young days that I thought it hilarious to make other people's lives miserable. Thanks to the Jamestown Police Department this crime spree didn't last very long, Thank God. During Halloween it was quite common in those days for young boys to run around at night raising hell. For instance, we would set sewer fires with the fall leaves off the trees on the ground. This kept the Jamestown Fire Department quite busy. Then there was the usual soaping of car windows, which was quite harmless. We also scared the daylights out of people with a very simple device. We would remove the thread off a spool and then with a knife we would carve notches on each end of the spool. Then we would re-thread the spool with string and stick a long pencil through the whole of it and put it against a house window, pull the string and it would make quite a noise against the window. Another really bad trick we pulled was letting the air out of car tires parked on the street. This was quite annoying for the victims, as they had to get a tire pump to get the air back in order to drive the car. If these people were still around today and I could find them, I would go around and apologize to all of them.

Those were just a few of the annoying tricks we played. But the really bad one was a device that my friend Dan Weinstein and I invented. I can't recall just how we put it all together but it was a small exploding device that we had in a paper bag. We would put it on the front porch of the house, light the fuse and ring the house doorbell and run like hell. Just about the time they opened the front door the bomb would go off. It was quite harmless but it did leave a burn mark on the porch. It also could have been dangerous if anyone picked the bag up before it went off. But of course Dan and I never thought those things out. The problem was we thought this was such a great prank that we decided to carry it on for weeks after Halloween. It didn't take too long for the Jamestown Police Department to catch up with us. They weren't too happy with us nor were the Fire Department. Needless to say, Dan and I were also in deep trouble at home.

I saw Dan Weinstein recently on a visit back to Jamestown and he told me that had his father not destroyed our laboratory, we both would have become famous chemists. Dan went on to graduate from Michigan State and became very successful in business around the world.

And it was not long after that period of hell-raising that I met a guy in school who played the trombone and got me interested in jazz.

**Jim – the neighborhood menace!**

## CHAPTER 4

# Discovering Jazz

RIGHT AROUND THE TIME WORLD War II ended there was a renewed interest in New Orleans jazz. Due to the large payroll of the big bands they were finding it hard to stay alive. Therefore, six or seven-piece groups like the New Orleans jazz bands were far more affordable. In the early part of the 1900s New Orleans jazz bands were very popular and musicians such as Louis Armstrong, Sidney Bechet and Kid Ory left the Crescent City for bigger and better things. Armstrong, for instance, went to Chicago to play with King Oliver's Creole Jazz Band, originally from New Orleans. Armstrong went on to fame and fortune and became one of the most celebrated jazz musicians anywhere. Bechet went to Europe when he was very young and became a well-known clarinetist and soprano saxophone star. Kid Ory ended up on the West Coast playing the Los Angeles area and wrote the well-known jazz classic, "Muskrat Ramble."

Not all the New Orleans jazz musicians left the city. Some stayed behind to play locally. Many of them could not make a living just playing music and ended up working on the docks as stevedores. One of them, a great clarinetist named George Lewis, was caught up in the New Orleans Jazz revival along with cornetist Bunk Johnson, who didn't even have any teeth left to speak of. With the help of Sidney Bechet, whose brother was a dentist, he was fitted with false teeth and able to play again. This New Orleans Jazz revival caught fire and spread all over the United States and eventually to Europe. Kid Ory was ready for a comeback on the West

Coast, as well as Sidney Bechet on the East Coast. Armstrong however, went with the flow of the big bands and remained popular during the big band era. Small band jazz was back and so were the jazz nightclubs and concerts.

On the West Coast, players like Lou Waters and Turk Murphy started what they liked to call San Francisco Jazz. In Los Angeles there was a band formed mostly from musicians working for Disney. Their leader was Ward Kimball and they were called the Firehouse 5 +2. The cornetist with that group was Danny Alguire, who years before had played with the country band, Bob Wills and his Country Playboys. Oddly enough, many years later, after I had moved to Portland, Oregon, Danny ended up working in my band and recording with me. His most asked-for tune from our fans was a number we recorded called "Little Orphan Annie." To this day I love to listen to it. Another popular LA band was led by Pete Daly, a great cornet man. But, his drinking did him in. Where have I heard that before?

I did finally get involved with the band at Lincoln Junior High. This is where I met a trombone player by the name of John Jacobson. John asked, "Have you ever heard of Bunk Johnson or George Lewis?" I shrugged my shoulders and said, "Who are they?" Well, I soon found out. John Jacobson invited me over to his house after school to listen to some of his records of New Orleans jazz. It sounded good to me and he only lived about three or four blocks away from the school at 169 Hallock Street. When we arrived at his house, I could not believe it. I had been there before. This is the house my father had taken me to buy my rabbit, and John and his younger brother, Jim, were the two young boys that sold it to me. So here I was back at the same house, only this time for a much different reason. He led me up to his bedroom where he had an old wind-up record player, or Victrola, as they called them in those days. The Victrola played 78 rpm recordings. There was a song on each side and you had to be careful with the record because it was very fragile and broke very easily. The first tune was the Bunk Johnson band playing "Alexander's Ragtime Band". I couldn't believe it as I had never heard such beautiful music played, deep from the heart, as this jazz band was doing. The clarinet player was George Lewis. I never knew a clarinet could be played with such feeling. I was hooked, but good. We listened to those recordings for the rest of the afternoon until it was time for me to go home for dinner.

John also had a pretend radio show that he broadcast for an hour a day out of his bedroom. He even put an "on the air" sign on his door when he was doing the pretend broadcast. He had a bunch of old records that he would play not just jazz, but all types of music. He even had fake sponsors from around the Jamestown area. He would give the time now and then; do the news and a weather report. He even asked me to be a guest on his show and I was flattered. After I got to know John better, he hired me and gave me my own show. No pay of course.

John was so happy that I enjoyed jazz that he suggested we start a band. I thought it was a great idea, but I told him that probably just a clarinet and trombone wouldn't sound that great. John said, "No problem, John Andrea, a guy I know at school, plays the drums."

In those days Jamestown was a very segregated city. The Swedes had their own little neighborhoods, as did the Italians. Jamestown had very few black people, but the ones that did live there had their own separate neighborhood, with their own bars and clubs. For instance, there was the white Elks Club and what was called at the time, the colored Elks Club.

There was also a very large Albanian population and they had their own neighborhood as well. As my mother and stepdad were Swedish, I don't know why we lived there. Probably because the rent was lower there.

John Andrea was an American-born Albanian whose parents were from the old country. He was tall, lanky and stood almost six-feet, five inches tall. He seemed like a nice guy and he loved jazz. So it looked like we had ourselves a new drummer and he lived right across the street from our school, which made it handy for rehearsals. John Jacobson could also play chords on the guitar, along with playing trombone. I blew the clarinet and our new drummer was our rhythm section. We had our first rehearsal the next day at John Andrea's house. I was quite surprised when I found out that our drummer did not have any drums. He said, "No big deal," and appeared from the kitchen with an assortment of pots and pans. I thought, this is not going to work, but the rhythm and sound that he got out of his mother's pots and pans was unbelievable.

Now I had quite a thing going for me. The junior high band, my pretend radio show with no real sponsors, as yet, and playing clarinet in a jazz band with a drummer that played with pots and pans. Of course, there was one minor problem: We didn't know any tunes. Learning songs was a major production. We had to learn the jazz songs from John Jacobson's small New Orleans jazz collection. So we would sit and listen to those recordings over and over until we were able to play them. But we had lots of time. John Andrea's parents were from the old country and I think he had a lot of freedom to do things. He was born with a natural talent for the arts, not only in music but he could sit down and draw beautiful paintings, especially wildlife. He loved the outdoors, fishing, hunting and trapping, and still does to this day. I was not supervised very closely as well. My mother worked all day at the bank and my stepdad was well on his way to becoming an alcoholic. John Jacobson's family life was about the same as mine. He had a lovely mother who worked at the *Jamestown Post-Journal* newspaper, a younger brother Jim, a sister Joan, who had married and moved away, and a father who got drunk every day after work, came home and raised hell. So the three of us had plenty of time to learn how to play jazz.

We still had very few jazz recordings to listen to and that was a problem, until John Andrea remembered that there was an older man in the neighborhood who loved jazz and had a huge jazz record collection. His name was Art De Meyer, and we set up a time to stop by his house and listen to his fabulous record collection. It turns out that he not only collected jazz recordings but made frequent trips to New York City and had met many of the well-known jazz musicians of that time. This was great because I got to listen to all the top jazz artists around, such as Sidney Bechet and Wild Bill Davison.

Now that I was in junior high school I was old enough to go downtown on my own. It wasn't that far, just down the hill and through the park and I was there. I missed my German prisoner friends and wished that we had exchanged addresses as it would have been fun to know what happened to them after returning home. The main street running through Jamestown was Third Street. It was a busy place with businesses, restaurants and department stores. The biggest department store was Bigelow's. If you ever watched the "I Love Lucy" show on television, whenever Lucy went shopping she used the name of that store. She also used her old Jamestown girlfriend's names on the show. She never forgot her old hometown.

The next street down was Second Street. Second Street was busy as well, but only because it was full of taverns and saloons for several blocks. Guess what? That's were my dad lived in his apartment. Instead of him picking me up on Sundays for our brunch at Aunt Lizzie's, I would walk downtown and meet him at his apartment. It was on the second floor above a bar. It consisted of one big room with a bed, dresser, refrigerator, stove, and a kitchen table. He also kept a girlfriend there by the name of Mary Crumb. She was a nice lady and often would slip me ten or fifteen cents. The room smelled just like a tavern; whiskey, stale beer and ashtrays with cigarette butts were all over the room. I would wait for my dad to finish his whiskey and beer and then we would be off for our Sunday visit with the British relatives and lots of roast beef and Yorkshire pudding.

My dad still had that old Chevy. We didn't do the movie thing anymore as I was now old enough to go on my own. I loved spook movies with Frankenstein, Wolfman, and Dracula. I also loved comedies. My favorites were Laurel and Hardy. I usually walked home from my dad's apartment as I enjoyed walking through town and looking at new cars. I was especially interested in the big expensive cars, such as Lincoln's, Cadillac's, Chrysler's and Packard's. I later found out that many of these cars belonged to members of the mob.

The big deal around that time was really something: Television! My cousins Ruby and Hibby, who lived on the second floor above Aunt Lizzie's, had one of the early television sets. Usually, when my dad and I were there, nothing was on but a test pattern. But I would sit there and watch it anyway. If I could get back there later in the day I could watch Milton Berle's comedy hour. He was hilarious and became known as "Mr. Television." There was also the Friday night fights that were very popular. We did not have a television in our home until a few years later.

We did get our first telephone on William Street, and boy what a thrill that was to call some of my friends. We had what they called a party line, which meant we had to share the phone time with our neighbors. So you had to be careful what you were saying when you were talking with someone as your neighbor could very well be listening in. Sometimes I would make up ridiculous things to say when I felt that someone was listening to my conversation.

The really big thing in music was a new recording process. The record industry came out with a vinyl, 33 1/3 rpm record that recorded twenty-five minutes per side. This was really a big deal and the old fragile 78s were history. So now our little band, the Dixie Kats, could learn tunes much more rapidly with so many tunes on each disc. We did have to buy a new record player that would play them. I don't remember how we managed the money to buy one, but we did and somehow our drummer, John Andrea found the money to acquire a drum set. Maybe one of us broke into a music store, I can't remember. But we were now looking and sounding like the making of a real band.

While in junior high school we did have a little diversion away from trying to learn jazz. My band buddy, John Jacobson, had joined the Civil Air Patrol as a cadet and convinced me to do the same. The Civil Air Patrol was an organization that began very early in the Second World War. It started as a group of guys with the love of flying wanting to put their private planes and flying skills in use for the defense of the United States. During the war thousands of civil air patrol members answered the call and did National Service by accepting and performing wartime missions.

After the war the Civil Air Patrol continued to provide valuable services to both local and national agencies. Congress passed a law permanently making the Civil Air Patrol an auxiliary of the United States Air Force. Their primary mission was aerospace education, cadet programs, and emergency service.

So there I was, after missing action in World War II because of my age - a cadet in the Civil Air Patrol. After a few meetings I got a khaki uniform plus a set of wings for my shirt and cap. We had meetings on cadet classes and the occasional ride-along on a flight around our area, mostly the Lake Erie coast line. During my time on duty we were never invaded, even by the Canadians. As cadets, we were never taught to fly but occasionally the pilot would let us handle the plane for a while. As time went on jazz became more important and the civil air patrol dropped to the sidelines. However, I'm glad for my time with them and I think it helped me out with my flying planes years later. I was familiar with the Jamestown Airport and the surrounding territory and it all came in handy in my later flying days.

John Jacobson, John Andrea and I spent more and more time at Art DeMyer's house listening to all the great recordings he had collected. Art was a car salesman at a local Chevy dealer and lived with his elderly mother. She was a nice lady and somehow tolerated us hanging around listening to records. Until now I had just heard Bunk Johnson and George Lewis playing their brand of New Orleans jazz. But now a whole new world of music was in Art's amazing collection of hot jazz. Sidney Bechet played the clarinet and soprano sax. I had never heard anyone play a soprano sax before because they had gone out of style during the big band era. They were also extremely hard to play in tune, but Sidney certainly didn't have any trouble in that department. I told my dad about Bechet and he thought that I was crazy to like anything like that. My dad was a dance band musician and I guess never paid any attention to the jazz world. He could talk about Benny Goodman and that was about all. So right from the beginning I never got any encouragement in music from my dad. I also heard recordings of Bechet playing with cornetist Wild Bill Davison. Wild Bill was one of the most exciting players I had ever heard and to hear Wild Bill and Sidney playing together was just too much. I knew that somehow I had to go to New York City and see them for myself. I eventually did, even though I was underage for drinking. Of course it wasn't even in my wildest dreams that Wild Bill and I would become friends and work together many years later.

Sometimes I would go over to Art's house on my own when the guys were not around. It was fun hanging out with Art and all his collection of jazz recordings. I guess he was sort of like a father figure to me under the situation I had been in all my life. Unfortunately, I came to find out that Art not only liked jazz but he also liked young boys. He approached me one day and I let him know that I was very uncomfortable with what he had in mind. So that was the end of that. It was never the same and I ended my visits to Art's house, but we remained friends for years afterwards.

John Jacobson was still running his pretend radio station, but he was getting a little more mature and decided to go for the real thing. There was another older fellow in the neighborhood, just up the street from John who was a DJ and worked for one of the local radio stations, WJOC. His name was Bill Kirby. He was married and had a little boy. He had a radio program every afternoon called the *Hurdy Gurdy Show*. He would play the popular tunes of the day and throw in some jazz along the way.

This was our chance to get involved in real radio with real announcers and real sponsors. WJOC had recently been purchased by a couple from the deep South, Mr. and Mrs. Layman. There was a station manager by the name of Art Borgason who managed the station and also spent a great deal of time on the air, along with Bill Kirby. The only other employee was a janitor and that was it. I felt sorry for that janitor, as one Christmas he gave everyone at the station a little gift. Mr. and Mrs. Layman, being from the South, were insulted, because he was black, and would not take his gift.

Quite often, after school, John and I would head down to the station and spend the afternoon learning the radio business. Everyone there was so nice and helpful and it got to the point where if anyone got sick John or I could step in and take over. That never happened. But what did happen was that the station manager, Art Borgason, asked me if I would like to hear an organ recital, since I was into music. It turns out that he was the organist at a church in town. Well, it turned out that I was the only one in an empty church listening to him play the organ. But he was excellent and I enjoyed it very much. After he finished playing, he asked me if I would like to join him watching a movie at a nearby theater. It sounded good to me and I was always game for a free movie as I was not flush with money. But here we go again. Shortly after the movie began he had wandering hands and what was I to do? So I sat through the whole movie like that and that was the end of my radio adventures.

I went back to my interest in jazz. Sometime later, Bill Kirby stopped by my house one afternoon. He was very serious and said, Jim you have to be very honest with me and I need your help. It seems that somehow the word got out at the competing radio station, WJTN, that there was a pedophile at WJOC and all fingers were pointing at Bill Kirby, because he was so friendly and nice to us kids. I told Bill what had happened at the movie theater and the two of us went down to the radio station and I gave my story to the station's owners, Mr. and Mrs. Layman. The station manager was fired and my friend Bill was off the hook. It's amazing that at my age I had to handle this by myself and to this day I doubt if my parents ever knew. My mother was just too busy working and trying to keep the family together and everybody else was too busy drinking.

One funny thing to end this story was that at Christmas time, John and I went out one night and stole a Christmas tree and delivered it to Bill's house. Radio announcers in those days did not make a heck of a lot of money, so he appreciated the tree. There was a trail from the tree lot all the way to Bill's house because we dragged it through the snow, but we got away with another caper. Speaking of some of my evening adventures, I had a friend at school whose brother had returned home from WW II with a German flare gun. It was in a case, and wouldn't you know there was a shell along with it. This was too much for me to pass up. So, I convinced my friend that we should wait until dark and go to the Third Street Bridge and shoot the flare over the city of Jamestown. It was a spectacular sight and there was a big article in the *Jamestown Post-Journal* the next day. I suppose my friend's brother was not very pleased about the one and only shell being missing, but I'm sure he got over it.

I had fun at Lincoln Junior High School. In addition to my jazz buddies, I was involved in stage productions, often taking the lead part. I loved acting and everything that went with it; the rehearsing every night after school, the costumes and the staging, not to mention dress rehearsal, makeup, and the general excitement of putting on a big production. Opening night was always a nervous but exciting time. But there was one thing missing every time and that was that my family was seldom there to watch it. It hurt, but then, I was getting used to that. I can't blame my mother for not being there as she worked at the bank every day, had my young sister, Linda, to take care of, and had to make dinner and worry about what condition her husband might be in when he returned home at night. It must have been a very stressful time in her life. However, I remember how lonely I felt when the curtain went down and I was the only one in the play that didn't have a parent there to congratulate me and tell me how great I did in the show.

I also was in the junior high band. I enjoyed that very much but I was much more into playing with our little jazz group, such as it was. It was also during that time that I thought I would like to be a funeral director. How this got into my head, I don't know. It might have had something to do with my fascination and love of horror movies and the Frankenstein monster, Dracula and the Wolman. Why does anybody decide what they would like to do in life in the first place? Who knows?

So it was business as usual for me dealing with the awful Western New York snowstorms, beautiful springtime, gorgeous summers and Chautauqua Lake and one of the most colorful fall seasons you'd ever want to see. In the wintertime I would save a lot of travel time by running in back of a car and holding on to the bumper until I got to where I wanted to go. If that car wasn't going all the way I would let go and wait for another one. Sort of like a transfer. Plus you could always count on a snowball fight every day.

One beautiful spring day, my friend John Andrea and I were out hiking in the woods. This is something the two of us often did. As I've mentioned before, John had a natural born talent in music and with his painting, and still has. I think our hikes out of town and into the woods were just a release to get away from everything. One day we ran across a small farmhouse that had goats. We sort of fell in love with this one goat and played with it at great length. Finally the farmer saw us with the goat and asked us if we wanted it. We couldn't believe it; now we were the proud owners of a goat that happened to be female and as we later found out, was pregnant. We put a rope around the goat's neck and the three of us headed back to town. John had a shed in his backyard and that was the goat's new home. Trouble was we were a couple of young kids that knew nothing about the goat business, let alone taking care of a pregnant one, who by the way, we named Julie. Fortunately for us, John's father came to the rescue. He was from Albania and was out of work and probably saw a small profit in goat milk and the future baby goats, or kids. But then again, that's what my Dad called me. Anyway, Julie gave birth to three cute baby goats. John and I went back to playing jazz and turned the goat business over to his dad.

It was now time to move on to high school. Jamestown high school was located in downtown Jamestown. To get to school I had to walk over Second Street past my dad's apartment and all the bars he spent his time in. I also discovered that a few of the guys I saw driving those big beautiful cars had newsrooms, a place for me to hang out after school, and a new adventure began.

**Jim's first band**

**Early solos**

CHAPTER 5

# The Mob

MANY THINGS STARTED HAPPENING DURING my high school years. My father had started going out with a new girlfriend by the name of Isabel. Everyone called her Belle and she was a good match for my Dad because she could throw the drinks down with the best of them. They seemed to get along fine, except when they both had too much to drink, and then they weren't much fun to be around. Belle tried to be a second mother to me and treated me well, along with slipping me a few bucks along the way. My dad and Belle both worked at the MRC Ball Bearing Company and between the two of them made a very good income. My father finally got rid of his old Chevrolet and bought a big, black, 1946 Buick Roadmaster four-door sedan. It was a beautiful car and I was excited because I was close to getting a driver's license.

My Dad and Belle also bought the Lawrence Hotel, a small, rundown hotel on Second Street in downtown Jamestown. They bought the hotel as an investment and lived there as well. The hotel occupied the second and third floors of a three floor building. The bottom floor was a restaurant supply business that was owned by the guy who was the owner of the building and he rented the top two floors to my dad and Belle. It was by no means a first-class hotel and I guess by today's standards it would be called a flophouse. Nevertheless, the two of them had a nice big family room/bedroom overlooking Second Street. They also had a kitchen down the hall that was mostly used for drinking and smoking. In all the years that I knew my dad I never once saw him take a bite of food. Unbelievable but true.

They eventually got married and I was the best man. One Sunday we drove across the New York border into Pennsylvania and found a justice of the peace that married Mr. and Mrs. Percy Beatty. For the wedding party we drove back into New York and went to a restaurant in Bemis Point, New York, on Chautauqua Lake. Belle and I sat down and had a wonderful wedding dinner and my Dad, true to form, spent most of his time drinking at the bar. A very bizarre way to spend the honeymoon, but that's the way it was.

In high school I became more and more interested in New Orleans jazz and less interested in the high school band. There were two new additions to our jazz group: Matt Passamonti on trumpet and John Jacobson's younger brother, Jim, on banjo and piano. Jim wanted to be in the band and he taught himself on both the instruments…a bright and very clever young man.

Now our band looked like a New Orleans jazz band, even though we probably didn't sound like one. I was spending time between my two groups of friends, the academic/theater friends during the day and my jazz friends at night. Playing music for a living never entered my mind. My dream was to someday be a funeral director and embalmer. I talked this over with my career counselor in high school and we found out that to get in to the funeral business you had to go to an embalming college for two years and then apprentice at a funeral home for another two years. I found an embalming school not too far away, in Syracuse, New York, so that was the first step. Now came the money part, and for that the only one I knew that could help me was my dad because my mother and stepdad were in poor financial shape.

One Sunday when my dad and I were at our weekly gathering with the Beatty clan I got up the nerve to tell him of my future plans and ask for some financial help. We were in the middle of our meal when I brought the subject up and my dad looked at me and said, "Are You Crazy?" He told me that he had never heard such a ridiculous thing in his life and said I had a good future ahead of me working at MRC and playing music on the weekends, just like he did, and he wanted to know where I got such a stupid idea in my head in the first place. I was crushed and hurt and all I could do was to leave the table and run out of the house and cry. I walked and walked around the neighborhood until I put myself together and returned to the house. Everyone was concerned where I was and my Dad told me never to do that again. As far as I can remember, plans for any kind of college were never spoken of again.

When you mentioned the name Johnny DeVita around Jamestown you got everybody's attention. During prohibition Johnny was a bootlegger, getting his liquor shipped over Lake Erie from Canada. Following prohibition he settled into other illegal businesses that mostly involved gambling, including running his own bookie joint above his newsroom on First Street in Jamestown. He was also Lucille Ball's boyfriend in her early Jamestown days and had a helping hand in getting her on the inside track of show business in New York City with the help of his mafia friends.

His newsroom was used for money laundering from his gambling businesses and I passed it to and from high school every day. On the way home in the afternoon there was always an array of beautiful new Cadillac's, Lincoln's, Packard's and Chrysler's parked in front that belong to the various bookies around town. One day after school I got up enough nerve to walk into the newsroom pretending to buy a magazine or comic book. There was a stocky fellow behind the counter, nicely dressed with a shirt, tie, Cardigan sweater, cigar, and a beautiful fedora. I soon found out that this was Johnny's brother, Pete, and he was friendly to me and a very nice guy. After he found out my name was Beatty and that Percy Beatty was my father, that led to more conversations due to my father's musical popularity around town. After a few trips into the newsroom and buying lots of comic books, it became a regular hangout for me, and Johnny's brother, Pete, and I became friends over a period of time. Johnny came in and out several times while I was there but was very busy and never paid any attention to me.

Johnny had his office in the back of the newsroom and upstairs there was a gambling hall with the bookie joint and telephones for the latest updates on all the horse racing, plus card tables and roulette wheels and whatever other gambling device you could think of. The funny part of the whole situation was that the building was owned by the Present family, who had a jewelry store on the first floor right next to Johnny's newsroom. Jess Present, one of the two brothers in the family, was a New York State Senator and had a money laundering newsroom and bookie joint as tenants in his building. That's the way things worked in those days.

After a time, Johnny DeVita started noticing this young high school kid hanging around every afternoon. He asked his brother Pete who the hell I was and Pete assured him that I was okay, so he struck up a conversation with me that led to a friendship with one of the nicest guys I ever met in my life. Johnny never had children and I became the son he never had.

There was one Christmas with the Beatty's that didn't work out very well. I had my driver's license now and drove my Dad and Belle up to 11 Shaw Avenue for the big Christmas brunch. After we got there my dad had his usual shots and beers. Then he said, Jimmy, I need you to drive me somewhere for a while but we will be right back. So off we went and now that I had a driver's license my dad did not have to worry about drinking and banging up his beautiful Buick Roadmaster.

What my Dad had done was accept invitations to stop by and visit many of his drinking buddies on Second Street for a Christmas drink. So we drove from one house to another for a drink or two. Often his drinking buddies would have their whole family assembled for Christmas dinner and I'm sure they wondered what the hell we were doing there. This went on all afternoon until we arrived at one house where everybody was in the middle of Christmas dinner. Of course, being in the Christmas spirit, we were invited in, but it was very awkward. About that time I was getting very nervous because I knew we missed the entire Christmas gathering at the Beatty's and it was now time for me to head over for Christmas evening with the other side of the family. So back to 11 Shaw Avenue we went. When I opened the door I could feel the chill in the house. We were probably the most unpopular two guys on the planet. We missed the Christmas social fun along with the big Christmas brunch and plum pudding and the opening of presents. Fortunately, no one held me responsible. In fact, they all felt sorry for me. My Dad was the one in the hot seat and he could have cared less. The food of course was all gone, but that was all right as I had lots of snacks at the other houses. I had two or three presents to open and then off we went so I could catch up with the Swedish side of my family. It's amazing to imagine how my Dad managed to stand out on his own two feet that afternoon with all the whiskey and beer he had and no food. Thank God I was driving. Looking back, I feel sorry for my dad, for he never knew what Christmas was all about and what we did that afternoon was just inexcusable. Unfortunately, when my dad thought of a holiday, whether it would be Christmas, Easter or whatever, to him it was just another day, except he could drink and party more.

It became my pattern on my way home from school that I would stop and visit Pete, Johnny, and the boys at the newsroom. I now was able to put faces on those beautiful big luxury cars that were often parked in front of the newsroom, like Rags Condella and Jimmy Amatoza. There was another fellow that was often there, Al Morgan, who was a big time bookmaker and had his own newsroom a few blocks away. Al was a sharp dresser with a suit, white shirt and tie along with beautiful expensive shiny shoes and a good-looking fedora. He had a mouthful of gold teeth that lit up the room when he smiled and carried a wad of money that would choke a horse. Al Morgan's newsroom wasn't much, with very little to read and stale candy and gum. Let's face it, it was strictly for money laundering and you didn't get a friendly reception if you came in to buy something legitimately. It was right next door to Pete and Owen's, a local bar and restaurant that was a popular place to place bets with your favorite book maker. Being on 2nd St., Pete and Owen's was also a bar that was popular with my dad because he was really into baseball and bet on many of the major league games. It was also right across the street from the Jamestown Furniture Mart where all the Jamestown furniture factories displayed their products. Right next door to the Furniture Mart was the small, three-story building where my dad operated the Lawrence Hotel along with Belle.

Another fellow that was a regular at Johnny's newsroom was "Bang Bang." He had the barbershop across the street and I never knew him by any other name. Needless to say, that's where I started getting my haircuts. It was a little awkward because my Uncle Charlie had been cutting my hair since I was a kid. But when the word got out around the family who I was hanging out with, I'm sure he understood. How Bang Bang got his name I never knew and didn't want to find out. All I knew was that his barber's chair faced the front door and window of his small basement barbershop. There was another fellow there by name of "Coke." He never had much to say and I'm sure he got his name from drinking a lot of

Coca-Cola, because drugs were not in the picture with the guys in those days, it was simply gambling.

One afternoon a rookie patrolman wandered in the newsroom. It was obviously his first day on the police force as he had a bright new uniform and was very smartly twirling his baton. Johnny had a habit of double parking his car in front of the newsroom if there wasn't any room at the meter. If someone came back to their car and wanted to get out we could see this through the front window and we would go out and move Johnny's car. The rookie policeman wanted to know if we might know who the double-parked Buick belonged to. I said yes, I do, it was Johnny's car and he owned the newsroom. Well, the policeman said that car is double parked and I'm going to give him a ticket. "Where is he, I want to talk to him." I said okay and went back to Johnny's office and got him. This poor policeman had no idea who he was dealing with. Johnny came out and the cop began to give him a lecture about double parking and the ticket he was about to get. Johnny very politely said, would you hang on a minute officer? With that Johnny went to the phone, dialed a number, spoke briefly to someone on the other end, and handed the phone to the rookie policeman. After a brief time on the phone the officer apologized to Johnny for the misunderstanding and he became a regular, stopping by the newsroom as he was patrolling his beat.

I often rode around with Johnny when he went out on his errands. He had his Buick Roadmaster, with the license plate number JD 1. He liked to stop at his mother's home to say hello and I always looked forward to that because as soon as we walked into the house his mother had a nice glass of red wine poured for us and a dish of good old-fashioned Italian spaghetti. Johnny's mother was wonderful and she seemed always happy to see me.

There was a mystery in that house that I noticed but never ever questioned or talked about. There was always a young girl standing in the living room looking out the front window. She was around my age and always nicely dressed. But she made no attempt to come out to the dining room table and join us. In my presence neither Johnny nor his mother talked with her or acknowledged her existence.

For years there had been rumors around Jamestown that Johnny and Lucille Ball had a love child, and that rumor is still floating around to this day. One of the scandal magazines, *The Star*, had a big article about Johnny and Lucille's secret child. They claimed it was a boy and that he was put up for adoption. I don't believe that. If you followed the life of Lucille Ball you would find out that she went to New York City for a brief spell and returned to Jamestown for two years before picking up her career again.

So who was the mystery girl I saw in Johnny's mother's living room? Was she retarded? Was she told not to come out when there was company? Could she have been Johnny and Lucille's love child? She was about the correct age. However, I never talked with anybody in Jamestown that knew anything about it or would admit knowing anything. It's a Jamestown mystery that will probably remain just that.

By this time I had taken my driver's test and had passed. I took the test in my dad's Buick Roadmaster, so I was very good at driving a big car. Johnny was pleased when I got my license because now I could drive him and his friends to the many trips to the Buffalo Raceway. To get there we had to pass through several small villages from Jamestown to Buffalo. We were usually in a hurry and the speed limits through the small hamlets were around 25 mph, and they were speed traps. I could ignore the speed signs and go as fast as I pleased because the police were all paid off all the way to Buffalo. On the way there the car was completely silent as everyone was studying the horses that would be running that night.

I always hoped that the guys would have good luck betting on the horses, because it made for a more cheerful trip on the way back to Jamestown. Coming back, we made two or three stops for drinks and food. We always made a stop at the Sinclairville Hotel, where Johnny called Lucille Ball. One time I asked Johnny if it would wake Desi Arnaz up. Johnny said, Jim, they don't share the same bedroom. Evidently at that time, Johnny and Lucille might not have been romantically involved, but they were still good friends.

Johnny was having trouble with the law because the government was starting to crack down on gambling and he was in the hot seat. One day Johnny walked up to me and dangled a key before my eyes. It was a key to the gambling hall and bookie joint upstairs. Because of pressure from the government he decided to close it down. Johnny said, "I know you have talent for music," and I'm giving you the key to the hall upstairs to rehearse your band. He had taken everything out of the gambling hall/bookie joint, including the telephones for the horse races. All there was left in this big hall was a lonely piano sitting in one corner of the room and a few chairs. So there, in this empty bookie joint was the beginning of the Jim Beatty Jazz Band.

So that's where we had our first big rehearsal: Matt on trumpet, John on trombone, Jim playing a very out of tune piano, John Andrea on the drums, and Jim Beatty playing the clarinet. Halfway through our first tune, there was banging on the entrance door. I opened it and there was several officers from the Jamestown Police Department. I let them in, they looked around very puzzled, and I guess they couldn't believe that they just busted a bunch of teenagers playing jazz.

We were so wrapped up with playing jazz that we had little or nothing to do with girls. A high school hayride/barn dance came up and I decided to get a date and go to it. There was a girl that was very cute who I enjoyed talking with in school in the halls between classes. Her name was Joanne Bellevia and her father owned a very nice bar and restaurant on Second Street in downtown Jamestown. She agreed to go to the hayride/barn dance with me and I picked her up at her house on the night of the dance. Her father greeted me at the door and being a good Italian he offered me a glass of red wine while I was waiting for Joanne. Her parents were very gracious and having a drink of wine at my age in an Italian home was no big deal.

I agreed to have Joanne back home by 11 p.m. and off we went to the dance. It was a fun hayride to the barn dance and Joanne and I had a great evening dancing and socializing with our classmates. I had Joanne home ahead of time and even got another glass of wine. It was a fun night until my mother found out that I took an Italian girl out on a date. My mother was horrified and said, "Jimmy! What will the neighbors think? What will the girls at the bank think?" I guess my mother thought that her fellow employees at the bank were watching her family activities constantly and so I must have disgraced the family, at least on the Swedish side.

Years later my son, Jame, married an Italian girl, and of course my mother was fine with it. I recently talked with Joanne Bellevia at our 62nd high school reunion when I was back in Jamestown and we both laughed at that story. Joanne ended up marrying a Swedish guy, Robert H. Erickson, from our class, and they still live in Jamestown and have four children and nine grandchildren.

One afternoon I went over to John and Jim Jacobson's house to hang out and play some music. It was then that I met another member of their family. Their sister Joan was visiting along with her young son, Mike. Joan's husband was a newspaper man and they lived out of town and evidently Joan enjoyed spending time in Jamestown visiting with family and friends. She had never heard New Orleans jazz before and immediately fell in love with the music.

**Jim in front of Bang Bang's across the street from
the Newsroom and gambling hall.**

**A day of hunting with Jim Jacobson**

## CHAPTER 6

# New York City and the Jazz Clubs

My Dad, being a big baseball fan, was anxious to go to New York City and watch a few Yankee games. This could be done now as he and Belle purchased another brand-new Buick Roadmaster. This car was absolutely beautiful and it came with Buick's new automatic drive called Dynaflow. It was slow on acceleration but once it got moving it went like hell and drove like a dream. In those days you had to order a car to your specification and they built it at the factory just for you. It took a few weeks for delivery and when we went to pick it up my dad was frightened to drive it with the new automatic drive, so I drove it out of the car lot for a few blocks to teach him how to work the automatic shift. My dad and Belle were doing very well financially now with the two of them working at the MRC factory and the income from the Lawrence hotel. So it was off to New York City.

By that time the New York State Thruway was finished and was called the Super Dewey Highway, after Governor Dewey. But did we take the new highway? Of course not! Why? Because it had no roadside saloons to stop for drinks. So my Dad, Belle, Uncle Bill, and I set off for the big city, traveling the old Route 17 with me behind the wheel. Besides all the roadside stops, they had beer and a bottle of whiskey in the car and that's the way the trip went for a long drive, making friends with barkeeps along the way. When we did finally arrive in New York City we checked into our hotel absolutely exhausted and ready for some sleep. The next day was game day and all I wanted to do was roam around town listening to the jazz coming out from the jazz clubs all over the city. My dad, Belle and Uncle Bill went to the Yankee game and we made arrangements for all of us to meet in front of a jazz club called Jimmy Ryan's.

New York City was the capital of the world for good American jazz. Most of the jazz clubs were cellar clubs. They were turned into jazz clubs because in the cellar of the building the rent was cheap. You would walk down a short flight of stairs and enter a narrow, long room with the band playing at the end of the room. It was smoky as hell and everyone was packed in like sardines. There was nothing else like it and I loved it. The only problem was that I couldn't get in without adult accompaniment as I was only 17 and 18 was the legal drinking age in those days. So I would sit out on the curb as long as the doorman would let me and listen to all the jazz greats of that era do their thing.

Since I loved New Orleans jazz so much, on my first free night in New York I went to Jimmy Ryan's and sat out on the curb listening to the Wilbur De Paris Jazz Band. They had New Orleans musicians that played original New Orleans jazz and were part of originating it. I was in seventh heaven. On the first intermission the musicians came out gasping for air. I couldn't believe my eyes. There standing next to me was a New Orleans clarinet legend by the name of Omer Simeon. Omer was the clarinetist on the famous New Orleans classic recordings of Jelly Roll Morton and The Red Hot Peppers. He was one of my idols and he was standing next to me, probably wondering what this white boy was doing sitting on the curb. Omer lit up a cigarette and it looked like he was going to hang out for a while. So I lit up a cigarette as well, took a deep breath and got up the nerve to walk over to him and introduce myself and tell him how much I admired his playing through the years. Omer was a very charming, modest man and that conversation that we started turned into a long, long friendship. I told him I could not get in the club because I was under eighteen and did not have my parents with me. Omer suggested that to get in he would tell them he was my uncle. We thought about that for a second and then looked at each other and laughed.

After the Yankee game my Dad, Belle, and Uncle Bill showed up as planned and we all went in and heard some beautiful jazz. My Dad had a way of criticizing the music that I liked, and he could be very obnoxious when he had a few drinks. I don't think he was very pleasant to Omer that night and I was embarrassed. Looking back, sometimes I think that he was jealous of me, my love for the music and my musician friends. But that's another story for later on. It was time to head back to Jamestown and reality. The trip back was the same except in reverse. I could not wait to get home and tell the guys in the band all about my time with Omer and the night I spent at Jimmy Ryan's.

If I ever had a chance to do any part of my life over again, I think my high school years would be on the top of the pile. I was in the high school band, theater, a good fraternity, and lots of nice friends from all walks of life. I dropped out of the high school band, the theater, and was kicked out of the fraternity for drinking and smoking. For the most part I hung out with my jazz friends. Don't get me wrong, they were all nice fellows and we had a ball learning and playing jazz music and hanging out together. But like the rest of the guys, I had very little supervision or support from my family. So I guess I found it elsewhere.

Now that I had my driver's license I drove my Dad's Buick every Sunday to the Beatty brunch on 11 Shaw Avenue. I had a regular Sunday routine where I would stop by my Dad's, pick up the key to the car so I could take it out and give it a good wash and cleaning, and then I would pick my dad up and drive him to our weekly roast beef and Yorkshire pudding brunch. Afterwards I would take my dad back to Second Street where he could continue his visits to the many bars there. If he was in a good mood I would often ask him if I could borrow the car for a few hours. He usually had enough to drink and was in a good mood and would let me have it for the afternoon. That was a terrible mistake on his part.

I had this beautiful big Buick Roadmaster to pick up my friends and go joyriding for the afternoon. We didn't worry about gas because in those days it was around fifteen cents a gallon. But that Buick could go like hell and I would often take it out on country roads and floor it. The cars then were built like tanks and could survive my ridiculous and careless driving. I had a friend, Warren Erickson, whose father owned a big construction company in town. His Dad had an identical Buick except a year newer. Warren and I would take those two Buicks, along with our friends, and drag race around the football field of the local junior high school. Another friend, Gary Hunt, drove his father's Oldsmobile 88. That was a hot car of the time, but Warren and I never raced him. We would never have won anyway because those Oldsmobile 88s really could move.

I took it a step further and had a car key made for the Buick and when I knew my dad was busy with his bar hopping or passed out on his bed, I would go joyriding with the boys and surprisingly enough was never found out. To make sure and to cover my tracks I disconnected the speedometer so all the miles I put on didn't show. Fortunately, I never had an accident and my friends and I got through it in one piece. Not my proudest moment.

On top of all this nonsense, my grades at school were tumbling. I was happy if I just squeaked by with a C. I really needed some spending money so I wouldn't have to depend on handouts from my Dad and Belle.

A friend of mine told me about a part-time job opening at the Jamestown Stamp Company. It was a popular company for stamp collectors all over the country, and it was just a block away from the high school. I applied for the job, which consisted of working in the mailroom and being the general cleanup boy around the office. I went in to work after school every day and on Saturdays, when the place was closed; I cleaned and polished floors along with the assistant manager. He was the owner's brother and his name was Norm Patrick. I found out that he was a local drummer and an acquaintance of my dad. He had the stage name of Pat Norman so not to embarrass his brother, who was a very prominent businessman in Jamestown. His name was Marvin Patrick. So I got to work about 12 to 15 hours a week and was paid fifty-seven cents per hour. Norm, being a musician, enjoyed jazz and he would often have me over to his house to listen to records and feed me beer. It turns out that he wasn't that great of a drummer, but oh well; he was the leader of the band.

Norm Patrick's piano player, Paul Wick, owned an early recording device. It was a wire recorder and was sort of like fishing tackle on a spool except it was wire and more sturdy. I borrowed it from him and we brought it over to John Jacobson's house and made some recordings. Boy, did we feel like we were professionals now. But recording on wire was something else, because if it went off the track, like fishing tackle, you have one heck of a mess on your hands. It was hilarious when it went off the track as we had wire all over the place that we had to straighten out. But at least we got to hear ourselves and to this day when I tell people I made my first recordings on wire, they think I'm crazy.

Our band started falling apart with John Jacobson, now of age, thinking about joining the U.S. Navy. I never saw much of John after that and I understand he dropped his music. But John's brother, Jim, was still around to play the piano and banjo. My family life with my mother, sister Linda, and my stepdad, Pop, was going on about the same. I wasn't around much and still sleeping in my curtained room off the dining room. We now had a telephone, television set, and an old Ford. Things were looking up. One night I was at home babysitting my sister Linda and got in to the wine supply. I can assure you that this was the cheapest wine you could find anywhere. I think if you offered the wine to some bum in the gutter, he would turn it down. But I got into it and was having a ball for a while until I started throwing up all over the house. I thought I was going to die. And there was no way to cover it up by the time my mom and pop came home. It took me a while to live that one down and from then on the wine was hidden. Not that I would want it anyway. My mom told my dad about it and he gave me a lecture the next Sunday about the evils of drinking. Can you imagine that?

My mother was out working at the bank all day so she had hired a lady from upstairs to look after my little sister Linda. The ladies name was Alberta Sonholm and I think I drove her crazy and made her job with us a hard one. I was just full of my usual tricks; not bad ones, just practical jokes. I wish she was here now so I could tell her I was sorry, but then again she might have enjoyed it and it might have brightened up her day. I hope so. I had fun putting my mother on too, and she knew I was doing it. I asked my sister once what I did to drive my mom crazy the most. Two things I was doing deliberately for a laugh was opening the refrigerator door and staring into it forever, trying to figure out what I wanted to eat. The other one was something I do to this day, and that is wander around the house shaving with my electric razor.

My mother was something else. She was so nice to us and everyone. I think she just had one flaw. She wasn't very good at picking husbands. After many, many years and many hellish alcoholic episodes, Pop quit drinking and joined Alcoholics Anonymous and her life became much better. After pop passed away, she had many happy years in New York, later moving to Ohio, where my sister lived and watched after her, and lived to be 93 years old.

I listened to jazz recordings around the house when I was a kid, so much so that my mom began to know the bands and its personnel. For instance, I could ask, mom – who was playing with Louis Armstrong's Hot Five? She would rattle off, Johnny Dodds, clarinet, Louis Armstrong, Cornet, Kid Ory, trombone, Lil Hardin, piano, and Johnny St. Cyr on banjo. All correct. She was a fun wonderful mother and I miss her. It must have broken her heart not being able to spend more time with my sister and me. But she had to work every day to keep the household going and feeding us all. My stepdad's work was sporadic. Because of his drinking he went from one job to another. The unfortunate part of the whole thing was that he was an excellent salesman and if you went into a clothing store to buy a suit or whatever, you couldn't find anyone better to help you. He had a wonderful personality, was immaculately dressed and made you feel like you were somebody when you came into the store.

We continued our rehearsals at the Jacobsen household and things even got a little more interesting when we started making our own home brew. We were all getting close to being 18 years old and the legal drinking age. A little marijuana even entered the picture. I can't remember how we got it but it was in small quantities and we didn't smoke it that often. Jim and John's sister Joan started to spend more and more time in Jamestown with her young son. Joan was terrific and a lot of fun. I didn't know why she spent so much time in Jamestown away from her husband. I just thought at the time that she enjoyed coming home and spending time with her family. Joan was a free spirit and fell in love with New Orleans jazz and being at our rehearsals. She would just sit there hours at a time listening to the music. We guys never really had any girlfriends except for our high school dances and fraternity functions.

One afternoon after one of our rehearsals Joan took me by the hand and led me up the street. We went midway up the hill to a field with lots of tall grass. It was there she taught me a crash course on how to have sex with a woman. We did this several times during her visits to Jamestown. The only trouble was she was a married woman in love with a 17-year-old boy. I didn't have a clue what a 17-year-old does at that point in his life. I wish I could say that this little fling ended here, but it didn't.

I was burning the candles on both ends and I began to feel rundown, with a lack of energy. On my own, I went to a doctor. A friend of mine at school recommended Dr. Zabo, and I just walked into his office without an appointment. He was a short, middle-aged, Jewish man and he saw me right away. The two of us sat in his office smoking cigarettes, while I told him how I felt. He examined me and after our consultation he diagnosed me with rheumatic fever and admitted me to the hospital for observation.

My parents were worried sick as I lay there with an intravenous drip and all kinds of nurses taking care of me. I know now that he was wrong with his diagnosis, but in those days there were not the tests that they have now. It really screwed me up and put me out of action for some time. I even missed the graduation ceremonies at Jamestown High School. I wonder who would have come to see me graduate anyway. I'm sure my mother and sister would have been there. But with all this behind me, I was looking forward to getting on with my life. I was soon to turn 18 years old and that would open up a lot of new doors for me. For one thing, I would then be of legal drinking age and able go to the jazz clubs in New York City on my own. It also made me eligible for the draft for the Korean War.

Turning 18 was a big deal and I don't think that anybody was happier about it than my Dad. I now could meet with him at his hangouts on Second Street and have a drink and a smoke with him. Of course, I was expected to order a shot of whiskey with a beer chaser just like he and his friends did. This was heavy duty drinking and I could not even think about attempting it now. I was my Dad's new drinking buddy. He would usually buy the rounds of drinks, but they were not much, around 25 or 30 cents for a shot and a beer chaser. You didn't have to worry about the police in those days, because they could care less if you were drinking and driving. All the bars had a bottle of whiskey in the back room along with some beer for the patrolman on the beat to come in and take a break. During the Christmas season all the bars served Tom and Jerry's. They were liquor mixed with a heavy sweet batter and sprinkled with cinnamon and served hot. And boy did that taste good on a cold December evening in New York. It was sort of like the TV show, *Cheers*, but instead of one bar you were known and knew everyone at ten bars on Second Street.

The drinking had its bad side as well. Home, with my mother, step-dad and sister Linda, was not getting any better. My stepdad's drinking problem was not good and I felt sorry for my mother who was trying to keep the family together. There was never any violence on his part but he just got falling down drunk and could not hold on to a job. He had joined AA but kept falling off the wagon. He was so likable a fellow, I felt sorry for him and it all caught up to him down the line.

The trips to New York City and the Yankee games continued, except now I was of drinking age and could go into the jazz clubs on my own. This was terrific because when the bands took their intermission I took advantage of the opportunity to introduce myself and get to know the players. Many of the musicians were a major part of creating New Orleans jazz back in the early 1900s. I knew them from all the recording's they had made years before. I was still spending a great deal of time at Jimmy Ryan's Jazz Club on 52$^{nd}$ Street. I loved it there because of the Wilbur De Paris Jazz Band and his clarinetist, Omer Simeon. We became great friends and on his intermissions we would walk down 52nd St. to a little bar and have our shots and beers for 35 cents, and that was in downtown

New York City. Often I would hang around until Omer was finished playing, and at three or four in the morning we would go have breakfast together. In our talks he taught me so much about playing jazz clarinet. I got to be a frequent visitor to the Big Apple.

Turning 18 now made me eligible for the draft, and that meant the same for all my friends in our little jazz band in Jamestown. John Jacobson, for instance, did not want to be drafted into the Army so he planned to join the Navy for four years. He had been drifting away from the band anyway, because he was becoming interested in modern jazz or bebop, which of course I didn't care for any more than I do now. But that was a big thing in those days, a new way of playing jazz, drifting farther and farther away from the melody of a song. The musicians and fans of that new type of jazz even had their own dress called zoot suits and peg pants.

I had to start to make some real money. I was on my own financially and wanted my own car. There were job openings at MRC Ball Bearings, which offered me much more money than the fifty-seven cents an hour that I was making at the Jamestown Stamp Company. I applied and got the job, probably because of my dad and stepmother who both worked there. I got a job working in the inspection department as a Magnaflux inspector. This was a job inspecting the ball bearings for very minor cracks that could be major problems after assembled and installed. Everyone in my family was very happy for me and I think that they saw a great future for me doing this for the rest of my life and playing music on the weekends. I knew I did not want to do this the rest of my life, but at the moment the money really came in handy. My first major purchase was a 1942 Cadillac. This car was built at the beginning of the Second World War and instead of chrome on the car, it had plastic. It was probably quite a ridiculous car to own, but if I had it today it would be worth a lot of money.

I was eligible to be drafted into the Army, and sure enough I got my notice to report for a physical examination. I was in perfectly good health and believed that I was misdiagnosed with rheumatic fever from Dr. Zabo. I reported for my physical and recognized almost everyone there from high school. It was hysterical. You could not believe the excuses of ill health those people came up with to get out of going into the service. One friend of mine, a strapping Swedish boy, showed up with a huge neck brace. Others were limping around like they could barely walk. But the doctors, of course, were always on to this and off they went to serve their country whether they wanted to or not. But me?

Of all things, Dr. Zabo was on the draft board and one of the examining physicians. He took one look at me and said "This young man is not eligible for service, due to the rheumatic fever that damaged his heart". So there I was 4F, and not fit for service in the US Army. I knew this was wrong, but how do you fight the doctors at the draft board? But it gave me an opportunity to better prepare myself for music later on.

Our band got its first and only job at the Sons of Italy Club in Jamestown. It was a big night for us. We had all started playing together and learning jazz in junior high school and now here we were accepting money for playing. It was quite a night and even my mother and stepdad showed up to hear us. My mother brought her movie camera along and took some footage that I have to this day. Trouble was, the Musicians Union was big in those days and we were not members. The union representative showed up and told us we should join immediately. My dad had been a member of the Musicians Union for years and to avoid any problems I joined as well.

The rest of the guys in the band sort of drifted off their own ways. John Jacobson in the Navy, Matt, I think, moved to Florida, and John Andrea, being a talented artist, went in that direction and later was drafted into the Army, ending up in Germany. That left Jim Jacobson and I and the two of us went out and played as a duo with Jim on piano and me on the clarinet. I'll never forget our first job at the Lakewood Rod and Gun Club. We called ourselves The Two Jims, and the newspaper had a misprint in the ad for us that read, The Two Gins. I cut that ad out of the paper and it has survived all these years. Saving newspaper ads and stories about my music engagements became a habit for the rest of my life and has been a lifesaver in writing this book. Jim Jacobson also found a job at MRC on the night shift. So now we both worked at MRC and played our music on the weekends. We became very good friends.

I tried to get into New York City as often as possible as time permitted. Omer was my new best friend in the city and was still playing with the Wilbur De Paris Jazz Band on 52nd Street. Omer and I were talking one night about Jelly Roll Morton and those recordings he made with him came into the conversation. I told him how much I enjoyed listening to them and how great they were. Omer said, Jim, I have never heard them, because back in those days after you made the recordings there was no such thing as a playback; you could not hear what you had just recorded. It was almost 30 years after he recorded them with Jelly Roll, and he still had not heard them. After I got back home I played the records into my tape recorder and the next time I went into the city I brought my tape recorder and played the recordings for Omer. He was thrilled. I learned a lot from Omer about New Orleans jazz and will always be grateful. We saw a lot of each other over the years because of my frequent trips to New York City to hear the jazz greats.

Another jazz club, of the many that I used to frequent in New York City, was a place called Eddie Condon's. Eddie Condon was a very popular guitar player and jazz promoter. He grew up and played in Chicago during the roaring 20's and the Al Capone era. He ended up in New York City and opened his own jazz club backed by the Mafia using his name.

He always had a great band playing what was known as the Chicago style jazz, a white man's version of New Orleans jazz. His club was located on W. 3rd Street in Greenwich Village. But the extra big attraction for me was his cornet player, Wild Bill Davison. Wild Bill, originally from Ohio, got his name honestly. He smoked and drank like a madman and played the cornet like it was going to catch fire.

Like Eddie Condon, Wild Bill Davison played in and around the Chicago area during the Al Capone era. He moved to New York City in 1941 playing in many jazz clubs and became a well-known musician. He spent World War II in the Army and after his discharge became a regular at Eddie Condon's. He was a cornet player on all those great Sidney Bechet recordings that I heard when I got interested in jazz while in junior high school. I made it a point to meet him and talk with him, and the way to do that was to buy him a drink on his intermission. Wild Bill, like most of the famous musicians I met in those days, always took the time to talk with me about music and encourage my playing. I made it a point to visit Condon's and Wild Bill every time I came to town. Little did I know then that later in my life we would become great personal friends and play music together?

And then there's Sidney Bechet. Wow, what a talent. I met him only once. In the early 1950's, Bechet moved to France and became a national hero there, only returning to play in the US occasionally. I learned that he would be playing in New York City at the Paramount Theater lounge. So off I went with my old buddy Jim Jacobson to hear this great musician play his soprano saxophone. The Paramount Grill was huge with a very large stage. It was an upscale place to go hear music with white tablecloths and all. Sidney was backed by a band called the Salt City Six. Oddly enough, that was a band that I would be playing with in later years. Meeting Sidney wasn't anything that I thought would happen. However, a crazy coworker of mine at MRC knew that I was going to New York to hear Sidney Bechet and he sent me a telegram in care of Sidney Bechet at the Paramount. Of course, Sidney got the telegram and said, "Who the hell is Jim Beatty?"

As luck would have it, a piano player by the name of Dick Wellstood was with Sidney at the time and told him he knew me and that I was in the lounge. Dick Wellstood was a great piano player and I got to know him from listening to him play with many bands in the city. It looked like musicians were starting to know who I was. Dick came to my table in the lounge and said "Jim, Sidney wants to talk with you!" You could've knocked me over with a feather. I was taken into a large office and there was Sidney Bechet, seated behind a big desk. He looked at me and said, "So you are the famous Jim Beatty? Well, I have a telegram for you." He had a good laugh and I knew everything was cool. He couldn't have been nicer to me and we had a nice chat until he had to go back and play his second show. I'll be ever grateful for my coworker, Gil Siverson, at MRC for sending me that telegram. Bechet wrote several wonderful tunes. His most famous one, "Petite Fleur," went to number one on the hit parade. The hit recording of it was made by a British clarinet player, Monty Sunshine, and many years later I would have the opportunity to play with him as well.

Back in Jamestown things were going fine. I was working at MRC making good money and playing music jobs on the weekends. I was ready to go back to New York City again when I found out George Lewis and his band from New Orleans was going to be performing at the Paramount Lounge. I had patterned some of my clarinet style after George Lewis. He was the clarinet player on the Bunk Johnson records that I heard while in junior high. Many of the musicians in New Orleans in the 1920s left the city to make names for themselves in Chicago, however, George and a few others preferred to stay home in New Orleans and play their music. George was a small man, around 100 pounds or so, and worked as a stevedore on the docks of New Orleans during the day and played jazz at night. When the New Orleans Jazz revival came, he was at the forefront, playing and recording at first with Bunk Johnson and later forming his own band, which was outstanding. His clarinet playing was so beautiful and full of soul that there was none other like it. He also wrote a pretty tune that he named "The Burgundy Street Blues," and it was his signature tune. In later years he made many tours around the world, especially in the UK. When I tour the UK, I hear so many of the British clarinet players trying to copy his style. There was only one George Lewis of course, but there is an English clarinet player that does a good job of playing like George. His name is Sammy Remington.

When I got to town I naturally went to see Omer first. I told him that I planned to go hear George Lewis. Omer, being a New Orleans musician himself, said "Jim, tell him hi for me." So off I went to the Paramount Grill and as I walked into the lobby, who did I come face-to-face with but George Lewis himself. He was on intermission and heading for the restroom, all dressed up and smoking a cigarette with a cigarette holder. I had never had any trouble meeting and talking with all these great musicians in New York, but here was my big opportunity to strike up a conversation with George Lewis and I froze. I could not get the courage to introduce myself and tell him that Omer Simeon sent his greetings. I did hear the band that night and it was wonderful, but that's as far as it went. The next night I headed back to Jimmy Ryan's to hear the De Paris band with Omer playing the clarinet. On Omer's intermission the two of us made our little trip down to the corner bar for 35 cent shots and beers. Omer asked me about my night with George Lewis. I had to tell him that I didn't have the nerve to engage him in a conversation. Omer laughed, and suggested that the two of us go see George Lewis the next evening, as Omer had the night off.

We had a ball. Not only did George Lewis join our table but his whole band did as well. I imagine that people watching could understand a bunch of black musicians from New Orleans catching up on old times. But who in hell is that young white boy? George and I became friends and I saw him many times after, in New Orleans and Los Angeles. A few years later, when I was in the Army School of Music at Fort Dix, New Jersey, I would take a bus into the city to listen and visit with him when he was in town.

Another adventure I had with Omer Simeon was quite unexpected. Omer's nights off were Sundays and we decided to go to a jazz club in Times Square called the Metropole. It was a long, long room, not too wide, but the bar ran from one end of the room to the other. The stage was right behind the bar and equally as long. There were alternating bands and because the stage and bar were so long they had one band set up on one end and the other band set up on the opposite end. The musician we came to see that night was Henry "Red" Allen. He was a big, boisterous, entertaining trumpet player that got your attention, whether you liked it or not. He recognized Omer, of course, standing at the bar with me. So, on his intermission he came right down to visit with Omer and we were introduced. Henry had a one half hour intermission while the other band played and he suggested that we take the short walk down to the Basin Street East, where Louis Armstrong was doing a show.

Henry knew Louis very well, as they worked together many times over the years and knew that he was on intermission at the time. So off we went: Omer Simeon, Red Allen, and Jim Beatty, on their way to see "Satchmo." When we got to the Basin Street East, Henry walked in like he owned the place and we marched right through to the dressing room door and walked in. And there was Louis Armstrong himself. He was stark naked with just a small towel around his middle. His face lit up when he saw Henry and Omer, two old buddies from New Orleans. I was introduced and the party began. There was a tray full of drinks of all sorts plus all kinds of snacks if you wanted them. Satchmo, of course, was known for his fondness for marijuana and he was doing just that. I didn't join in, as I was happy with that tray full of assorted cocktails. Everyone had lots of laughs and then it was time for Armstrong to take a shower, get dressed and do another show. That was quite an experience, and one I'll never forget. Later on I was to have another meeting with Armstrong which was just as interesting.

Besides driving to New York City listening to the jazz greats, life in Jamestown went on. I bought a boat and in the summertime just buzzed around Chautauqua Lake. There were a few restaurants and bars on the lake and also the Moose and Viking clubs. My mother loved to go for boat rides with me, although she could not swim and was terrified by the water. I could not swim very well but it never bothered me. Like the young idiot I was, I took a liking to sniffing the gasoline tank on the boat. It really gave me a high until one day I took one too many sniffs and passed out briefly. That wised me up big time and I never did it again, but I still love the smell of gasoline. I also enjoyed fishing on Chautauqua Lake noted for its huge muskellunge. I never caught one but was satisfied with getting my fill of bass or perch because if you caught enough of them you had yourself a great meal.

I was still working at MRC, playing the occasional music job on the weekends and hanging out with Johnny DeVita and the guys at the newsroom. I still loved cars and became friends with a car dealer named, incredibly, Jack Sharkey. He was a "Sharkey" and first-class crook of a used car dealer, but a nice guy and fun to be around. Jim Jacobson and I would buy old cars from him, detail them and make them look presentable. We would put an ad in the paper and sell them to people who said they would never buy a car from a used car dealer, only a private party.

Jim and I would make a few extra dollars on the side and had a lot of fun doing it. Of course, Jack Sharkey taught us one of his favorite tricks:

Turning back the odometer so we could advertise it as a car we got from "My grandmother who only drove it back and forth to church." So when you think about it, we were no better than the used car dealers, but that's the way it worked in those days. One day Jim told me he had purchased a 1929 Franklin with an air cooled engine. Everyone laughed at that car and there were no buyers. It ended up going to the junkyard and selling it for $50. I hate to think what that car would be worth today.

Rumors had been floating around MRC about a layoff. If and when this happened, I would be one of the first to go as I was low man on the totem pole. I liked my job at MRC and had worked myself up to a good paying position in the gauge room. Making ball bearings was very delicate and precise work and the measurements during the manufacturing process had to be perfect. After all, many of the bearings we made were for jet aircraft and it was just unthinkable to have one of your bearings fall apart at 40,000 feet in the air. So in the gauge room we checked and rechecked everything before it went out the door. I worked the evening shift from 3 in the afternoon until 11 at night. That gave me three hours every night to hit the bars and party on the way home. It was sort of fun because you could sleep as long as you wanted the next day and on the weekend you were finished work on Friday night and did not have to go back until Monday afternoon.

My Dad and Belle were still working at MRC and running the hotel. They were doing well financially and even bought a new Buick every couple of years. The British side of the family were doing well and of course I was always welcome to join in for roast beef and Yorkshire pudding on Sundays. On the Swedish side I did lose my favorite aunt, Hildur. She was the eldest of my mother's sisters and of course she brought me up along with my grandmother in my early years. Her favorite hymn was, "Beyond the Sun Set." Many years later in my career I was able to record it on a Christian album. My mother was well, but still had to contend with my stepdad's drinking problem. My little sister Linda was growing up and we were becoming good friends. So everything was cooking along fine in Jamestown and at the time I thought that I could live like this the rest of my life. But it was not to be.

The layoff happened and I was one of the first to go, along with my friend and musical partner Jim Jacobson. It was unemployment time and hanging around Jamestown without a job did not sound good to me. I thought it time to follow the music in other parts of the United States. I asked Jim if he wanted to go and he was game. So, off we went, the two of us on a new adventure, in a 1953 Dodge Ram.

## CHAPTER 7

# Road Trip, First Stop
# New Orleans

JIM JACOBSON AND I TOOK off on an adventure to "follow the music." I had a 1953 Dodge Ram two door with fluid drive. Fluid drive was Chrysler Corporation's version of an automatic transmission. It had a clutch and you could shift gears if you wanted, or leave it in second gear without using the clutch and drive by simply pressing and releasing the gas pedal to change gears. Of course it was antiquated by today's standards, but back then I thought it was great. Dodge stopped producing their cars with fluid drive in 1954.

So off we went, fluid drive and all. Our first stop was the "Mecca of Jazz," New Orleans, where it all started back in the late 1800's. I was really looking forward to catching up with George Lewis and his band after meeting them in New York City. George's band was full of great musicians. Besides George on clarinet, there was Kid Howard, trumpet, Big Jim Robinson, trombone, Alton Purnell, piano, Slow Drag Pavageau, bass, Lawrence Marrero, banjo and Joe Watkins on the drums. Of course, New Orleans was famous for many musicians playing there at the time. Probably at the top of the heap was clarinetist Pete Fountain. Pete was a marvelous clarinet player and gained national fame when he was playing on the Lawrence Welk television show on Saturday nights. (Some years later I became friends with Pete and he gave me a helping hand.) He later returned to New Orleans, opened his own nightclub and was very successful with it.

Another well-known New Orleans musician was trumpeter Al Hirt. He had his own nightclub as well. Al was a big heavy man with a beard and the ability to blow the roof off the room. There was also a well-known band called the Dukes of Dixieland. They were what I would call the white man's version of New Orleans jazz. They wore fancy jackets and straw hats and played loud and fast. They were all excellent musicians and really put on a great show. There was also a jazz club that was a must see in New Orleans. It was a hole in the wall called Preservation Hall. The club hired old time musicians to come and play. They were the real thing and it was wonderful to listen to them and their old jazz songs from the past. When you listened to the music you went and got your own beer and sat in rickety old chairs. It wasn't a very big room and if you could not find a chair you simply stood or sat on the floor. So, besides all the music in New Orleans, there was the history, the restaurants with New Orleans food, and of course, Bourbon Street at night. There was nothing like it in the world.

Jim and I took turns driving to save money on motels and to get there faster. I would drive and he'd sleep and vice versa. When we pulled off the freeway and drove into the city of New Orleans, I could not believe it, standing on a corner was none other than Big Jim Robinson, trombone player with the Lewis band. I pulled over and got Jim's attention. "Hey Jim, do you remember me from New York City and Omer Simeon?" He replied, "Ya man! What are you all doing in New Orleans?" I filled him in and he told me that the Lewis band was playing at a jazz club on Bourbon Street. That's all I needed to know as that was going to be our first stop of the evening. We needed lodging and found a small apartment right downtown. The rent was low so it was great for our budget. We moved our luggage in, freshened up, and went out on the town for the night. The bars on Bourbon Street in New Orleans are open 24/7, so we had a big night ahead of us. Little did we know at the time this would be our first and only night in New Orleans this trip.

New Orleans, the land of dreams. At least that's what I thought when I arrived on Bourbon Street. Talk about a party. I had never seen anything like it. Everyone was in a gay mood and there was hot jazz blaring out of all the nightclubs. It was super hot and muggy and my shirt was ringing wet from sweat and not many places had air conditioning. But that's all right, I thought, I'd just have to learn to live with it. We found the club where the George Lewis band was playing and we couldn't get a table because it was so packed, but found some room at the bar. I waved at George, but did not get much reaction from him and when the band took intermission, they disappeared out a side door. And then it hit me: Segregation. My first real encounter with it. In the South, a black band could not mingle with white customers on their break and had to go to a back room or out in the alley. Unbelievable but true. So Jim and I went out to the alley and said hello to George and the boys. It was a rather uncomfortable situation under the circumstances and we kept our conversation short. We did get some bad news. George said that he and the band were leaving to play in Los Angeles for a month. That was a bummer because I was planning on hearing a lot more of them in New Orleans. But there was a lot of other groups to listen to and we wouldn't be starved for music. Jim and I were like kids in a candy store, so much to see in one night- impossible!

During the course of the evening we went to several bars for drinks and found out that if we wanted to go we did not have to finish our drinks, just get to-go cups and take it with you. That was a surprise. We did talk to some locals that were interested in chatting with two young teenagers from New York. We were told that New Orleans had a very high crime rate and we had rented an apartment in a very bad neighborhood. We were also told that it wouldn't be a good idea to park our car near our apartment with out-of-state plates. In fact, we were told that wandering too far off Bourbon Street was not a good idea - a good chance of being mugged. We also found out that the musicians playing late at night carried pistols to protect themselves. So I was beginning to see that New Orleans was not necessarily a bed of roses. Then it started raining. It rained like I had never seen rain before and the two of us were drenched to the skin. But what the heck, it was warm and muggy and rainy, and we were having fun. At about 4 a.m. we decided to give it up and go to our apartment for a good night sleep.

We didn't park the car near our apartment, but found a brightly lit place fairly close. We got to our apartment building soaking wet, opened the door and saw several hundred cockroaches scurrying about the place. God, I could never crawl into bed here, it gave me the creeps to think about it. I looked at Jim and said, "I think we've seen enough of New Orleans for now." He agreed and we picked up our luggage and left. Fortunately we had not paid any money for the apartment and had not used anything or slept in the beds. All we had done was leave our luggage there for a few hours. So we did not feel guilty about slipping away in the early hours of the morning.

So far, we had driven from New York through Pennsylvania, Ohio, West Virginia, Kentucky, Georgia, Alabama and Louisiana. We got in the car and looked at each other and I said, "Now what?" New Orleans, despite all the great music and history, was not the place for me to live for any length of time". And the segregation was intolerable. So I said, "Jim, you know that old saying, 'Go West young man!'" We pointed the car toward Los Angeles and off we went through Louisiana, Texas, New Mexico,

Arizona, and finally, California. The old Dodge with fluid drive was doing great and thank God that gas was cheap in those days.

Arriving in California felt great. The sun, perfect temperature, and palm trees were sure a welcome sight. Los Angeles was also a fantastic town for traditional jazz. Trombonist Kid Ory was playing there, along with Pete Dailey, a local favorite cornet man. There was also the Fire House Five, consisting of musicians that worked at the Walt Disney Studios. Their cornet player, Danny Alguire, would play with my group in Portland, Oregon years later. There was also a few old New Orleans jazz players that moved out to that area and a huge active jazz club. Plus, George Lewis and his band were on their way in a week or so to play at the Beverly Caverns Jazz Club in Hollywood. This looked more like it...beautiful, sunny weather, great temperatures and even an ocean nearby. The traffic was a nightmare during rush hour and the smog could be annoying at times, but what the heck. We were a little smarter this time around and found a motel so we could take our time looking through the paper for apartments. After searching around for a couple of days we found one that we liked and within our budget. It looked like a great place to settle in for the moment and we started searching for jobs.

After looking through the want ads, we found that the General Motors Chevrolet plant was hiring and we both got jobs. They put me to work on the assembly line. They gave me a rivet gun and a big bucket of bolts and I was to rivet them on the engines as they came by. Well, I didn't weigh much back then and that rivet gun just about shook me to death. On top of that, many engines were flying by me with no bolts. It didn't take too long for the foreman to come up and tell me that I wasn't doing a good job and they were going to transfer me to another department. They gave me a broom and sent me to the men's restroom/smoking lounge and promoted me to janitor. The men's room was so thick with smoke you could hardly make out who was standing next to you. All I had to do was keep the toilets and urinals clean and sweep up the cigarette butts. This was a job that I could do and I was proud of myself.

One day while I was doing my janitorial duties, a very well dressed gentleman stopped in for a pee and cigarette. He looked at me and said, "What's a nice young man like you doing working in a place like this?" I told him my story and my failure on the production line. He was an office manager and had a lot of pull and I was transferred into a cushy office position. Now I came to work every day all dressed up like I was some-body very important and I could go to the men's restroom for a pee and cigarette without my broom. Things looked good. I had a nice apartment with a motherly landlady, a well-paying job and lots of jazz to go listen to at night. What more could I ask for?

Los Angeles is where I really had to start putting my clarinet skills to the test. I attended the Los Angeles Jazz Club activities and was play-ing alongside some real hotshot musicians. The musician that I really was thrilled to play along with was none other than Johnny St. Cyr. He was the banjo player on the early Louis Armstrong Hot Five recordings made in 1925 and 1926. These were historic recordings that I still enjoy listening to. I would also go listen to local bands and have my clarinet ready in the trunk of the car hoping that I would be asked to sit in. I can understand now that if I wasn't asked it was because I had a heck of a lot to learn. Running around nightclubs and coming up with the rent every week was expensive and I often saw myself picking up cigarette butts, tak-ing the tobacco out and rolling my own cigarettes. Those were the days.

One Saturday afternoon while relaxing around the apartment, there was a knock on the door. I opened it and just about fell over. There stood Joan with her luggage. She had left her husband Scotty and children and followed me to California. She spent the night with her brother and me, then found her own little apartment nearby. Her husband must have been a wonderful guy and really in love with her, to put up with all this. Joan came along to all my musical activities and met many of my musician friends. It was now obvious to her that there was no future for us and that I was just an immature young teenager. Joan still loved jazz and took a liking to a trumpet player by the name of Johnny Lucas. Johnny was handicapped and was in a wheel chair. He couldn't completely bend his arms and had a trumpet especially built for him. He was a nice, cheerful guy and a decent trumpet player. I was happy to see the two of them get along so well and it sure took the pressure off me.

After only a few months in LA I got a phone call from my mother saying I had a letter from MRC that they were getting ready to hire back the people that they had laid off. Now what to do? If I did not go back to work I would lose all the little bit of seniority that I had built up. But on the other hand, I had a job at Chevrolet and was breaking into the jazz world in LA. Then another phone call from mom. A letter came from the draft board to report for another physical. I probably could have transferred to the draft board in LA but decided to go back to New York. I could always return to California later as I had my foot in the door now. My buddy Jim also had a job that he could return to at MRC and he was ready to head back as well. I gave my notice at Chevrolet and once again we packed up the Dodge and headed across the country to Jamestown. I went back to work at MRC and waited for the physical at the draft board. I figured that my old friend Dr. Zabo would reject me again and I would restart my life. I was in for a surprise.

Back at MRC everything fell into place and it was great to see a lot of my old friends again at work. A few of them were involved with the United Auto Workers Union. They thought I was good with people and asked me to represent the union members in the inspection department. It was an elected position and I won. It was interesting because I had to deal with my fellow workers and the department foreman and night superintendent.

Sometimes we had a lot of grievances going on and it could get hectic, but the nights went very fast. Included with the inspection department was the polish room, which was the end of the line for the ball bearings because all that was left was polishing the insides of the bearings where the balls rolled around. This was terribly dirty and greasy work with the finishing compounds that they had to work with. Nobody wanted that job, so they gave it to black employees. It was a separate room, closed in, and no one would even think about entering the room, especially management. You could very likely go into that room with clean clothes on and come out looking like a grease monkey. The greasy compounds were flying all over the place in that room and if you got splattered you would never know who the person was that did it. Fortunately, I was friendly with the polish room guys and was the only one at MRC that could venture in the polish room and come out without a speck on me.

Now that I was back at MRC I was making good money, along with playing the occasional music jobs on weekends in clubs and private parties. I went out and bought myself a used 1952 Buick Roadmaster with Dynaflo transmission. Jet black with white sidewall tires. The Dynaflo transmission was Buick's version of an automatic transmission. It was smooth but slow on acceleration, but boy did it burn the gas. It had a nickname in those days: "Dynaslush." This car was the cat's meow and it was a big hit with the gang at the newsroom.

Nothing much changed with my family. It was great to see my mom, Pop, and sister Linda. My dad and Belle were still plugging away on the day shift at MRC and running the hotel. They even had Aunt Lizzie working there now. I guess you could call her the maid. She changed and cleaned the bed sheets and the rooms. My dad still played on weekends with the Viking Orchestra. He used to get so drunk on his jobs, I don't know how he made it through the night. On the other hand, a few of the other musicians in the band were not too far behind him.

Then I got the letter I was waiting for. It instructed me to report to the draft board for another physical. I thought it would be the same deal with Dr. Szabo pulling me aside and saying that I was not fit for service. Much to my surprise, Dr. Szabo was not there and I had a new doctor. He gave me the once-over and said, "I see you have been rejected in the past, but I can't seem to find anything wrong with your health. How do you feel?" I said I felt great and didn't think there was anything wrong with me. So, my papers were stamped, "Fit for Duty."

## CHAPTER 8

# Fit For Duty

So "FIT FOR DUTY" IT was, and I was ready. Trouble was, I wanted to be in the Army band, but when I talked to the Army recruiter he said if I was drafted I would have a slim chance of getting in. The band was a cushy assignment and everyone that played an instrument wanted to get in. The only sure way of being assigned to the Army band was to enlist in the Army for four years. If you were drafted, you are only in for two years. What do I do? I had discussed this many times in the past with Johnny DeVita and he told me, "Jim, let them draft you, you'll get in the band." So I decided to sit back and wait for my orders to report for duty.

A letter did arrive in the mail from the President of the United States. It said, "Order to Report for Induction on December 5, 1956." I showed up at the assigned place and there was several other young men waiting to board a bus. Everyone from both of my families were there to see me off. We all said our goodbyes and I boarded a bus that was headed for the train station in Buffalo, New York, that would take me to Fort Dix, New Jersey. The bus arrived at the Buffalo train station and we had a half hour or so before the train departure. I knew that this would be my last night to party for some time to come. So I ran up the street to the nearest liquor store and bought me a pint of whiskey and a couple of packs of cigarettes. I used to smoke Camels or Lucky Strikes in those days, no filters, just the raw tobacco. I was in a sleeper car and compartment that I shared with a stranger. So I took my pint of whiskey and cigarettes to a smoking compartment. I had a few guys come in and join me for a cigarette and if they were interesting to talk to I gave them a sip of whiskey. The train rolled on and I managed to polish off my bottle. I went into my sleeper car and had just nodded off for a bit when we arrived at our destination, Fort Dix, New Jersey. We got off the train and I felt terribly hung over. To make matters worse, there were Army sergeants yelling at us. I realized now that the party was over, and I was in the United States Army and I was nothing but a pile of manure as far as they were concerned. And, the worst was yet to come.

I did get a great farewell present a couple of days before leaving for the Army. Louis Armstrong and his band came to Jamestown for a concert on December 3, 1956, just two days before I was to report for induction. And there was an added bonus: My good friend, clarinetist Edmund Hall, was now playing with Armstrong. I came to know Edmund Hall from when he was playing at Eddie Condon's in New York City, along with Wild Bill Davison. Edmund took the job with Armstrong because it paid good money, $500 a week, all expenses paid, and you could take your wife along on the tours. Edmund was a New Orleans musician and blew a beautiful, woody tone out of his clarinet. He had his own style of playing that you can pick out easily on a recording. He was also a very well-educated gentleman and always dressed immaculately.

When shows came to town, the performers usually stayed at the Hotel Jamestown, so on the afternoon of the concert I called Edmund and we agreed to meet at the hotel before the concert. When I got to the hotel I called his room and he said that he and his wife were on their way down and to meet them at the elevator. The elevator door opened and there was Edmund and his wife and to my surprise Louis Armstrong and his wife were with them. I had not seen Louis since that night in his dressing room at the Basin Street East with Omer Simeon and Red Allen. He remembered us coming to see him that evening and said he was pleased to see me again. I told Louis that I was going in the Army in two days. He actually puckered up and tears came to his eyes when I told him. It was like I was going off to battle or something. We had a quick bite to eat at the coffee shop and then they were off in a cab to get ready and set up for the concert. It was too early for me to go with them so I walked over to the Jamestown High School auditorium for the show. It was a great show and at intermission time I went back stage to the dressing rooms and said my goodbyes. Armstrong's wife, Lucille, was very busy sewing a button on his jacket. What a sendoff for the next two years in service.

As soon as we got off the train we were herded into a large hall with tables and chairs. In front of each chair on the table was a stack of papers and a pencil. This turned out to be an IQ test. After consuming a pint of whiskey on the train trip and having a short nap, I didn't feel that great. All I could think of was to get some sleep. However, that was out of the question and I sat down and did my best to get through the IQ test. My brain wasn't functioning at 100% and I knew it. But what the heck, it was just a test that probably no one would look at in the first place.

After we finished testing, the next stop was the barber shop. I knew that they were going to cut my hair short, so I thought I would outfox the Army on this one. So, the day before I was inducted, I went and got my own haircut from my barber in Jamestown and told him to cut it nice and short. Then when I sat down in the Army barbershop's chair, he just took a look at me and cut it shorter still. So that little plan of mine backfired.

The next stop was a physical examination with shots and a vaccination. At this point I was hoping that I might see Dr. Szabo there, but of course, no such luck. I passed the physical with flying colors, just as I expected, even with the giant hangover I had and no sleep. The next stop was to stick my arm out and get a series of shots, and then the last doctor in the lineup gave me a vaccination.

Then on to what they called the supply room. It's there that they passed out your uniforms. You passed by one window and they would say, you look like a medium, and give you an overcoat and a raincoat. The same with fatigues, shirts and the like. They also gave us our dress uniform, which was at that time an Eisenhower jacket and pants. The Eisenhower uniform was of course named after General Eisenhower, the supreme commander of the Allied forces during World War II. At the next window they asked you your shoe size and gave you a pair of boots and dress shoes. Then they gave you your hats, socks, a tie and a belt. And last but not least, a duffel bag that you soon learned how to cram all this clothing into.

This whole day was beginning to seem like one big dream. We all filled our duffel bags up with our new duds and were led to buses that took us to our barracks and new home for two months of basic training. When we got there my bunk sure looked good. But before we could go to bed we had to make our bed, according to Army regulations. And that included flipping a dime on the bed sheet and making it bounce in the air. This I learned very quickly. I needed some sleep.

It seems like I just settled in to my new bunk and closed my eyes for a nice evening's sleep, when all of a sudden the lights came on and someone was yelling, "Wake up, you poor excuse for soldiers!" A sergeant walked by every bunk hitting each sleepy person on the arm where he had just had his shots and vaccination, and boy, did you hop out of bed fast. We were told we just had a short time to get ourselves cleaned up and dressed before reporting to a formation in front of our barracks for reveille. It was quite a sight watching everyone trying to figure out what to put on that first morning. After reveille we were marched to the mess hall for breakfast. It wasn't a nice leisurely breakfast by any stretch of the imagination. We went through the line in front of the kitchen where a few soldiers would plop food on your plate. It was usually scrambled eggs, bacon, sausage, potatoes and some kind of fruit. I never once heard anyone ask me how I liked my eggs, sunny side up or scrambled? The mess hall also had coffee that was so strong that you had no choice but to wake up and wait for the next surprise they had planned for you. I also soon found out that working in the kitchen mess hall was assigned as extra duty and that I would find myself cooking bacon, sausages and scrambled eggs at 4 a.m. and being yelled at by the mess hall sergeant.

The Army had two months to make you into a soldier. So every day was jam-packed with activities that you couldn't have imagined. At the end of the day nothing looked better to you than your bunk bed to climb into, even for a short while.

Shortly we were assigned rifles. The rifle was an M1 and we were taught that they would be our best friend while we were in service. They issued the M1 to us without ammunition and when not in use the rifle was kept the arms room. Oddly enough, the M1 was developed by a Canadian guy named John Garand. They were first produced on a small scale in 1938. But with the expanding war in Europe and the attack on Pearl Harbor the government made the M1 a top priority and four million of them were produced by the Springfield and the Winchester rifle companies. They were an automatic loading rifle and the United States was the only country using them. They had a very large advantage in firepower over the other rifles made at that time. After World War II the M1 was mothballed and put in storage. But during the Korean War, one and a half million more of them were made from 1950 through 1958. We spent hours in the classroom taking our M1's apart and reassembling them over and over again. We did this until we could do it blindfolded and for a while that's all that was in my dreams at night.

We had a couple of strange characters in our company. One guy obviously wanted to get out of the service badly, so he peed the bed every night. This went on for a while until they discharged him, and our Sgt. said, "We don't want anyone like him in the service, anyway." Another fellow was a real mess. He was sort of shaped like a pear and no matter what you dressed him in, he looked ridiculous. They sent him to the supply room several times to see if they could find him uniforms that would make him look halfway fit for duty. But no matter what he put on, it just didn't work. Besides that, he had zero personality. They finally sent him home and I felt a little sorry for him because he was not trying to get out of service. I don't know if his family were happy to see him back or not.

A good share of our training was outdoors. It was December and colder than hell, not to mention the snow. Our fatigues were quite warm and with our boots, gloves and hats with earmuffs, we were quite comfortable, despite the freezing temperatures. But I hadn't learned my lesson yet about trying to outfox the Army. One of my newfound buddies came down with a little case of the sniffles and reported for sick call and they put him in the hospital. Well, if that's all you had to do to get in to a nice warm hospital for a few nights, it sounded good to me. I did have a little cold, so I reported for sick call. I told the doctor that I felt terrible and he admitted me. So, there I was, in a nice, clean, warm, hospital bed and eating great food. I got to talking to the guy next to me and he said that he was being recycled. In other words, he was starting basic training from the very beginning again. Well, it seems that if you were gone from your company too long you were sent back to start your training all over again. I immediately called for a doctor and told him I made an amazing recovery and I was ready to go back to duty. He must've thought me strange, as I just got there. That was the end of me trying to take shortcuts in the Army. From then on in, I just went with the flow; after all, I was in the same boat as everyone else and we were starting to become a tight knit group of guys.

We did all the usual things that you do in basic training. Lots and lots of physical training, bayonet training, marching (close order drill), chemical/biological/radiological training with exposure to CS gas. We also completed the Infiltration Course, compass training and land navigation.

We did have a little problem with the compass training. I was loaded into a truck with a group of fellow soldiers and taken out in the middle of nowhere in the woods and dumped off. The Sgt. assigned me the leader of the group and gave me the one and only compass and told me to lead my men back to base. Well, that compass needle seemed to be going every which way and we wandered and wandered through the woods for what seemed forever. I had two guys in my group that were from New York City and probably had never seen a tree before and they were both in tears. But then a miracle happened. We accidentally came to a clearing in the woods and there was our home base. Everyone thought me a hero and I didn't have a clue how we got back.

We also spent a lot of time on the firing range. I wasn't too bad to at that, as I had done a little bit of hunting in Jamestown. We were using real bullets and it was actually a lot of fun, except lying on the ground in the freezing cold. Then one afternoon a jeep pulled up with a Sgt. driving. He got out of the Jeep and yelled, "Is there a private Beatty here?" I raised my hand. He said to hop in the Jeep and that I was going for an audition for the Army School of Music/Army Band School. My God. I had forgotten all about this possibility and what Johnny had told me back in Jamestown.

I gave my rifle to the Sgt. at the range and got into the Jeep with the Sgt. who took me to the Army Band School. I was led to the instrument room where I was given a clarinet and some reeds. I found a good reed and was all set to go. In the meantime there was another clarinet player waiting for his audition that was warming up his clarinet and playing scales and chords like you would not believe. He was a master of the clarinet. I thought, oh boy, I don't stand a chance. Anyway, after a short wait, a smartly dressed, good-looking black Sgt. came out and got me for my audition. I later found out that he was the band drill Sgt. and he was in charge of the Army band students. He also made out the weekly duty schedule, so he was a good man to be on the right side of if you did not want to be cleaning latrines every day. His name was Sgt. Kent and I liked him immediately. He gave me some sheets of music and asked me to play for him. He was pleasant and patient and made me feel very comfortable and relaxed. He was really listening and watching my fingering while I was playing different passages and asked me why I fingered an Ab a certain way. I gave him an answer and he seemed to be okay with it. Other than that, he sat there grading my playing.

It was all sight reading, which isn't easy, and I tried not to make too many mistakes. To get into the school you had to have at least a 75 percent on your audition, and that's what he gave me. I was in! I thanked God, my clarinet teachers and of course, Johnny DeVita. The strange part of this story is that that great technician on the clarinet who I had heard earlier did not make it. I think that the band school was looking for good musicians with pleasant personalities. After all, in any kind of band, the musicians have to get along with one another or the music suffers. I'm sure that Sgt. Kent was very impressed with this guy's clarinet technique but probably felt that he fell short on the personality side. Now the audition was over I had to get back to basic training; after all, I still had a couple of weeks left, along with a lot of hard work.

It seemed like a long two months, and actually it was more than two months because we got a 10-day leave over the Christmas holidays. And those 10 days were not counted for our basic training. That 10-day leave for Christmas at home was very interesting. Actually, I had only been in the Army about three weeks and in those days we had to stay in uniform while on leave and I was treated like a national hero when I got home. My mom and stepdad actually cried when I walked in the door and sister Linda was so excited to see me again. My dad, of course, had to be tracked down at one of the bars on Second Street. When I finally caught up with him, he was so proud to show me off to all his drinking buddies. Of course, it was shots and beers once again and I wasn't allowed to buy anything.

I had my usual British Christmas with my dad at Aunt Lizzie's house on 11 Shaw Ave. I say Aunt Lizzie's house but it wasn't, as Uncle Bill had bought it when he came over from England many years before. But Aunt Lizzie ruled the roost and made the roast beef and Yorkshire pudding, so to make her feel good, we all pretended that it was her house. As it was Christmas we also had a figgie pudding served for dessert. Aunt Lizzie poured the 151 proof rum on it and brought it out to the table ablaze with fire. We all had a wonderful dinner as usual. But even at Christmas my dad would not join in the feast. He sat at the table drinking his whiskey and beers and smoking one Camel cigarette after another.

The Swedish side of my family had its usual Christmas celebration on Christmas Eve. We got together with my mom's sisters and brothers and their families for lots of good Swedish treats with some *sylta*, pickled herring and liverwurst served on hardtack. We also had the usual *korv*. And then of course there was the Lutfisk. It was lye soaked cod in a cream sauce over mashed potatoes. This I could not eat and still can't to this day. Fortunately, they also served a turkey with all the trimmings and that saved the day for me. For drinks we had Swedish *glogg*. It was a spiced wine served warm and made with port wine and brandy. If you didn't watch out it could knock you on your fanny.

I can't remember the sergeant's names that trained me nor can I remember the names of some of the guys I became friends with. I did have one Jewish friend that I went to services with at the synagogue every Friday evening. It was fun because after the service we went to a party room where there was lots of great food, music and girls that were shipped in from New York City to dance with. After the party the girls were quickly put into buses and taken back to New York City. So there was no chance of any romance.

Sundays were our day off and I got out of the barracks first thing in the morning as I had learned that if you hung around lying on your bunk doing nothing, sergeants would roam around looking for guys for work details. So I would be gone all day, usually by myself, going to church, the PX, a movie, or anything else to help whittle the day away. I would get back to my bunk before lights out and be ready for duty on Monday morning. Our final bit of training was more of the same with our rifles and the firing range, bayonet training, PT, close order drill and the infiltration course. At the very end of basic training they brought out the hand grenades. That was rather spooky because you didn't know if the guy next to you was going to screw up and blow everybody to bits. It didn't bother me because I treated the hand grenade like a hot potato and couldn't get rid of it fast enough.

On our last day we dressed in our Class A uniforms and went to the basic training graduation ceremony. In a way, it was rather sad to see that part of your life over with. We then packed all our belongings into our duffel bags and were loaded onto buses that took us to our special training units. I got off at the Army School of Music to the sound of cheers and jeers from my fellow soldiers going into infantry. The band school was located in a fairly new, block cement two-story building. The first floor is where the main office was located along with some private offices for some of the officers and sergeants. The arms room was located there as well as a couple of latrines. At the far end of the building there was a very large rehearsal hall and music storage rooms for our horns and music. Our barracks were located on the second floor and I noticed that everything there was spit and polish, including a very shiny, spotless floor. There was also a long hallway down the middle of the building with small rehearsal rooms on each side along with a couple of latrines and showers.

After reporting for duty I was told to wait and someone would come get me and show me to my quarters. It didn't take too long before Sgt. Kent walked into the room and called my name. He was the sergeant that auditioned me a couple of weeks before. I liked him because he was calm, cool and collected. He brought me up to my barracks and assigned a bunk to me and then showed me around and introduced me to some of my new band mates. Sgt. Kent told me to take my time to unpack, make up my bunk, and he'd see me in the morning. My God, what a change from basic training. I felt like that I just moved into a resort hotel. I knew better, however, because there was going to be a lot of work to do and things to learn in the next two months. But I also knew that I would probably be meeting some incredibly great musicians.

I got my things put away and settled in. A few of the guys in the band stopped by and introduced themselves and invited me to join them for dinner. They filled me in on the ins and outs of the band school. As I suspected, Sgt. Kent was a good one to be on the right side of, because besides being in charge of the student's, he was the drill Sgt., and shaped us up to look good on parades and military functions. On top of that, he made out the duty roster. It was a big building and the grounds had to be policed, windows washed, floors mopped and waxed, and the latrines cleaned and stocked with toilet paper and paper towels. If an officer came around and found something dirty, it was Sgt. Kent that got his ass chewed out. And you did not want that to happen.

We fell out for reveille the next morning and then went for breakfast. It was a nice leisurely breakfast compared to basic training and it seemed great not to have to gulp my food down. After breakfast, since it was my first day, I reported to the arms room and was issued my M1 rifle. Just because we were in the band we still had to have a weapon and know how to use it if the occasion arose. After just finishing basic training I needed no instruction. I could take an M1 apart and put it back to gather again in my sleep.

I was issued a metal clarinet. I had brought my personal wood clarinet back with me after my Christmas leave, but wooden clarinets crack easily when the weather turns hot or cold. The trouble with the metal clarinet was that it was made of silver and had to be polished constantly. If we played outdoors and it was cold we wore gloves with the fingertips cut out of them so we could cover the keys of our horns. I was beginning to find out that there was going to be a lot more to the Army Band School then I realized.

In order to know what chair a student in the band would play he had a lesson and evaluation. I was sent to a music room for my evaluation and was there at the appointed time and sat outside waiting to be called in. While sitting there I heard a clarinet playing in the next room, warming up with very difficult scales and chord progressions. I figured he was probably playing all those difficult passages to intimidate me, which he did. Finally the door opened and I was called in. Much to my surprise, he was only a PFC with one lonely stripe on his sleeve. He was a young, cocky, short little guy that had a chip on his shoulder, the type of person that I certainly would not want to hang out and have a beer with. My guess was that he was from a symphony somewhere and drafted into the Army, and boy, the Army got themselves one hell of a clarinet player. To play the way he did you had to practice for five hours a day easily. There were two chairs in the room and a music stand with some clarinet charts on it. He asked me to sit down so we could get to work. I put my clarinet together and sat down next to him and before I blew a note he exploded with rage: "How do you think you can play the clarinet with the dirty fingernails you have? You get out of my office you dirty soldier and don't come back until your fingernails are spotless!" You're nothing but a dirty, dirty, soldier."

I packed up my clarinet and got out of there quick. I blew it. I looked at my fingernails and they were a bit dirty. That was probably because I just finished basic training and I had spent a good part of two months crawling around in the mud and dirt. I went back to my barracks and into the latrine and scrubbed and scrubbed my fingernails until they shined. Was this incident going to get me expelled from the band training school? I could just picture myself in an infantry unit running around with an M1 again. I thought the best thing to do was go directly to Sgt. Kent and tell him what had happened before he heard it from that crazy PFC clarinet wizard.

I knocked on his office door and told him I had a very serious matter to discuss with him. He asked me in and I told him what had happened. He exploded with laughter. "So that little pile of shit bastard got you, did he? That son of a bitch has been nothing but a pain in the ass since he's been here. Thank God, he is due to be discharged soon and good riddance. Don't worry Beatty, you won't see him again, even with clean fingernails."

To this day I'm fussy about my fingernails. And every time I look at them I think of that cocky little PFC.

One morning at band practice the quartermaster Sgt. interrupted us to tell us that our unit had been selected to model a new Army summer uniform. They were Bermuda shorts with matching dress socks up to the knee. The Bermuda shorts were one inch above the knee. The uniform also came with a tan shirt and dark tie and standard belt and buckle along with our regular black dress shoes. Actually, this uniform originated with the British Army for wear in the tropical countries. During World War II the German Africa Corps, under the command of Field Marshal Rommel, wore them too. Well, we weren't in the tropics, we were at Fort Dix, New Jersey and it was not quite spring. Nevertheless we were issued our uniforms and they looked rather nice. When we were in parade you would've sworn that the British Army was marching down the street. At Fort Dix we did get a lot of ribbing at first, but that subsided when everyone got used to it. I must admit that those of us with nice legs looked pretty snappy in that uniform.

It was rumored from the very beginning that the Eisenhower uniforms would be a thing of the past. During the Second World War Eisenhower thought the old uniforms to be too restricting and not suitable for combat. Ike came up with an all-wool field jacket that was quite short and comfortable. It was known as the Ike jacket and was issued to US troops in 1944. It was a standard Army uniform until a general phase out began in 1956 and new uniforms were fashioned.

Shortly after the Bermuda shorts were issued they gave us the new Army Dress Greens. They were a snappy new uniform jacket with brass buttons on the front and on the pockets, along with matching pants, tan shirts, cap and our black shoes. I really liked this uniform. So now I'm up to my neck in uniforms and it looks like I'm going to stay for a while.

It didn't take long to get to know everyone at the Army music school. I met and made friends with a couple of guys that I would be close to for the rest of my life. I heard that there was a new fellow that just arrived from basic training and he was from Sweden. His name was Roy Landgren and I went over and greeted him in Swedish. Boy, did his face light up. I filled him in on my Swedish background, being raised by my grandmother and aunt at an early age and I also told him when I was young, Swedish was the language spoken in the house.

Roy had been in the Swedish Army band playing the clarinet and after being discharged from the Swedish Army he and his mother moved to America for a new life. He was immediately drafted into the United States Army and after basic training, because of his Swedish band training, was assigned to the Army School of Music. Roy was rather tall, maybe six-foot one or two, a typical Nordic with blonde hair and blue eyes. Had he been German he would have made the perfect model of a Nazi soldier. Roy and I hit it off immediately and decided that I would help him with his English and he would help me brush up on my Swedish. His only problem was that he loved modern jazz, but then nobody is perfect.

We became really good buddies throughout the band school training and oddly enough we were both assigned to the same Army band unit following our graduation from the music school. Now I had a partner to share shots and beers with, and we did plenty of that.

Another friend I became close with was a neat guy from New York City, accent and all. His name was Dick Henzel and he played the hell out of the old-fashioned ragtime piano. Like me, he loved New Orleans jazz and had spent lots of time at Jimmy Ryan's in New York City listening to the Wilbur De Paris Band. He also loved to go to Eddie Condon's club and listen to Wild Bill Davison go crazy on his cornet. Dick couldn't believe that I was friends with Omer Simeon and Wild Bill and couldn't wait for the two of us to go into the city for a weekend of jazz. It was up in the air as to how long the two of us would be able to hang out together as he had applied for an early hardship discharge from the Army because his father had passed away and he was the sole supporter of his mother and younger sister. As it turned out, we spent the entire rest of the Army band training together and he was still there waiting for news about his early discharge when I graduated from the school and went to my next assignment. We did end up spending a few nights in NYC and enjoying the music and drinks. It wasn't easy to do on $76.50 a month, but somehow we managed. Although we parted, we kept in touch and after our discharge from the Army got together occasionally. Dick, by the way, did get his early hardship discharge shortly after I left Fort Dix. He got home only to have his mother pass away a month later. It's interesting that many years later he promoted Long Island tours for me that were lots of fun and financially rewarding.

Besides being an Army band training unit, Fort Dix was also the home of the 19th and 173rd Army bands. They consisted of 70 or so musicians that had graduated from the music school under the direction of SFC Francis Janenko, chief instructor. There were different teachers for the many sections of the band such as the chorus, percussion, horn and read instruments. The band and music school was under the direction of CWO Alexander DiFronzo, who I seldom saw.

Army bands date back as far as the Army itself, and today, although they have grown in size and skill, their main purpose remains the same: To foster morale. We all had busy lives as we had to carry out our administrative and domestic duties, in addition to long hours of practice and actual band duty. Speaking of administrative duties, I was walking past Sgt. Kent's office one day as he was sitting at his desk typing out the duty roster on his typewriter - the hunt and peck system with one finger. He obviously could not type. I poked my head in the door and kidded him about taking forever to type out a duty roster. It was obviously a frustrating job for him and he said, "Beatty, can you do it any faster?" I told him that I could because I took typing in school. Sgt. Kent asked me to sit down and demonstrate. Then he said, "You have a new job typing out the duty roster." I said okay and asked him to write it out in longhand and I would type it with carbon copies and post it in the appropriate places. Sgt. Kent said, no, I want you to make out the daily duty roster and type it up yourself. In other words, he turned over the entire job to me.

Now this was a potential problem. No one liked extra duty, especially on the weekends. On the other hand, I knew all the guys in the school and what their habits were. For instance, a few of the guys lived in or around NYC and liked to go home on the weekends, while many of them didn't necessarily want to go anywhere. They were happy hanging out on base or perhaps going in to Wrightstown, a small village just outside of camp that had a few saloons. So with me assigning the daily extra duty to the guys didn't become a problem because I was flexible and so were they. In fact, there were a few cases where extra favors where requested of me and I often got gifts of cigarettes and whiskey. So it worked out fine all the way around. The guys were happy, I was happy, and most of all,

Sgt. Kent was happy. I reported to Sgt. Kent's office every morning and he sent me out to get coffee and doughnuts for us. So from then on that's how my day started, sitting in Sgt. Kent's office, drinking coffee, eating donuts and shooting the breeze, and making out the duty roster. Still, my main job was to improve my musical skills and I took advantage of every opportunity that came along.

I tried to go into NYC as often as time and money permitted, usually accompanied by Dick Henzel, as he enjoyed the same style of jazz as I did. One day I read in the paper that the George Lewis Band would be playing in NYC. Henzel was busy and Roy Landgren preferred modern jazz (or I had him scheduled for duty that weekend), so I asked a trumpet player friend of mine to go along with me. We could always get a room at the YMCA called the Slone House for one dollar a night if you were in uniform. A darned good deal even in those days, but you had to sleep with one eye open.

The first stop we made was to hear Omer Simeon and the Wilbur De Paris Band at Jimmy Ryan's on 52nd Street. On Omer's intermission the three of us walked down the street to a saloon where we had our 35 cent shots and beers. I mentioned to Omer that we came into town especially to hear the George Lewis Band from New Orleans. Omer said, "Jim, you're too late as George and the band played their last show last night." Omer thought that they might still be in town because they were going to do some recording before they went back to New Orleans.

We walked over to the hotel where George and the band were staying and I asked the desk clerk if George was still there. Fortunately he was. I got on the house phone and called his room. George answered the phone and was probably surprised to hear from this kid who had been following him all over the country. Anyway, George told me that he and the band were on their way down to the lobby, as they were being picked up to play a private party on Park Avenue. George asked if my friend and I would like to come along as his guest - boy what a deal we ran into that night. Here we were, two young soldiers in a fancy penthouse apartment with all the food and drinks we wanted, listening to the George Lewis band. Wow! What a night. When we got back to base we told the story to the guys in the band and from then on when I went into NYC everybody wanted to come along.

Sadly, that night in NYC was the last time I saw George Lewis. His fame spread the world over and he spent a great deal of his time traveling out of the country. He became so popular in England that even to this day a great deal of the British clarinetists have copied his style of playing. He also wrote a beautiful tune called the "Burgundy Street Blues." He was a small frail man but very close to God, and you could hear it in his playing. I'll always cherish the times I spent with him.

I was sorry to see the end of my time at Fort Dix. I think I accomplished a lot musically and in growing up a bit. There were lots of band practices along with practicing on our own. We did have those sound-proof rehearsal rooms and they came in handy for individual practice or jam sessions, although sometimes they were used for smoking weed. There was a fellow in the band that sold it. I later found out that he was busted and sent to Fort Leavenworth, an Army jail in Kansas. I often pass by Leavenworth when we are at our other home in Topeka, Kansas, and always give a wave as we pass, just in case he is still there. I was never much on smoking marijuana. I figured that I spent enough money on alcohol, and besides that, the two don't mix. But I usually never turned it down if I was offered a free smoke.

I had mixed feelings when graduation day came, as I had to say good-bye to many of my good friends that I had met along the way. On the other hand, I was anxious to leave for my permanent assignment to an Army band. I was assigned to the 184th Army band in Fort Eustis, Virginia. I packed my duffel bag and along with my good Swedish buddy, Roy Landgren, took a train towards a new adventure.

**Army Band School, 1967**

**With Omer Simeon, New York City, 1967**

## CHAPTER 9

# Fort Eustis

As I WAS RIDING THE train on my way to Fort Eustis, I had a lot to think about. Before I walked out the doors of the music school for good, I stopped by to say farewell to Sgt. Kent. He wished me well, good luck, and said "Oh, by the way Beatty, did you know that you will be one of the first white guys in the 184th band at Fort Eustis?" I couldn't believe that after all these years they were just getting around to integrating the band.

Discrimination in the US military against African Americans went way back to the Revolutionary War in 1775, the war of 1812, World War I from 1914 – 1918 and World War 2 from 1941 to 1945. President Harry Truman signed an Executive Order in 1948 that ended segregation in all branches of the US military. So how could this be? Eight years later and they're just getting around to implementing it now? As I well knew, many things happened slowly in the Army and I guess that something like this is a major transition and would take some time. I suppose that they didn't disrupt this all-black band because no doubt they had been playing together for years, so I guess that the sensible way to do it would be to assign the white musicians to the band as the older black musicians were transferred or retired. At any rate, I wasn't concerned about it, just curious. On top of all that, I realized that I was also going to be stationed in Virginia, a southern state that was segregated. How was all this going to work out? As the train rolled along I knew that I was soon to find out.

I arrived on a Saturday to report for duty at the 384th Army band barracks. To my surprise it was an old wooden barracks similar to the one I had during basic training. A far cry from the plush accommodations at the Army Band School. When I walked in there was no one around except for a barracks orderly, who greeted me. He told me that the band was off for the weekend and most everyone had left and probably wouldn't be back until late Sunday. So he suggested that I just go upstairs, find an empty bunk, and make myself at home. I grabbed my duffel bag and went upstairs. There was a private bedroom at the top of the stairs with the name, Sgt. Sloan Williams, on the door. The rest of the room was filled with bunks and footlockers. I found a free bunk and unpacked my duffel bag, hoping that my uniforms were not too wrinkled. There were a couple of guys laying on their beds either sleeping or reading and not paying too much attention to my presence. At dinnertime they took me and Roy to the mess hall and later we all went out and drank a bunch of beers. As I lay in my bunk I was looking forward to the next day, Sunday, when everyone returned for duty and I would meet my fellow musicians.

The next morning I slept late along with everyone else, went to lunch at the mess hall, and then decided to have a walk around the base. Fort Eustis was the home of the Army Transportation Corps. To my surprise the Army had a Navy, Air Force and a railroad training center, along with 44 miles of tracks right there at Fort Eustis. The soldiers were taught how to be train engineers on both steam and diesel engines. There was a flying school there on-base that taught soldiers how to be helicopter pilots. At graduation they became warrant officers or lieutenants. The Army naval ships were also here but most of them had been mothballed after World War II. I soon found out that the transportation Corps had a very important function in the Army. In combat, for instance, the Army is useless if they have no supplies, no ammunition or food. That's where the transportation Corps came in, along with many other functions. There was a famous trucking system in Europe during World War II, called the Red

Ball Express, that got supplies to our troops, and they even made a movie about it. There was all kinds of training at Fort Eustis for watercraft operators, watercraft engineers, truck drivers, railway training, and helicopter school. There was also an Army band that I was yet to see.

After dinner at the mess hall I went back to the barracks and the absent members of the band came trickling in. One by one I met them, all nice guys. A real neat guy came over to me and introduced himself. His name was Harley Baritz and he was the company clerk. He was a New York Jew and his father was a very successful physician in the city. Harley had a shiny new Chrysler at camp and when he flew back to New York on furlough or weekends, he gave me the keys to his car as we became very good friends. His nickname for me was Beetle Bailey after the popular comic strip.

The fellow that had the bunk next to me arrived, his name was Len, and he was a tall blonde good-looking guy. He reminded me of one of the southern belles from the movie, *Gone with the Wind.* On top of all that he was a racist. His family history went back to the old plantation days of the South and he lived with his family in an old southern mansion. He had gone home for the weekend and brought a few band members with him. He told me that he would love to have me to his house sometime, but he would never dare bring a Yankee home to his parents. So that's how we started out. But besides all the negatives in our thinking he was a really nice guy, we became good friends, and Len played the clarinet too.

Later that evening a large black man arrived, Sgt. Sloan Williams, and he was our first Sgt. He had been in the Army for 37 years, including 25 years in the infantry, and had been in the band at Fort Eustis for 10 years. During World War II he served as an infantryman in the Pacific theater. Before retiring for the night I mentioned something about seeing everyone in the morning for reveille. Everyone went into a hysterical laugh. I was told that there was no such word around the 384th and to never say it again. That was my first clue that the band was run loose as a goose and a PT notice I had seen written on a blackboard did not mean physical training, but instead, meant personal time.

I rolled out of bed early that first Monday at Fort Eustis because I was anxious to finally report for duty and meet our company commander, chief warrant officer Mario S. Petrelli. I even went over to the mess hall and had breakfast, which turned out to be one of the few times I would be doing that. When I returned to the barracks, Harley, the company clerk, told me that the company commander wanted to see me. I went downstairs to his office, knocked on the door, went in and saluted, and said Private James Beatty, ER 51393187, reporting for duty. Sir! He smiled, put me at ease, and welcomed me to the band.

Mr. Petrelli was about medium height, receding hairline, glasses, very Italian looking and wearing a summer dress uniform. A few of the guys in the band had filled me in on his history in the Army. He was born in 1920, graduated from the American Conservatory of Music and entered the Army in 1942. Working his way up from a private in the Army band he performed in many shows with World War II entertainers such as Bob Hope and Red Skelton. As a Sgt. at Fort Ord, California, he played with a great Army band that consisted of musician draftees from the big bands, such as Les Brown, Stan Kenton and Charlie Barnett. He got a Warrant Officer commission and his first assignment was at the 384th Army band at Fort Eustis. He told me to keep my eye on the blackboard and I would know what was going on from day to day or week to week. In parting, he happily said that we had a real nice job coming up soon to play for Queen Elizabeth of England. I had arrived at a perfect time and couldn't wait to write to my British relatives back in Jamestown.

There was a rehearsal that morning at 9 a.m. in a separate rehearsal hall a few buildings away. It was large with a stage, instrument repair room, and arms room. To my surprise we did not use the M1 rifle that I was trained to use all those weeks in basic training. Instead I was issued a smaller carbine rifle and was told that I would be given training with it later on. I was also issued a metal, silver-plated clarinet like we had back at the band school at Fort Dix. I was told by Sgt. Kent that I would be going to an all-black band and I was yet to see a black guy with the exception of our first Sgt., Sloan Williams. But the mystery was soon solved when the rest of the band moseyed in to the rehearsal hall and every one of them were African Americans. These were the guys that had been in the band forever and lived in rented apartments on or off base with their families. Many of them even had purchased their own homes off base. So it was like a regular job to them coming to work every day. And boy, were they all terrific musicians. I could see that this was going to be a great musical experience for me.

It wasn't too long before I got to go on a road trip with the band. We had a huge bus painted army gray with a sign that said 184th Army Band on the front. There was luggage space under the passenger seats of the bus that accommodated all our instruments and music stands. All the black bandsmen were professional soldiers and all sergeants. They were career soldiers while guys like me were just passing through. They had been in the band so long that over the years they had claimed their bus seats and each of them sat in the same seat on every trip. As we know, in the South in those days the black people had to sit in the back of the bus on public transportation. So when I got onto the bus for the first time I looked at all the black Sgt.'s sitting in their seats up front and said, "I suppose that I have to sit at the back of the bus!" At first there was dead silence and all the white guys looked at me in horror. But then all the black sergeants started laughing hysterically. I had just reversed a bad situation for them and they really thought it was funny. After that, every time I got on the bus everyone joined in and said, "Back of the bus, Beatty!" It always got our trip off to a fun start, until we passed through the gates of Fort Eustis into the deep South and reality.

I soon found out how awkward it was on our road trips when we had to stop for lunch or dinner. We made one stop so the white guys could eat and one stop so that the black guys could do the same, but that took much longer as there were more of them. It would have been easier had there been fast food places like we have now, McDonald's, Burger King, and so forth, but there wasn't. I got a bright idea one day and went to Mr. Petrelli with it. I told him that we knew the black guys could never come into a restaurant and eat with us, but who says that we can't go to one of their restaurants and eat? It would save us a lot of time and there's not very many of us white soldiers. We all have the same uniform and we could try to blend in. Mr. Petrelli thought it was worth a try, anything to shorten our road time. So the next trip that's what we did and it went over like a lead balloon. The black proprietor of the restaurant said, "What are you guys trying to do, get us all killed?" He said any white folks passing by might see us and throw rocks through the windows or worse yet a bomb. He told us to please leave. Well, so much for my suggestion. As it turned out Mr. Petrelli found a solution that solved the whole situation. He merely had the mess hall prepare box lunches for us. It wasn't very popular with the mess Sgt. but that's the way we did it from then on in.

Then for very long trips Mr. Petrelli thought, "Hey, We are the transportation Corps." So we were assigned two helicopters for long trips. They were very large helicopters and it was like riding on an egg beater. One day we had a flight to play at Fort Story, Virginia. Some big general was coming in and they were going to put on a show for him. As we approached the field for a landing there were soldiers waving frantically at us. We thought it was a welcoming committee and they were just happy to see us. We landed and a few of the guys started to get out when they discovered they were walking in green paint. The grass had been painted field green so it would look good for the General's ceremony and it hadn't dried yet. What a mess! Just another day in the Army band.

The big day finally arrived when the 184th was to play for the arrival and tour of Jamestown and Williamsburg, Virginia by Queen Elizabeth and Prince Philip of England. The event was to celebrate the 350th anniversary of the founding of Jamestown as the first colony of the British Empire. The Queen was to arrive at nearby Patrick Henry Airport from Ottawa, Canada, via a Royal Canadian Air Force plane. That plane had been practicing takeoff and landings a number of days before the Queen's arrival. Before we boarded the bus for the event we were inspected by some of the high brass of Fort Eustis, as we had to look absolutely at our best spit and polish. Our bus left early as we had to get there well ahead of time to set up and prepare for a long day. I got on the bus and made my way to my usual seat at the back of the bus and to the laughter of all the guys.

When we got to Jamestown Festival Park we noticed a very strange thing. All the "Colored" and "White" signs on the rest rooms and drinking fountains were taken down. The plaques had been there for years and of course there was an outline of them where they were taken off. This was done so the Queen would think that everyone was equal in the United States, as if she didn't know that there was segregation in the South. At any rate, on that day all the black guys in the band got to go in the white restrooms and drink from the white water fountains as well. One of the black sergeants told me that he was going to make sure that he took a dump that day. I took a peek into the black restroom and saw that it was exactly the same as the white one. So I guess the old Southern expression, "separate but equal" was true, at least in Jamestown.

The Queen arrived exactly at 1:30 p.m. to a 21-gun salute. There was an estimated 10,000 people there at the airport to greet the royal couple. The band played "God Save the Queen" and there were lots of officials there to greet them, from the State Department, Gov. Stanly of Virginia, and the British ambassador.

President Eisenhower sent his personal presidential Cadillac limousine with a bubble top for the Queen's ride into Jamestown. There were two other bands playing; one Marine band and an Air Force band. The Queen acted very relaxed and didn't seem to be in a big hurry to go anywhere. She wore a lightweight blue coat and a hat entirely made of pheasant feathers. We played for her as she toured Jamestown and Jamestown Festival Park. The Royal couple also visited the College of William and Mary. She had a luncheon and later on in the evening an early dinner along with speeches and so forth. Later in the evening, the royal couple went back to the airport and boarded President Eisenhower's presidential plane, the Columbine 111, for Washington DC. This is before there was an Air Force One. I assume he sent his plane for her to make sure that he got his limousine back.

So that was the end of the very long busy day. All the guys in the band were happy and it was fun for us all to take a whizz together, not to mention drinking out of the same water fountain. I had purchased a cheap camera in the hopes that I would be able to get a couple of snapshots of the Queen. It was no problem and I got plenty of good pictures as she passed by. I sent copies of the photos to my British relatives and they were very proud of me. My Aunt Lizzie sent the pictures off to friends in England and they were amazed at how close I got to the Queen. Many years later when I played in England and was in London, I never missed an opportunity to go to Buckingham palace for the changing of the guards. It brought back many happy memories.

After we played for Queen Elizabeth I realized how she could have spent much of her day in the Jamestown/Williamsburg area. If you are at all interested in history and especially the history of this nation, then that was the place to be. And it was re-created just the way it was many years ago. For instance, there were replicas of the three ships that the first settlers made their first journey from London, England in 1607, starting the first English colony. These were open to the public to go through and I took advantage of this many times. The ships were the *Susan Constant*, *Godspeed* and *Discovery*, and were moored at the Jamestown Pier. The three ships brought a total of 105 passengers and a crew of 39 on the transatlantic trip from London, England. It was amazing because they were not that big.

I was lucky, as we were asked to come back several times to play and I always took advantage of my breaks and intermissions to walk through history. We also played in Williamsburg, the home of the College of William and Mary. It's the second oldest college in the United States and would have been the first had there not been Indian uprisings and the building was delayed and consequently Harvard became the first college.

The College of William and Mary is called the alma mater of the US because so many of our founding fathers went there. It's where George Washington received his surveyor's license and presidents John Taylor and James Monroe received their education. It was the first college to become a university and it had the first law school in the United States. The original building, called the Wren building, is the oldest structure in the United States. I love history, so I soaked it up every time that we played in that area.

Meanwhile, back at the barracks, it was business as usual. We were getting some new people arriving every few weeks and the band was looking more integrated each day. It was taking some time but it was happening. I became friends with two of the new arrivals. One was a trumpet player from Rhode Island and his name was Chuck Hinkley. He was a tall, lanky guy, very friendly and a good trumpet player. Another new musician that I became friends with was a French horn player named Johnny Canupp.

He was a small likable kid from North Carolina. He told everyone that he was from Granite Falls, North Carolina. And when we asked him where the hell that was, he would reply, "It's just 10 miles from Hickory." Of course no one ever heard of either one of those cities but we used to ask him that question quite often just to hear the answer.

Not everything in the Army was a bowl of cherries. I got in trouble twice. The first time, when we were playing a public relations concert off post, we had our usual uniform inspection before we left for the job and everything was fine. However, when we got to our destination and were setting up, I opened my clarinet case, and to my shock there was no mouthpiece there. Going on a job without a mouthpiece in the Army band is like going into battle without your rifle. The clarinet section sat right in front and I could not hide from our conductor, Mr. Petrelli, so I had no choice, I had to go to him and tell him the situation. He wasn't very happy with me and when we got back to Fort Eustis he gave me company punishment, which was an Article 15. He had no choice and I understood. I think I policed the area, cleaned all the windows in the barracks and the latrines for a day or two. To this day I check my clarinet case a few times before going on a job.

I got another Article 15 when I disobeyed an order from a corporal who was in charge of a formation. He had everyone in Class A uniforms and I knew that we were supposed to be dressed in fatigues. I knew this because Mr. Petrelli had told me. So I stayed in my fatigues while everyone else was in their class A's. Stupid! I was right and everybody else ended up changing into their fatigues. But nevertheless I did disobey an order and spent some time doing extra duty around the barracks.

Christmas leave was coming up and I was really looking forward to going back to Jamestown, New York and seeing all my family and old friends.

Our band was given leave over Christmas and New Year's and I was excited to get home. But before we left for the holidays, the band had a big project ahead of it. We were going to put on a Christmas concert along with the Fort Eustis Chorale, under the direction of our commanding officer, Mario Petrelli. We were performing the show on the 19th and 20th of December, so that gave everyone time to get home for Christmas. The concert was held at the Transportation School Theater which was fairly new and impressive. So it meant a lot of rehearsing for us along with the chorus. The band played the usual Christmas favorites like "Sleigh Ride" and selections from the *Nutcracker Suite.* The chorus did Christmas favorites as well like "Jingle Bells" and "White Christmas." The band joined in for "White Christmas" and it was quite beautiful. On top of all that there was a pageant about the birth of Christ compiled by the post Chaplin and along with background music from the band and chorus it went over very well. The chorus consisted of enlisted men, officers and the Officers Wives Club. It took a lot of rehearsal and time for everyone involved, but it turned out to be a beautiful production.

I arrived in Jamestown in time for Christmas Eve and Christmas. Nothing had changed as far as the routine went. We had our big Swedish smorgasbord on Christmas Eve along with lots of whiskey and Swedish *glogg*. My sister Linda had grown up a lot and it was nice to see her again. My stepdad was still into the heavy drinking and I felt sorry for Linda to have to be around it day after day. My mother looked great and seemed happy and was still at her job at the bank. My mom and pop were members of the Vikings, a Swedish Lodge in Jamestown and they spent just about every Saturday night there dancing away. And oddly enough, my father was in the band there...one big happy family.

On Christmas day I walked downtown and picked my dad up at his hotel. He and my stepmother, Belle, still ran the hotel. We dropped Belle off at her relatives and my dad and I continued on to 11 Shaw Avenue. There, the Beatty family was still going strong and everyone was in a happy Christmas mood. Of course the first thing they asked about was my day with Queen Elizabeth. They couldn't have been more excited and proud of me. In reality I was just a clarinet player in the band that played for her, but that didn't matter. All the guys, Uncle Bill, Uncle Walker, Uncle Walt and cousin Hibby were into a bottle of Seagram's 7 and feeling very happy. It didn't take long for my dad to join in with them and I probably did too.

After dinner we opened presents. As I said, I was in the service and didn't want any civilian clothes, so guess what I got from everyone? Cartons of cigarettes. Each one that I opened I acted surprised and said that this is just what I wanted. Getting cigarettes was no big deal because I bought them at Fort Eustis for ten cents a pack. However I was grateful and they did eventually get lit up and smoked.

I spent a lot of time just visiting friends and hanging out at the house. I went downtown to the newsroom but it wasn't the same because Johnny DeVita had had a heart attack and passed away, but his brother Pete was still there holding the fort. It was usually cold and snowy out and every saloon you went in to would serve hot Tom and Jerry's. And boy, did they taste good. Before I knew it and it was time to go back to Fort Eustis. And you know, I was looking forward to seeing all my friends there again. Fort Eustis was my home now.

When we all arrived back at camp we went back to our usual routine of rehearsals, concerts and looking forward to the springtime when we participated in outdoor concerts and parades. We also went back to our favorite saloon, The Knotty Pines. It was a cute place just outside the gates of Fort Eustis. They served big jugs of beer at a reasonable price and also had great burgers. One of our favorite nights there would be when the Gary Moore Show was on television. He found a great new female comedienne by the name of Carol Burnett, and we all know now what happened to her career. If there was nothing special going on with the band in the evening this is where a bunch of us would always end up at the end of the day.

By now we had our own little clique of guys and I was sort of the ringleader because I was a bit older than everyone else. In fact, the company clerk, Harley Baritz, who nicknamed me Beetle Bailey, also jokingly called me the Company Drunk. He even found a nickname for the Knotty Pines: The Nitty Not. That nickname caught on because nobody knew where we were going. We would sit there slugging down beer, smoking cigarettes, (I had lots of them), and talk about nothing. Actually, Jerry Seinfeld did a very successful TV series doing just that - talking about nothing. At any rate it was always a fun night with a lot of laughs. Unfortunately it was just outside the camp and naturally it was white only, so we never got to socialize with our black friends in the band.

When nice weather arrived, which was early in Virginia, we used to have integrated band parties because there was a park on-base near a small lake. So every now and then Mr. Petrelli would put a barbecue together at the park and everyone was invited, including the wives and children. It was always fun and we barbecued burgers and hot dogs with all the fixings. We also made sure that we had plenty of beer on hand and everyone brought their favorite brand of liquor. On one of these occasions we were all having a ball when I noticed that I hadn't seen my Swedish friend, Roy Landgren, in a while. I asked around and nobody else had seen him either. It was worrisome because of the lake there but none of the swimmers had seen him near the lake. So we got a big search party going. There were some woods with a little swamp close by and I went looking there.  I found him! He was laying in the swamp, out cold. Evidently he had a lot to drink and had to take a whizz and ducked into the woods to do it. So, there he was lying in the swamp with his head above water, thank goodness. However there was another issue: he was covered head to foot with leeches. We picked him up and drove him back to the barracks and onto his bunk, got his clothes off and proceeded to get the leeches off by burning them with our cigarettes. He came out of it okay but he had a lot of marks all over his body. From then on for our trips to the lake for barbecues, Roy was assigned a companion to stay with him for the afternoon, and of course nobody ever let Roy forget about that afternoon barbecue.

We got word that the headman of Fort Eustis, Major General Lincoln, was going to inspect various units on camp and the band was one of them. This inspection became our top priority above anything else. So we very busily started to get the barracks in tip-top shape. This meant that the windows had to be glistening, the floor shined and waxed, and the outside grounds policed for cigarette butts and anything else that wasn't supposed to be there. As for us personally, our belt buckles and brass insignias for our uniforms had to be shiny, with the help of Brasso. We all got our hair cut, teeth brushed, and our nails clipped and clean. Of course I learned all about clean nails back at Fort Dix. Our foot and wall lockers were to be left open and everything in them in its proper place. First Sgt. Sloan Williams ran around with white gloves on looking for dust, and there better not be any or you would hear him shout his favorite expression – "Piss, Shit, Fart and Puke." Believe me, you did not want to hear that. Our horns had to be spotless and shiny. That meant that most of us had to take our clarinets apart, to do a good job, and then put them back together again. I noticed that Roy Landgren was spending quite a bit of time with his clarinet. He had it all apart with the keys and springs spread all over the bed and shining the hell out of it. But that was Roy, he was pretty fussy about everything being neat and in its place.

So the big day arrived and Mr. Petrelli came around for a last minute look around the barracks. He was interested in our horns looking good and wanted to see them all. Well, Roy produced his clarinet and it looked like it just came from the jewelry store. It sparkled so that it just about blinded you. Mr. Petrelli had a fit because Roy's clarinet was so beautiful that it made the rest of us look like a bunch of ragged musicians. So, Mr. Petrelli told Roy that we had to hide his clarinet and he gave him another one from the instrument room, I don't know what he did with Roy's clarinet but it wouldn't surprise me if he took it out and buried it somewhere.

Now the last thing we did was to slip into our Class A uniforms because they were all freshly starched and we didn't want to wrinkle them, and also our shoes were perfectly shined. Our uniforms were stiff as a board and could almost stand on their own. They were so heavily starched and pressed that the buttons on our shirts looked like they were glued to the fabric. I slipped into my pants, put my shirt on and started to button it and one of my buttons popped off. There was nothing I could do because it was crunch time. So I put my shoes and tie on and hoped that nobody would notice. The general arrived accompanied by his staff, all holding clipboards and taking notes. They stopped and looked at each one of us, standing tall with our instruments. Well I was busted. I saw one of the captains pointing at me and making notes on his clipboard. Of all the times this could have happened it had to be the day that the General came by…but what was done was done and as it turned out we got a very high score on our inspection and my little button didn't hurt us that much. Mr. Petrelli and the first Sgt. did look at me and shake their heads, but that was the end of it. Now we could go back to our regular routine, thank goodness.

Late afternoon one day, we saw nothing important coming up for the next day, except for a mid-morning rehearsal. Landgren, Canupp, Hinckley, Lewis and I decided to take a trip up to Richmond, Virginia to a jazz club for an evening of jazz music and drinks. Hinckley had brought his old Buick Super with Dynaflow drive on it to camp. Although the transmission was slipping it was okay if we stopped now and then and added transmission fluid. We decided to wear civilian clothes for the evening, and off we went. We had a heck of a good time. The band was great and we stayed the night and closed the club. We got a couple of six packs and headed back to Fort Eustis, getting there early in the morning. As we pulled into the parking lot in front of our barracks, to our surprise and horror, we saw the band in Class A uniforms in formation with the bus standing there running and ready to go. First Sgt. Williams spotted us and said, "Piss, Shit, Fart and Puke! Where in hell have you guys been? Get your ass inside and change in to your Class A's, grab your horns and get on the bus. I'll give you two minutes." I bet that you have never seen five guys change outfits so fast in your life. It seems that after we had left for Richmond, one of the top brass on camp discovered that it was the General's birthday and it would be a wonderful surprise for him at reveille to have the band playing "Happy Birthday."

Mr. Petrelli was beside himself because it would have been terrible to have three clarinet players, trumpet and a French Horn missing from the band. We silently got into formation in front of his house and at reveille we played "Happy Birthday." General Lincoln, accompanied by his wife, came out of the house in their pajamas, robes and bedroom slippers and went through the ranks of the band thanking us individually. So all was well. It was a close call but we got through it. After we got back to the barracks, Mr. Petrelli got me aside and said "For God's sake Beatty, the next time you pull a stunt like this, chew 'Sin-sin." That was a breath freshener that would be like the Scope of today. We went to the mess hall and had breakfast and then as long as we were all there we had an early rehearsal. I guess our punishment was no sleep.

We had one more encounter with General Lincoln. One afternoon four of us decided to go to the golf course for an afternoon of golfing. Now I really didn't know how to play golf and I don't think the rest of the guys did either, but that didn't seem to bother us. We changed into our civilian clothes because it would not look good for four Army privates to spend a leisurely afternoon on the golf course. As we were hacking our way from one hole to another there was a single player behind us and naturally catching up to us. As he got closer we looked back and, to our horror, it was General Lincoln. He said, "Excuse me gentlemen, do you mind if I play through?" We said by all means, pretending that we had no idea who he was. He was in civilian clothes as well, probably playing hooky like we were. Thank goodness that he didn't ask if he could join us! We let him get quite a bit ahead of us before we resumed our game. I did learn how to play golf a few years later from an ex-Nazi SS Officer while I was working in the Bahamas.

There was a music insignia that band members could purchase and put on their caps in place of the standard issue with the eagle in the middle. I bought one, and as I was walking around camp one day I discovered that from a distance it looked like an officer's cap. Everyone was saluting me, including officers, until they got right up to me and realized that I was nothing but a lowlife private. Nevertheless, I enjoyed being saluted instead of being the "saluter." This all came to a screeching halt when I was promoted to a Private First Class and received my first stripe. I could no longer pull off my impersonation, with a private stripe on my shirt, so I took the music insignia off and put the standard issue eagle back on.

I had another fun time with salutes. Mr. Petrelli was going on leave and taking his family with him. He told me that if I would drive them to the airport I could use his car while they were gone. I told some of the guys that we had another car at our disposal. So, that night we put on our civilian clothes and headed for the Nitty Knot for our mugs of beer.

As we went through the gate of Fort Eustis the MPs on guard duty snapped to attention and saluted. I realized that Mr. Petrelli's car had an officer's identification sticker on the front bumper. Boy did we have fun with that one, and we took that car every time we went for beers at the Nitty Knot.

I did have a few encounters with the MPs. For extra duty I was assigned to play at the NCO Club. I used to get that duty because I could play songs without any music. But that was good extra duty. I usually played during happy hour and dinner time. They always fed me a great meal and when I was done for the evening I got a six pack of beer to go. I usually took my six pack back to the barracks and shared it with a couple of friends. The band barracks was quite a walk from the NCO Club, but on a nice evening it was a pleasant and relaxing one. One particular evening a Military Police car pulled alongside of me and asked me where I was going. The band barracks, I replied. "Well soldier, what are you holding in your hand?" I told them it was a clarinet." Not that hand, the other one." I explained that that was a six pack of beer that is given to me at the end of each evening I played. One of the MPs got out and opened the back door and said, "Get in." I wasn't sure if I had done anything wrong or not. I thought it was okay to be carrying a six pack with me. Come to find out they were giving me a cab ride back to the barracks and the fare was two bottles of beer. I arrived back at the barracks with only four bottles, much to the disappointment of a few of my buddies that were waiting for me, but I did make two MPs happy. That night became a pattern and the MPs watched for me every time I got off from playing. Many years later my son, Jame, joined the Army and asked me what branch of service he should sign up for. I suggested the Military Police. "I think you'll enjoy it." And he did.

One night at the Nitty Knot we were having a great time with lots of beers, shots and laughs. When we got back to camp I think we went to the Post PX for more beers. We had an easy day the following day, so what the heck. Back at the barracks we had a quiet little party downstairs in our lounge with more drinks, and then made our way upstairs to our bunks and called it a night. At least I wish we had. At the top of the stairs, First Sgt. Sloane Williams had his own private little bedroom. During the day he always kept it secure with a combination lock attached to the door. At night, when he went to bed for the evening he closed his door and left the combination lock hanging on the hinge of the door unlocked. I was in one of my moods and thought it would be hilarious if Sgt. Williams woke up in the morning and found himself locked in his room. So, I very quietly snapped the lock closed with the Sgt. trapped in his room. All the guys had tried to talk me out of it, but to no avail.

Early the next morning our sleep was interrupted by a very loud voice yelling, "Piss, shit, fart and puke!" It was the first Sgt., pounding frantically on his door threatening to have whoever did this's ass for breakfast!!! After locking him in, I wrote on a slip of paper, "The Phantom," and slid it under his door for him to read in the morning. He shouted the combination to his lock to one of the guys and when he got out of his room he went into a tirade that I had never heard before. He said that he was going to find out who the hell the Phantom was and put him in the stockade for the rest of his life. So, things were pretty tense around the band for the next few days as Sgt. Williams suspiciously eyed everyone. But as time passed things went back to normal and the whole matter became history.

One afternoon we all saw a notice on the blackboard that said, because we had a rather easy schedule ahead of us, three-day passes would be available. All we had to do was to sign up and say when, why, and where we were going. Landgren, Canupp, Hinkley and I thought it would be fun to drive to Jamestown. They had all heard me tell of my friends and family there and what a fun area it was to visit along with viewing Chautauqua Lake and Lake Erie. We were going to take Hinkley's Buick with the slipping Dynaflow transmission, but if we loaded the trunk with transmission fluid we'd be okay to go. We could also take turns driving and sleeping so there would be no motel bills and we could get there in good time. So a few days later we were told that we were granted our three-day passes.

Before we left, Harley Baritz, the company clerk, told me that the first Sgt. would like to have a word with me before I left on my pass. I went down to his office and he was sitting behind his desk holding a piece of paper with the word "The Phantom" written on it. It was the paper that I had slipped under his door that evening some weeks ago. In his other hand he had the sign-up sheet for the three day pass and my explanation as to when, where, and why I was going. He looked at me and said, "Hello, Mr. Phantom." What he had done was to compare the handwriting from my note to my writing on the sign-up sheet for the three-day pass. I was busted. I just stood there and looked at him, waiting to hear what was in store for me. Sgt. Williams looked mean and gruff, but he had a very loving side to him and a very pleasant smile. As he sat there looking at me his face lit up with that big smile. He said, "You know, Beatty, I figured it was you all the time, and it wasn't a very smart thing to do. But I told my friends about it at the NCO club and they thought it was hilarious; even more hilarious when they found out it might be you because they knew you from playing at the club." He just wanted me to know that I didn't pull one over on him and told me to have a fun few days leave. I dodged the bullet on that one and I noticed that from then on he brought his combination lock in to his room every night.

The trip to Jamestown was fun, even though we didn't have that much time. By taking turns driving and sleeping and pouring in transmission fluid every now and then, it didn't take long to get there. We all stayed at my house. We spent some time with my dad and his friends on Second Street and with our uniforms on it was free drinks for all of us. You didn't see very many soldiers in Jamestown so we were treated royally. My sister, Linda, was at that age in her life and I think I remember her having a crush on both Roy Landgren and Johnny Canupp. My friends also got a taste of some good Swedish food along with a trip to 11 Shaw Avenue for our fill of roast beef and Yorkshire pudding. It was a quick trip, but we all had a ball and it was talked about for some time after.

There was to be an all-Army entertainment contest at Fort Eustis. The winner would represent the post at the all-Army entertainment contest at Fort Belvoir. I got the idea to form a Dixieland Jazz band consisting of a few of the guys in the 384th Army band. I got Specialist Bill Owens (our bus driver) on trombone, Pfc. Chuck Hinkley, trumpet, Pfc. Roy Landgren, piano, Pfc. Mike Siskal, bass, Pfc. Barry Fuller, drums, and myself on clarinet. We rehearsed some nifty jazz tunes and got sounding quite good. We started taking jobs at the service club, the Field House, during sporting event intermissions, and William and Mary fraternity dances. We became quite popular around Fort Eustis and I'll be damned if we didn't win the entertainment contest. We went on to Fort Belvoir and won that as well. We were pretty proud of ourselves. But the trouble was the winners were to tour US army camps and entertain the troops. All of us didn't have enough time left in the Army to make it worthwhile. So we ended it there. We had a lot of fun doing it and it was a great learning experience, it was also my very first jazz band.

Mr. Petrelli received a telephone call from the top brass. They told him that the Secretary of the Navy was going to visit the US Naval base in Norfolk, Virginia. Trouble was that the fleet was out on ocean maneuvers, along with the Navy band. So the Navy wanted to borrow the 384th Army band for the various ceremonies involving the Secretary of the Navy.

You might wonder why he would want to visit a naval base while the Navy was out to sea on maneuvers - but I guess that's the US government for you. It sure sounded good to us because it was a long trip and it would be a change, playing a Navy base. We were told to get there early and have breakfast and then we would greet the Secretary of the Navy, Thomas S. Gates, as his plane arrived from Washington, D.C. We had to get up early, dress into our Class A's, load the bus with our horns and drive to Norfolk, Virginia. We got there in good time for breakfast. I had never been in a Navy chow line before and couldn't believe the variety of food that was laid out. I almost fainted when one of the servers asked me how I wanted my eggs. Was I dreaming? At Fort Eustis I ate whatever they put on my tray.

We were ready when the Secretary arrived and played a few marches as he got off the plane and shook hands with the naval officers and dignitaries. For the rest of the day he was busy inspecting the base and attending different ceremonies, and we played when it was appropriate. There was a nice luncheon and we got to eat as well. I might add that we looked very out of place in the middle of all the white naval uniforms. At the end of the day we went back to the airstrip and played for the farewell ceremonies. They were the same as the welcome ceremonies except in reverse.

The Navy brass were very pleased that the day went off so well, and we were a little bit responsible for it. As a way of thanks, we were invited to the NCO club for food and drinks. Now that sounded like a party to all of us, especially the Nitty Knot gang. Mr. Petrelli could have gone to the officer's club, but he always seemed more comfortable hanging out with his fellow musicians. Being a warrant officer he could fit in at either the NCO club or Officer's club, but he told me one time he did hang out with the officers and they looked at the insignia on his cap and uniform and treated him like he was some kind of visitor from a foreign army. So he partied with us and the Navy guys. There was lots of food and we especially took advantage of the free drinks. When it was time to go we were offered six packs to go, if we wanted them. I took advantage of that, as did many of the other guys. We said our goodbyes and everybody hoped that we would come back and play again sometime.

We boarded our bus and got in our seats ready for the ride back to Fort Eustis. I settled into my seat and opened a beer out of my six pack, looking at the scenery from my window. We were passing through the city of Norfolk and it was just starting to get dark, but I was able to take it all in. And then all of a sudden there was a "Bang, Bang, Bang, Scrape, Scrape, Scrape." My God, we just sideswiped seven cars driving through downtown Norfolk. How could this be? Specialist Owens was a wonderful driver and we had never had any problems driving around with him the whole time I was in the band. However, it seems that our driver got carried away at the NCO club along with the rest of us and had a bit too much to drink.

But there we were. We pulled over and it wasn't too long before the Norfolk police arrived. We were the Army and the police had no jurisdiction over us except to detain us there until they could call the military police at Fort Eustis. It took them awhile to arrive and of course I was chugging my beer trying to destroy the evidence, not thinking of the empty bottles. When the military police arrived they brought an empty bus with them. They secured our bus for evidence and told us to get on the empty bus, bringing nothing with us. After we were loaded into the new bus they went through our band bus and found all the six packs and pint bottles of whiskey some of the guys had brought. They came back to our bus and informed Mr. Petrelli that we were all under arrest and when we got back to Fort Eustis we would be confined to our barracks under house arrest.

I looked at Mr. Petrelli on the drive back to Fort Eustis and I could see he was watching his military career fly out the window along with a bunch of the career sergeants in the band. I didn't have that worry as the

Army was not my career, but I could see myself in the stockade along with my buddies. We got back to our barracks that night and we all got a very restless sleep. The next morning I looked out the window and there were a few military police outside our doors. It was a gloomy day and we just were waiting for the bad news, whatever it may be. First Sgt. Williams wasn't with us on that trip, nor was Harley Baritz, the company clerk, so they were free to come and go. Box lunches were brought for food, but nobody was very hungry anyway.

The next morning we woke up and I noticed that the military police were gone. First Sgt. Williams told us to report to the rehearsal hall and that Mr. Petrelli wanted to talk to us. When I walked in the hall I noticed Mr. Petrelli looked happy! What the hell is going on? He asked us all to sit down at our seats and said, "Gentlemen, what happened in Norfolk the other night never happened! The cars that we hit going through town will be taking care of by government insurance. Specialist Owens is responsible to pay for the damage on our bus." he said that he was sure that we would all pitch in with some money so our driver didn't have to pay the whole bill. So the matter was closed and we were told never to talk about it anymore.

What had happened, of course, would have been a big embarrassment to the US government, the Department of the Navy and the Department of the Army. The news of an entire Army band getting arrested would be unheard of and embarrassing to all concerned. After all, we were down there in the first place playing for Secretary of the Navy, Thomas S. Gates and the drinking party courtesy of the US Navy. So I guess you'd call it another one of those government, "It never happened" deals. To top things off, the band was awarded the post safety award for the month. My only complaint was that I recognized a couple of the MPs that night as my taxi drivers. This time they really made off with a bunch of six packs.

Our band bus trips became so routine that when we left the post into segregated Virginia territory, we didn't pay too much attention to it. That's just the way it was and there wasn't a damn thing we could do about. We went to a lot of small towns to play parades and concerts. If there were black restaurants and bars our black friends would go there and we would end up at a whites-only place. The food was usually better in the black restaurant anyway, so no one complained. And then we always had the sanctuary of our band bus with comfortable seats and box lunches. As far as segregation went, we figured that we'd leave that to the civil rights leaders.

We did have one interesting trip on the band bus that could have led to disaster. It had a happy ending, fortunately for all of us. We had a new recruit assigned to our band a few months before my discharge. His name was Dan Lewis. He was very shy and bashful and of all things played the flute. As we got to know him a little better we found out that he was a very nice person, a good flute player, and of all things, a virgin. Now, that was not a good thing for the guys in the barracks to know. First of all, he got the nickname, "Virgin Dan," and the poor guy was harassed constantly. I felt sorry for him but that's the way it was in a barracks full of horny young men.

One Sunday afternoon we were assigned to play a public relations concert at a small township in Virginia, just a couple hours from Fort Eustis. It was a low-key job and our company commander, Mr. Petrelli, was on leave. We had a corporal in the band that conducted that afternoon. Nobody was really in charge and nobody especially wanted to be in charge. And, there was nothing much to be in charge of because we knew how to get there, play the concert, and get back to post. The audience loved us and we loaded the bus and headed back to camp. It was a Friday and we had the weekend off and didn't have to report for duty until our Monday morning rehearsal. On our drive back to camp a car with three good-looking girls drove along the side of our bus, waving madly. This wasn't unusual as people often passed us and gave us a wave as the

384th Army band was written on the front and side of the bus. This time, however, the girls persisted and kept on passing us and waving and then letting us pass them and they waved. After this went on a few times I suggested to our bus driver, Tom Owens that we pull off to the side of the road and see if the girls did the same.

Sure enough they did pull over behind us. A few of us got out and talked to them and they told us they were vacationing and just looking for company. It is then I thought of Virgin Dan. I told the girls that we had a very good-looking young man in the bus that was very shy and bashful and never been with a girl before. I went back to the bus and got Virgin Dan and brought him out to the girls. I told Dan that this was his chance of a lifetime. The girls thought he was really cute and so we coaxed him into their car. Before they drove off I told the girls that they had to bring him back to Fort Eustis, Sunday night, without fail, or he would be in big trouble. They promised they would have him back and off they went.

We got back to Fort Eustis less one musician. We were off for the weekend but technically Virgin Dan was AWOL. I thought it best to tell First Sgt. Williams. At first he said "Piss, Shit, Fart and Puke! Now what have you guys gone and done?" The Sgt. wasn't happy, but he wrote Virgin Dan a weekend pass; however, he had to be back by sunrise Monday. He said if he is not back Monday morning you all better start running - especially you, Beatty!

Now I started to worry. We put this poor young boy in a car with three horny women that we didn't know anything about, other than the fact that they were on vacation. We didn't even get the make of their car or the license plate number. I felt responsible because I told the bus driver to pull over in the first place. He had no business taking orders from me as he was a Cpl. and I was only a private first class. There was also a bunch of Sgt.'s on the bus with us but they acted like they were just along for the ride. Sometimes I think that everybody thought that PFC meant Personal Friend of the Colonel.

So, that Saturday a bunch of us went to the Nitty Knot for our usual beer session and we all hoped that when we got back, Virgin Dan would be there waiting for us. He wasn't. On Sunday, I stuck pretty close to the barracks waiting and watching for Dan to walk in. So far there was no sign of Dan and we all went back to the Nitty Knot and worried over a few beers. When we got back there was still no sign of Dan. Every now and then the First Sgt. would walk past me just looking at his watch. I think the first Sgt. was a bit concerned as well, because with Mr. Petrelli on leave he was the highest-ranking person in the band, and probably should have been with us on that bus trip.

Then it happened. The front door opened and Dan wandered in with a big grin on his face, as if he didn't have a care in the world. I was never so happy to see anyone in my life. Dan would never have passed inspection. His shirt was open, his tie was hanging loose around his neck, and he needed a shave badly. We all gathered around him anxious to find out where he had been and what he had been doing for over two days.

Well, evidently his name wasn't Virgin Dan anymore. We renamed him, "Dan the Man." He told us he spent the entire time at a motel with the three girls, going to bed with them one at a time and then all three at once! We all looked at each other kicking ourselves for not getting off the bus with him.

I never did like goodbyes. But they were starting to come along, as some of the old gang was getting close to being discharged or assigned to other bands. Our band was pretty much desegregated now; I had even taken a seat at the front of the band bus. And, there was even talk about the band being quartered in a new building similar to the one I stayed at while I was in the Army Band School. Times were changing.

A few of my buddies were leaving before me. Chuck Hinkley, our trumpet player with the Dixielads, was one of the first to go. He lived in Rhode Island, just a short distance from the ocean. He gave me his address and I agreed to come visit him the summer following my discharge. Roy Landgren, went back to his home in Holden, Massachusetts. I told him I would visit him as well. I did visit them both that next summer.

When I got to Hinkley's house I found him down by the ocean with his boat, ready to take a spin, so I jumped in for the ride. Come to find out he had built that boat himself and this was its maiden voyage. I spent the entire ride looking for leaks. Fortunately, he was a good boat builder and we got to back to shore with no trouble. Hinkley and I lost track of each other after that visit and I can only hope that he had a successful career with music or building boats.

I stopped by Roy Landgren's house that he shared with his mother. He took me to some bars in town and we got caught up over a few shots and beers. Roy and I did keep in touch over the years and he and his wife even came to visit many years later. Unfortunately, he was battling prostate cancer, but it was in remission. A few years later I called to wish him a Merry Christmas. His wife put him on the phone and he sounded terrible. He told me the cancer had returned but he was going to fight it and win again. He passed away a short time later. I had to say goodbye to Johnny Canupp as well. He was a real swell guy and a good French horn player. He went back to his old hometown, Granite Falls, North Carolina. I suppose that when he wanted a big night on the town, he took the short drive into Hickory.

Len was being discharged about a month before me. We had become very good friends as he had the bunk next to mine and we talked constantly. Len was obviously gay. But back then there was no such word as gay" or concept such as "coming out of the closet." If you were gay you never told anyone except your very closest friends, because if the word got out it would destroy any career you had for yourself. And, in the Army it was totally unacceptable. But everybody in the band enjoyed Len and his company and accepted him for the way he was. He had come out to me and told me that he had a boyfriend that was waiting for him when he got out. Before he left he came to me and asked if I would be interested in moving to Washington, DC, with him after my discharge.

I told him that we were going in two different directions. I wanted to make music for my career and someday fall in love with a gal, get married, have children and live happily ever after. I told him that I was flattered, but he had somebody waiting for him and he should take advantage of it. Len's feelings were hurt, but we parted as friends and he made me promise that I would visit him someday in Washington, DC. One of my Army Band buddies and I did take a drive and visit Len and his friend in Washington. After that we lost contact.

My discharge day finally arrived and it was time for me to say the final goodbyes to all my friends. I had an airplane ticket to Buffalo, New York, and a ticket for the Greyhound bus from there to Jamestown. On the way out I stopped by Mr. Petrelli's office. He said, "You know Jim, as your company commander I am supposed to try and talk to you into a four-year enlistment in the Army. In your case I'm not going to do it, as I see a different future for you." Mr. Petrelli was later promoted to Capt. and commanded a few Army bands around the country. He ended the last four years of his career as a Lt. Colonel, commanding the West Point Band. My last stop and goodbye was to first Sgt. Sloane Williams. He shook my hand and with a big grin said, "Goodbye Mister Phantom, I'm going to miss you." With that I walked out the door, sad to see this part of my life come to an end.

The Dixielads – winners of the All Army Talent Show

Queen Elizabeth and Prince Phillip

**Gag photo in front of Ft. Eustis stockade!**

CHAPTER 10

# Welcome Home

I FLEW INTO BUFFALO, NEW York, December 6, 1958, with a duffel bag
full of my worldly belongings, some separation cash, and a Greyhound
bus voucher good from Buffalo to Jamestown. I arrived in Buffalo too
late to catch the last bus so I stayed overnight and planned to get to the
first bus out in the morning. I phoned my mom that night and told her
my plans and what time my bus would arrive in Jamestown and to let
all interested parties know. I decided to go out on the town that night in
Buffalo, see the sights and hit a few bars, as it would be the last night I
would be able do that in uniform. Buffalo wasn't a big military town and
you didn't see many servicemen. So, as in Jamestown, I got a lot of free
drinks from the bartenders. I found a nice restaurant, had a wonderful
dinner, and called it a night.

The next morning I boarded the bus and took the very familiar ride on
the New York State Thruway. The bus took the Dunkirk exit and then a
beautiful drive through the country and through the little townships that
I passed a few years before when I drove Johnny DeVita and some of his
guys to the Buffalo Raceway. I was getting excited now as we drove into
the Jamestown city limits and passed the very familiar sign –"Welcome to
Jamestown – The Home of Lucille Ball."

We pulled into the Jamestown Greyhound bus terminal and I looked
out the window, searching for familiar faces. I thought perhaps there

might be somewhat of a welcome home group waiting for me. I got off the bus, grabbed my duffel bag and looked around the bus from one side to the other and saw nobody. No mother, no father, stepmom, stepdad, sister, aunts, uncles or cousins. I waited around for a while in hopes that maybe a few people were just late. Finally, I gave up, grabbed my duffel bag, and walked home. I walked in the front door and there was my reception committee - my dog, "Spot." I dropped my duffel bag and for the longest time "Spot" and I rolled around the floor together. It just didn't get any better than that!

Later on my mom, stepdad, and sister came home and of course were very happy to see me. I took a walk downtown and dropped in the newsroom to say hello. Johnny's brother Pete was still there holding the fort. I went up to Second Street and it did not take long to find my dad in one of his saloons. He and his friends were happy to see me and the shots and beers were flowing. Most of my good friends were gone now. John Jacobson was in the Navy, John Andrea, the Army, and Jim Jacobson was married. So things had changed and now I knew that I had to work on my goal of becoming a professional musician. In order to do this I had to make some money and buy a car and hopefully find a paying music job in the Jamestown area. It didn't take too long before all the pieces came together.

Fortunately for me, my job at MRC was waiting for me, because when you were drafted into service, whoever you were working for had to keep your job open for you when you were discharged. After having such a fun and interesting two years in the Army I was not looking forward to going back to work in a factory for eight hours every day. I needed the money however, and MRC gave me my old job back in the inspection department. The pay was good and of course much more than I made in the Army. It was fun to see my old friends again at work and it didn't take me long to get involved with the United Auto Workers Union once more. The Union did its best for good wages and working conditions for its members. It was a closed shop, meaning that if you worked at MRC you had to belong to the union and pay dues. The local Union wasn't necessarily on the up and up; all the meetings were rigged for the way that the union officers wanted them to go. But that's the way things worked in those days and you went with the flow. I became a low ranking union officer and saw everything firsthand.

I worked the evening shift...3 p.m. until 11 p.m. I liked this shift because if I wanted, I could party from 11 p.m. until the bars closed in the early morning, then go home and have a few nightcaps and go to bed and sleep until around noon, then go back to work again at 3 PM. These hours were also great because I was living at home with my parents and helping them with their rent. Because of the odd hours I kept, I only saw my family on the weekends and was out of their hair most of the time.

Early one afternoon the doorbell rang and when I opened the door there was a middle-aged Italian-looking fellow standing on the front porch. He told me he was looking for Jim Beatty, and I introduced myself as such. He said that he had heard that I had just been discharged from the Army band and that he had a local dance group and was looking for a reed player. I invited him in and he introduced himself as Joe Prince. He was obviously an Italian that had changed his name to distance himself from the reputation that Italians had in Jamestown. Joe said that he had a quartet and that they played every Saturday night at the Jamestown Moose Club and during the summer months they played both Saturday and Sunday at the Moose Summer Home on Chautauqua Lake. The job paid $13.25 a night and the hours were 9 p.m. till 1 a.m. I agreed to give it a try the following Saturday and if I liked the band and Joe was happy with my playing, we had a deal.

I showed up at the Moose early the next Saturday evening, so I could meet the guys in the band and look over some of the tunes they played. Well, it was a far cry from a jazz band. In those days I guess you would call it a cornball or "Mickey Mouse" band. The piano player, Ed Schultz, was a very small, friendly, bald guy. I was horrified when I saw him drinking expensive whiskey (7 Crown) mixed with Coca-Cola. You could dump any rotgut booze in with a Coke and never know the difference. To my surprise I found out he could play nothing without the music, including "Happy Birthday." The drummer, Frank Richardson, was in his 60's and was a friendly, happy-go-lucky guy that drank like a fish and had a nose like W.C. Fields. He wasn't the greatest drummer in the world but it was fun just being on the bandstand with him as the night wore on the more happy and buzzed he got. The leader, Joe Prince, was a good-looking, happy guy in his mid-40s. He played the cornet and sang. He had a baritone voice that tended to get on my nerves as the evening wore on. The Moose members were very nice and greeted me warmly, and I think my playing lit a fire under the band because several people mentioned how much better they sounded. So what the heck, I accepted the job because I had to get back to playing for money, and God knows I needed it.

Fraternal lodges were big in Jamestown. In addition to the Moose Club, there was the Eagles, Elks, Vikings, Thule Lodge, The Rod and Gun Club, and the Marco Polo Club. It was suggested to me that now I was a member of the Moose orchestra that I should join the Moose Club. That sounded okay to me because it was a nice place to stop by for a cocktail or dinner with friends. I got the membership application and started to fill it out when I got to the part that said that I was a White Christian. That floored me. It meant that no blacks or Jews would be accepted as members. I reluctantly signed it because I remembered from my time in Virginia that I couldn't change things by myself. And selfishly I wanted to keep the music job there.

Before entering the service I had joined The Rod and Gun Club and they did not accept Italians as members. The saying around the club was, "Once you let one in, they take over." It was not in black and white that Italians were not allowed, but new member applicant's names were put in a hat and pulled out once a year. The reason for this was that the club was so popular since it was situated right on the shores of Chautauqua Lake. An Italian could fill out a membership application but it never made its way into the hat. The black people of Jamestown overcame their club exclusions by forming their own club – "The Colored Elks." The Thule Lodge accepted only Scandinavians, and to be a member of the Vikings you had to be 100% Swedish. The Marco Polo Club was Italian, but anyone could join. There was an undercurrent of racism in Jamestown, and with me belonging to the Moose and the Rod and Gun, I was part of it! Looking back, it's not something I'm proud of.

I got my taste of reverse racism when The Vikings Lodge changed their policy of being 100% Swedish. Now you could join if just your mother or father was Swedish. The Vikings was a nice club in downtown Jamestown. It had a bar, restaurant and a large ballroom for their banquets and dancing. They also had a very nice summer home on Chautauqua Lake. Because my mother was Swedish, I decided to join, and looked forward to getting my membership card in the mail. The day my card arrived I thought I would take advantage of my new membership and go down to the club for a beer or two. I got there and took a seat at the bar and eyed the bartender, but he acted very busy and did not wait on me. I waited a little more and he really did not seem that busy. So, I took my membership card and laid it in front of me on the bar, thinking he might have thought I was not a member. He still did not wait on me and passed by me several times taking care of other people. I smiled at him and waved at him, but it was like I was invisible. And then it became obvious to me that I was not going to get any service. I didn't have blonde hair and blue eyes, instead black hair and brown eyes. I could've been a Jew or heaven forbid, Italian! I picked up my card and left. So, then I knew a little bit about how it felt to be treated like a piece of dirt. The funny part of it was that my dad was in the Viking orchestra and a few years later I played several dances there. But I never ventured into the bar again.

The summer of 1959 started out on a sour note. One of my musical idols, Sidney Bechet, died in France of lung cancer. I had no idea that Sidney had been ill and was very surprised to read it in the evening edition of the *Jamestown Post-Journal*. What a loss to music, but thank God he left behind hundreds of recordings and compositions. I had purchased a used 1955 Ford sedan to get around with and shortly after the death of Bechet I took a trip into NYC to take in some jazz and to visit and listen to my old friend Omer Simeon. Omar looked frail to me and he told me that he too had lung cancer. Omer passed away the following September. So, two great musical friends of mine died just a few months apart. The smoking did them in.

The Moose Summer Home on Chautauqua Lake was now open for the season. It was a beautiful home overlooking the lake and had a dock for people to come and go by boat. It dawned on me that if I had a boat I could take it to and from music jobs at the Moose. Not a smart move. Going to work was fine, but the coming home at night after many drinks was not such a good idea. I docked my boat at a friend's house on the lake near Jamestown, and always managed to find myself back safely. My boat was an 18-foot, wooden Penn Yan with a 40 horse Johnson motor. It was a fun toy and I used it a lot for fishing and pleasure.

Every week there was a floor show at the Moose and we had to accompany the entertainer. It was usually just a vocalist and he or she might have music for us to go over. If not, we just talked the show over with the entertainer. One of the favorites was a vocalist from Buffalo, New York, who was wheelchair-bound. He was driven to Jamestown by a midget companion and they were both very nice people. When the show started the vocalist would wheel himself out on to the dance floor and sing his songs, finishing with a tear-jerking rendition of "You'll Never Walk Alone." Watching and listening to a man in a wheelchair singing a sad tune brought everyone to tears, including me. One night he came in to do the show and we had our usual rehearsal with him in a private room. He brought some new music that he passed on to us but still ended the show with his signature tune, "You'll Never Walk Alone." When we were all satisfied with the rehearsal, we went back to the bandstand and played a few dance tunes before the show started. When I got back to the bandstand I realized that I had forgotten my music in the rehearsal room. I quickly ran back to retrieve my music and opened the door to the room, only to find our "handicapped" vocalist in a wheelchair standing and mixing himself a drink along with his little companion. The three of us just stood there motionless for what seemed like hours. I had to get back, so I grabbed my music and went back to the bandstand and never said a word to anyone about it. After all, why should I ruin a perfectly good floor show and spoil the illusion? But when he sang his finale number I was probably the only one in the room without tears in my eyes. Years later I would remember this episode while watching the *SCTV* comedy program, where Joe Flaherty played TV station owner Guy Caballero, who could walk, but used a wheelchair. When caught, he would say he was in the wheelchair, "For respect."

I met many interesting people while playing at the Moose. The band was not overly good, but the guys were so much fun it made it bearable. I did learn a very valuable lesson while playing at the Moose. One Saturday afternoon I was tearing around the lake with a friend and a case of beer in the boat. We stopped at different saloons around the lake for a drink, including the Rod and Gun Club. I bumped into a musician friend - or so I thought - who played clarinet by the name of Franklin Fritz. Franklin was an ok guy but wasn't much of a musician as far as I was concerned. I had heard that he had always wanted the job with Joe Prince and the Moose orchestra. It was time to go home, have a bite to eat, get dressed, and go play my job at the Moose. When I got to the Moose to play, Joe Prince was waiting for me. He said, "I understand that you have been partying all afternoon on your boat and I don't think that you are in any condition to play the job tonight." However, he said that if I did not have any more to drinks I could stay and play the evening. I told Joe that that was fine and that I really didn't have to have a drink to play. Of course, what he didn't realize was that I had a huge capacity for alcohol and was perfectly capable of playing that night. Clearly, after I left the Rod and Gun Club that afternoon, Franklin Fritz called Joe and told him that I was bombed and was going to show up for work in bad shape. Franklin wanted me fired and wanted my job, but it didn't work. Halfway through the night, Joe came up to me and laughed and said, Jim, you are fine, if you want to have a drink go ahead. I remembered that night for the rest of my life: If you have a job to do, you have no business showing up half in the bag. And it was one of my number one rules after I became a bandleader. Thank you, Joe, and I guess, reluctantly, thank you Franklin Fritz.

I met a terrific couple at the Moose Summer Home that had a rented cottage on the lake: Dewey and Bernice Vickroy, who were in the business of flying. Dewey was a corporate pilot and Bernice was a flight instructor and operated out of the Jamestown Airport. On top of that they were amateur country musicians. Bernice sang all the old Hank Williams tunes and Dewey accompanied her on the banjo. They were quite entertaining and a lot of fun. And oh boy, were they country! They became friends of the band and we started to have jam sessions at their house. I didn't fit in very well with country clarinet but I did play the bass fiddle with them while they did their thing. I don't know what I was doing playing the bass because I knew absolutely nothing about it.

Dewey flew a twin engine Piper Comanche. It was a wonderful airplane and after I got to know him better I took flights with him. Every now and then when the weather permitted he let me take the controls. What a thrill! One time at one of our jam sessions I played a record of George Lewis playing the "Burgundy Street Blues." Dewey got tears in his eyes and said he had never heard anything so beautiful. I had Dewey hooked on George Lewis and New Orleans jazz and because of Dewey, I had the flying bug. Something good might come from this.

Playing dance jobs was great but I was always looking for an opportunity to play some jazz. As a rule this was done in the form of a jam session; just a bunch of guys that liked to play. Keyboards were rather new at that time so we'd usually go to someone's house that had a piano. In doing these jazz sessions I started meeting a lot of new musician friends that offered me casual jobs. One of the first interesting guys I met was Leo Matson. He played the piano and bass and was one swell guy. I did notice that he consumed a huge amount of beer. He lived a strange life with his mother and a brother who was rather out of it. His brother did absolutely nothing. He just lay around the house, also consuming huge amounts of beer. How Leo's mother put up with all this, I'll never know.

I also met a very good cornet player who patterned his style after the famed Bix Beiderbecke. He was another Italian fellow that changed his name for the usual reasons in Jamestown, to Sam Brady. He preferred to be called Bix. And, I got a call from my old friend from the Army band school, Dick Henzel. He lived outside of New York City and had a job playing a boat club in Dobbs Ferry, New York, on the Hudson River. It sounded good to me, and besides that I thought it would be fun to see Dick again and get up-to-date on our life after discharge.

One Sunday evening after playing a country club dance in Warren, Pennsylvania, I decided to stop in town and get something to eat. As I was walking down Main Street I heard the sound of a trombone drifting out of the second floor window of a building. I couldn't believe it! Whoever the trombone player was, I knew that he had listened to my old friend Big Jim Robinson of the George Lewis New Orleans Jazz Band. I looked on the door of the building and it said, Sons of Italy – Private Club. I walked up to the second floor and rang the buzzer and when somebody came to the door I told them I was a very good friend of Johnny DeVita. Of course I was let in immediately.

I walked into the room where the music was coming from and sat and listened to the trombone player's wonderful sound and interpretation of New Orleans jazz. His name was Pete Pepke. He was real country look-ing and wore a pair of farmer trousers and a bandanna around his neck. I soon found out that he was just a character and was quite on top of things. After we chatted a while I zipped out to my car and got my clarinet and spent the rest of the night playing New Orleans jazz with Pete. That start-ed a friendship that was to last over sixty years.

Pete Pepke had an interesting background. His mother and father met when they played in a Minstrel show together years before. His mother conducted the orchestra and Pete's dad played the trombone in black face. After minstrel shows went out of style his mom and dad moved back to Warren where Pete was born. They bought a house on Conawongo Creek in Warren, Pennsylvania. Pete's dad went into the printing business and was also an expert at leather working. He made beautiful saddles and harnesses for horses. When Pete graduated from high school in 1954 he joined the Von Brothers Circus and played trombone in the circus band. He played for the summer and then came back to Warren and got a job as a banker. He was a banker by day and a musician by night and he became very popular in the Warren community.

I also got to know a very good cornet player who also played some exciting ragtime piano. His name was Brian Johnson, and besides being a musician he was somewhat of a character. He was a guy about medium height, slightly stocky, and to look and talk with him he didn't come across as too bright. But he was a good friend and a good addition to any band.

Another musician I got to know was a drummer by the name of Darrell Jones. He was an engineer at a company in Jamestown and loved to play drums on the side. He was quite an athlete and into gymnastics. Needless to say, he had a lot of energy when he played the drums.

Then I met a bass player who had a rather unusual occupation; he had a mink farm and did very well with it. He was a tall, good-looking guy, slightly balding, and his name was Austin Main.

I knew that somewhere down the line I wanted to put together an authentic New Orleans jazz band. I now knew enough musicians to put a band like that together. I was, however, missing one important ingredient - the banjo! Dewey played the banjo but he was country and besides that he was often flying his plane around the country. I went to my dad and asked him if there were any old banjo players still around that he knew from the 20s and 30s. He remembered one, Don Peterson, but didn't know if he played anymore or was even interested. I called Don and he couldn't believe it when I mentioned the banjo. He had quit playing it years ago and switched to guitar. But, if I was serious about starting a New Orleans jazz band he was in and would go out and buy a banjo. I met Don for a beer one day and he was a lot younger than I expected him to be. He was on the short side but in good shape and he had managed to keep all his hair. He was also a shot and a beer man. I'll never forget when he ordered a shot of Ten High Bourbon with a beer chaser. Looked like that he was one of the boys and he turned out to be a great friend with a great sense of humor and fun to be around. He had a nice wife, Ann, and they had a daughter, Dorothy, who was in show business in Las Vegas. Don also drove a Swedish Volvo, and they were few and far between in those days. Don was very excited and said that he would find a banjo, brush up on it, and be ready whenever I called.

I got to know Dewey Vickroy quite well because he often showed up at our jam sessions. He was really a country banjo player but he fell in love with New Orleans jazz. As a corporate airplane pilot he was gone a lot and was on call 24/seven. However, if he had started drinking and got a call to fly, he would tell them he couldn't do it because of the alcohol and would have to take them to their destination the next day. I should have learned a lesson from that but I didn't and learned the hard way later on.

Occasionally, when Dewey had a flight and there was an extra seat available, I went along for company on his solo return flight to Jamestown. He had a twin engine Piper Comanche that sat five adults comfortably. On the return flight, if it was just the two of us, he would let me take the controls. I really enjoyed doing that and he suggested that I take flying lessons from his wife, Bernice. She was an excellent pilot and instructor.

So I did it. I started my flying lessons with Bernice on April 27, 1961. I know this because I still have my pilot flight record and logbook. It's all in the log, starting with day after day of takeoff and landings. After I was proficient in this part of the instruction I went on to the four basic flight maneuvers: The straight and level flight at different speeds, the climb, the turn, and the glide along with the descent of power. The flight lessons were a lot to take in but I was lucky because if I screwed up I knew Bernice was there next to me to save the day.

After four months of flying instructions, I was OK'd to solo. After our takeoffs and landings during instructions, we always turned around and went back to the end of the runway, ready to take off again using the full-length of the runway. After landing one afternoon, Bernice looked at me and said, "Jim, you're on your own and ok to solo." With that she got out of the plane and told me to take it up on my own. I was so excited that instead of turning the plane around and going back to the end of the runway I took off right there, in the middle of the runway. Bernice and others were looking in horror as I just made it off the runway, skimming the trees at the end. I was so excited that I never knew this until I was told after I got back to the field. Very embarrassing. But I made it and everyone was relieved.

Taking off from the middle of the field was a very serious mistake and could have had a terrible ending for me. The Piper Colt that I was flying was new to the airport, as they only started making them in 1961. Prior to that the Jamestown Airport used Piper Cubs. The Cub was a very popular training plane and they were made for ten years, 1937 to 1947. They were one of the most popular private planes ever. The Piper Colt that I was flying had a climb rate of 610 feet a minute, and by taking off in the middle of the field I just skimmed the tree tops at the end of the field. Had I been flying the older training plane, the Cub, I would have crashed at the end of the field right into the woods because the Cub only had a climb rate of 450 feet a minute. Someone was watching over me that day.

I was having a jam session with the guys when Dewey stopped by on his way back from the airport and told me there was a new Piper Cherokee that had just arrived at the airport. I was anxious to see that plane because there had been so much talk about it. At the end of the session I hopped into my car and drove out to the airport to see the new plane and I hoped that someday I would get checked out on it and take it up myself. I noticed my Piper Colt was sitting there and as long as I was at the airport I thought I would take it out for a spin around the area.

I had had a few beers at the jam session and knew that alcohol and piloting an airplane did not mix, but what's the harm in a few beers? So I checked the plane out, taxied it to the end of the runway - I had learned my lesson- and took off. I think I took my favorite route that day, over Chautauqua Lake and then on to Lake Erie and circling back to Jamestown and the airport. While I was gone, a cross wind came up and when I came down to land, I just could not line up with the runway. The wind was blowing me all over the place, so I gave it full throttle, came around, and tried again. The same thing happened and the wind was not that bad; it was my coordination. It took me five attempts before I was able to land my Colt, and I was a nervous wreck. Now I knew why Dewey turned down flying jobs after he had had a drink. I was finally starting to realize what a responsibility it was to pilot an airplane and it took your total concentration and coordination at all times.

One afternoon after getting back from a flight, I became involved in a very bizarre situation. After landing the plane and on my way to my car, I noticed it was busier at the airport than usual. I had purchased a brand-new French Renault, a small four-door sedan that probably was supposed to compete with the Volkswagen Bug. I pulled out of the airport and headed for Jamestown. After a while I noticed that I was sort of boxed in between the car behind me and the car ahead of me, and we were going slowly. I stuck my head out the window and looked front and back and I realized that I was in a motorcade. I also noticed some police motorcycles escorting us. Now what have I done? Where am I and where are we going? I started to put two and two together and remembered that Governor Nelson Rockefeller was coming to Jamestown and was flying in to the Jamestown Airport and I was in his entourage in this funny looking little car from France. I was just hoping that his bodyguards and the state police would not think that I was some sort of an assassin. Fortunately, the cavalcade drove into town and to the Hotel Jamestown. There was a big crowd there waiting for him. As he arrived and as the cars pulled in front of the hotel people got out one by one and then the next car pulled up and so on. I had to sit in my car until it was my turn to pull in front of the hotel. Of course, I was the only one in this funny looking car and people were just looking at me like I was someone from outer space. I quickly pulled away from the hotel and luckily nobody I knew saw me, or I never would have heard the end of it.

In later years Nelson Rockefeller became Vice President. Thank God that he wasn't vice president then, because with the Secret Service I'm sure I wouldn't be around to tell the story today.

It was time for me to make a move to my goal of getting in to the music business full time. This was not going to happen as long as I was working at MRC and playing music at the Moose Club with Joe Prince. These jobs got me back on my feet after the Army but now it was time to start thinking about a change. I thought the first thing I would do was to form my own band. I had met enough musicians now and I knew who I wanted in the band. Don Peterson was waiting for my call with his new banjo and trombonist Pete Pepke was eager to get started. Leo Matson was to play piano and Austin Main, the bass. I picked Darrell Jones for my drummer and called Brian Johnson to play the cornet. With me on clarinet, we had ourselves a seven-piece New Orleans jazz band.

People thought I was crazy, including my dad, because there was nothing like it in Western New York and there was a good chance it might not go over. I thought differently, because if we practiced and worked up a good repertoire, it would be something new to our part of the state that hadn't been seen since the 1920s. Good jazz music never dies but gets better with age. I decided to take the same name of my little group in the Army band – The Dixielads.

I said farewell to the Moose Club Orchestra and they were all sorry to see me go, but understood what I wanted to do. Now there was a big job ahead of us, and that was getting enough material together for a four-hour job. With the quality of the musicians this job was an easy one and we were ready to go. I have a scrapbook with the newspaper ad of our first job. It was at the Knights of Columbus Hall in Warren, Pennsylvania on November 22, 1961, from 9 p.m. till 1 a.m. Admission was $3.00 per couple.

Early in the fall I read the help wanted ads in the Musicians Union paper: "Wanted, New Orleans style clarinetist to play the winter season in Nassau, the Bahamas." It was the Wolverine Jazz Band out of Kalamazoo, Michigan. I called and talked to the bandleader, Jens Jensen. He was interested in talking with me and asked me to come to Kalamazoo for an audition. This is what I had been waiting for, so I took a few days off from MRC and drove my little French Renault to Kalamazoo. I found Jens Jensen quite a character; he liked to think of himself as an old Kentucky Colonel and preferred to be called "Colonel." I played for him and he liked it. The job he had going in Nassau was not for sure as yet, but I told him no problem, that I was in the process of forming my own band anyway, but if the Nassau job came through I would take it. We left it at that.

Meanwhile back in Jamestown I had car problems. That damn French Renault had an engine in the rear of the car. I was out bar hopping one night and the car began to spit and sputter. I looked out the rear window and saw smoke. I pulled over and found that the water hose had come loose and water was not getting in to cool the engine. It was toast. It was drivable, however, and I took it to the Pontiac dealer and traded it in for a new,1961 Pontiac Tempest. This was a beautiful car in those days and with my job at MRC and my music casuals, I could afford it. Or I should say, I could afford the payments. At this point of my life I still didn't know how to save money and it was going to take me a few more years to catch on. In the meantime I spent my money as fast as I made it.

In early November I got the call from Jens Jensen. The Nassau winter engagement was on and I was hired as the clarinetist for the band. This was sort of a bummer because I had just started my band in Jamestown. However, I knew I had to move on and agreed to meet Jens and the rest of the band in Miami, Florida at the end of November for rehearsals and our flight over to Nassau. I had a piano player friend in Jamestown, Paul Wick, that had a brother who lived in Miami, and his brother let me leave my new Pontiac Tempest in his driveway while I was away in the Bahamas.

I didn't know at the time, but this trip to Nassau was the beginning of an adventure that would change the rest of my life.

**The Moose Orchestra, Jamestown, 1959**

**With Piper Colt and new Renault**

CHAPTER 11

# Wolverine Jazz Band

So THE TIME HAD COME. I was officially a member of the Wolverine Jazz Band and we had a four-month engagement in the show lounge of the Emerald Beach Hotel in Nassau, Bahamas. One of the hardest things I had to do before leaving Jamestown was to quit my job at MRC. I was making good money and had built up quite a bit of seniority. However, this is the life I decided to live and I had to get started on it sometime. I said goodbye to my family and friends. My sister Linda was all grown up now and had a nice boyfriend. She cried when I said goodbye.

It was the end of November with winter and snow in Western New York in full force, and I agreed to meet Jens and the rest of the band at a motel in Miami. We were to have a rehearsal and fly out the next morning for Nassau and open at the hotel that evening. I thought it rather rushed, but I wasn't the band leader. I grew up in Jamestown, with all the snow, so I never gave it a second thought. I had no snow tires or chains, just a full tank of gas, a carton of cigarettes and a case of beer; I was all set to go. I drove through New York, Pennsylvania, Ohio, West Virginia, North Carolina, Georgia, into Florida, and then Miami. I made it to the motel in plenty of time, and one by one the rest of the band showed up.

The bandleader, Jens Jensen, the "Colonel," dressed and acted the part as he affected a phony southern accent and smoked a cigar. It was part of his show business deal and we all went along with it. The trombone player was a guy by the name of Joe Rotis. I had heard of him when he was a member of a famous New Orleans band called the Basin Street Six. Pete Fountain had also been a member of that band before going with Lawrence Welk and making a big name for himself. The piano player was a guy named Bernie Schroder. The only trouble I saw right off the bat was the drummer, Red Moore. I've been around enough boozers in my day and I spotted it in him, but again, I wasn't the bandleader and it wasn't my worry.

We had a rehearsal late that afternoon. I was surprised because when you bring a new band into a club that hasn't worked together very much; you play tunes that everyone in the band is familiar with. Instead of doing that, Jens was calling numbers that most of us did not know. He said; let's try "The Buzzards Parade." What the hell is that! Jens knew it and played the lead on his cornet and expected everyone to follow. He had no music or chords or anything. Things weren't going well until I suggested that we play tunes that everyone knew.

It was then the band started to sound like a professional group, with Jens playing a good lead melody on his cornet, me filling in with my clarinet part, and Joe Rotis playing tailgate trombone. We only had two guys in the rhythm section, piano and drums, and it sounded rather empty. I could see where we desperately needed a bass player to take up the slack. This problem would be solved after we got to Nassau. Everyone in the band was on their best behavior of course, trying to make friends with one another. As far as forming personal opinions about one another, that would come after working together on the bandstand for a few nights. But I did know, after observing the drummer a little more and having cocktails during rehearsal, that he wasn't going to last very long. I was sure he was a full-blown alcoholic...too bad, because he was a real nice, happy guy from Texas.

After the rehearsal and dinner I made arrangements with my friend's brother to drop my car off at his house. Turns out that he was a Miami lawyer and a very nice guy, just like his brother Paul. He had room in his driveway and I didn't feel bad about letting my new car sit there for four months because of the beautiful Florida weather. So that was it. We were to fly out of Miami early the next morning. I was looking forward to it, and in those days it seems that I was looking forward to every day.

Nassau is only a few hundred miles from Miami and our flight was a short one, just under one hour. I had done a little research on Nassau so I wouldn't be totally out of touch when I got there. Over the years Nassau had given refuge to pirates, freed slaves, rum smugglers, and the like. In 1629, Charles I of England claimed the Bahamas for England. In 1648, the first English settlers arrived. Later, wrecked ships became a livelihood for some of the outlaw settlers. They would put lights on the reefs and fool ships into coming in and grounding themselves. The British government did not condone this type of activity but the pirates ran wild because the Royal Navy was too busy fighting their wars. Pirates ruled the island, including the well-known Blackbeard. In 1718, the British outlawed piracy and sent Governor Woodes Rogers to Nassau along with three warships to restore order there. That's when the Bahamas became an English colony. During the American Revolution many plantation owners fled to the Bahamas along with their slaves. In 1807, the British Parliament banned the slave trade and the Royal Navy stopped slave ships that were on their way to America and the slaves were set free in the Bahamas. By 1834, three quarters of the Bahamian population were from Africa.

During the American Civil War, England and Nassau continued to trade with the southern states. In the movie "Gone with the Wind," Rhett Butler was a popular man in Nassau. Later, during prohibition in the United States, Nassau did a very nice business smuggling liquor into the southern states. In the early 1940s the King of England, Edward VIII, gave up his throne to marry a divorced American. He was also pro-Nazi and the embarrassed British government sent him to Nassau to be the governor. That was just a way of getting rid of him during the war. So, here I was on my way to this island full of history and mystery.

We were greeted at the Nassau airport by Bob Chase. He was the entertainment director for the Emerald Beach Hotel and our boss. He had two cars waiting for us along with a truck for our luggage and instruments. Bob was a tall, nice-looking fella who had a big job managing the entertainment and putting together and coordinating all the conventions that were continually running at the hotel. The band did not stay at the hotel because the rooms were too valuable; instead they put us up in different housing in downtown Nassau. There was one double room in a very nice complex called The Cumberland House. For some unknown reason the piano player, Bernie, and I decided to share that apartment. It was very nice with a small living room and dining area along with a tiny kitchen and the rest of the guys had single rooms in houses just a block or two away from us. The bandleader, Colonel Jens Jensen, had his own accommodations somewhere and for our whole stay there we never found out where he lived. I soon found out that not only the island was mysterious, but so were a few of the guys in the band.

We had to be at the hotel for opening night, so we showered, dressed and followed instructions on how to get the free Emerald Beach Hotel bus. It ran 24/seven, every hour on the hour. It couldn't get any better than that and it was no problem getting back and forth to work every night. Not only that, we were told that we could dine in the main dining room for breakfast, lunch, and dinner, on the house. We also had the use of the swimming pool and, of course, the ocean. The hotel had its own golf course that we could use. A real nice bonus we had was at the end of our job each night, we could go to the kitchen and they would make any kind of sandwich we wanted to take home with us. All this and we were getting paid as well.

We found out that on our first night we were alternating with a bohemian steel drum band. We played a half hour set, as did they, and this went on from 9 a.m. to 1 a.m. This was getting better all the time. I always loved the steel drums and looked forward to my intermissions when I could listen to them. The first night, however, Colonel Jens brought some marijuana along. He turned the steel drum band onto it and I never have heard a steel drum band play so far out in my life. Our group played just okay, although the audience loved us.

I was right about the drummer. He showed up buzzed and continued to drink all night. He was a full-blown alcoholic and I knew he had to go. But again, I wasn't the bandleader and this was something that Colonel Jens would have to deal with sooner or later; probably sooner. I could also see that my roommate, Bernie, was a lightweight drinker. He was a redheaded guy and after a couple of drinks his cheeks became very rosy - a dead giveaway. But he played fine and seemed to be having a good time. I found Joe Rotis, our trombone player, another heavy drinker, but an old pro and in control of himself. He was a happy-go-lucky musician and I liked him. As for Colonel Jens Jensen, he was a decent cornet player but was really too much into himself. The Kentucky Colonel act and the phony southern accent were too much for me, but it seemed to work for him. As for me, the rest of the band probably thought that I was a teetotaler because I was so straight and sober. Little did they know that I was brought up with shots and beers and could out-drink all of them. Because I was the kid of the band, somehow the name Jim was dropped and I became known as "Junior." Our opening night was really enjoyable. The hotel made a big deal about it and we had a packed house. We had about 16 weeks ahead of us doing this six nights a week.

As it turned out my hunch was correct. After a few nights it became quite apparent to Jens that the drummer was a hopeless alcoholic. Jens put in a call to the Miami musicians union and they sent over a replacement. He was a middle-aged guy called Roger. He played okay but I wasn't that impressed with his personality. At least he showed up for work each night sober.

There was another thing that still bothered me and that was the rhythm section. We really needed a bass. Part of the problem was that Bernie, our piano player, didn't have much of a left-hand. If he was a strong player, we might have squeaked by. Then I remembered what Dewey and Bernice had told me before I left Jamestown, that after I got settled in Nassau they would take the Comanche and fly out and see me. The Comanche seated five and had a huge luggage space -enough room for Leo, his luggage and bass. I knew that Leo would love to come to Nassau and join me, just for a room, beer money, and food. He didn't eat that much anyway

I suggested this to Jens and he was elated. He then had to present this to the Entertainment Director. Bob thought it doable and gave the go-ahead to Jens. I called Leo and he was ready to go. Within a week Dewey, Bernice and Leo landed at the Nassau airport and the band had a complete rhythm section. The hotel gave Leo a single room in my complex at the Cumberland House. He was outfitted with a new black suit and a white dinner jacket. I'm sure he never looked so distinguished in his life.

Everything was cheap in Nassau. For instance, Bernie and I hired a housekeeper for twenty-five cents an hour. It was next to slave labor for the native Bohemians. I went out and bought myself a tailor-made black suit for practically nothing compared to what it would have cost in the United States.

The band sounded much better now with the added bass. It was decided to change our hours to 8 p.m. – 12 a.m., which was fine with me. The hotel was full of wealthy people from all over the world enjoying a relaxing vacation in Nassau. The first celebrity we had in the lounge was Sean Connery - Mr. James Bond himself! He was there filming *Dr.No.* Lady Oakes, a local socialite, was also a regular. Soon I was to become friends with a few other celebrities, not to mention - royalty.

I found that it doesn't take long to get to know your fellow band members, on and off the bandstand. My roommate, Bernie, talked in the third person and he referred to himself as "Dad." He had been married and divorced and thought of himself as a real womanizer. He'd say things like, "Dads in love," or "Dads going to get laid tonight." I never saw him with a date the whole time we were in Nassau, except one afternoon I came home and he was in bed with our Bohemian cleaning lady. Bernie wasn't a good drinker and it didn't take much to make him feel good. After a few drinks he also had a nasty streak. For instance, he would play wrong chords on his piano to try to screw you up while you were taking a solo. Also, on the bus back to town after work, he would talk softly to himself, but just loud enough so everybody could hear. Things like, "Junior squeaked a lot tonight on his clarinet," or "Leo is a drunken stumble bum." All these things did not bother me; in fact, I thought them amusing.

I liked Joe Rotis very much. He was a short, stocky guy with black hair, black moustache, and big smile. He had quite a beer belly and had also suffered a heart attack a few years earlier. Like Bernie, Joe also liked the women, but had very unconventional ways of having sex with them. Also, like Bernie, I never saw Joe with a date the whole time of my stay in Nassau. Joe and I became good friends and rode the bus to and from work together. On the other hand, Bernie and the new drummer teamed up and rode the bus together. We were starting to have our own little clique within the band.

Colonel Jens had purchased a car and never took the bus. Nor did he ever offer any of us a ride. He kept himself separate from the guys in the band, although he would occasionally join us for dinner in the dining room before work. I found him boring and a braggart and I think he was living some kind of a fairytale life. The whole thing was crazy to me - the title of Colonel, along with a southern accent, beard and big cigar was just too much. But at the end of each week he handed me a lot of money - this I liked.

And then there was Leo. He never rode the bus to work with us because he didn't take advantage of the great dinner in the dining room. He took a later bus in time to play the first set of the night. Leo was a sweet guy and he called me "Brother Jim." After the job each night he would get a sandwich from the kitchen to take home, so he did eat something. Poor Leo was skin and bones and it was obvious that if he kept up this lifestyle, he wouldn't be around for too many years.

Roger, the new drummer, was not very social. I never did get to know him and he didn't seem interested in knowing me. But we were friends on the bandstand and after all that's what we were there for…to play music.

I had a lot of free time during the day in Nassau. There was certainly a lot to do and I took advantage of it. Quite often I would go downtown and hop the bus to the hotel and have lunch in the dining room. The hotel had a beautiful oceanside swimming pool and it was enjoyable just to relax in the sun and cool down in the pool. There was also the ocean, and although I was far from being a good swimmer, I would wade out to my waist and just dog paddle around. One afternoon I was doing this and to my horror I spotted a shark fin some distance away heading my way. Oh boy! What do I do? Do I make a mad dash back to shore? Or should I just freeze on the spot? The shark was getting closer and I decided turning around and heading for shore would just cause an attraction, so I froze! The ocean in the Bahamas is crystal clear and I stood there and watched the shark, who was bigger than me, swim by. I watched him head back to sea and then I made my move to dry land. The hotel had shark nets all around the property but every now and then one would find his way through. This ended my oceangoing playtime and I confined myself to the pool after that.

There was also a beautiful golf course at the hotel. I had never played golf but I got to know the golf pro. He was a tall, blond, blue-eyed German and I could just picture him in a Nazi SS uniform. A lot of Germans came to the Bahamas after the war but I didn't ask any questions. He offered to teach me how to play golf. It was fun and a good way to kill some time, but in the long run I found it boring and usually lost interest after the fourth or fifth hole. I feel the same to this day, even on a miniature golf course. I sure would have made a poor businessman, as that's where all the big deals are made.

I also made a lot of friends with the daytime employees of the hotel. Consequently, I was up-to-date on all the gossip going on; like who were the important VIPs staying at the hotel and what company they owned. I found out that David Beck was staying at the hotel. He was a big labor leader and having problems with the US government. However the big scuttlebutt around the hotel was that the King of Bulgaria would be spending his honeymoon there. There was a good chance that I would see him and his wife in the dining room. They might even come into the lounge and hear the band. They were coming incognito and we were not supposed to talk about it. The Emerald Beach was one of the most elegant hotels on the island with its 215 rooms. It was built in 1954 so it was fairly new when I was there.

When I didn't spend my time at the hotel I would often wander around town and people-watch. All the big cruise ships would stop there and people would get off and purchase their Bahamas souvenirs from the natives. I loved to have lunch in town as well, because I really enjoyed *conch*. That is the meat from those giant seashells you see. My favorite was the deep-fried *conch*, called fritters. *Conch* was good in a salad as well. I also headed for the docks when I knew that a British battleship would be in. That would always be impressive and it was the British way of letting the native Bohemians know who was the boss. After my day of leisurely afternoons I had to return to my apartment and get dressed for another night's work. I should've learned my lesson of warning Bernie I was coming home, especially after walking in and finding him with the cleaning lady. Another time I came home and walked in on him pleasuring himself. He was just as embarrassed as I was, but I couldn't resist saying, "Looks like Dad's in love with himself." He didn't think that was very funny and swore me to secrecy. I have kept that secret all of these years - until now.

After work, if I wasn't in the mood to call it a night I would often stop at a certain bar on the way home. It was an old building and looked like it had been there since the beginning of time. It had a high ceiling with three or four fans buzzing around and they were swaying back and forth as if they were ready to come off their hinges and fall down on all the customers. It reminded me of some establishment you might walk into in India, so I called it The Taj Mahal. I tried to keep this my own personal hideaway and most of the time the guys in the band didn't know that I was there. When I was alone I could mingle with the customers at the bar and strike up some interesting conversations.

As it turned out this was a hangout for many of the entertainers on the island. It was also a place for celebrities to come and not be harassed by fans. For instance, Raymond Burr often stopped by with his entourage of good-looking young men. Raymond Burr was Perry Mason on television, one of the most watched shows at that time. He later went on to do another hit TV series, *Ironside*. He was a big, good-looking man, and when he walked in the door he had to duck so as not to hit his head. When he saw me he eyed me up and down. I know it was an open invitation for me to come over to his table and introduce myself. I didn't feel comfortable about doing that, or maybe I was just too shy about approaching a celebrity of that status. In hindsight, I should have gotten acquainted with him because he must have been very interesting to talk with, not to mention some of the show business doors he could have opened for me.

Another show business celebrity that frequented The Taj Mahal was Burl Ives. He was an actor, writer and a folksinger and made several movies including, *Cat on a Hot Tin Roof,* with Paul Newman. He later became popular as the snowman in the TV classic, *Rudolph the Red Nosed Reindeer* and sang "Holly Jolly Christmas" and "Silver and Gold." He was a big, happy guy with a beard and drove a small scooter around the island. I always knew when he was at the Taj Mahal because he always parked that little scooter right out in front. He liked to buzz around the island with his scooter and drink beer at some of the saloons and asked me to join him one afternoon. We must have looked pretty funny on that little scooter with me sitting in back of him hanging on for dear life.

Another regular was Lloyd Bridges, who was in another popular television show at the time, *Sea Hunt*. He took the part of a scuba diver and had an exciting episode each week. Bridges was the father of two popular movie stars, Beau and Jeff Bridges. One night on my way home I passed by Leo's door. The door opened and out came Lloyd Bridges. I looked at Leo and said "What's Up"? Leo said that he was just having a few beers with a friend he had met at a saloon. Leo had absolutely no idea who Lloyd Bridges was.

One busy night in the lounge the band was in the middle of a set when I noticed five men walking in. With all the conventions and business meetings going on at the hotel, this wasn't unusual. But these men were different and stood out among everyone else in the room. They were definitely mafia. I thought that perhaps they were in from Miami. When our intermission arrived a waiter told me that I was invited over for a drink at the table with the five strangers. One of the men stood up, greeted me, and introduced himself as Reggie Freno. He said we had a mutual friend from back in New York and I knew immediately that he was talking about Johnny DeVita. So that connection had followed me in the Army and now the Bahamas.

Reggie explained that he had moved to Nassau after living in Cuba for several years. Right away I knew I was talking to someone important in the Mafia. The Mafia had been big in Cuba since the 20's when they ran rum out of there. They were also dealing cocaine many years before it became popular in the United States. President Batista was in cahoots with the Mafia and gave them hotel and gambling licenses as long as he got his share of the profits, which were 10% to 30%, and he protected them for a very lucrative seven years. Batista was corrupt and the Cuban public knew it and hated him. In the early part of 1959 the Cuban rebels, led by Fidel Castro, marched into Havana. Batista had already taken his money and fled to Spain. The Mafia leaders ran around to all their casinos and got millions of dollars and left as well. Many of them went back to the United States, but obviously at least one decided to come to Nassau. You are talking about dangerous men here, and people like Lucky Luciano were people you didn't want to fool around with.

Reggie seemed like a very nice chap and fun to hang out with. He loved the music and asked me if I, along with the rest of the band, would like to come to his house for spaghetti dinner on our next night off. He said he loved to cook, and spaghetti was his specialty. He offered to send his car for us but I told him that our bandleader had a car and all we needed was directions. So it was all set - I talked to the guys in the band and they all wanted to go. I walked Reggie and his friends out to the parking lot when they left. He had a beautiful new Cadillac that he said he didn't trust the Bohemians with and he shipped it over to Miami for oil changes.

So on our next night off we drove to Reggie's house. It was in a very secluded part of Nassau. When we drove up the driveway there was a gate with two guys carrying shotguns standing outside. I told them who I was and they said they were expecting me and opened the gates. Reggie was waiting at the front door with an apron on and looked quite harmless. I had told the rest of the fellows in the band that he was a friend of a friend. They all had a very puzzled look on their face but never said anything. Occasionally, a silhouette could be seen through a window of a guy with a shotgun over his shoulder. But other than that it was just another spaghetti dinner in the home of a Mafia boss. Dinner was great and wine flowed like there was no tomorrow. At the end of the night when it was time to go Reggie gave me a huge stack of mail, all addressed to people in the United States. He asked me if I would please mail them when I got back to town. Oh great! Now I was a runner and I was never so happy to get something in the mailbox in my life. Reggie gave me his phone number and said to call him anytime if I needed a favor. I never did because this situation made me nervous. When you're dealing with people who are in the drug business, along with gambling, you are getting in dicey territory. Johnny DeVita never had anything to do with drugs. It was strictly gambling, and the whole time I was associated with him I never knew of any murders… that all happened way before I entered the picture.

The guys in the band had a ball. And it was the first time we got a ride in Jen's car. I don't know how we all got in because it wasn't very big. At any rate, I had gotten lot of respect from Bernie after I walked in on him with the housekeeper and then again when he was having his "private moment," but now I got a lot of respect from the rest of the band members. So, I guess it pays to have the right kind of friends.

The hush-hush gossip among the employees of the Emerald Beach was that the King of Bulgaria had arrived with his new bride. They were incognito but it wasn't hard to recognize them in the lobby and various places around the hotel. They seemed like a nice young couple around my age and I spotted them around the pool and in the dining room.

King Simeon is the son of King Boris III and Queen Joanna. He was born in Sofia, Bulgaria, in 1937, so he was just three years younger than me. In his younger years as a prince he lived with his parents and younger sister in the royal palace. His father was an ally of Hitler and Germany during World War II. His father died suddenly - and mysteriously - in August of 1943 after coming back from Germany from a meeting with Hitler. Some write that the meeting did not go well and King Boris turned down Hitler's request for Bulgarian troops to aid Germany, and he also opposed the liquidation of Jews. The Nazis were suspected of poisoning him. So, Simeon II ascended to the throne as King of the Bulgarians at the age of six.

After a communist takeover of Bulgaria in 1944, King Simeon remained on the throne, although his uncle and a great number of the Bulgarian elite were executed. In 1946 he left Bulgaria along with his mother and a few other members of the royal family. Their Majesties went to Egypt, where they lived until 1951. While there, young King Simeon studied at Victoria College. Thanks to the Spanish government's hospitality, the Bulgarian royal family arrived later in 1951 in Madrid, where he resided in exile. In 1958 the King entered Junior College at Valley Forge Military Academy in Pennsylvania, graduating in June, 1959, as a Cadet

2 <sup>nd</sup> Lieutenant. He speaks Bulgarian, Spanish, English, French, Italian and German.

The King's new wife, Margarita, also had quite an unusual young life. Her father and mother were executed by Spanish loyalists in 1936, when she was one. A friend of the family sheltered her and her brother in his house. From there they went to France and then entered northern Spain. She and King Simeon were engaged in 1961 and married in the first part of 1962. For their honeymoon they picked the Emerald Beach Hotel in Nassau the Bahamas.

Since we had been playing at the hotel for a few weeks, the band was starting to take shape and sounding much better. We were still alternating with the steel drum band and they were starting to drive me nuts after listening to the song "Yellow Bird" hundreds of times. On our intermissions I would often grab a drink and my cigarettes and go out on the dock and relax with the fruit bats flying all around me. One night a rocket from Cape Canaveral buzzed over my head on its way to outer space. That was quite a sight. I never did figure out why the fruit bats were flying around the dock. They were quite large but seemed quite harmless and never bothered me. I enjoyed my time on the dock with the steel band playing in the background, but I didn't get to do this often because lounge customers usually asked me to join them for a drink on my intermission.

The band was swinging along one night when in through the door came the King and Queen of Bulgaria. They sat at a table near the band. I knew who they were, but never told the rest of the guys in the band because I thought it would be awkward if they were staring at them. When intermission came a waiter told me that the couple at the table near the bandstand would like me to join them for a drink and pointed to the

King's table. Why they asked me I don't know, perhaps because I was around their age. How do you address a King? But then again I'm not supposed to know who he was! So, I went over to their table and just said, "How are you guys doing?" I sat down with them and had a drink and lit up a cigarette after noticing that the King was smoking. We started out with just small talk. They wanted to know all about me, where I was from and so forth. The King introduced himself as Simeon and his wife as Margarita, so that's how I addressed them.

It was still an awkward conversation because I knew who they really were but I felt that I could not let them know that I knew. But then the ice was broken. Simeon must have felt comfortable with me and told me who he was and where he was from. It still seemed strange at first, sitting having a conversation with a King and Queen. The King told me that they were enjoying their honeymoon in Nassau but were disappointed in the night life there. They wondered where I went after work and what I did. I told them that if they wanted to see the real Nassau that the late-night partying went on over the hill in the native Bohemian district. I had been over the hill several times, even though I had been advised not to do so.

I had become friends with a lot of the Bahamians working at the hotel. The hotel had two buses running, one bus went back and forth into town and the other bus went over the hill, doing the same for the Bahamian employees. Every now and then I would hop on the bus with my Bahamian friends and would hit a few of the bars, having drinks, listening to the bands and dancing. There was nothing but poverty over the hill. Many of the houses were made with just plain wooden boards and had tin roofs. Some of the homes were just old shacks like you would see in the backyard of your house. There were also old, abandoned cars around that should have been in a junkyard. Most of the streets were very dark and probably had no electricity. I also heard that many of the homes had no running water. The bars were not fancy but everyone had loads of fun and I never felt unsafe. Simeon asked if I would take them there the next night after work. He had a rental car and both of them were excited to party.

So the next evening the two of them came in, had a few drinks and listened to the band. When the band was finished for the night we piled in to their rental car and headed over the hill. Few white people did this, but I had gotten to know so many native people now that I felt very comfortable. The native musicians were marvelous and I really loved to hear them play. We went to several bars that night and Simeon and Margarita had a ball. We even did the native dance called the *Limbo*. That's where you form a line with a group of people and dance under a pole. Each time you go around, the pole is lowered until you fall on your rear...lots of fun when you're drinking.

The three of us enjoyed ourselves, just talking and getting to know one another. At one point the King was talking about his mother and her health problems as she was getting older. I told him about my mom and that she was in pretty good health. Then I realized that he was talking about the Queen of Bulgaria and I was talking about a Swedish lady from Jamestown, New York. I thought it quite amusing. Every time Simeon sat down at a table he always placed what looked like an oversized pen next to him. One time he went to the boy's room and I asked Margarita what it was. She told me that it was a small gun and that there were people who would like to see Simeon dead. That's just great, I thought. Here I am sitting at a table with someone who might be a target for assassination. But then again there was little chance that anyone would find him hanging out with a jazz musician over the hill in Nassau.

After that night the King and Queen bid me farewell and went back to their home in Spain. We have always kept in touch and I send them a new recording when I make one. Over the years much has happened politically for Simeon. The Berlin Wall came down and the Communists left Bulgaria. In 1996, Simeon visited Bulgaria and most of his royal property was returned. In 2001 Simeon became Bulgaria's Prime Minister. Through all of this, he still found time to send me Christmas cards, pictures of the royal family and letters always praising my music and good luck in the future.

One evening, while playing at the Emerald Beach, a group of British Naval Officers gathered at the Lounge Bar for a drink. On our intermission they invited the band over to join them. As it turned out they were Officers with the *HMS Troubridge*, now docked in Nassau. The *Troubridge* had a long and distinguished record as a destroyer with the British Navy. It was commissioned in March, 1943 and was involved in the invasion of Sicily and Salerno. The *Troubridge* also was credited with the sinking of the German submarine U–407, using depth charges.

After the Second World War the *Troubridge* became the leader of the 3rd Destroyer Flotilla in the Mediterranean. In 1957, the *Troubridge* was converted into a fast anti-submarine frigate and was recommissioned and became part of the 8th Frigate squadron on the America and West Indies station. The ship was 358 feet and ran at 36 mph with a full load. It had a crew of 174.

The British Naval officers explained to us that they were having a ship's party at one of our convention rooms at the hotel. They said that we would make a lot of sailors happy if we joined their party during our next intermission and played a tune or two for them. We all agreed and during our next intermission put on a show. The captain of the *Troubridge* came over, thanked us, and wanted to know if we could join him for dinner the next evening.

Early the next evening we all met at the dock. As we approached the *Troubridge* we couldn't believe our eyes. The entire crew of the ship were all on deck in their dress whites greeting us; the whole deal - whistles blowing, piping us aboard - salutes and all. It was just like we were the British Royal family. After we were aboard the captain invited us down to the officer's dining room, where we had our choice of rum or beer or both. Naturally, I drank both.

While we were drinking and chatting, smartly dressed orderlies would bring us little tidbits to nibble on, like cheese and crackers. I was looking forward to the dinner - Yorkshire pudding, perhaps? Well, we drank and drank and drank. The Captain of the ship, who incidentally was wearing a monocle, was really getting loaded. He took off his monocle and insisted that we all try it on. I stuck it on my eye and it just kept falling off, much to the amusement of the captain. By this time we were all falling down drunk and were ready for a nice British dinner. But suddenly the captain managed to get up and announce that the party was over and thanked us so much for coming. No dinner, no Yorkshire pudding... nothing, but a lot of beer and rum. The *Troubridge* left the next morning. I often wondered how they managed to get out to sea.

The Emerald Beach played host to many conventions while I played there. They had a big one coming up for the Carling Black Label Beer Company. It was about a week long and at the end there was to be a big show with a number of headliners from the U.S. We were asked to play the show in the main showroom, backing up all the acts. Those attending the convention were top-notch employees and distributors of the beer company. It was free beer all week and although Carling's wasn't my favorite beer, I made an exception for that week.

When it came time for the big show we found that we only had the afternoon before the show for rehearsal. Hugh Downs was to be the master of ceremonies. He was one of the top radio and television announcers around at that time and was also Jack Parr's sidekick on *The Tonight Show*. He showed up for the rehearsal in a wet suit, just coming out of the ocean. Turns out he was a wonderful guy and fun to work with. Vocalist, Roberta Linn, was also on the show; she gained fame as Lawrence Welk's first "champagne lady." There was also a great comedy team at the time, Phil Ford and Mimi Hines, who was famous for putting a cymbal on her head, squinting her eyes like an Asian and saying, "Rots of Ruck." There was also comedian Alan King, who had an attitude and was not very friendly. To round out the show was one of the greatest vocal teams of all times – The Mills Brothers. They were four black guys that were really a class act. I became friends with Harry, the spokesman for the group. He liked his marijuana and asked if I could get some for him, which I did. The show went great and it was a very rewarding time for the band, as we did a good job backing everyone up. The next day everyone left, including all the entertainers and the free beer.

A very wonderful lady who worked at the hotel as the official social hostess was Louise Campbell, and she was not only popular at the hotel but on the entire island. She lived in a suite at the hotel and she drove a real cool green MG convertible. She was a tall, tan, dark-haired lady, with a gracious and friendly smile. She was very flamboyant - in personality and dress. Louise was an active volunteer on the island and raised money and coordinated a summer camp for native island children. She was also on many charity community boards and known all through Nassau as "Auntie Mame." She was originally from Vancouver, BC, Canada and moved to Nassau in the mid 50's as Social Director for the hotel.

Louise approached me one night in the lounge in and told me that friends of hers were sending their daughter down from Vancouver as a graduation present from nursing school. Her name was Pauline and she thought I might enjoy meeting her and help to show her around the island for the short time she was there. Sounded good to me, and I told Louise to bring her around to the lounge so we could get acquainted.

Louise explained to me that before she came to Nassau she had lived on a houseboat on the Fraser River in Vancouver and became friends with Percy and Tannis Vickerstaff who had a boat moored on the river. Pauline was the Vickerstaff's daughter and Louise would often babysit her when she was young. Although Louise was not a blood relative, the Vickerstaff's would call her "Auntie Louise."

Louise told me that Pauline was graduating from the University of BC/VGH School of Nursing mid February and after completing her nursing board exams, she would take off for Nassau, arriving early March 1st. Louise knew that Pauline also had secretarial skills so she arranged a job for her at the front desk of the hotel as a secretary to the Assistant Manager. She also was to help Auntie Louise with various social functions - entertaining guests, help with children's activities and running bingo night. With her busy social functions she didn't have much time to spend with an American jazz musician, so it would be a while before we became acquainted.

Although I saw Pauline and her Auntie Louise in the lounge while they were on their social functions, we never officially met until March 18th, 1962. We met at the hotel hostel which was located on the hotel grounds. It was a small recreation hall with a bar and a young, very friendly native bartender (and drinks were only a couple of shillings). Hotel management employees and the white band were allowed to hang out at the hostel in the evenings. Pauline was entitled to one of the 12 rooms there, along with laundry, dry cleaning, housekeeping and meals.

Pauline was a tall, blonde, very good-looking lady with a great personality. We seemed to hit it off right away and I knew that I wanted to see more of her. The first time I asked her out was to play golf at the hotel golf course. Little did I know that she came from a golfing family and was quite good. I had just taken a few lessons from the golf pro and thought I knew it all, until she beat me. Not a good impression for the first date.

I really enjoyed her company and we started to meet often during days off and evenings after work. Many nights we never got back to the hotel until 4 a.m. and poor Pauline had to work in the morning while I slept in. On weekends we went to the beach during the day, walking, lying in the sun and swimming. Again, I was not the greatest swimmer while she was excellent because her family had a cottage on a lake in Canada. We went snorkeling on the other side of the island at Lyford Cay, we walked on the beach and pier at night - stargazing, moon-walking and talking. We even took a water taxi over to Paradise Island for lunch and fun on the ocean - that was way before the bridge over there was ever built. One day we took eighteen kids from the hotel into town to the Wax Museum, then ice cream on the beach. We even went to church on Easter Sunday. The Howard Johnson's restaurant was near the hotel and we often enjoyed their hot fudge sundaes. We just seemed to like talking and being together as much is possible.

Every now and then, after I was done playing, we would go over the hill and party at places like the Conch Shell, Coconut Palms, and The Flowers, dancing the merengue until dawn. We also went to the Goonbay to watch exotic dancers. There were several nightclubs in downtown Nassau that we also frequented... The Cat and the Fiddle, Dirty Dicks, the Junkanoo, the BaMa, and the Esquire. There were just so many places and we seemed to make time to do them all.

Pauline was a different kind of lady then I had ever gone out with before. She came from a good family and had good values and I respected that. So I didn't push anything on the beach, not that I didn't think about it...but time was getting short as our band was winding up its engagement and thinking about packing up and going back to the states. Pauline had an opportunity to go on a medical mission to the Bahamian out-islands with Dr. Steven George in April so she left Nassau before the band did. She was returning to Vancouver May 17ᵗʰ via Toronto, Canada. Since Jamestown was so close to Toronto we agreed to meet there. We said our goodbyes and I started thinking about my next move. Nassau was heavenly - what a way to start a career.

**The Wolverine Jazz Band, Nassau, 1962**

**Joe Rotis, Jim and the "Colonel" putting on a show, Nassau**

Pauline and Jim, a stormy night off, Nassau, 1962

King Simeon and the royal family, 1972

## CHAPTER 12

# The Jazz Saints

IT WAS GETTING DOWN TO my last two weeks in Nassau. By this time the band was sounding really solid, but we were all tired of Colonel Jens Jensen and all his nonsense. There was even talk about ripping his tailor-made southern Colonel-type suit off him on stage during the last number of the last night. I didn't want any part of this because I wouldn't humiliate anyone like that.

I was planning on returning to Florida, picking up my Pontiac Tempest, and driving back to Jamestown with Leo. We would somehow have to strap his bass to the top of the car, but we were going to worry about that when we got there. Everyone else in the band was going home as well, because that was the end of Colonel Jens Jensen and the Plantation Jazz Band. Trombonist Joe Rotis was going home to New Orleans and then joining up with Murphy Campo and his Jazz Saints for a US and Canadian tour. It sure had been a wonderful four months in the Bahamas and I hoped to return sometime, which I did with Pauline, some 51 years later.

And then the unexpected: Joe Rotis got a call from Murphy Campo in New Orleans. Murphy's clarinet player could not make the tour with the band and Murphy wanted to know if I would be interested in the job. I jumped at the chance. This meant that I would not be going back to Jamestown and Leo would have to fly home or take the Greyhound bus.

So it came down to the last night at the Emerald Beach Lounge. Somehow, Jens got wind of the story that his suit might be ripped off on the last tune, so he simply disappeared and didn't play for it. Joe Rotis, like the rest of us, had a tailor-made suit and he was so disappointed that he didn't get to help tear Jens suit off that he started to tear his own suit off and asked everyone in the band to help him out. He didn't have to ask us twice and he was soon standing there with a trombone and his underwear. That was the end of our last set in the lounge, much to the amusement of the customers, but certainly not very professional.

The next day Joe Rotis and I flew to Miami and picked up my car. My New York license plates had expired and before Joe and I left for New Orleans I had to get Florida plates. I remembered that Pauline and I were going to meet in Toronto, Canada, but with this new music job I knew that it wouldn't work out, so I wrote her a letter and explained the situation with hopes that we could make other arrangements in the near future. And then we were off for a rather easy drive to New Orleans. Joe lived with his sister Helen Prestopnik. She was the wife of the late Irving Prestopnik, whose stage name was Irving Fazola. Irving was a well-known and respected clarinetist in his day and played with many notable orchestras, including Glenn Miller. Here I was sleeping in his bed with all his pictures and memorabilia on the wall along with loads of music he had played over the years. Joe's sister, Helen, was most gracious and opened up her home to me along with some wonderful New Orleans cooking. This certainly was a far cry from my last adventure in New Orleans a few years before.

The first thing I had to do while in New Orleans was to go to an instrument repair shop with my clarinet, as it was a mess after being played six nights a week for four months. I had rubber bands over some of the keys so they would work and the clarinet pads were worn out. Joe Rotis was a good friend of clarinetist Pete Fountain and suggested that we go talk to Pete some night at his club on Bourbon Street. Lawrence Welk had a very popular television show every Saturday night featuring Pete and several other musicians and he called it "champagne music." Pete Fountain left the Welk orchestra in 1959, having said that champagne and Bourbon didn't mix, and went home to New Orleans, opening his own club on 800 Bourbon Street.

I only had one week in New Orleans before I went on tour with Murphy Campo and his Jazz Saints. Joe Rotis and I stopped by Pete Fountain's club one night before he started his show. Pete came out to the bar and Joe introduced us. Pete was a very gracious man and we had a wonderful visit over a drink and I explained to him about my clarinet being in bad shape, asking him to recommend a good repair shop. At that time I played a LeBlanc clarinet, the same as Pete. He wrote down the name and address of the repair shop and a little note to go along with it. Pete then went to do his show and Joe and I sat and enjoyed it - a masterful clarinetist! The next morning I went to the repair shop with the note from Pete Fountain. I told them I was going on tour and needed my clarinet repaired as soon as possible. To my amazement they told me they would have it ready late that afternoon. I went back to pick it up, the repair man opened my clarinet case and there sat a shiny bright clarinet that looked like it just came from the factory. The clarinet was totally rebuilt like new and to top it all off there was no charge! It's nice to know the right people.

The Murphy Campo Band was managed by Mike Gendel and the Continental Booking Agency out of New York City. This was no small time tour and it paid well. The night before we left for the tour I was invited over to Campo's home along with the rest of the band for a little get-together rehearsal and spaghetti dinner. Compo was another stocky trumpet player with a beard, like Colonel Jens, except he played a less traditional jazz horn and he was showboating with a lot of loud high notes. In other words, he wasn't a real jazz team player on the bandstand; but he was the boss. The spaghetti dinner was great and as it turned out half the band was Italian; Murphy Compo, Johnny Sansone, piano, and Joe Nastasi on bass. The band was rounded out with me on the clarinet, Joe Rotis on trombone, and Chubby Wreath on the drums.

At the spaghetti dinner I found out there was a catch to our tour that I was not aware of. It seems Murphy Compo's band bus was a Volkswagen with the engine in the rear and could only go 60 mph, tops! It would be absolutely ridiculous to load six guys, their instruments, drums and luggage in that bus. At that rate it would take us two weeks to get to our first engagement in Reno, Nevada. It was obvious that we needed to take another car on the tour. Everyone looked at me! I agreed to take my car as long as I was reimbursed for the gas money.

Joe Rotis and I decided to ride together in my car. We loaded our luggage and instruments into the trunk and had room for some of Chubby's drums in the backseat. We had a long drive ahead of us to get to Reno, Nevada. At first we decided to caravan with the guys in the Volkswagen bus, but it was too painful because they would get to a hill and slow down to 30 or 40 mph. In fact, I was wondering if that damn bus would get there at all. Anyway, we told them we would meet them in Reno and off we went.

This was just the first part of a long traveled tour, because after our two weeks in Reno our next stop was Cleveland Ohio, and that's a hell of a drive. But I saw that we had a couple of weeks in between jobs and Jamestown, New York, was only a four hour drive from Cleveland. We were also scheduled to play in London, Ontario, Canada, and Toronto, Canada, another short distance from Jamestown. It was sounding better all the time.

Joe Rotis and I pulled into the outskirts of Reno in the wee hours of the morning and checked in to a motel there. I did all the driving because

Joe didn't have a license, but that was ok because I preferred to drive anyway. We had managed to consume all our stash of booze in the car and arrived at the motel without a drop to drink. Just to show you what a couple of dumbbells we were, we never thought of the fact that we were in Nevada and could have gone out and had drinks 24/7. So we went to bed thirsty, which was probably for the best.

The next day we drove to the motel that the casino had arranged for us and waited for the rest of the band to show up. They finally arrived in that damn Volkswagen bus looking like a bunch of refugees. We all freshened up and went down to the Nugget Casino to let them know we were there and to check out the lounge showroom where we were to perform. It was really a beautiful hotel/casino and was absolutely jammed with customers.

Come to find out the Lounge Casino Showroom had just been built and we were one of the entertaining groups chosen for the opening along with the Russ Morgan Orchestra, The Lang Sisters, Buddy Greco, and comedian Jack Marshall. The show went from 8:30 in the evening until 3:30 a.m. Wow! That was seven hours a night for seven nights a week. But in those days I could've cared less as long as the cigarettes and drinks were plentiful.

I was anxious to get to work on the first night because I wanted to meet Russ Morgan. I had listened to his weekly radio show, *Music in the Morgan Manner*, for years. He was a musical genius and legend. Morgan played the trombone and piano, composed, and arranged and conducted to perfection. He arranged music for musicians like John Philip Sousa all the way to Louis Armstrong. He composed "Does Your Heart Beat for Me"- his theme song - and also wrote, "You're Nobody 'till Somebody Loves You," and many others. My band favorites of his were "Forever and Ever"

and "Cruising down the River." He also made the trombone "wa-wa" style popular. He was from Scranton, Pennsylvania - my neck of the woods - and I knew we would have lots to talk about.

I arrived at the casino early on opening night to familiarize myself with the bandstand and to meet all the musicians and entertainers that I would be working with the next two weeks. There was a large musician's dressing room right behind the bandstand. This is a room where we could leave our instrument cases, uniforms, and change our clothes for the show. When I arrived, Russ Morgan's musicians were busy setting up their music stands and sorting their music out for the show. It was an eleven-piece orchestra with piano, bass, guitar, and drums, along with seven horns. Buddy Greco was there as well, getting organized with his musicians for their part in the show. He had a three person rhythm section and a sax player. The Lang sisters were there and were to be featured with the Russ Morgan Orchestra. The only one missing was Jack Marshall, the comedian, and all he had to do was show up and go into his routine.

Soon after I got there, Russ Morgan walked in and he was exactly what I expected - just a regular guy and drinking beer out of the bottle- a real Pennsylvania coal miner. He was of average height and dressed in a tailored tuxedo. I was impressed by how pleasant he was to everyone and how he always had a friendly smile on his face. I introduced myself and told him where I was from. He said - Jamestown is on the Pennsylvania border - do you know Pete Pepke? I told him that I sure did and we had been playing together before I went on the road. It seems that Pete was a real fan of his and they corresponded often. Now I knew where Pete got his "wa-wa" trombone style. Russ Morgan had two sons and they were working in the band with him. Jack Morgan played the trombone, like his dad, and David Morgan played the guitar. The Morgan band were given rooms at the casino and both of the boys went to their rooms on intermission time until their next show. Daddy Morgan was protecting his boys from the waitresses who were always waiting to go out with the musicians after work.

In addition to the casino lounge there was a big showroom called The Circus Room, where the big-names of the day performed. For instance, while I was there Liberace was the main attraction and after him, The Osmond Brothers. The casino also had their own in-house star – "Bertha the Elephant." Bertha entertained in the Circus Room (I bet the stars loved that!) and was often paraded around the casino in-between all the slot machine and gambling tables. I talked with Bertha quite often and I swear she got to know me.

Buddy Greco was a talented young singer around my age who had done very well for himself. Greco started his career playing piano, arranging and singing with the Benny Goodman Orchestra. He went out on his own and became very successful with a few big recording hits like "Lady Is a Tramp," selling one million copies, and was awarded a gold disc. He did a TV show with Buddy Rich and George Carlin and starred in the movie *New Girl in Town,* playing the part of a vocalist. He also did some things with the Rat Pack and was close friends with Frank Sinatra. Greco was also a close friend of Marilyn Monroe and he and Frank Sinatra were two of the last people to see her before she died. In the band dressing room Greco wasn't very friendly and I could see where he was really into himself, but then again, he might have been in a bad mood. The casino had a huge advertisement in the paper about the big show in the new Casino Show Lounge - it mentioned everybody's name except his. So as far as anybody reading the advertisement knew, Buddy Greco wasn't even there.

The Lang sisters were three very pretty dark-haired girls that looked amazingly alike, especially when they were dressed the same at show time. They were really nice, friendly girls, and were also carefully under the eye of Russ Morgan. They were not impressed with wildish, casino behavior. After their engagement was over at the casino they found God and switched to playing religious music. The Lang sisters were shocked at people dropping off their children at the casino's day care and then spending hours upon hours drinking, smoking and playing the slots. They also didn't approve of the behavior of the musicians and the waitresses after show time. It was quite easy for the musicians in the show to get a date after work and if you didn't luck out - there was always Bertha. The Lang sisters were very talented, beautiful singers, and they went on to do great things in religious entertainment.

The first couple of days got off to a rocky start. For one thing, the Casino management didn't think that our band looked sharp enough on the bandstand. So they sent us to a tailor in Reno to be fitted with new jackets, shirts and ties. The casino picked up the tab, so there were no complaints and we now had new outfits for all our future engagements. It's amazing that back in those days, money was no object and the sky was the limit. Today it's rare to even see a single or a duo musician in a lounge, let alone a six-piece jazz band or an eleven-piece orchestra like Russ Morgan's.

The other problem we ran into was with Buddy Greco. Russ Morgan started the show and he had seven or eight music stands with a big RM on them. After their show his musicians moved the music stands to the back of the bandstand rather than lug them and their music offstage to the musician's room. It made sense, and when we followed the Morgan Orchestra we simply played in front of his music stands - no big deal. But, I arrived at work one night to find Buddy Greco and Russ Morgan in a heated argument. It seems that Buddy Greco did not want to play as long as Russ Morgan's music stands were on stage. I heard Russ Morgan shout out some real Pennsylvania coal miner's language to Greco. He said, "Listen you fucking kid! I was a star before you were even born!" This went on for some time and finally Greco went to casino management, but to no avail. The music stands stayed and Greco was in a foul mood in the musician's room for the rest of our engagement.

Our band was starting to get it together and we were pleasing the crowd. Unfortunately, the same thing happened in Reno as it did Nassau. Probably because I was the youngest, best looking (?), and exuberant on the bandstand, the newspapers always put a picture of me in the story and wrote favorably about me. This did not go over well with bandleaders as they wanted and should have had the headlines. However, there was nothing I could do about it.

But, for the most part all the guys in the band got along very well. We had one little problem with our bass player, Joe Nasasi. He was an albino and could not stand the sunlight - sort of like a vampire. He made arrangements with some of us to bring lunch to him in the afternoons. When it was my turn I would knock on his door and he would just open it enough for me to slide his lunch in. I felt sorry for him but he sure came alive in the evenings. At the end of our show every night he reminded me of Bela Lugosi as Dracula as he rushed back to the motel before sunrise.

One night, or I should say early-morning, there was a knock on my door. It was Chubby Wreath and he was in a big panic. He told me Murphy Compo was down at the casino losing big-time, using the band payroll. Knowing my association with Johnny DeVita and gambling during my Jamestown days, he asked me if there was any chance of me coming down and helping Murphy out. I told him I didn't know - but it was worth a try, because if he lost all the money, the band would not be paid. I went back to the casino and found Murphy at the craps table. I sat down next to him and we slowly started winning and making his money back. He wanted to keep going but I managed to drag him out of there. This was pure luck, because believe me you cannot beat the casinos in the long run. The band got paid that week and I was the big hero.

Spending all that time working at the casino was fun, but after a while it started to get on my nerves. It was the same thing every night; most people were not necessarily jazz fans and you could play almost anything and they would be happy. Russ Morgan was the hit of the show, as he should have been. And, I was starting to hear the "Ding Ding Ding" of the slot machines in my sleep every night. As we became closer to the end of our engagement I looked forward to our trip cross country to Cleveland, Ohio.

One night I went into work at the casino and there was a message for me to call Dewey Vickroy back in Jamestown, New York. He had a favor to ask. His son, David, from his first marriage, was coming to visit him. Dewey wanted to know if I would mind picking him up in Salina, Kansas, on my way back East. Chubby Wreath asked me if he could ride along with Joe Rotis and me because he felt he could not survive the trip to Cleveland in that Volkswagen bus. Chubby was a real neat guy and I told him yes. So, it looked like it would be a real fun trip traveling from Nevada to New York.

We played our last show in the Casino Lounge and said our goodbyes to Russ Morgan and his guys. By the way, Russ was missing one horn player after he hit it big at Keno; he packed up his horn and went home. Also goodbye to the Lang sisters and comedian Jack Marshall, who was very funny and had become a friend of mine. I don't recall Buddy Greco saying goodbye - but then nobody seemed to care. Before I left I had to make one last trip out to the floor of the casino and say goodbye to Bertha, my Reno girlfriend.

The next afternoon after our last night at the Nugget we all got up and organized our two vehicles for the long haul ahead. Joe, Chubby and I loaded our luggage and instruments into the trunk of my Pontiac. We sat two in front, one in back, and we still had to pick up Dewey Vickroy's son, David, in Kansas. I did all the driving and it was up to the other two to keep the beers and cigarettes coming.

At one point I had thought it might be possible for me to make a trip up to Vancouver and visit Pauline before going east. That thought became unworkable as I had Joe and Chubby with me and it would have been impossible for them and their luggage to fit into the VW bus. I wrote Pauline a note to that effect and told her that at least for the time being our relationship would have to be limited to letters, postcards and phone calls.

Pauline had left Nassau in early May to go on the medical mission with Dr. George, and she wrote and told me that it had been a wonderful adventure for her traveling from island to island in a four seat seaplane helping the natives with their medical needs. Pauline returned to Nassau from her mission on May 24th and I had left on the 20th. She flew home to Vancouver for her graduation ceremonies on June 8th and started working as a nurse in pediatrics at Vancouver General Hospital.

In the meantime the Three Musketeers were having a merry time driving east. The weather was beautiful and we had great conversations talking about our time at the casino and our future engagement at the Theatrical Grill in Cleveland. We picked up David in Kansas and squeezed his luggage into the trunk and off we went for the rest of the trip to Jamestown, which was still quite a drive and a few more motels.

Murphy Campo's agent had arranged for the band to do a recording with New York City-based clarinetist, Peanuts Hucko. He was an
excellent clarinetist with a good name and had played with the Glenn
Miller Orchestra during WW II. I had heard him occasionally at Eddie
Condon's in New York playing with Wild Bill Davison. I didn't have to
make the recording session since they had Peanuts on clarinet, so I spent
a few days in Jamestown before meeting everybody in Cleveland. I was
happy to stay in one place for a while. We arrived in Jamestown and I
dropped Joe and Chubby off at the Greyhound bus terminal so they could
get their ride in to NYC. I then delivered David to Dewey at his house,
had a few drinks and then went to my mom's place. Sound complicated?
Well, that's the music business.

I had a few days in Jamestown and it seemed nice to be home and see a
lot of my old friends. Over the years I had heard Johnny De Vita talking about some of his friends in Cleveland. Johnny told me that there
was a long line of associates in Cleveland, going back to the 1920s with
such names as Big Joe Lonardo, Frank Milano, "Big Joe" Porrello, Alfred
Pollizzi, and the list goes on. There were also Teamster Union bosses like
Anthony Milano, Bill Presser and Milton Malisheo, and Teamster leader
John Nordi. It looked like I wasn't going to be in the company of amateurs there, but then again I was only a jazz clarinet player minding my
own business. Come to find out, the Theatrical Grill was Cleveland's
oldest jazz club. It was also a front for owner Morris "Mushy" Wexler,
who ran his gambling wire service there. He gave all the odds for the
bookies that bought in to his service, and this is where Johnny DeVita
got his odds from. The club was located at 711 Vincent Avenue in downtown Cleveland. The street was only a block long and was nicknamed
"Short Vincent." That little street had many clubs and bars that were the
entertainment attraction for all of Cleveland. On that street the police
looked the other way and the Theatrical Grill was the place where sports

and entertainment celebrities gathered, along with the mobsters, not to mention people from the legal profession, like judges and lawyers. And of course it was the place to go to hear good jazz

Over the years it was a meeting place for anybody who was anybody, and Judy Garland, Frank Sinatra, Jimmy Durante, Dean Martin, Joe Louis, and Jane Mansfield all graced the doors along with Cleveland mobsters. Although the place opened in 1937, there was a disastrous fire in 1960 and the Theatrical was rebuilt and opened a year later. So, actually I was going to play in a fairly new club. I was excited to follow in the footsteps of such jazz greats as Gene Krupa, Wild Bill Davison, Dizzy Gillespie, and Oscar Peterson.

I went to my job at the Theatrical Grill in Cleveland a day early. It was only a 3 ½ hour drive from Jamestown, so no big deal. I found an affordable hotel just two blocks away from the club. The club was beautiful, with a dining area and a circular bar with a revolving bandstand in the middle. I was wondering if I would get dizzy while I was playing but found out the bandstand went around very slowly.

We had a packed house on opening night and since it was a jazz club we went into all the Dixieland songs that people expected. We played tunes like the "Muskrat Ramble," "Way down Yonder in New Orleans," and "Dixie." We looked sharp because we were wearing those snazzy outfits that the casino in Reno bought us. We played forty-five minute sets and on our intermissions the Chet McIntyre Trio entertained. It was a fun, well-dressed, audience from all walks of life and you would never know it was possible for you to be sitting at the bar next to a mob boss.

On our very first week we were playing away and as the bandstand circled the room I spotted one of my favorite actors sitting at the bar: Forrest Tucker. I had watched his movies in the 40s and 50s and loved his acting. He was a big man, 6'4", and was in good shape, I would say around

200 pounds or so. He was blonde and good-looking, just like in the movies. For the most part he made Western and science fiction films and was the leading man in a few hundred other movies. I was a spook movie buff and one of my favorite films of his was the *Abominable Snowman*, which also starred Peter Cushing, the British horror star. The film was made in 1957 and scared the daylights out of me. One of his most famous roles was in the movie, *The Yearling*, and he was also Beauregard Burnside in *Auntie Mame*. He played the part of Mame's first husband and the film had the highest gross of any movie in 1958. Later on he was Sgt. Morgan O'Rourke on the TV series *F Troop,* and also appeared on TV in the series *Gunsmoke.*

As the band was playing and slowly revolving around the bar crowd I thought that if Forest Tucker was still at the bar on intermission I would take the part of a real fan and tell him how much I have enjoyed his films. It turns out that I did not have to do that because on our next pass Forest Tucker looked up at me and said, "Hey Mr. Clarinet Man, you'll never get any place in showbiz without wearing a nice pair of glasses." He had obviously had a few drinks and he took off his horn rimmed glasses and handed them to me. So I wore them on our next circle around the bar and we all had a good laugh. It was then intermission time and I joined Forrest at the bar and returned his glasses. Turns out that he was a regular guy and was in Cleveland doing Summer Theater and the Theatrical was his night time headquarters. He told me we'd be seeing each other every night, which we did, and the glasses routine became a nightly event.

There is one inside story about Forest Tucker and that is the reputation he had in Hollywood circles for having a very large "John Thomas." A big joke about him was that one time he was playing golf with bandleader Phil Harris. Tucker putted the ball so close to the hole that he didn't bother to putt it in all the way. Phil Harris gave him a bad time and insisted he finish his putt and Tucker said that it was so close he could putt it in with his manhood, which he did to the amazement of everybody in the viewing area. There was another Hollywood celebrity, Milton Berle, who had a big one as well. He was interviewed one time about the size of his member and Milton said – "I don't know, but every time I get an erection, I pass out." So much for Hollywood gossip.

Louis Armstrong and his All-Stars were in town to play a concert one evening and after the concert his clarinetist, Joe Muranyi, stopped by the Theatrical to say hello. Armstrong played the same program of tunes night after night because that's what his fans wanted -all his hits like "Hello Dolly" and "Mack the Knife." Muranyi wanted desperately to play some different songs and asked if he could sit in with us. We said yes, of course, and we had a heck of a good time playing with him the rest of the evening. Muranyi was five or six years older than me and passed away in 2012 from congestive heart failure.

Our engagement at the Theatrical Grill was for two weeks and that was the normal run for all the bands. I was now on tour with one of the top jazz bands in the country. How I got this far so quickly was probably a lot of luck. But nevertheless I was there and I was hoping that some of my family would take the 3 ½ hour drive to come and hear me play. Nobody showed - no mother, father, aunts, uncles, cousins - nobody. So it was just like coming home from the Army that day - nothing had changed. But now I was starting to wonder if my father was jealous of my success. Could that be?

After our Cleveland engagement at the Theatrical Grill we had a two week gap without work. Half the band, including Murphy Campo, hightailed it back to New Orleans, while Joe Rotis, Chubby Wreath and I headed for Jamestown. My sister Linda had married in March and had moved out of the house, so there was an extra bedroom for Joe and Chubby to share. Well, as it turned out, my Mom and Pop loved having me home again and they really got a kick out of Joe and Chubby. Joe was a cutup and had my mother in stitches all the time.

I introduced the guys to my dad and all his cronies on Second Street. They were treated very well by everyone in the bars, somewhat like my Army buddies when they came home with me. I took them down to the newsroom to pay respects to Pete DeVita and the guys, but it wasn't the same without Johnny there. We also had a reunion party with Leo Matson and Joe was especially happy to see him after working with Leo in the Bahamas.

When we were in Jamestown I got the bright idea to pick up a casual music job as long as I had Joe and Chubby with me. This way we could get a little extra cash to help ease the pain of two weeks with no work. I called the Governor of the Moose Club in Jamestown and told him I was in town with a few musicians and would love to play for them at the Moose Summer Home on Chautauqua Lake. He thought it was a great idea and we set the date for the Sunday before we left for Toronto, Canada.

In the meantime the three of us kept busy buzzing around Jamestown, including Sunday brunch with the Beatty family and Uncle Bill's routine with the Yorkshire pudding. I had warned Joe and Chubby about this and we all made sure that there was lots of Yorkshire left when the plate came down to Uncle Bill. We also visited some of my Swedish relatives and we had some shots and beers. I think the Swedes come to life and are more fun during the Christmas holidays.

When you visit Jamestown in the summer, Chautauqua Lake is a must. It's a beautiful lake about eight miles long and full of fish, especially muskies. I borrowed a friend's boat and we spent the day on the lake trying our luck at fishing and stopping at a few of the bars along the way, including my old haunt, The Rod and Gun Club.

We played our Saturday night job at the Moose Club on Chautauqua Lake the weekend before we left for Toronto. The band consisted of Joe, Chubby and me, plus we added Leo Mattson on piano and Dewey Vickroy on banjo. I don't know who had more fun, the audience or us, but it was a huge success. It was one of those nights that I would go back and do all over again.

Our two week break was over and now it was time to head for Toronto, Canada. It was a short drive from Jamestown, just a mere 175 miles, which was nothing compared to our drive from Reno. The drive was a pleasant one, taking us through the New York grape country and the home of the Welch's Grape Fruit Company. From there it was down through Buffalo and Niagara Falls and up to Toronto.

Toronto is a huge town, one of the largest in Canada, with a population of 18,500,000. We were playing at the Colonial Tavern on Yonge Street, one of the main roads that went through the city. The Colonial Tavern was a family affair and was owned and managed by two guys that were brothers-in-law. When you think of a tavern you think of a small club. Believe me, the Colonial Tavern was not small. It was huge, with a high stage on the left hand wall as you entered. Above the stage was a beautiful, old-fashioned disco ball revolving around. The entertainers had their own dressing room in back of the stage and if we wanted we could stay in some rooms above the Tavern. I chose not to because I did not want to live at the same place that I worked. There was also a balcony that went all the way around the room for drinking and dining with a good view of the band. I found a nice hotel just a couple of blocks away from the Colonial and was all set to go for our opening night.

We had a full house for our first night of playing, and that included the balcony. This is good because we were not the only act in town. Our competing jazz venues were the Savarin Tavern, The Palace Royal, George's Bourbon Street, The Town Tavern, George's Spaghetti House, and The Imperial Room at the Royal York Hotel. There were lots of places you could go to hear jazz. We also wanted to make a good impression on the jazz critics who were always there opening night. It was important to get a good favorable review in the paper the next day. Unfortunately, the top jazz critic in Toronto, Patrick Scott, gave us a so-so review. It partially read –

*This is a band with several good features, such as a liquid–toned clarinetist named James Beatty, a muscular fender-base man named Joe Mastasi, and the infectious, harmless vocals of Mr. Campo himself, who unfortunately has delusions that he can also play the trumpet.*

Those words about our bandleader probably jinxed this band forever from getting a return engagement. We never got a bad review in Cleveland, because if we did I'm sure the jazz critic would have ended up at the bottom of Lake Erie with a cement overcoat on. One wouldn't say anything bad in the paper about the Theatrical Grill as it was a hangout of all the big mob bosses in the city.

I was once again following in the footsteps of many great jazz musicians, such as Benny Goodman, B.B. King, Oscar Peterson, George Shearing, Gene Krupa, Dizzy Gillespie, and Wild Bill Davison. I knew that my dad would never come to Toronto and hear me play because he never dared venture over the border to Canada since he never became an American citizen or got a green card. He really didn't have to worry because he didn't have a British accent and in those days all you showed at the border was your driver's license. However, my mom and pop drove in from Jamestown to hear the band. After Joe and Chubby's visit with them they felt that they knew half the band. It was fun to see them and we had a good time that night.

The only big incident on this particular engagement was one night just as we finished playing a set and we were ready for intermission a guy yelled at me from down on the floor. He told me how much he enjoyed my clarinet playing and he wanted to shake my hand, so I leaned down and bent over to shake hands and I'll be damned if he didn't pull me right off the bandstand down about eight feet to the floor. Fortunately he caught me and I wasn't hurt. He obviously had had too much booze and he told me he just wanted to buy me a drink. I think I got him for two or three drinks.

While I was in Canada I called Pauline and filled her in on my playing and travels. I told her that I was playing in Canada, but the opposite coast from her...somehow or another we would figure out a way to get together again soon. Pauline did say that she and a nurse friend were toying with the idea of getting work in Montréal, Canada. Montréal is not that far from Jamestown, probably around 350 miles by car and just a short hop by airplane. Who Knows?

Following our job in Toronto we were scheduled to open in London, Ontario, Canada, at the Hotel Iroquois. We had a week off between jobs so Joe, Chubby and I went back to Jamestown and hung out, while the other guys in the band went sightseeing. Thank God we had Jamestown to go to on our weeks off because it saved us a lot of money.

Our opening at The Iroquois Hotel was a huge success. It had a very nice lounge with quite a sizable dance floor, as this was a place where people came to listen to music and dance. To top things off we got a wonderful review in the local paper. It said:

*This group, in which each player is a first-class musician in his own right, presents a toe-tapping, always danceable program of authentic Dixieland, New Orleans style.*

Our music had such an appeal for dancers that the management decided to let couples dance on the stage throughout the entire program. This was always a little worry for me because I was always on the lookout for someone banging my clarinet into my mouth. It all turned out fine and the customers were happy, as well as the hotel management. This went on for our entire engagement and it was a pleasure to go to work every night. On top of that the hotel gave us rooms and meals - all I had to do was ride the elevator down to the hotel lobby to work.

**Joe Rotis, Jim, Russ Morgan, Murphy Campo.**
**Sparks Nugget, Reno, NV, 1962**

**Murphy Campo and the Jazz Saints, Theatrical Grill, Cleveland, OH, 1962**

CHAPTER 13

# Musician/Bartender

AFTER OUR CANADIAN ENGAGEMENTS THERE was another three week gap between our next job at the Famous Door on Bourbon Street in New Orleans.
This jazz club was more or less the headquarters of the band and they played
there often during the year. That was fine because the rest of the band lived
in New Orleans and had family and a home there. I loved New Orleans and
its musical history, but if I went to play there I would have to rent an apartment and set up housekeeping in a city where I did not know anybody except
my friends in the band. Even George Lewis was seldom in town anymore
because his newfound celebrity kept him out of town, mostly in Europe and
the United Kingdom. The weather in New Orleans was another factor. I was
never fond of the hot muggy rainy weather, and when it rained, it came down
in buckets. There was also segregation, which I didn't like. I had a lot to think
about before I made the next move.

When I got back to Jamestown I made up my mind to stay put for a
while and examine future musical possibilities. I thought about getting
my own apartment but my mom and Pop insisted I stay at the house
since my sister had now married and moved away. I guess they didn't
like being empty nesters. I called all my musician friends and told them
my plans to hang around for a while and they were all eager to go back
to work with me again. Now the big job lay ahead of rustling up some
work.

Of all the bars and saloons on Second Street in Jamestown, I had a favorite called Cala's Restaurant. It was a very friendly place with a nice clientele and great Italian food. The owner was a fellow named Al Cala and he was from an old Italian family in Jamestown that had an Italian restaurant for years. Al decided to break away from the family business and opened his own restaurant with himself behind the bar and his wife in the kitchen cooking up the best spaghetti anywhere.

One evening I stopped by Cala's for a drink and Al approached me. He said, Jim, I understand that you are going to be back in town for a while and I am looking for a bartender to spell me when I need a break or time off. He said, I need someone I can trust and train in the art of mixing cocktails - would you be interested? I told Al that I thought I would like to give it a try as long as I could work the hours around my music jobs. He agreed and we had a deal. The interesting thing about the New York laws in those days was that the bartenders could drink and smoke behind the bar while they worked. So what the hell, I could party and get paid for it - just like playing music.

There was not a heck of a lot to learn about bartending on Second Street. A good share of the old gang just came in for their shots with a beer chaser. Fleischmann's Whiskey was a big seller along with Ten High Bourbon - both bottom of the line booze but not too bad taste wise and, as I recall, were $.35 a shot. We had draft beer on tap - that probably was the hardest part of the job, wrestling those kegs around and tapping them without squirting beer all over the place, including yourself. Many of the customers just drank bottled beer - the popular one in Western New York at the time was Genesee Beer. Other popular drinks were mixers like whiskey and seven-up, gin and tonic, and scotch and soda. I had to learn how to make a Martini and Manhattan, two drinks that were not popular calls but when someone did order them - look out - they really got loaded.

When you entered Cala's the bar area was on the right-hand side of the club. The dining room area was on the left-hand side and there was a partition in-between the bar and dining room. The partition had flowers along the top so that the diners would have privacy from people sitting at the bar. Al's wife, Marion, was a fantastic cook. Her meatballs were made from the best ground beef available and seasoned to perfection. I used to slip into the kitchen when she was making the meatballs and eat them raw - that's how good they were. That's something you would never dare do today. There was also a bottle of whiskey standing on a table in the kitchen. That bottle was for the policemen on foot patrol in the city, and all the bars on Second Street did that. Consequently we had a very happy police department. Al Cala and I never thought of it, but because I was so well known in town due to my music the bar business picked up considerably with people just dropping by to visit, along with all my musician friends. So it became a very happy place to go to work

I had gotten together with my old band members for a few rehearsals and things were sounding pretty good and slowly but surely jobs were starting to trickle in. One of our first engagements was playing at my old haunt - The Lakewood Rod and Gun Club on Chautauqua Lake, along with a few casuals at the Moose, Eagles, Elks and Marco Polo Club. So things were starting to look good and between Cala's and my music jobs I was making a fairly good living. Unfortunately, I still hadn't learned the art of saving and living within my means and managed to spend my money just as fast as I made it.

One little glitch did happen. One Saturday night we played a dance at the Hotel Jamestown Crystal Ballroom. At the end of the job, as usual, I was not ready to call it a night and wanted to keep the party going. So we decided to have a party at our banjo player's house in Gerry, New York, which was only a few miles from the Jamestown city limits. On the way home I really had to go to the bathroom. It was snowing like hell and I was out in the country so I decided just to pull over and relieve myself. Well, wouldn't you know it; a sheriff's car came by and caught me in the act. He wasn't a Jamestown policeman - so I was screwed. He said he was arresting me for indecent exposure - my God - I was in the country and in the middle of a snowstorm - who was to see me? However, he could also have charged me with a DUI, but he didn't. I also had Florida plates on my car, which confused him totally. He took me to the Falconer, New York, jail, which was on the way back to Jamestown. When we got to the jail the policeman behind the desk was a guy I had gone to school with - that helped. I was dressed in a white tuxedo jacket and looked quite out of place. However, I was locked in a cell and told I had the right to make one call. I called my banjo player, Don Peterson, where we had the party, and told him the situation. I asked him to come and get me later in the morning, because he was pretty drunk and I didn't want him to get arrested as well. So, here I am all dressed up sitting in a jail cell at four in the morning. The only one I had to talk to was a fellow in the next cell who had been arrested for a bar fight, and I think he was looking for another one. Thank goodness for the cell bars!

Morning came and Don was there to rescue me. The jailer came to my cell to unlock the door and I'll be damned if the keys did not work. They screwed around and screwed around and couldn't get that door open - I was stuck. Finally, they found someone who came and busted the lock and got me out. After the police talked back and forth to a judge on the phone they decided to reduce the charge from indecent exposure to failure to produce a registration for the car. I had misplaced the registration for the Florida plates and couldn't show it to the arresting policeman. There was a small fine but I was told if I came back to the police station with the registration, everything would be forgotten. I must say that that was not a fun night for me and to this day I never get in my car with a full bladder.

To make my band affordable I also worked as a quartet with myself on clarinet, Leo Matson, piano, Don Peterson, banjo, and Austin Main on bass. When somebody wanted the New Orleans sound, I added Pete Pepke on trombone, Brian Johnson on cornet and Darrell Jones on drums. It was starting to make sense to me that I made the right decision in getting off the road, at least temporarily. Murphy Campo's booking agency did not do a good job for him. You just could not make it financially by working for two weeks and then nothing for another one or two week. Fortunately for me the jobs with Campo were fairly close to the Jamestown area and I could go home when there was no work. Had I not been close to home it would have not been financially rewarding. Anyway, things were looking good now and I was even getting a few inquiries about the band from other cities around New York and Pennsylvania.

On the home front, everything was about the same. My mom still was working at the bank Pop was still drinking too much and having trouble holding jobs. Sister Linda was expecting a baby. Linda and her new husband, Chuck, had moved to Hyde Park, New York, where Chuck had found a job after graduating from college. Dad and Belle were still working at MRC and running the Hotel Lawrence and driving new Buicks. My dad had more or less given up playing music, probably because he couldn't stay sober enough to play and nobody wanted him around. The Sunday roast beef and Yorkshire pudding brunches were still on at the Beatty's and I was always there unless I was playing a job or working at Cala's. I saw Uncle Bill just about every day when he stopped by Cala's for his shot and beer. That was his last stop for the day on Second Street before he caught his bus back to 11 Shaw Avenue. I got a kick out of Uncle Bill. He had a good outlook on life. One afternoon he walked into Cala's wearing a brand-new winter overcoat. I told him how nice it looked on him and he said in all seriousness, "Jim, this coat will last me twenty years." He was in his mid-80s at the time. It must have been all that good Yorkshire pudding...or maybe the shots and beers, or both.

One Sunday night in October, 1962 I was just relaxing at home when the phone rang and lo and behold the voice on the other end said, "Surprise! This is Pauline." I was shocked. I knew that she and a girlfriend had planned a trip but we had been out of touch for quite a while. I asked Pauline where she was and she said, "We're here in Jamestown at a place called The Ships Inn." Pauline added that they just happened to be passing through in a snow storm! Really? She was right in downtown Jamestown and I told her to stay where she was and I would be right down. The Ships Inn was a cute little bar/restaurant right in the middle of the city and it was a cut above all the bars on Second Street. When I walked in Pauline was sitting in a booth with her friend, Jan McGill, and it was so great to see her again after all those months. She said she barely recognized me with my long hair and big black wool coat.

Well, evidently Pauline and her nurse friend, Jan, decided to go to Montréal, Canada, to work. They each wired $300 to a bank in Montréal so they would have some cash when they got there. Jan had a bright yellow Sunbeam Alpine convertible sports car that they were driving on their trip. The Sunbeam was a snappy little British-made car with a very small trunk and a tiny storage space behind the two seats. It was the sports car that Cary Grant and Grace Kelly were driving in the Alfred Hitchcock movie, *To Catch a Thief.* Not a very comfortable car to take a cross-country trip in, especially in the wintertime, but what the heck - they were young.

They left Vancouver, Canada and drove through Washington, Oregon, Idaho, Utah, Colorado, New Mexico, Texas, Mississippi and Louisiana. They stopped in New Orleans for three nights for a breather - visiting bars and strip joints along Bourbon Street and the French Quarter. They inquired about me and the Murphy Campo band with no result. I would've thought that Murphy and his band would be at the Famous Door by then, evidently not. They continued on down the West Coast of Florida and then to Miami. From there they flew over to Nassau for a week, stayed with some of Pauline's friends, and showed Jan around Nassau. They also visited the Emerald Beach Hotel and all her friends there.

Returning to the United States they drove up the Florida coast. They visited Philadelphia, where they stayed with Pauline's Nassau friends. Then from Philadelphia they drove all the way to Jamestown in a snowstorm. That was one hell of a trip and they were not finished yet. It was wonderful to see Pauline again and we seemed to pick up right where we left off in Nassau like it was yesterday. I was happy to find out that they had a few days before leaving for Montréal, so I invited them to stay at my mom's house. My mother was so happy to finally meet Pauline as she had heard so much about her. I took a couple of days off from Cala's so I could show them around. We went to all the clubs and bars and I introduced her to all my friends. It was the snowy season in Western New York so I took Pauline and Jan for a sleigh ride. Then the girls had to leave - they went to Montréal via Toronto. The distance between Pauline and I was quite short compared to Vancouver, Canada. So I assured her that she would be seeing a lot of me and hopefully she would return to Jamestown for visits.

About a week later I got a call from Pauline and they were in Montréal safe and sound. Another nurse friend from Vancouver, Jackie Young, had joined them and they found a furnished apartment right across the street from the fraternity houses at McGill University. They also got jobs at the Royal Victoria Hospital just three blocks away from their apartment. Pauline worked on a urology floor and rotated through all three shifts on a four-week schedule. French was the primary language spoken throughout the hospital, but don't forget Canada is a bilingual country. I'm sure she and her friends didn't have an easy time of it being from the West Coast. Pauline said that she loved the city, the exciting French atmosphere, fashion, the winter-long snow and the lighted ice structures built on the McGill campus. She was all settled in and I was looking forward to my first trip to Montréal to visit her.

My band played New Year's Eve of 1962 at a place called The Starlight, just outside the Jamestown city limits and on the way to Chautauqua Lake. The owner of the Starlight was a Swedish fellow by the name of Ynguve Carlson. He was an excellent cook and had restaurants around the Jamestown area for years. To this day I have never had a better cheeseburger then Ynguve made. His stepson, Russ Eklund, was a high school friend of mine and tended bar. Everyone enjoyed the music so much that they asked us to stay on and play every weekend. So now we had a musical headquarters and a steady weekend job.

Now that Pauline was so close, we kept in touch just about every day on the phone. The first of the year 1963 I decided to drive to Montréal for a visit. I asked my piano player and friend Leo Matson to join me so the trip wouldn't be so lonely. Pauline somehow made room for us in their apartment and we had an enjoyable three days. We met the friends the girls had made, which were mostly nurses and doctors. There was also a charming young man across the hall from their apartment, Hugh Billings. He was from a very aristocratic and wealthy family in Ottawa, Canada. To this day you can see the name "Billings" all over the city of Ottawa, including the Billings Gate Shopping Mall. Hugh was a great guy and said that he would like to come to Jamestown with Pauline to visit and hear the band.

Meanwhile back at Cala's, things were going well and we even brought the quartet in occasionally on Sunday afternoons to entertain. Sundays were strange in Jamestown because the bars could not open until church was out. Consequently, Cala's didn't open until noon on Sunday and had to close at 10 p.m. The bars were also closed on election days. One election day, Don Peterson took me to a bar outside town for drinks. I asked Don how this place managed to stay open on Election Day and Don said - "That's easy, they don't have a license."

I made another trip to Montréal on my own later in January. I drove through a pretty wild snowstorm to get there, but it was worth it because Pauline and I enjoyed being together so much. The girls had a big costume party and Hugh dressed up as Julius Caesar. We all had a ball and it was great fun. But the drive back to Jamestown was not fun. It snowed like hell in that part of the country when it wanted to and I was right in the middle of a giant white-out snowstorm. I got as far as Watertown, New York, when they closed all the roads. You couldn't get in or out of the city. Fortunately, I found a bar/restaurant that said they would stay open all night to accommodate stranded travelers. So what the heck - I had drink and food with a nice booth to curl up in and catch a nap. The next morning after breakfast they had plowed the roads well enough for me to continue on to Jamestown.

I got a call from an agent that had heard about the band and wanting to know if I would be interested in playing jobs in some of the nearby towns in Pennsylvania. I explained to him that we were already booked every weekend at the Starlight Restaurant and Lounge in Jamestown. He said he could give me work on Sundays and during the week if I was available. I told him, "Sure, why not," and he explained to me that he wanted the full seven-piece band. He said he had a booking for me the next Sunday in Kane, Pennsylvania. We agreed on my fee and of course he wanted a 15% cut of the money. 15% was normal for a booking agent to charge so I told him that would be fine. Kane was a small town around fifty miles from Jamestown, but it was driving on all country roads and took a while to get there. Kane was an old Pennsylvania community founded in 1863 by a Civil War General,

Thomas L. Kane. It was a far cry from my engagements in Reno, Cleveland and Toronto, but what the heck it was a start.

Well, Sunday rolled along and we took off for our trip to Kane, Pennsylvania. There were seven of us, so we had to take two cars because of all the instruments and drums. We didn't have to worry about packing a keyboard because in those days all the clubs and dance halls had a piano and usually in tune.

When we arrived we found that it was an old dance hall and the place was already half-full. They charged admission at the door and it was first come, first served seating. I introduced myself to the dance promoter and he said that we should have a large crowd because they had heard good things about the band. That made me feel good because it sounded like my name was getting around the dance circuit.

Sure enough, by the time we were finished setting up the band, the place was absolutely full. I noticed that the crowd was quite young, which was very encouraging to me. Before we started our first set we went to the bar for a drink - the dance promoter said to the bartender – "With a crowd like this - drinks are on the house for these guys all night!" Besides that, he said that he would like to treat for dinner when we were through playing. Well, it couldn't get any better than that and all the guys in the band were patting me on the back for getting such a terrific job.

As I recall, for our first set we started out with the "Muskrat Ramble" because that was always a popular tune to get the crowd started. I expected the dance floor to fill up - but nobody danced, they just sat there and looked at us. Then I thought that they were enjoying the jazz so much that they just wanted to sit and listen. But that theory was blown to hell when I noticed table after table getting up and leaving - demanding their money back. At that point the promoter ran over to me and said - Jim! What in hell are you playing? I said that we were playing our dance music.

The promoter said this is a Rock and Roll club and that's what I want you to play. I explained to him that we didn't play that style of music and by that time the hall was empty and everybody wanted their money back.

The promoter and I called the booking agent and the agent said that he thought that I played rock. It was all a big mess and misunderstanding - regardless, we had to get paid. When you got right down to it, this was the fault of the booking agent. The promoter was a nice fellow and paid us anyway and said he dealt with the agent often and that he would get his money back. So we left Kane, Pennsylvania, with our tails between our legs, never to come back. Ever since then I have been leery of booking agents, and seldom used them, even when I started playing abroad.

CHAPTER 14

# Wedding Bells

PAULINE AND I HAD KNOWN each other now for about a year. We spent a lot of time together in Nassau and got along really well and enjoyed each other's company. We could sit and talk for hours. We had a long distance relationship because I was on the road and Pauline was back in Vancouver working as a nurse. Now we were back together again and nothing had seemed to change, we just had a ball together.

I figured that there was only one way to make sure that there would be no more long distance relationship. Now I'm even driving through snowstorms to see her. If this isn't love I don't know what is. So I bought a ring, gathered up Don Peterson and Leo Matson for moral support and we headed up to Montréal. We drove up through another snowstorm and Pauline and I were engaged on February 10th, 1963.

I drove home to Jamestown and bad news was waiting for me. Uncle Bill had passed away on February 12th. It was so sad for me because Uncle Bill and I had a special relationship and I wanted so much for him to meet Pauline, but that was not to be. I always missed his Ragtime piano playing and exchanging cartons of cigarettes with him at Christmas time.

A few weeks later Pauline and Hugh Billings drove to Jamestown to visit for a few days. My family was anxious to see Pauline after our engagement. Pauline and Hugh arrived in style. Hugh had purchased a new Mercedes- Benz 300 SF. It was a two-door coupe with Gull Wing Doors - an expensive car in those days and if you were lucky enough to have one today you would be looking at around $1 million dollars. It was built in Stuttgart, Germany and I'm sure there wasn't many of that model around anywhere. I didn't know the value of the car and was zipping around Jamestown showing it off to my friends. Had I known what it was worth I would never have driven it.

Hugh was an interesting guy and as it turned out he was very intrigued with flying after he heard that I had learned to fly. I told him I got the flying bug from Dewey and arranged for the two to meet. Pauline, Hugh and I went out to Dewey's house for a party and Dewey told Hugh that he'd be happy to take him out the next day in his twin engine Apache. I couldn't take him up flying because I did not have an instrument license and it was snowing like hell. The next day Pauline, Hugh and I met Dewey at the airport and the two of them flew around for about a half an hour in a snowstorm. Hugh was elated.

Hugh went back to Montréal and got his flying license, instrument license, and bought his own airplane in an amazingly short time. He really worked hard to accomplish such a feat. Next he got a job flying for Air Canada, even though he really didn't have to work. He later was married and raised a family, but sadly died of cancer in 1989 at only fifty years old.

Pauline and I decided that we wanted to get married right away so we could be together. Pauline's parents were very supportive from the beginning, even though they had never met me; I was an American, and especially, a musician. I had music and work commitments until June 1$^{st}$, so Pauline's mother agreed to book the church and reception venue. June 28th was the first open date for both the church (United Church of

Canada) and the Marine Drive Golf and Country Club, where Pauline, her father and her brother had all been members for years.

Pauline continued to work in Montréal until the end of March and around the first part of April I drove to Montréal picked her up and we drove back to Jamestown where my mother, aunts, uncles, cousins and friends had a bridal shower for her at the Sheldon House.

Pauline still had not met my father and my stepmother. So that weekend when I played at the Starlight they said they would come out and meet her. My dad arrived, but wouldn't come in to the restaurant part of the Starlight, probably because he thought it too far away from the bar and he also would have to sit and listen to me play. So, when an intermission came I took Pauline into the bar area where my dad and Belle were sitting at a table. My dad was absolutely loaded, had his dentures in his shirt pocket, and was using terribly foul language. He was a mess and I was very embarrassed. But that was his behavior when he drank too much - which was most of the time. Not a very nice first impression for Pauline.

A few days later I drove Pauline to the Toronto airport, where she flew back to Vancouver. I promised to drive out to Vancouver the first part of June and be there for my birthday on June 9th. She went back to work at the Vancouver General Hospital and started with the wedding preparations, including finding a wedding dress, having bridesmaid dresses made, cake, flowers, etc.

On June 1st I set out in my faithful Pontiac Tempest for my coast-to-coast drive to Vancouver, Canada. I pulled into Pauline's driveway a few days later in the late morning. Pauline's mom, dad, and sister, Val, were there to greet me. Pauline panicked when she saw my car and ran into the bathroom and locked herself in! After 20 minutes we coaxed her out and the rest is history. I quickly bonded with Pauline's family and of all things her father's name was Percy - the same as my Dad's.

We had about three weeks before the wedding to reacquaint our-selves, have a date or two, and for her family and me to get to know each other. Pauline's brother, Bob, took me around to the men's bars at dif-ferent locations around Vancouver. We spent a few days at the family's Sakinaw Lake cottage on the Sunshine Coast and went out on the ocean in Pauline's dad's cruiser. They also had a nice birthday party for me, and Pauline's Auntie Freda and Uncle Frank held of big pre-wedding party for us at Trader Vic's Bayshore Inn.

We went out one night to hear Lance Harrison's Dixieland Band. Lance was probably the best-known musician in Vancouver and oddly enough I often listened to him play his weekly jazz Session over the CBC. Jamestown, being so close to Canada, could easily pick up the Canadian radio stations. Lance played the clarinet, saxophones, and even banjo. He was a terrific guy and we hit it off right from the get-go. He asked me to sit in with his band that night and we had a ball. It was the beginning of a musical friendship that would last many years.

Lance was playing at a nightclub called the Pillar and Post that night, but there were many other nightclubs around Vancouver. The most popu-lar club in town was called The Cave, on Hornsby Street in downtown Vancouver. Everybody who was anybody performed there, including Louis Armstrong, Sammy Davis Junior and the Mills Brothers. Another popular club was called Izzy's and they also featured many of the jazz stars. There was music all over Vancouver, and many people, after a night out on the town, ended up at a White Spot hamburger restaurant, which had the best burgers in town. When I was with Pauline she always ordered "Triple 0," which meant lots special sauce.

Lance Harrison was bigger than life, 6 foot six with curly hair and rosy cheeks that arose probably because he drank so much gin. Early in his career he played with the big bands in Vancouver and during WW II he was in the Royal Canadian Army Band. After his discharge he formed his own Dixieland band and became one of Vancouver's most popular entertainers. Lance had many opportunities to join big-name bands in the States, but turned them down because he loved Vancouver so much. And I must say I don't blame him.

It was now time to momentarily stop the nightclubbing, lake parties and ocean cruises and get down to the main purpose of my Vancouver trip, the wedding. It was no surprise to me that none of my family were coming to the wedding. My dad of course was afraid to come because it was in Canada, but he wouldn't have come anyway. Probably my Mom just couldn't afford it and couldn't take that much time off of work. But my faithful friend, Don Peterson and his wife, Ann, drove all the way from Jamestown to attend. Pauline's brother, Bob, was to be best man. Hugh, our friend from Montreal and Don Peterson, along with a few other friends of Pauline's were the ushers.

Shortly after World War II, Pauline's dad, Percy Vickerstaff, and her uncle, Alec Smith, came across Sakinaw Lake while on a fishing trip off the Sunshine Coast in British Columbia. After pestering the British Columbia government in Victoria, the land around the Lake was surveyed and Percy and Alec were able to purchase several large pieces of property at the Northeast end of the lake, including two islands. The lake is seven miles long and a mile wide at its widest point.

It wasn't an easy trip getting to the Lake in those days and Pauline and her family had to take a passenger ferry as far as Pender Harbor and then hike a trail to the lake for about a mile. Percy packed a small outboard motor that they used on a rented boat to camp on an island, now known as Hemingway Island and owned by Pauline's sister Valerie and her husband, Brian Hemingway. It would often take Pauline and her family up to fourteen hours to make the trip to the lake and the same coming back home.

After a few years car ferries were put into service in the area, along with improved roads. Eventually, Pauline's dad constructed a small tin shack at the edge of the lake where they camped, until it was decided to build a bigger, more permanent cabin across the bay on a peninsula they owned, which gave them lakeshore property in front and a bay in the back for parking boats. Pauline's dad prefabricated this cabin in his backyard in Vancouver and brought up the sections in one of his friend's, named Gordy Shannon, trucks. Gordy owned a trucking company and he and his wife Marion would often caravan up to the lake with the Vickerstaff family, cooking hot dogs from the back of the truck on a Coleman stove while waiting for the car ferries. The Shannons built a cabin around the bay from the Vickerstaff cabin and it's now occupied by their daughter, Bev and her husband Rick, who have remained very good friends of ours.

This was the cabin I came to just a couple of weeks before Pauline and I were married. They brought me over in a little outboard tin boat from the end of the government road. There was no electricity and everything was propane or candles. Last but not least, no indoor plumbing, so when you had to go it was a creepy little outhouse in the woods in the back of the cabin. But there was plenty to drink, so nobody seemed to mind.

The big day of the wedding arrived - June 28th, 1963. Pauline looked so beautiful in her wedding dress and along with her bridesmaids they seemed as if they came out of a story book. I wore a black tuxedo, white tuxedo shirt, black bowtie and patent leather shoes, probably looking more like a penguin. The wedding was held at Pauline's church - the United Church of Canada. The chapel was full with Pauline's many friends and relatives along with Don and Ann Peterson. It was a lovely service and Pauline and I repeated our vows.

Following the church service there was a reception at the Marine Drive Golf and Country Club. Pauline's family had been members for years and her dad and brother Bob were extremely good golfers. As I found out in Nassau, Pauline was no beginner as well. The country club was a great backdrop for a gorgeous wedding reception that everyone enjoyed. We had a delicious sit-down dinner along with the usual toasts to the bride and groom. There was dancing after dinner and lots to drink. Later in the party Pauline and I changed into our street clothes and said our goodbyes. The boys had gotten hold of my Pontiac Tempest and decorated the hell out of it, so there was tin cans banging and sparking as we drove off. We drove to a hotel in downtown Vancouver and spent the first night before leaving the next morning for the main part of our honeymoon.

The first few days of our honeymoon were rather a mystery to us and it was very overwhelming. There was an old lodge on Vancouver Island a few miles from Victoria, BC. It was called Eagle Crest and it was strictly for VIP visitors. For instance, Queen Elizabeth and Prince Philip had been there a few weeks before on their Canadian tour. Evidently, Pauline's dad knew a guy who knew a guy that arranged for us to be guests at Eagle Crest. We were told not to ask any questions to anyone at the lodge, nor to tip, but just act like we were important.

So the next morning after spending the night at the Vancouver Hotel we took an early ferry over to Victoria, BC on Vancouver Island. From there we drove to Eagle Crest and pulled up to the front door. It was beautiful and very elegant in a very woody setting. A butler appeared in the huge wooden doorway and came out to greet us, opening our car doors and telling us that we were expected. Then a few maids came and took our luggage and showed us to our room. We later found out that our bedroom was the one that Queen Elizabeth slept in on her visit there - Prince Philip was in the bedroom across the hall. After Pauline and I were settled in and unpacked we wandered out to the main living room where our butler was waiting to fill us in on the lodge and to inquire about our needs.

The main living room was enormous with huge comfortable leather couches and chairs scattered about. Along the walls there were all kinds of stuffed animal heads, lions, tigers, bears, etc. There was also a couple of big writing desks with pencils, pens and writing paper. The dining room was just as enormous as the living room, with a long dining room table that could accommodate twenty or so guests.

Our butler explained to us that the lodge was totally self-sufficient. They had their own farm along with a few livestock. Most of the food that you ate there was fresh from their farm. My God, everything was delicious and even the butter was made there. For breakfast and lunch we could order anything. For dinner we were served a surprise every night and were never disappointed. Plus, we could have any kind of cocktail or beer along with a large selection of red and white wines. Pauline and I felt a little foolish, just the two of us sitting at this enormous dining room table, but we were loving it. And each evening when we retired we went into our bedroom to find the covers folded back with a red rose and a candy on our pillow. Just think, some people live like this their entire life.

Well, all good things must come to an end and we bid farewell to Eagle Crest and went on to the next phase of our honeymoon. Pauline's brother Bob was in the insurance business and lived and worked in Victoria, BC. He gave us the keys to his house and said for us to enjoy it for a few days and explore Victoria. So we moved into Bob's house and enjoyed the solitude until Pauline's family arrived and joined us for the last few days of our honeymoon! They came over on Pauline's father's cruiser, "The Pauline," so we all had fun cruising around for a couple of days.

Now it was time to go back to Vancouver, pack the Pontiac Tempest full of our wedding gifts and start off on the long journey back to Jamestown. We had received many very nice wedding gifts along with some cash that came in very handy on our trip through the states and for setting up housekeeping when we got back to Jamestown. We did have one last fling, however, and went out on our last night in Vancouver to hear Lance Harrison and his band. I sat in with him a good share of the night and a good time was had by all. The next morning it was a tearful goodbye to Pauline's family and the start of a new adventure.

The first stop on our journey eastward was the American border inspection. To save time, Pauline had made a list of all the wedding presents we were taking with us and their approximate value. This helped tremendously and the border inspector peaked inside the car, looked in the trunk, wished us good luck and sent us on our way. The Pontiac Tempest had another big job to do and that was to take us through Washington, Montana, North Dakota, Minnesota, Michigan, Ohio, Pennsylvania, and finally arriving in Jamestown, New York, the end of our journey for now.

But when we were driving through Ohio I got the bright idea of taking a slight detour to Columbus, Ohio, where my cousin Winston and Annette Anderson were residing. When I was a little boy living at my grandmother's house they were a young couple, newly married, and would often come rescue me and take me to movies, playgrounds, Chautauqua Lake or their house for dinner... so the two of them had a hand in helping me grow up as a child. Later, they had four of their own children, Skippy, Diane Kathy, and Jeanne, and we became close as well. They were happy to see me and especially meet Pauline. Winston and Annette were fun people and loved to party. We had a lot of laughs and a great dinner that first evening. Before going to bed I picked up the Columbus paper and lo and behold I came across a good-sized ad for the Grandview Inn, a local jazz club. To my surprise there was a picture of Wild Bill Davison in the ad. It advertised him being there for the next two weeks, featured with a local Columbus jazz band. I showed the ad to Pauline and said – "Guess where I am taking you tomorrow"?

Pauline had heard me talk about Wild Bill often and she was just as excited about seeing and listening to him play as I was. The next evening we arrived at the Grandview Inn, and there he was - Wild Bill Davison in all his glory - making all that beautiful sound come out of a cornet like only he could do. I had known Wild Bill since I was seventeen years old going to Eddie Condon's club over the years and he recognized me as soon as I walked in the door. On his first intermission he immediately walked over to our table to say hello. We invited him to sit down and have a drink with us and filled him in on our wedding and honeymoon. He immediately started flirting with Pauline, but I had warned her about his roving eyes, and that was just one of the reasons why they called him "Wild Bill."

Wild Bill started to fill us in about what he had been doing since last I saw him at Eddie Condon's. He had built himself up a reputation of being one of the top jazz cornetists in the world. He had his own style of playing and there was just no one else like him. He said that he had been playing at Eddie Condon's for twelve years and it was time for him to strike out on his own. He formed his own band and in-between engagements he would go out and be a guest artist with other jazz bands around the country; that is what he was doing in Columbus, Ohio, playing as a featured guest artist with a local band. On that particular night he wasn't very happy with the group he was playing with because their tempos were too fast. As I was to find out in later years, Wild Bill was an expert on setting the correct tempo for any particular tune to make it sound better. He spent a considerable amount of time off the bandstand that night and when he wasn't on the bandstand he was sitting with us chatting the night away.

I don't know what got over me, probably too many drinks, and I said – "Hey, Wild Bill!" Now that you're doing guest appearances around the world, how would you like to play with my band?" He looked at me and said it would be a pleasure – When do I start? Oh boy! What did I just do? I had just asked one of the major jazz artists in the world to come play in my band in Jamestown, New York. My little band, "The Dixielads," were coming along just fine musically but I didn't think we were ready to play with a major jazz star such as Wild Bill - so it looked like I had a hell of a lot of work to do when I got back to Jamestown. Wild Bill told me that his wife Anne took care of all his bookings and gave me his card and said to call her and make arrangements for his appearing in Jamestown. We were getting into the wee hours of the morning when Pauline and I bid Wild Bill goodnight and said that we would be seeing him soon in Jamestown. The next morning we left Columbus for the last leg of our trip. Looking back now it amazes me that we were running around all this time with our car full of wedding gifts - we would never get away with it today.

Arriving in Jamestown we stayed with my mom while we looked for our first apartment together. We found what we wanted on Stow Street, in a fairly nice neighborhood in Jamestown. It was a small second floor apartment and we had a very nice landlord by the name of Charlie Clapper, who was a baker in town. We later found out that he liked to suntan in the nude in his backyard, which was rather hilarious because he was no Charles Atlas. We also found out that Charlie made his own *korv* at Christmas time and he was very generous with it.

I went back to work at Cala's soon after we got back to Jamestown and Pauline immediately found a job as a nurse at Jamestown General Hospital, so we had an income and a place to live. The apartment was small but cute. It had a tiny kitchen and dining area, a living room and a large bedroom attached to the living room, so not too much privacy if you had company. Now the next big job was to get the band back in shape and get ready for Wild Bill Davison.

Wedding Day - June 28, 1963, Vancouver BC, Canada

Town Hall Inn, Jamestown NY. Jim, Wild Bill, Pete Pepke, 1963

The Dixielads with Norm Robinson. Jamestown, 1963

The Dixielads, Town Hall Inn, Jamestown. Don Peterson, Leo
Matson, Jim, Darryl Jones, Brian Johnson, Pete Pepke

CHAPTER 15

# Wild Bill

AL CALA WAS HAPPY TO see me back at work behind the bar. He said that I had returned at an opportune time because he wanted to take a Sunday off and visit his relatives in middle New York. He wondered if Pauline would be interested in taking food orders and working in the kitchen. I told Al that that sounded like something Pauline would get a kick out of doing and we could both work together that day.

Al gave me the keys to the restaurant and Pauline and I opened it up the following Sunday at noon. Bars could not open until church was out at noon on Sundays. We made a few phone calls to our friends and families and told them that we would be in the restaurant business for one day and to stop by and say hello because we had not seen many of them since we were married. Well, that probably turned out to be the busiest Sunday that Cala's Restaurant ever had, as everyone showed, up including my mother and stepdad and father and stepmother and fortunately they got along fine.

All the guys in the band came in with their wives. Don Peterson was slugging down his Ten High bourbon with a beer chaser with Leo Matson right behind him drinking one draft beer after another. I filled them in about seeing Wild Bill in Columbus, Ohio and that I had asked him to come to Jamestown and play with our band as a guest. In unison they all said, "Jim, you got to be kidding us!" I told them that this was no joke and we had a lot of work ahead. First of all, we had to find a suitable venue to play in. I told them that I had all of Wild Bill's recordings with Sidney Bechet and in the next few days we would get together at my house and listen to them.

In the meantime Pauline was running around like crazy taking food and drink orders and cooking in the kitchen. There were all kinds of meats for sandwiches in the refrigerator and spaghetti for anyone who wanted it. I was running back and forth behind the bar and the cash register was ringing all afternoon and evening. Even though bartenders could drink while they worked I refrained because I didn't want to get the cash register all screwed up. Pauline and I did, however, have a few drinks when we were finished work.

I had an interesting conversation with one gentleman that came in that evening. His name was Norm Robinson and he was a popular figure around the Jamestown area. He owned a large, busy gas station on Third Street, just one block above Cala's. Norm kept himself busy with the different organizations, like the Rotary Club, Optimist Club and the American Red Cross. I believe he was one of the biggest blood donors in New York. He was also an officer at the Elks Club. In other words, when you mentioned Norm Robinson's name, everyone knew who you were talking about. On top of all that his picture was in the paper constantly.

Norm ordered a dry martini and asked if he could have a few words with me. He told me that he and a friend had purchased the Town Hall Inn from a retiring Swedish couple who had owned it for years. He said he would be opening in a couple of weeks and was looking for a bar/restaurant manager - would I be interested? I told him that the only experience behind the bar I had was the short time working at Cala's. Norm looked around the place and said - you sure as hell are doing a good job of running this place. With that he ordered another dry martini and told me that I made the best martini he ever had in his life. Would I be interested in the job - yes or no! I assured him that I was very happy working for Al Cala, but if it was to be a learning experience and more money – yes, I would certainly think it over. I also told him that music was first for me and I would have to take off for any music job that came along. Norm said he had several other people to interview for the job and that he would get back to me. I thought that would be the end of that conversation because he certainly would find someone far more qualified for the job than me.

Pauline and I were just about ready to wrap things up for the night. Shortly before ten, Al and his wife walked in from their trip. You could see by the expression on their face that they were happy to see a full bar and people dining. Al was especially happy when he cashed out and saw what a busy day we had. Al paid Pauline and me and was so pleased he gave us each a bonus. So, for at least one day in our lives, Pauline and I were in the restaurant business. It's interesting to note that the Cala's ran their restaurant and bar by themselves. I don't know how they did it, putting in all those hours, but they did. I was the only employee they ever hired and a non-Italian at that. Sort of the same situation I had with Johnny DeVita.

Unfortunately, my poor spending habits caught up with me. Being out of work all those weeks during the wedding, I got behind on my car payments by a couple of months. So one morning when I got up to go to work my car wasn't there; the bank repossessed it during the night. To make it more embarrassing, it was the bank my mother worked at. I went to my Dad for help and he loaned me enough money to bail the car out. I just couldn't handle money at that time of my life and if I saw anything I wanted I just charged it. For example, around Thanksgiving time we needed a turkey for dinner. I saw an ad in the paper that if you bought a portable typewriter they gave you a free turkey to go with it. So, I went and bought a typewriter, on credit, that we really didn't need. But we did have a beautiful big turkey for Thanksgiving dinner. It was then Pauline decided that she would be the banker and give me cigarette and beer money when I needed it. I never had a car repossessed after that. In fact, I usually paid cash when I bought one and still do.

On the bright side, I'll be damned if I didn't get a call from Norm Robinson offering me the job as manager of the Town Hall Inn. You could have knocked me over with a feather. It must have been those martinis that I mixed for him. Norm Robinson knew nothing about the restaurant and bar business and neither did his partner, Dick Brooker. So I went into the whole thing blind, but somehow managed to pull it off by just acting like I knew what I was doing. I didn't have to worry about the food end of it because Norm had hired a lady to make lunches and light dinners. All I had to do was to order the booze and the beer. We had about five or six draft beers on tap and the kegs were in a cooler in the basement. So, every time a keg ran out, I had to run down to the basement into the cooler and tap the keg without having it spray all over the place. It was a lot of work pushing those kegs around and they were heavy when they were full. The Town Hall itself was one of Jamestown's oldest bars. When you walked in the front door there was a long bar and bar stools on your right and tables and chairs on the left. On the left there was a door that led down a long flight of stairs into the basement where the beer cooler and rest rooms were. After you walked past the bar there was a big back room with tables and chairs and a bandstand against the back wall with an old, upright piano. It was an old place but a fun place to go for food, drinks and listening to music.

Dick Brooker, keep the books and ironically, he was also a piano player and played with a band called the Phil Oak's Orchestra. Brooker and Oaks lived in Westfield, New York, about a half-hour drive from Jamestown. They were scheduled to play weekends from 9 p.m. – 1 a.m.

I was looking forward to hearing them when I wasn't out playing somewhere myself.

The Town Hall was on Main Street in Jamestown in a section called Brooklyn Square. That was a busy little area of town with several bars and restaurants along with a very popular newsroom called Gunell and Carlson. That's where everyone went to buy their cigarettes, cigars, pipe tobacco, newspapers and magazines. And, while you're in there you could get caught up on all the Jamestown gossip. This also used to be my route to high school every day and Johnny DeVita's old newsroom/bookie joint was just up the hill on Second Street. I was in familiar territory.

It was time for the grand opening of the Town Hall and the night before the opening we all had a giant party and everyone got loaded. I even overslept the next morning. Norm called me and told me to get my ass to work because there were whiskey and beer salesmen waiting to talk to me. I felt terrible, but went down and took care of business. The salesmen were very competitive and if you bought more of their product they would give you nice perks. For instance the Schlitz Brewing Company re-rugged the dining area for just giving them a big order and letting them put a display in the front window. If you gave a whiskey salesman a generous order he might slip you a few bottles to take home. It was just playing the game.

The first weekend of the opening arrived and I got to hear the Phil Oak's Orchestra. They were not very good and I could see that all they were going to attract was the older generation – if that. Jazz was really popular then and it attracted college students, professional people such as doctors and lawyers, along with the older generation. I could see where my band might be just the ticket to make The Town Hall a successful musical venue. But it was very touchy because Norm's partner Dick played the piano in the Phil Oaks group. I even gave the band a nickname: "Phil Oaks for the Old folks."

Norm asked me what I thought of the Oaks Orchestra. I had to be honest and tell him that I didn't think it would attract much of a crowd. Then he said – "Do you think that you and your band could do better?" I told him that I thought the time was right for a New Orleans style jazz band in the Jamestown area and yes, I think we would be a good attraction. Norm explained to me that it would not hurt Dick Brooker's feelings, as he was a partner and he wanted to see the cash register ring. So it was a deal and we were going to give it a try. A seven-piece band was a large one, but we agreed on a wage of $11 per man, so $77 per night for the band. I called all the musicians involved and they were thrilled to have a steady weekend engagement playing our kind of music.

Norm put a big ad in the *Jamestown Post-Journal* with a picture of himself standing with my band in front of the Town Hall. Opening night came and as I left the house, Pauline gave me twenty-five cents to pay for my first beer. After that I was on my own and had to charm customers into buying me drinks, a process that I became very good at. Opening night was a smashing success and just as I had imagined there were customers there from all walks of life, including professional people and even executives from the Jamestown furniture factories and Crescent Tool.

There is an old joke about not being able to find a doctor on Thursdays because they were playing golf. Well, if you wanted to find a doctor on the weekend he might very well be at the Town Hall. Because there was standing room only, it took forever to get a drink at the bar, so we musicians went to a saloon a couple doors down from the Town Hall to get a drink on our intermissions - that is if I hadn't already spent my quarter. Norm Robinson and Dick Brooker became the bartenders on weekends and they were hilarious. One fellow ordered a Screwdriver from Norm. He said, "Coming right up," and he went to the tool drawer and grabbed a screwdriver and put it in front of the customer, saying, "That's what you ordered, right?" Our standing room only crowds continued every weekend and the Town Hall and Jim Beatty and the Dixielads became the talk of the town.

This also solved the problem of finding a suitable venue for Wild Bill Davison. I talked with Norm Robinson about bringing Wild Bill in as a guest artist and he was all for it. Now it was time for me to "walk the walk" and call Anne Davison and see about bringing Wild Bill to Jamestown. I gave her a call and she was just lovely over the phone. As it turned out I had met her very briefly years before at Eddie Condon's in NYC. I told her that we could do it anytime and she said that she would check Bill's schedule and see when he would be near Jamestown.

The guys in the band and I agreed to get together and listen to some of Wild Bill's recordings and have a few rehearsals as well. Our cornet man, Brian Johnson would not be playing because Wild Bill played the cornet, but Brian said he would be thrilled just to come and listen. The rest of the band would remain the same, with me on clarinet, Pete Pepke on trombone, Leo Matson, piano, Don Peterson, banjo, Austin Main, bass, and Darryl Jones on drums. The band was sounding pretty good now and I thought we were ready.

I got a call from Anne Davison telling me that Wild Bill would be playing in Toronto and it would be a good time for him to get together with my band in Jamestown. So we settled on a date in early October and booked him for a Tuesday and Wednesday. It would have been silly to bring him in on a weekend because we already had good crowds. The band and I got together a few times and worked up a few of the numbers that he had recorded with Sidney Bechet.

Wild Bill was born January 5th, 1906 and Defiance, Ohio and was in his late 50s when he came to play with us in 1963. At the time I considered him an old man and little did I know that I would someday reach his age and then some. He started his career in the 1920s but didn't became nationally and internationally famous until he moved to New York City in the 1940's and teamed up with musicians like Eddie Condon and Sidney Bechet. He got his name because of his heavy drinking, womanizing and generally getting into trouble. He was a great, superhot player, but he also could play beautiful ballads from the bottom of his heart that would bring tears to people's eyes. He was married four times and his fourth wife, Anne Stewart, was a former Hollywood starlet who devoted the rest of her life to promoting and taking care of him.

Just two weeks before Bill was to play with us, there was a big picture and article about him in the *Jamestown Post-Journal*. Evidently, after playing a jazz party in Aspen, Colorado, knowing that he was a gun collector, he had been presented with a. 357 Magnum pistol, along with a leather holster. Wild Bill packed the. 357 in his bag and took a plane back to New York City, where he grabbed a taxi and headed for his apartment in Manhattan. Wild Bill was a very friendly and sociable guy and wanted to show the taxi driver his new possession. He didn't realize that the pistol was loaded and as he took it out of his bag it went off, fortunately missing the taxi driver, but blowing the front window out of the taxi. Bill told the taxi driver that he would pay for the window and hopefully they could forget the whole incident. That didn't happen, because after dropping Davison off he went directly to the police station and reported him. The police came to the Davison's apartment and arrested Wild Bill, who spent some time in the cooler until Anne sent a lawyer to rescue him with $2000 bail money. Fortunately, all parties agreed that it was an unfortunate accident and the case was dismissed, but Wild Bill never did get his gun back.

The free publicity we got from the article in the Jamestown paper did wonders for the two nights Wild Bill was with us. We had a packed house both nights. We had arranged a room for Davison at the Hotel Jamestown. Come to find out that he hated being alone in a hotel room and asked me if he could just crash at our house. That was fine with me and I was sure Pauline would be okay with it as well.

Our opening night with Wild Bill went great. How could we miss with Wild Bill taking charge of the lead? Of course a lot of people came, not because they liked jazz, but because they wanted to see this madman musician who shot windows out of taxi cabs. Wild Bill loved the beer cooler in the basement and liked to go there to cool down and have a drink on an intermission. That's when I found out that he was a klepto-maniac and that he loved to pilfer things. That night after we got home he pulled out a bunch of hamburger patties that he found in the cooler and he was so proud of himself.

My dad and Belle showed up the first night with a couple of my Dad's musician buddies. He was drunk, as usual, and was looking for some way to criticize the music. He told Wild Bill that he didn't think Bill could play the verse to "Stardust." Wild Bill played it perfectly and shut him up - I was so embarrassed – again! But the rest of the night went perfectly, as did the next night, and Bill managed to steal more hamburger patties. This was the beginning of a petty crime wave that I would share with Wild Bill for the next several years.

After all was said and done, it was a musical success and just the be-ginning of a beautiful friendship with Davison. He loved to play with my band and told me he'd come back any time I called, which turned out to be numerous times, from the East coast to the West Coast. He said the next time he came to play he was bringing his wife, Anne, with him, and that meant good company for Pauline.

I received a phone call the first part of 1964 from Anne Davison telling me that Wild Bill was going to be doing a lot of work guesting with The Salt City Six, a very good band from Syracuse, New York. Anne said that would put Bill very close to Jamestown and if we wanted him back as a guest it probably could be arranged easily. We picked a date for the middle of the week in early spring. He arrived in Jamestown by plane this time because for some reason or another he had quit driving. So his previous trip to Jamestown was the last time I ever saw him drive a car. We had sold out crowds again at The Town Hall and the band was sounding better and better as we got used to playing with him.

Norm Robinson took Wild Bill and me out to lunch one afternoon. After lunch we were walking up Main Street from Brooklyn Square when Wild Bill noticed some beautiful jeweled pillboxes in a store window. He wanted to go in the store and look them over. So we went in and he checked them all out. They were beautiful, but he decided not to get one that time. When we got back to the house he took one of the pillboxes out of this pocket to show me because he was so proud of himself and his new possession that he'd taken. But when he lifted the lid of the pillbox he realized that the spring on the lid was broken. He said, Jesus Christ, I have a defective pillbox, take me back to the store! So back we go and he stormed into the store and went to the counter complaining about the broken spring. The sales lady behind the counter apologized profusely and told Bill to pick out another one with their apologies. He was happy now, the store had made amends and we could go home. So, I became an accomplice to another of his petty crime sprees. I also found out that when he was not happy he would shout, "Jesus Christ!" His wife, Anne, who was Jewish, would always say - William! Would you please leave that poor man alone!

After two very successful evenings of playing at The Town Hall with Wild Bill we got him to the Jamestown Airport and on the plane back to New York City, where he had several jobs to play. He sure was an amazing musician with unbelievable energy and I always was anxious for the next opportunity to work with him.

I didn't escape having unexpected wild episodes myself. One morning, Pauline was going to work at the hospital but I needed the car during the day, so I had to drive her to work early. I had played late the night before and hadn't had much sleep. At that time I wore silk shorty pajamas and I jumped out of bed in just my pajamas thinking that I would be right home and get back to bed for some more sleep. I dropped Pauline off at the hospital and headed back home, but going through Brooklyn Square my Pontiac sputtered and came to a dead stop. I was out of gas. What do I do? All I had on was those damn short pajamas - not even a pair of slippers, just my bare feet. I had no choice as there was no such thing as a cell phone in those days so I couldn't call for help. I just bit the bullet, got out of the car and walked to the nearest gas station. I must say that I really stopped the traffic that morning in Brooklyn Square and everyone just stared at me like I was a madman. Then I remembered that I knew the owner of the cleaners in Brooklyn Square where I would occasionally bring my clothes. I strolled in and asked if they would loan me a shirt and pair of pants. They just died laughing and gave me a pair of pants and a shirt. Of course, I still had no shoes - but what the heck! Luckily I went through high school with a friend, Marve Schuver, whose father owned a gas station in Brooklyn Square. I walked to his gas station and thank goodness, Marve was working. Everyone at the gas station got a good laugh as well. He gave me a gallon can of gas and I got my car started, drove home and back to bed – at last. Needless to say - the story got around town like wild fire and I was needled for several days after that. I did learn a lesson and to this day I always fill my car with gas when the needle points to half full and when I get in someone else's car I always glance at the gas gauge as well. I don't wear shorty pajamas anymore. In fact I don't wear any pajamas at all! I guess that would have been worse yet.

The band was getting busier and busier with work. We were featured in Jamestown's March of Dimes show and had requests to play engagements all over Western New York and Pennsylvania. I was also asked to be the musical director of the Miss Jamestown Pageant sponsored by the Jamestown Junior Chamber of Commerce. That turned out to be a big job - much more than I had anticipated, but I pulled it off with my band. There was a review in the *Jamestown Post-Journal* that read:

*Jim proceeded to play a clarinet solo that obviously impressed the capacity audience. His rendition of "Summertime" received an ovation that at least rivaled the one given when Miss America was first introduced.*

So my hunch was right - Jamestown was ready to join the jazz wave that was sweeping the country and the Dixielads were right in the middle of it. We even started to get so busy that we had to occasionally take time off from the Town Hall to fulfill our many booking requests - we did this with Norm Robinsons blessing; he would never hold us back.

With the band getting busier and Pauline's job at the Jamestown General Hospital, we were starting to feel a little more financially secure, but certainly not rich. We even traded the Pontiac Tempest in for a Ford station wagon. This was perfect because obviously the Pontiac had many miles on it and the station wagon could also be used for the band on road trips.

One evening Pauline told me that she had some exciting news for me. She said "Jimmy, we are going to have a baby." Wow! I was absolutely thrilled. It just couldn't get any better than this and I had absolutely no idea how wonderfully it would change our lives for many years to come. Since I didn't have a dad around in my younger years to learn from, it looked like it was going to be on the job training for me. But I was so excited and looking forward to it, I just started counting the days.

It looked like 1964 was to be a very busy time for the band. We were jumping all over the place, from the Town and Country Club in Warren, Pennsylvania to a jazz club in Olean, New York. I even got a fan letter from Florida and all that was written where the address goes on the envelope was a picture of me and "Jamestown, New York." That just shows you how much my picture was in the paper. Wild Bill came back to play with us for the third time and, as promised, he brought his wife Anne. I met them at the Jamestown Airport and Anne Davison was just as lovely in person as she was on the phone.

Anne Davison's parents were Russian Jewish immigrants and she was born on September 15th, 1914. Her mother and father were named Isadore and Dora Hendlin and they first located in New York, followed by moves to New Haven, Connecticut and then finally to Kingston, New York. Anne had two sisters. One, Elizabeth, was married to Dennis Peeples, a movie set designer who won an Academy award for *East of Eden*, and the other sister, Shirley, married the chairman of the board of Coca-Cola, Stanley Barbee. She also had two brothers that became businessmen.

Anne was a beautiful lady and in her younger days mixed with New York's high society. She fell madly in love with the Metropolitan opera and movie star Neno Martini and selected him to be the father of her child. She wanted a boy because she wanted him to be good-looking, like his father. The baby turned out to be a girl and she named her Diana. Anne then went to Hollywood to get into the movie business. She became a starlet, changed her name to Anne Stewart, and had small parts in several movies. She had non-speaking roles in the classic western, *My Darling Clementine,* with Henry Fonda and Tyrone Power and also again, with Power, in *Nightmare Alley.* She became quite the socialite in Hollywood and was friends with stars like Marilyn Monroe, Joan Crawford and Dana Andrews. She also had a love affair with Tyrone Power. She later married multimillionaire William McLauchlan II, but they divorced after five years.

Anne had an apartment in New York City and one night she went out on the town with friends and ended up at Eddie Condon's. That's when she first heard Wild Bill Davison and that was to change her life forever. They fell in love, married and she devoted the rest of her life to Wild Bill and his music.

Pauline and Anne hit it off and became friends instantly. Bill and Anne had traveling down to a science. She only wore black and some jewelry and a gold necklace. Bill wore a blue blazer, white shirt, tie, gray slacks and dress shoes - usually loafers. Anne did everything for Bill, including getting him dressed for work and combing his hair before he went out the door. As she often said – I am an all-around slave for Wild Bill Davison.

On that particular trip, the four of us had a great time together, but we also had a lot of playing to do. We played the Town & Country in Warren, Pennsylvania, The Red Coach Inn in Lakewood, New York, and of course two nights at our home base, the Town Hall Inn. We had great crowds at all the events and Anne and Wild Bill said they couldn't wait until the next time. The feeling was mutual.

In late summer/early fall Pauline and I decided it was time for a little vacation. We were anxious to go on a road trip with our new Ford station wagon, so we decided to hit the road and drive to Vancouver, Canada and visit Pauline's family. We also had a few more wedding presents to pick up that we couldn't fit into the Pontiac Tempest. Of course there was a lot to talk about with the arrival of a new baby the first part of 1965.

We decided to drive across Canada for this trip and that meant traveling through Ontario, Manitoba, Saskatchewan, Alberta, and finally British Columbia. It was a big country but we got to go through some cities that we had not seen before - such as Winnipeg and Regina. The new station wagon drove like a charm.

It was fun to hang out with Pauline's family again and we even found time for a few days at their cottage on Sakinaw Lake. Of course there were a few evenings where I caught up with Lance Harrison and his band and played the night away. After Lance was finished playing for the night we always found an after-hours club to jam. Lance and I had worked out a cute head arrangement of the tune "Sentimental Journey," and we were asked to play it wherever we went. You never had to worry about running out of drinks when you were with Lance - he always had a couple bottles of gin in the trunk of his Cadillac.

Two weeks pass quickly on vacation, especially when you take off days for travel time on the road. But it was fun and we enjoyed seeing everyone again. We were at a party before leaving and I was talking to a guy that happened to be a doctor. He said that Pauline should not be on such a long road trip when she was expecting a baby. It scared the hell out of me. During the drive, near Cleveland, Pauline started to feel sick. We pulled into a motel and got her to bed. She got a good sleep and felt great the next morning. I had been up all night worrying about Pauline and the baby, smoking one cigarette after another along with a few beers and I was a basket case the next day. Thank God we didn't have too many miles drive to Jamestown. We were back home now after a very enjoyable vacation and ready to go back to work.

CHAPTER 16

# Making Babies

LEO MATSON'S LIFE OF DRINKING beer and not eating caught up with him. His physical condition became so bad that he had to be admitted to the alcoholic ward of the Buffalo Veterans Hospital. Actually, drinking had started to become trouble with the band. Brian Johnson and Don Peterson often showed up for work under the influence of liquor and it affected their playing. I had learned my lessons about drinking before a job, but they didn't seem to get the picture. One night Don Peterson was so buzzed that he fell asleep playing the banjo on stage. Looking back at it now it seems humorous, but it wasn't then. Musicians that couldn't handle alcohol or drugs became a problem that I would have to deal with for the rest of my career.

Wild Bill Davison had been playing as a guest with The Salt City Six. They were a long established group that was quite popular in the New York and Pennsylvania area, although they had also played jazz clubs all over the United States. They were organized in 1952 as The Salt City Five by clarinetist, Jack Maheu and trombonist, Will Alger. Maheu was one hell of technician on clarinet and he must have put in a lot of hours practicing. Ironically, they were the band backing Sidney Bechet at the Paramount in NYC when I went to hear him play back in the early 50s. Maheu was co-leader and arranger for the band and Will Alger was co-leader and front man. Alger was a character, with his balding hair, horn rimmed glasses, handlebar mustache and drank beer like it was going out of style every night on the job.

For some reason Jack Maheu left the band, Will Alger inherited it and was now the leader of the Salt City Six. The band was in the middle of a concert tour called "Dixieland Jazz, U.S.A." It was a history of jazz show reviewing jazz from its earliest inception on the back streets of New Orleans to the big band styles of the 30s and 40s. It also included a commentary by George Hoefer. George was a distinguished author, eminent jazz critic and historian and associate editor of Jazz Magazine and Down Beat columnist. He was co-author of *Music on My Mind*, published in 1964 by Doubleday. He could also be found as author of numerous jazz record album notes. He talked the band through the past and present, painting vivid descriptions of the people, moods and music of jazz.

So, there was a position open playing clarinet with The Salt City Six. Wild Bill recommended me for the job and I got a call from Will Alger offering me the clarinet chair. Even though my group, The Dixielads, was doing well, I just could not turn this down. The Salt City Six was a good band and the money was good as well. They also kept quite busy, especially now that they were doing the history of jazz tour. Not only that, but Pauline was out of a job because she was pregnant and showing. Back in those days a nurse could not work after showing that she was expecting. So, the extra money would come in handy, plus Pauline could go on the road with me. Most of the work was going to be in the Western New York area and would not involve long road trips. So it was settled - I took the job and Pauline accompanied me on the trips. We stored our stuff with my mom and gave up the flat. It was the fall of '64.

After playing several Dixieland Jazz, U.S.A. shows we were scheduled to play a jazz club, Florrento's, in Syracuse for three weeks. It was a road house just outside of Syracuse and luckily there was a motel right next door. Pauline and I settled in to the motel and I just had a few yards to walk for work. To save money on meals Pauline bought a hot plate and cooked some amazing things on it. Back then you could get turtle soup, which was my favorite, and Pauline often served it to me for lunch.

After finishing the three weeks at Florrento's we went back to doing our History of Jazz shows. This meant that Pauline and I would have more time to go back to Jamestown and house hunt. There was going to be three of us in just a few months and we needed a bigger apartment in preparation for our new little baby. We found a cute little apartment ($45 a month) on the second floor of a very nice house on Front Street, that wasn't too far away from my old neighborhood and just about one block away from my old school, Lincoln Junior High. I got a break from the road during the holidays and took some local jobs for extra money. We had another fun Christmas and New Year's Eve with the British and Swedish side of the family.

With the holidays over I went back to doing more history of jazz shows before opening at a jazz club in Niagara Falls, Canada. We played at the Park Motor Hotel right in Niagara Falls, Monday through Saturday with Sundays off, which was nice because if we wanted to drive to Jamestown, it was less than 100 miles away and we could be there in 1 ½ hours. It's funny, but Niagara Falls is a favorite destination for honeymooners, and Pauline and I would walk around the city hand-in-hand with Pauline ready to deliver in just a few weeks. People would look at us and I am sure that they thought - Boy! They just made it!

Our new baby was due at the end of March and we thought it best that Pauline was back in Jamestown near her doctor and hospital - just in case. So I drove Pauline back to Jamestown on my day off and played the last week of our engagement by myself. I thought that this would be the best time to leave the Salt City Six because we were getting so close to delivery time and that's one thing I didn't want to miss. I also knew that this road tour would be my last one for a good many years and any children I had would never be abandoned by me traveling all over the country.

Now that I was back in Jamestown I called all my guys in the Dixielads and told them I was back for good and ready to start the band up again. It didn't take too long because Norm Robinson welcomed us back to the Town Hall with open arms. I had to get things going again musically in Jamestown, including bringing in Wild Bill when he got back from his European tour.

We were getting close now to the arrival date and Pauline's mother flew in from Vancouver, Canada to be here for the big event and to help out as much as she could. So now it was just a waiting game. Would the baby be a boy or a girl? We were soon to find out.

When I got back to Jamestown, Pauline had some exciting news for me. It seems that the downstairs apartment of our new home on Front Street was going to be available to rent and we had first dibs. That would sure be handy, especially with the new baby. The only trouble was our rent would go from $45 to $60 a month. That was a big increase in rent for us but we decided to bite the bullet and take it. By this time Pauline's mother was with us and between the three of us we got everything moved from the second floor to the first. It was really great because we had a nice big master bedroom and a second bedroom for the new baby. We also had a living room and kitchen with a gas oven and a good size yard with a storage shed in the back.

So we waited and stared at Pauline. We were now at the beginning of April and still no labor pains. Pauline and her mother even went to work with me at the Town Hall so I could keep my eye on her. As I looked out into the audience I saw her doctor, Dr. Dickson, sitting there - I thought this would be a perfect night for the baby to arrive because all the major players were there. But that was not to be, the weekend came and went and still no baby. We waited some more without any luck - it was now the second week in April.

We played another weekend at the Town Hall and again Pauline and her mother were there along with Dr. Dickson. Another perfect time for a delivery - we could all have walked up the hill to the hospital and had our baby delivered. But again, that was not to be and we waited some more. The three of us sat around the house and twiddled our thumbs, occasionally going out for lunch or dinner.

I remembered that somebody once told me that if you wanted to hurry a baby along, just take a ride on a rough country road. I never thought too much of that, but what the heck, it was worth a try and after all it was the 12th of April and Pauline was way past due, getting bigger and bigger. I had a friend that had an old Nash pickup that I borrowed and I loaded Pauline in the front seat and off we went. I knew all the old country roads around Jamestown like the back of my hand and we went up and down hills and over ruts in the road and stirring up dust like you wouldn't believe. After our drive I took Pauline home and went and returned the truck to my friend. When I got home there was Pauline, her little bag packed and ready to go to the hospital - she was in labor at last! Because Pauline was hungry we stopped by the new McDonald's for a 19 cent hamburger on the way.

In those days the husbands waited patiently in a waiting room. Finally, Doctor Dickson walked in and said – "Jim, you are the father of a very healthy baby boy." I went to see Pauline and to take a look at my new son for the first time. He was 8 lbs. 4 oz. with blonde hair and blue eyes. I couldn't have been prouder. Only trouble was that when Pauline lost her job she also lost her health insurance. We didn't have the money to pay the hospital bill so we had to make payments on the baby, who we decided to name William James Beatty. This is one payment I wouldn't miss because we didn't want the hospital to come and repossess him. William James quickly picked up the nickname of Jame and we were anxious to get him home.

Pauline's mother stuck around for a few days after we got Jame home and helped out a lot. But she never expected to stay that long and soon had to leave to get back to Vancouver. Everyone was anxious to see our little addition to the family and we had lots of visitors coming and going, including (Uncle) Pete Pepke. Now I had much to learn - making formula, changing diapers and getting up in the middle of the night for bottle feeding, but I caught on quickly.

With the new member of the family I had to get busy and hustle up some playing jobs that paid good money. It turns out that this would not be hard to do because word got around that I was back in town and my band was back in business. The phone started ringing with job offers - and the Dixielads were ready.

The Dixielads were back at the Town Hall again and playing to our usual full house. We were also asked to play for the annual March of Dimes show, which was always a big event in Jamestown, and we also started playing Tuesday, Wednesday and Thursdays at a new place in town called the Town and Country, just across the street from the Jamestown Furniture Mart, where our furniture factories displayed their products to potential buyers around the country. It was also just up 2nd Street from my dad's hotel. Speaking of my dad, he was getting close to retirement from MRC and that worried me because he had absolutely no hobbies and I could just see him hanging out at all the 2nd Street bars every day drinking himself into oblivion.

I received a call from the Hotel Jamestown asking for my availability to play a few jobs at their Colony Room and also for a Dixieland Jubilee that they were planning. This was a big deal because the Hotel Jamestown was "thee" place to play in town. I also got a call from the Red Coach Inn telling me that they were interested in booking my band along with Wild Bill Davison. Now this really made my ears perk up because Wild Bill was back from his European tour and I was anxious to get together with him again. Bill also told me that he couldn't wait to see our new home and little Jame. The Jamestown Jaycees called as well and wanted to do a show with Wild Bill and me. So things were looking up and it seemed like a busy year ahead. Thank God – because we still had to pay for Jame.

A friend of mine, Earl Olson, followed the band around wherever we played and he owned a construction company that built prefab homes around the Jamestown area. The houses were quite small but affordable to own. I was looking to make some extra cash during the day when I was not playing. So I asked Earl if he would put me on as a part-time salesman - and he was happy to do it. He always had a model home to show and that's where I would be, just waiting for customers to come and look around. As I said, these homes were on the small side, so he furnished them with extra small furniture to make the rooms look bigger. It was boring sitting around that house day after day, so I started to bring my clarinet along to practice and that worked out fine. It was easy for people to get financing to buy the house but the interest rates were out of this world. Young couples came in to look around and couldn't really afford the house any more than I could, but we could get them financed easily. That was my downfall because I just didn't have the heart to sell the house to them and consequently I was a complete failure in the sales business. Years later I started driving Lincoln Continental's and Town Cars. I drove them because I honestly believed that they were the best car made in the United States. So I could have easily been a Lincoln salesman - which proves you really have to believe in what you are selling.

I got a call from the Davison's and they had a very successful European tour and were happy to be home in New York City again. I told Anne that things had become busy with the band and people were anxious for Wild Bill to come and join in. We agreed on a date and I told her that I'd line up some work around Jamestown and Pennsylvania including our new venue at the Red Coach Inn.

Realizing that I was a failure in my sales venture, I still needed to get a day job of some kind to generate more income. So I went to an employment agency and we discovered that I wasn't suited for many jobs because I didn't have a college education. They did, however, have a job opening at an automobile parts store that I might possibly qualify for. The company was called CMK Auto Parts and was the biggest of its kind in the Western New York area. I made an appointment with the manager and applied for the job, realizing the only thing I knew about a car was how to start it, drive it, and occasionally wash it. But somehow the manager decided that I must have had enough brains to catch on to the auto-parts business and I got the job. CMK had enough auto-parts in stock to build a car and had everything from tailpipes to mufflers to spark plugs. They started me out filling phone orders and getting them ready for the delivery driver. I was slow finding things at first but as the days went by I started to catch on and got quite good at it. All the guys I worked with were wonderful, including the owner who lived a few blocks down the street from us but in a nicer neighborhood and in a big beautiful home. The only downside was that I had to be to work at 8a.m. and one thing that I was definitely not good at was getting up early in the morning, however, with baby Jame stirring every morning, he became my alarm clock.

Wild Bill and the Dixielads were booked into the Red Coach Inn for two nights and a Sunday afternoon show at the Greek Club for the Jamestown Jaycees. Wild Bill came alone on this trip and left Anne home in NYC to recuperate from their European tour. We met him at the

Jamestown Airport and he was as full of life as ever and was anxious to tell us about his new hobby - antiquing furniture. This is what he did at our house all day long with Pauline and baby Jame while I was at work. It was great because we had a lot of used furniture and he made it look quite elegant. I had to keep reminding him that he was in Jamestown to play music with me and not set himself up in the furniture business.

The two nights at the Red Coach went well and we had a big crowd, even with the $1.00 cover. Wild Bill became acquainted with the owner of a furniture hardware factory in Jamestown and the next day he, Pauline, and Jame were down at the factory helping themselves to hardware for all the furniture he was antiquing at our house. Pauline, of course, was taking the place of his wife Anne and taking care of his needs all day while I was working. In other words - she had two babies to take care of.

We did have a little surprise waiting for us on the way to the Greek Club job on Sunday afternoon. There was a cute little bar on the way there and Pauline, Wild Bill and I stopped in for a drink. As we were sitting at the bar having our drinks, Wild Bill said "Look what I have!" - and with that he pulled out a revolver! Somehow, somewhere, someone had given Wild Bill another gun. I couldn't believe that after all he went through with his gun charge in NYC that he would even think of having another one. If Anne knew about this she would have a fit! And she trusted us with him. The Greek Club was out in the country and I guess Wild Bill thought he could do some target practice on his intermission. When he pulled the gun out at the bar the other patrons, including the bartender, were horrified. It's a wonder that they didn't call the police, but Pauline grabbed the gun away from him and put it in her purse and scolded him like he was a naughty little boy. We went on to play our job and it went well; there was even a $1.50 cover at the door. On our way home Wild Bill pleaded for Pauline to give him his gun back. He had consumed lots of Scotch by this time and wanted to shoot the front window out of the Town Hall as we passed by. I reminded him that that was one of our places of employment and shooting the place up was not a good idea. We compromised with him and let him shoot the window out of our backyard shed. The glass was cracked and broken anyway and Wild Bill was happy. I'm sure our neighbors wondered what was going on that night but I never heard a word about it. After all our music jobs we put Bill on a plane back to NYC in hopes that on his next visit he would be accompanied by Anne.

The rest of the year was going by rapidly with me working days, playing nights, and Pauline back at the hospital. She went on the evening shift at the hospital so we only needed a babysitter for just about an hour or so until I got home from CMK each day. Jame was crawling around like crazy now and starting to make attempts at walking. The two of us would enjoy cocktail hour together when I got home. Sometimes I brought a buddy from work home with me and the three of us would have a little party.

In early November, '65 Pauline and I discussed going back to Vancouver, BC, for her sister's wedding. The wedding was in December and we both got permission from work to attend. We booked a flight to Vancouver via Air Canada departing from Toronto. We planned to go for a week before the wedding and we were looking forward to seeing family and friends again and of course everybody was anxious to see Jame. I also planned to take my clarinet with me and have some musical fun with my pal Lance Harrison.

As we were making plans for our trip Pauline said, "Jimmy, I have some news for you. I'm pregnant again and we are having another baby." What! It seems like we just had one, we're going to do it again? I was stunned, but thrilled to death in hopes that the next baby was as great an experience as the first one. Pauline and I decided that we would not tell anybody about our new baby, especially on our trip to Vancouver, because we were just showing off our first one.

The trip to Vancouver was great. It was a fun wedding and although it was a short time there, we got to see everyone and I even had a few sit-ins with Lance Harrison and his band. Now it was back to Jamestown for the holidays.

Christmas was always a jolly time in Jamestown, with family parties and all the other activities around town, including the bars on 2nd Street serving hot Tom and Jerry's. We brought the New Year in with the band at the Town Hall. The Dixielads were off to another busy year, traveling on weekends to out of town cities such as Erie, Warren, Kane, Bradford and Hershey, Pennsylvania, along with Western New York cities including Syracuse, Rochester, Ithaca, Corning and Buffalo. We also had plenty of local jobs to play during the week. So between the music and my day job, I was a pretty busy boy, but I wasn't complaining.

We had an interesting job at the Corning Country Club, playing a Saturday evening party and planning on driving back to Jamestown after the job. A gentleman came up to me during an intermission and introduced himself as the president of the Corning Glass Company. He said that after hearing the band he would like to have an afternoon luncheon at his home the next day and wanted to know if we would stay over and play for him. He said that he would pay me my regular fee and pick up the hotel bill for the night. I checked with the boys in the band and everyone was for it.

The next afternoon we showed up at the president's home, and it was a mansion with a butler, maids and the whole works, and the band was a big hit. When we were finished and packing up the band, the president asked me if I was married and if so, would my wife like some Corning ware. He took me to his car and we drove down to the Corning factory. He told me to pick something out and he'd have it shipped to Pauline the next day. I picked out a hot water kettle, Pauline loved it, and it was with us for many years.

I got a letter from Will Alger of the Salt City Six telling me that his band had broken up due to lack of work on the road. Things were beginning to change in the jazz world and the jazz clubs were starting to have a difficult time. Bebop and modern jazz was attracting different crowds, and the rock and roll craze was going strong with people like Bill Haley and the Comets, the Beatles and Elvis Presley. Now, Will Alger was asking *me* for work. With our popularity around the area I told him that I thought we could bring him in as a guest artist, like we did with Wild Bill. So we set up a date at the Red Coach Inn and again it was a full house. Will Alger was an excellent tailgate trombone player, good showman, and the people loved him and wanted him back. I was beginning to discover that I was getting good with music and also becoming a successful promoter.

My dad was retired now and just as I predicted he drank the days away on 2<sup>nd</sup> Street. You could set your clock by him. He left the Hotel Lawrence every day exactly at noon and started making his rounds from one side of 2<sup>nd</sup> Street to the other returning home between 6 p.m. and 7 p.m. Then he would sit in the kitchen drinking shots and beers and maybe eating a little food until he went to bed and started all over again the next day. When I could I would stop and see him in one of the bars. If he wasn't too far gone we would have some fun conversations, because he did have a great sense of humor, but unfortunately he got mean and nasty when he stepped over the line and had too much alcohol. Belle still worked at MRC and had to come home to him drunk every night. She finally couldn't stand it any longer and they separated. My dad moved over to a sleazy apartment on 2<sup>nd</sup> Street not too far from where he lived when I first met him as a kid. I knew then that for him it was the beginning of the end.

Pauline was beginning to show her pregnancy and that meant she would have to leave her nursing job again. Although she was working part-time it still meant a loss of income, but on the bright side she had been working at the hospital long enough to qualify for family insurance. That meant that the next baby would be paid for, and thank God because we still hadn't finished paying for Jame. Jame was getting to be a handful running around like crazy and getting into everything. I just couldn't imagine another one to take care in a few months; maybe it would be a quiet, little girl.

Fans were still asking for more Wild Bill, so I booked a few jobs with him at the Red Coach Inn. We picked him up at the airport and again he was without Anne. Evidently she trusted Pauline and me to take good care of him and it would also give her a rest. Wild Bill was still antiquing furniture, but the trouble was we were running out of furniture for him to work on. Pauline and Jame had the big job of keeping him entertained during the day while I was at work. Often he would take off and go into downtown Jamestown and hit a few bars on his own. He always hit the bars on 3$^{rd}$ Street so he never ran in to my dad – thanks be to God!

It was a full house as usual for both nights at the Red Coach Inn. They just couldn't get enough of my band with Wild Bill and couldn't wait to do it again. We did have a private affair to play at an old legion hall outside of Jamestown. Bill spotted an antique bench that he could not keep his eyes off. He was just fascinated with things like that. After we finished playing, Wild Bill and I went out to my station wagon to head for home. I lifted the back trunk and found the antique bench sitting in there. Wild Bill struck again and I was the proud owner of a new piece of furniture for our house. Wild Bill was happy as he had pulled off another theft. That antique bench followed us around for many years after that. We got Bill on a plane the next day to NYC as he had a huge tour ahead of him in Europe.

On a sad note, we lost Leo Matson to alcohol. We all knew that this was coming and even after his stay at the Veteran's Hospital in Buffalo he couldn't stop drinking. I hated to see him go down this path because he was such a great guy with lots of talent. He was a big asset to the band, not only musically, but personally. This was just the first of many friends that I would see commit slow suicide such as this. Many of my musician friends drank like crazy, but they also ate good meals.

One late evening I got a call from the Jamestown Police Department informing me that they had my dad in a cell and asked me to come down to the station. I went down immediately and a police captain told me that they had picked my dad up wandering around on 2nd Street in his bare feet and wearing only a bath robe. I said "Dad, what were you doing?" He replied, "Just taking a stroll." I looked into his eyes and they were glassy; no one there. The first thing I did was to call Belle. We decided to admit him to Jamestown General Hospital for observation and they suggested that he be taken to the Gowanda State Hospital for the mentally ill for further treatment. It broke our hearts, but it had to be done, and on the way to the hospital he kept asking me where little Jimmy was. I told him that I was little Jimmy, all grown up, but it didn't register.

We left him there for a few weeks and I think they gave him shock treatments. One day Pauline and I visited him and we sat in the lounge area that he thought was a bar. He asked us what we wanted to drink and recommended the screwdrivers. We told him that sounded delicious and with that he called an orderly and asked for three screwdrivers. The nurse immediately delivered three orange drinks to our table and my dad was happy. He was later released and Belle took him back home where they both stayed until they sold the Hotel Lawrence and rented a home nearby. My dad was never the same again, but he was at peace with himself even though he didn't know what was going on. Years later we realized that he had dementia or Alzheimer's disease, something that we knew nothing about in those days.

Then I got great news at CMK auto parts. The parts delivery truck driver was promoted to a better job and I was asked if I wanted the vacant position. The delivery truck left every morning after being loaded and went all over Western New York and into Pennsylvania. Every day was a different route and you're out on your own, free as a bird, just delivering auto-parts to gas stations and automobile repair shops. You are pretty much gone all day and return to CMK just in time to clock out and go home. One day of every week brought me through Warren and Pete Pepke. I timed my route so I would be in Warren at lunch time and Pete and I would have our lunch in the bank vault where he worked, surrounded by millions of dollars. One of my routes was up around Lake Erie and once in a while Pauline and Jame would meet me at a beach there and we would have a picnic lunch. I loved my new job and the freedom it allowed.

There was so much going on that Pauline's due date for the new baby came before we realized it. But with our experience with Jame being two weeks late we really didn't start to panic when the due date came. However, within a day or two that the new baby was due Pauline told me that she thought she was getting a few minor labor pains. To be on the safe side she packed her bag and we decided to have a nice dinner on the way to the hospital at one of our favorite restaurants called The Pub. It was a restaurant that specialized in beef on weck and was and still is one of our favorite meals. It's made with rare roast beef on a kummelweck roll. The sandwich is named after the kummelweck roll that is topped with caraway seeds and kosher salt. You very rarely see this on any menu except in Western New York. Anyway, you take your kummelweck roll stuffed with the thinly cut, rare roast beef, dunk it in 'au jus" and you have the best sandwich ever. Pauline really wanted this treat because she knew when she got to the hospital they wouldn't give her anything to eat.

So we leisurely sat there devouring beef on weck and I'm sure that I was having a beer or two to go along with it when Pauline looked at me and said, "Jimmy - we have to go right now!" With that we ran to the car, drove down Main Street and up hospital hill and rushed into the maternity ward. Our new baby was ready for the world immediately and luckily Dr. Dickson just happened to be there. I sat in the waiting room smoking one cigarette after another when Dr. Dickson came out and said – "Jim, You have another healthy baby boy - congratulations! Then he said – "Hell! Come with me and take a look for yourself." And there he was all, 8 pounds, 10 ounces of him, with long black hair. It was August 10th, 1966 and he was right on time, much to our surprise and to everyone else. They had a pool going at CMK as to how close you could come to the birth date. I know I didn't win because I was expecting the baby to be late; in fact, I had the Nash pickup truck standing by. We named our new baby Robert James Beatty, Bob for short.

The next day I realized we ran out of the Pub without paying our bill. Luckily I was a friend of the owner, Big Jim McCusker. Big Jim was two years behind me at Jamestown High School and was a fantastic football player. He became a professional American football defensive tackle in the (NFL) and the (AFL). He was with the Chicago Cardinals (1958), Philadelphia Eagles (1959-62), Cleveland Browns (1963), and the New York Jets (1964). After he retired from football he came back home to Jamestown and opened his new restaurant – The Pub. Big Jim always stood behind the bar slicing his roast beef for the beef on wecks. I walked in the pub and spotted Big Jim and I said – Guess I owe you some money. He laughed and wanted to know all about our new baby. He even gave me a beef on weck, on the house!

Bob was lucky because I did all my practicing on Jame. Diapers were held together by safety pins and I used to prick my fingers on my first several tries. I also was an expert on making baby formula and burping. So Bob's survival rate looked pretty good. Jame was walking now and as I looked into the future several months I could see Bob walking as well. It was going to be like herding cats.

Anne Davison called and informed me that Wild Bill's European tour had been delayed by a few weeks, so he was available again. I got hold of the Red Coach and they were elated, I also asked them if they would like to add Will Alger on trombone and make it a doubleheader. The show was a huge success and the band was fantastic, with Wild Bill and Will Alger in the front line with me.

I had booked a couple of more jobs with Bill, one of them being the Moose Summer Lodge on Chautauqua Lake. It turned out that I got myself involved in another one of Wild Bill's crazy capers. Just as the two of us were leaving the house for the job, Wild Bill noticed my cuff links. He said – Jim - I love your cufflinks, could we trade cufflinks for the night? What the heck. I said that that would be fine and we exchanged them. On our first intermission a gentleman invited Bill and me over to his table for a drink. During our conversation our host mentioned to Bill that he thought his cufflinks were beautiful. Well, Bill said, If you like them that much I'd like to give them to you. Bill then looked at me and said that he would like me to give him back his cufflinks because he could not play without them. Now I'm without a pair of cufflinks and some stranger is running around with mine on and thinking what a generous man Wild Bill was. I scrounged up a couple of safety pins and used them as cufflinks for the rest of the job. Another crazy night with the Wild One.

The next night we played at the Moonbrook Country Club in Jamestown. This is where the doctors, lawyers and the wealthy of Jamestown hung out. I introduced Wild Bill to Dr. Dickson and his wife. Bill looked at Mrs. Dickson and said "Where did you get that ridiculous looking hat?" Of course only Wild Bill could get away with a comment like that and everybody just bent over with laughter. I did notice, however, Mrs. Dickson later in the evening without the hat. Other than that the evening went smoothly and everybody enjoyed the music. It was foggy going home that night and Wild Bill was guiding me as I drove. I think that's called, "The Blind leading the Blind." The next morning in the paper a headline read: "Robbery at the Moonbrook Country Club"! My God! Could it be? No – he couldn't have – I was with him every minute! Or did he? I guess we will never know for sure.

I started to notice that my beard wasn't coming in quite as heavy as it used to and I didn't have to shave as much. I didn't think much about it as I just thought that happened as you got older - what did I know? Then I started noticing a lot of hair on my pillow when I got up in the mornings and quite a bit of hair was coming out onto my comb when I parted my hair. I was losing my hair and it started to come out in clumps. I had a doctor friend, Chuck Sinatra, who I went through high school with and I went to see him about my predicament. It turned out that I had a condition called "Alopecia." This is hair loss that could be caused by several things, but in my case he thought that I was burning the candle on both ends, playing music late in the evening, drinking, smoking and then driving a truck on my day job. I was becoming a nervous wreck. Dr. Sinatra told me that I should change my ways and slow down. This I couldn't do - I wanted to keep playing and I needed the day job to supplement my income. I told him that I would work my way through it somehow. He prescribed a shot of Vitamin B every other day and luckily Pauline was qualified to give it to me.

To make matters worse I was starting to get anxiety attacks. It bothered me to be around a group of people talking to me at the same time. I felt boxed in and had to get away and be by myself. This was not a good thing because I played for large crowds, but fortunately I felt safe when I was up on the bandstand away from everyone. On intermissions I would sneak in to another room or go outside with my drink and cigarettes. I also felt very self-conscious because I knew everyone was staring at me because of my hair loss. Going to a movie or walking through a mall was out of the question. In other words I was having a nervous breakdown! But with medication, Pauline's help and support from family and friends, I knew that things were bound to get better. Besides, I had a wife and two little boys who needed me. As the weeks went by things did start to get better. My anxiety attacks became less frequent, although I still didn't look good without a full head of hair. But it was starting to fill in, a step in the right direction.

As the year was coming to a close we enjoyed my family's company. Pop had finally tackled his drinking problem, with the help of Alcoholics Anonymous, and was doing pretty good with it, except for an occasional setback here and there. My mother was still at the bank and doing well and my sister and her family were back in Jamestown again. With the passing of Uncle Bill and my dad's deteriorating mental condition, the Sunday brunch roast beef and Yorkshire pudding parties were a thing of the past. Fortunately, I had watched Aunt Lizzie enough and picked up the skill of making a good Yorkshire – So it was Jim Beatty to the rescue!

It was obvious that sooner or later we had to solve the problem of me making a living in music or not. I was a big fish in a little pond and could not make enough money in the Jamestown area to support the family, buy a house and take care of the rest of the responsibilities of being head of a household. I really didn't see myself driving the CMK truck around

Western New York and Pennsylvania for the rest of my life. It was going to take some thought as to how to approach our next move, and that would be first on the list for 1967. In the meantime the band and I played in the New Year at the Town Hall Inn. In the audience was Dr. Dickson and his wife, along with Pauline. This time Pauline was having a cocktail with him - she wasn't pregnant! *"Auld Lang Syne."*

With the arrival of 1967, nothing much had changed. My band was booked solid right through the summer and fall. We wouldn't be having Wild Bill back with us in the foreseeable future because of his popularity around the world. In fact, a few years would pass before we played together again. In the meantime, I brought Will Alger in occasionally as a guest, because our fans really enjoyed his trombone playing and showmanship. When we were playing in the Jamestown area, the Town Hall and Red Coach Inn kept us very busy playing jazz.

I was feeling much better now and my hair was starting to grow back in. The hair came back as white soft baby hair and I really looked ridiculous - but it was coming back, and that was a step in the right direction. Pauline was busily back at the hospital part-time and we were finding out what a production it was to bundle up two little boys in their snow outfits and take them for a ride on their sled. Jamestown winters were brutal, but beautiful, and the boys really loved the snow.

I got a booking for the band at a very exclusive country club in New Hartford, New York, called the Yahnundasis Country Club. This was over 200 miles from Jamestown and the engagement was February 18, which meant driving through the snow. I charged them a good price and they put us up for the night at a local hotel. When we got to the country club and set up the band I noticed that the event was called *"Return to New Orleans, featuring Jimmy Beatty - The Renowned Recording Artist - Direct from the French Quarter in New Orleans."* I just hoped that no one would come up to me and ask how my tour was going, when I only lived

200 miles away. It was quite an evening with a free cocktail hour from 7 - 8 p.m. and a hot buffet from 8 -10 p.m. and dancing. It was a huge success and we were treated well with drinks, food, along with a first class hotel. I don't think anybody realized that we were not the real thing from New Orleans. Actually, the Dixielads had become a very professional group over the years and it showed in our playing because we didn't have to take a backseat to anyone. We were handicapped, however, because of the fact that we all had day jobs and couldn't wander too far away to play engagements. So, I realized that if I wanted to play music for a living I had to somehow situate myself and the family to a bigger city. That way I wouldn't have to supplement my income by having a day job.

Spring had sprung and it looked like the beginning of a beautiful Jamestown summer on Chautauqua Lake. It was May 18th and I had just pulled in to CMK after coming back from my auto parts delivery route. As soon as I walked in the door the manager told me that I was needed at home immediately. Now that scared the hell out me! Was something wrong with Pauline or one of the boys? I hurried home and my dad and Belle's car was parked in front of our house. When I walked in the door Pauline and Belle were waiting for me with the news that my dad had passed away early that afternoon. You're never prepared for this type of thing, even though in the back of your mind you were expecting it. He passed out at his house and Belle called Dr. Sinatra, who came over immediately and pronounced him dead. The cause of death: cirrhosis of the liver.

My dad did have an interesting life, at least at the beginning. He was a World War 1 veteran of the British Army, enlisting in Canada and assigned to the Kings Own Yorkshire Light Infantry. He was underage when he enlisted but the Army never found out until he was in the battlefields of France, at which time they assigned him to guard duty. He was the youngest veteran of World War I residing in Jamestown.

He was born in Kidderminster, Worchester, England on May 15th 1901. After World War I he returned to Jamestown and entered the professional music business, touring with the Culver and Jordan Orchestra. In 1925 he composed a popular tune at the time, "The Girl with the Golden Hair," a tune that I have recorded twice.

We had a wake for him on Saturday and Sunday of that week and the funeral service was on Monday. He was buried in Pine Hill Cemetery in Falconer, New York, and to get there the funeral procession had to go via Second Street and pass all my dad's drinking spots. As we passed the different saloons I could see the proprietors and customers giving a toast to my dad as the hearse drove past.

I thought about my dad and our relationship over the years from those first Sunday roast beef and Yorkshire pudding brunches and taking me to the Sunday afternoon movies that I watched alone as he sat at a bar next door to the theater. I thought about the black market stores we used to frequent on Sundays so he could purchase liquor and cigarettes. He did start me in the music business by buying me a clarinet when I was eight years old. But he never gave me a lesson nor in all those years did we play a single note together on our clarinets.

It wasn't until after I turned 18 and I could drink shots and beers with him that we got to know each other a little better. I very seldom talked to him when he was sober and never saw him take a bite to eat other than those little bags of peanuts he used to carry around with him. He loved baseball, and usually wore a baseball cap, and he had bets on the games with different friends along 2nd Street. Trouble was that he drank to the point that it was questionable whether he could make it home or not because he would stagger from one side of the sidewalk to the other. Thank God he didn't drive much but I remember one time he drove through the fence of his parking lot. Very embarrassing for him and he never lived it down being kidded by his friends.

The thing I could never figure out is why he never gave me any credit for my success in the music business and my clarinet playing. The only thing I can think of and I hate to say it, but maybe he was jealous of me. I believe I did something that he would have loved to do: The Army band, the Bahamas, on the road with some of the top jazz bands around, and then my band being so successful in Western New York.

After my dad's death I did learn a big lesson about greed. My dad had a beautiful diamond ring which obviously should have been passed on to me. But somehow it disappeared after his death and Belle couldn't figure out what happened to it. She said that perhaps somebody in one of the Second Street bars stole it from him; I doubt that because he had nothing but friends there. There was also a framed discharge paper from the British Army in World War 1 that hung on the wall at Aunt Lizzie's house, and I remember seeing it there since I was a little boy. That disappeared as well and that was a big mystery. Aunt Lizzie had always told me that my dad had a small insurance policy that was to go to me after he died and it was in her name. But after he died Aunt Lizzie had no recollection of that. This of course was small potatoes when you look at it now, but at the time it meant something to me and I could never figure out how family could do this at a time of death. After the will was read I ended up with some war bonds in my name worth $1700. This was a lot of money then and it came in handy for Pauline and my future plans.

My stepmother, Belle, got the bulk of my dad's estate and she bought a home in Florida. Pauline, the boys and I did visit her a couple times over the years. It was a beautiful little house right on the gulf and is still there to this day. When Belle died she left everything to her relatives. That's Show Business!

After my dad's passing Pauline and I started to think seriously about making a move. The West Coast was the most logical choice because of Pauline's family, Sakinaw Lake, the mild weather, and the thriving music business there. It was early summer of 1967 and I had several music engagement booked for the Dixielads that paid good money and I didn't want to let the guys in the band down.

We had a big concert coming up in two parts called, "Fifty Years of Recorded Traditional Jazz." It covered recorded jazz from 1917 on. It was a big production that involved a lot of research and rehearsals and went over very well. We also played a full weekend at Lakewood, New York's Summer Festival. That was an interesting job because a big fan of the band and good friend, Ray Anderson, lived about one half a block away and at every intermission he would take us over to his house for drinks, and believe me he was well stocked with any kind of liquor you wanted. Needless to say, the band was feeling pretty happy the entire weekend. Pauline and I became very good friends with Ray Anderson and his wife Dorrie. Ray was a very successful local attorney specializing in labor relations. He was in the US Navy during World War II and then graduated from law school. He was Labor Relations Advisor to President Nixon before moving back to Jamestown and becoming a senior partner with the law firm Johnson, Peterson, Tener and Anderson. He had three children at that time and they loved it when we came over with Jame and Bob for a visit. Wherever and whenever my band played, you could be sure to see Ray and Dorrie in the audience.

With the summer coming to its conclusion, Pauline and I decided to leave Jamestown for the West Coast in early fall, before we had to deal with any snow. It was hard saying goodbye to family and friends but it was time to move on to a new adventure. The last performance of the Dixielads was held at the Town Hall on Friday, September 15th and it was called "The Last Blast." It seems like the whole town was packed in there that night, and was standing-room only. The furniture people in town got together and presented Pauline and me with a beautiful, leather inlaid card table with four folding chairs that was made at the Jamestown Furniture Company.

There was an article in the *Jamestown-Post Journal* called "Rambling and Roving." It read, in part:

*The local curtain is coming down on a beautiful character who un-doubtedly was the leading exponent in late years of bringing tra-ditional Dixieland jazz to the Jamestown area. He brought real Dixieland music here when they said it couldn't be done and had a long packed house stand at the Town Hall Inn plus many other head-line dates out of town. Jim is a clarinetist of the first order with long plaintive notes that come clear from New Orleans. The best of luck, Jim, and may you rock 'em on the West Coast.*

So now the fun began. We put our furniture in storage with a trucking company and told them we'd tell them where to ship it when we got to the West Coast. We packed what we would need for the trip into our station wagon, plus a big supply of diapers for Jame and Bob, made a quick stop to say goodbye to my mom and pop, and then we were on our way. On this trip we went through New York, Pennsylvania, Ohio, Illinois, Wisconsin, Minnesota, South Dakota, North Dakota, Montana, Washington and finally, Vancouver, BC.

I did the driving and Pauline had the big job of keeping the boys entertained. Don't forget, in those days there were no car seats for chil-dren, so Jame and Bob were crawling from the back seat to the front seat and back again and then over the backseat into the tail end of the sta-tion wagon. Pauline was constantly changing diapers and feeding them. Somewhere along the way the fuel pump went out on the car. Luckily it happened going through a small hamlet and I limped into a gas station. They didn't have a new fuel pump but said they could order one and have it there the next morning. We found a motel nearby and spent the night, got a good rest and took off the next early afternoon with the new fuel pump. Other than that it was a smooth trip and as we got nearer to Vancouver we called ahead and told them about what time to expect us.

When we arrived at Pauline's parent's house the whole family was there, including her sister Val and brother-in-law Brian, as well as her brother, Bob, and sister-in-law Gail. They had a big welcome party for us with plenty of food and drink. But now Pauline and I had to get busy and decide where we were going to set up housekeeping. There was a lot of territory between Vancouver, BC and San Francisco, California and we were going to try and find an ideal place for us to live and bring up the boys and hopefully find work for me in the music business.

Vancouver was a huge city with lots of opportunities for playing music, but my friend Lance Harrison had things pretty well locked up in the Dixieland jazz department, and the last thing I wanted to do was to start a competition with him for work. We were thinking about it, however, and I even applied and received a Canadian Social Insurance Card so I could work in Canada. We decided to weigh all of our options and take a look at Seattle, Portland, and San Francisco. We had great babysitters to look after the boys and drove off to look for our new home.

## CHAPTER 17

# Portland

PAULINE AND I LEFT VANCOUVER, BC, crossed the border into the United States, and headed south on Interstate 5. We decided to pass up on stopping in Seattle and would look it over on our way back because I had a cousin, Sandy Howard, in Portland that we had called and told we were coming for a visit. Sandy told us that she had an extra bedroom in her apartment and would love for us to spend our time in Portland with her. Pauline's sister and brother-in-law, Valerie and Brian, also had some good friends in Portland who said they would be happy to show us around town.

We arrived in Portland to a light misty rain and I remember thinking that everything seemed so fresh and alive. It was fun to see cousin Sandy again as it had been a few years since we had last met. Sandy had moved to Portland for Peace Corps training, but she did not join due to a medical issue and decided to stay in Portland anyway, finding a job at the local newspaper, the *Oregonian*. When we stayed at Sandy's house we had to be quiet for one hour on Sunday while she watched her TV show, *Mission Impossible*, which I didn't mind because it was a very exciting TV series.

We called Pauline's sister's friends, Bill and Dorothy Compau, and they told us they would be very happy to take us out for dinner and show us around the town. I really got my eyes full that evening when I realized that there was so much music around Portland. There were bars and lounges that had everything from a single musician up to a fifteen piece big band. I was very impressed when they took us to the Hoyt Hotel, which had four separate bars and a large showroom with stage shows nightly, backed by a big band.

The Compau's invited us back to their home for after-dinner drinks and conversation. Bill Compau was in the car business and was a partner with a well-known Portland businessman, Bud Meadows. Bill told me the automobile dealers often used music for their parties, car showings and so forth. One musician that they used a lot was a fellow named Monte Ballou, who had a popular band in town called the Castle Jazz Band. Bill called Monte and we had a nice talk. He was very interested in hearing all the news about musicians I knew on the East Coast. Monte was playing an office party with his band the next afternoon and invited me to stop by and say hello. I took advantage of the offer and showed up at the party. Monte and his musicians were very nice and encouraged me to give Portland a try because there was lots of work. The next day Pauline went to the Good Samaritan Hospital and interviewed for a potential job. They loved her credentials and told her that there was a job waiting for her if and when she wanted it.

When moving into the new area my big hurdle was the Musicians Union. Each local union had its own laws and some made you wait several weeks or months before you could start playing full-time. I stopped by the union office and luckily the local union President, Joe Dartis, was there. He invited me into his office and we had a long talk. He was also interested in what was happening on the East Coast and wanted to know about the musicians I had worked with. Come to find out, there was no waiting time before you could start working and he said that I would be more than welcome in Portland. And on top of that, he added, if you have talent, there is more than enough work here.

Well, it seemed like everything was laid out for us. We had a relative here, new friends, Pauline had a job, and I had plenty of opportunities for work and didn't have to get a day job. So we said – This is it! - Let's go for it. We rented an apartment about a block away from Cousin Sandy and now that we had an address we called the moving company and asked them to ship our furniture. With the furniture on the way we then drove back to Vancouver to pick up the boys and to fill Pauline's family in on our decision. They were probably disappointed that we didn't decide to stay in Vancouver, but the opportunities in Portland were far better and besides that Portland wasn't that far a drive from them. However, her family was very supportive and happy for us.

So here we go again, Pauline, Jame, Bob, and I said our farewells and drove off on a new adventure. We were hoping, depending on the work situation, that we'd be back for Christmas. I was really excited and couldn't wait to get things started in Portland.

Our furniture arrived and we set up housekeeping with our living and bedroom furniture along with two cribs and a carload of diapers. Pauline started working the day shift at Good Samaritan Hospital and I called Monte Ballou and let him know that I was in town and available for work. Monte had a few casual jobs for me, including office Christmas parties when we were nearer to the holidays. I also got a call from a trombone player, Archie Thomas, who heard I was in town, offering me a New Year's Eve job. So this was great considering that I just arrived in town and already had a few music jobs trickling in. I was in charge of the boys during the day and luckily there was a park one block away from our apartment with slides, swings and all the things little boys liked to do.

When Christmas rolled around we did arrange to find the time to drive up to Vancouver and spend two or three days with Pauline's family. I even had a visit with Lance Harrison, who was happy to know that I was staying on the West Coast and he wanted to get together with me and play some jobs in Vancouver. Back in Portland I played the New Year's Eve job at a place called the Sweetbrier Inn, about 8 miles south of Portland on Interstate 5. I didn't know it but this venue was one that I would be doing a lot of work at many years later. Archie Thomas was a terrific guy and a very good trombone player and the rest of the musicians in the group were good as well, even though it was primarily a pickup band. It was a good deal because I met more musicians for more contacts and Archie told me he was in another group, the Muddy River Jazz band, which played every Sunday from 4 p.m. until 8 p.m. and asked me to come and sit in any time I wanted.

In the meantime I was told there was a very good traditional jazz band playing nightly in downtown Portland on 11th Street. The band was called the 10th Ave. Jazz Band and its leader was a trombone player by the name of Ed Zimbrick. The name of the club was Orleans Alley, and it was a basement club that you entered through an alley. As I walked in the band was swinging away, sounding very good and very well-rehearsed. I was particularly impressed by the clarinetist and the cornet player. Standing at the bar I ordered a beer and next to me was a nice young fellow with a handlebar mustache, smoking a pipe. He introduced himself as Fred Bowman and said he was a very good friend of the cornet player, Jim Goodwin. (Bowman and Goodwin became important names in the micro beer business in Portland years later, but that's another story and further down the road.) At intermission, Jim Goodwin came over to the bar and Fred introduced us. This was the beginning of a lifelong friendship. I told Jim about my job with Archie Thomas and come to find out Jim was in the Muddy River Jazz Band with Archie. I really wanted to go sit in with that band now because I knew two of the players.

The Muddy River Jazz Band played in a nightclub called the Longhorn Steak House, and it was located at 82nd and Sandy Boulevard, not too far from the Portland Airport. The club featured Dixieland jazz in the late afternoon until 8 p.m., after which the place turned in to a strip club. The band was led by co-leaders Don Kennedy and Paul Sabrowski, both banjo players. Sabrowski was a marginal musician on the banjo and he taught Don Kennedy how to play. They never considered themselves superstar material; they just had a lot of fun doing what they did. Don Kennedy turned out to be a great friend of mine and he was instrumental in helping me musically around Portland. Like Bill Compo, Don was in the automobile business; he owned the Portland Auto Auction along with his partner, Roger Sheik. A number of years later the three of us staged the biggest jazz show ever seen in Portland at the Civic Auditorium.

It was great to see Archie Thomas and Jim Goodwin again and they introduced me to the rest of the band: Nat Pope, piano, Bill Stauffer, tuba, Axel Tyle, drums, and Jim Buchmann, clarinet. Jim Buchmann also played with the 10th Avenue Jazz Band that I'd heard previously at Orleans Alley. The Muddy River gang were a very happy good time band that were fun to be around and listen to.

At intermission Don Kennedy asked me to get my clarinet and sit in for a few numbers with them. I went out to my car, got my horn and went backstage to assemble it when I noticed that Jim Buchmann was putting his clarinet away and leaving. I thought, "What in the world is going on?" Well, it seems that Buchmann had a conflict on Sundays and was looking for a convenient way to leave the band, and I was it. I played the next set with them and at the end Don Kennedy offered me the job permanently every Sunday. I got on the phone to Pauline and told her the circumstances and that I would be coming home late. I'll never forget stopping at a pizza place on the way home and bringing take-out for Pauline, the boys and me for a little celebration.

There was a big difference between East Coast jazz and West Coast jazz. On the East Coast we dressed up to play; usually a suit, white shirt and tie. The West Coast musicians were very casual and often dressed to look like they came out of the 1920s. For example, when I worked with

Monty Ballou I had to wear a candy-striped jacket, red bow tie and straw hat. I recall that the 10th Ave. Jazz Band wore wild striped jackets as well and the Muddy River boys had matching shirts and ties that looked like they came out of the 1800s, and over their shoes they wore old-fashioned spats. I don't even know where they got them because they went out of style in the 1920s and I had never even seen a pair before.

Another big difference, other than the dress, was the style of the jazz. All the bands seemed to have a rhythm section of banjo and tuba. The West Coast also had a different repertoire of tunes they played. On the East Coast the more common rhythm section was banjo/guitar and stand-up bass. This is a formula that the New Orleans bands used as well. The tuba sounded exciting at times, but after a while it got on my nerves. To me it sounded like an elephant passing gas. I wasn't about to complain about the tuba because I was so happy to have work. I was curious, however, whether there were some groups around Portland that had a rhythm section of piano, standup bass and drums. I asked Jim Goodwin if he knew of any bands with this instrumentation and he said he thought there was a swinging group playing at the Flame Super Club at 122nd and Halsey.

The next Sunday rolled around and I went to work at the Longhorn with the Muddy River Jazz Band, really my first full day's work with them. It went well and I had to learn a lot of their West Coast tunes and arrangements, but I could see where I was going to enjoy my time with them, especially hanging out with my new friend, Jim Goodwin. After the job I packed up and headed for the Flame Supper Club. It was a rather large lounge with a nice bar and in the showroom there was seating for several people. They served very nice meals in the showroom and there was no dancing. There was a large bandstand with an upright piano and I noticed a standup bass and a set of drums on the stage. I sat at the bar while the band started their first set, sounding very good and pleasant to listen to. It was the closest to what I was used to playing since I left New York, other than Lance Harrison's band.

At intermission time there was a comedy team that performed named Mike and Brian (Mike Neun and Brian Bressler) and they were hilarious. The band came over to the bar and I introduced myself. John Picardi, the drummer, was the leader, Ed Fontaine played the standup bass along with vocals, and Henry Estelle was on the piano. I told them that I had just finished playing with The Muddy River Band and they asked me to please sit in with them on the next set. I joined them and we played several tunes, much to the delight of the audience and the owner, Mr. Kavanaugh. Before I left, John Picardi asked me for my address and phone number in hopes of getting together again sometime.

The next morning Pauline woke me up and said that there was a man at the door wanting to talk to me. I thought, who could that be? I didn't know that many people, especially people that are up at that time of the day. I came downstairs and there was John Picardi, the drummer and leader of the band at the Flame. Johnny said that everyone loved my playing the night before, including the owner of the club, and he was there to offer me a steady job six nights a week at the Flame. I was flabbergasted! This is the last thing I expected just being new in Portland. Of course I said yes, even before talking about salary, because I knew it had to be at least union wages. And then he said, "Another thing Jim, I would like you to be the leader of the band because I don't like the responsibility and it's only logical that the lead instrumentalist front the band." I started to think that perhaps I was dreaming all this - but no - it was really happening - not only did I just get a steady Sunday afternoon job but on top of that I was the leader of the band playing six nights a week in one of the top nightclubs in the city of Portland. Someone is looking out for me.

All the new work that I suddenly had was great because now Pauline could cut back to four days a week which was still enough working time to qualify the family for health insurance, which was very important. But also with me working so much, we needed to buy another car. Now why I didn't go to my friend Bill Compau or Don Kennedy for help finding a good used car, I'll never know, but I didn't. Instead I went to Canyon Road where all the used car lots were. I found an old model French Renault Dauphine like the one I had back in Jamestown and it seemed to run okay. However, after I bought it and drove it home it didn't take too long to figure out that I got screwed. The car burned oil and smoked when it was hot like you couldn't believe. So I had to carry extra oil cans in the car and stop periodically to pour oil into the engine. I couldn't believe I let this happen to me after all my wheeling and dealing with cars back in Jamestown. I had to get rid of it and the only place I could think of was to take it back to the place I bought it from. There was a hill on Canyon Road that I drove to and parked with the engine off until it cooled down. Then I filled it up with oil and water and coasted down the hill and into the used car lot. The owner, who I had bought the car from, was there and probably forgot what a mess the engine was. I told him that he gave me such a good deal on my car I wanted to trade my Renault in for a little newer car. He was very thrilled that he had a satisfied customer and took my car for a ride around the block with the nice cold engine. When he came back I had picked out the car that I wanted, which was a midsize Nash Coupe that I had checked out thoroughly. We made the trade and I drove off in my Nash and left that mess of a Renault behind me. I thought, thank God I'm not in the car business, I'd hate to go through something like this every day of the week.

Bud Kavanaugh was the owner of the Flame Supper Club and he was looking for someone he could trust to take over the entertainment end of the business so he could concentrate on the liquor and food. He told me that I was in charge of the music and could hire anyone I wanted as long as we were getting big crowds. The first thing I did was to add Jim Goodwin to the band on Fridays, Saturdays and Sundays. The 10th Ave band was no longer at Orleans Ally, and Jim had been looking for work. I played Tuesdays, Wednesdays and Thursdays with my quartet and then added

Jim on Friday Saturday and Sunday. On Sundays I also added Archie Thomas on trombone and Monty Ballou on banjo. The Sunday crowds became unbelievable, with standing room only. After I finished playing on Sunday afternoons at the Longhorn, much of that crowd would follow me over to the Flame. It was like New Year's Eve every Sunday!

Mike and Brian (they used to say that they were "An act as exciting as their name") were very good at comedy and they both played guitar and sang folk-type tunes. They later became nationally known after they appeared on Johnny Carson's TV show. Mike Neun later was on the *Dinah Shore Show* and also became a popular standup comic. Brian Bressler went on to be one of the comics on the *Laugh-In* television series.

They also performed in a nightclub in Aspen, Colorado and were good friends with the Kennedy family, who skied there frequently. Mike and Brian had a ski routine that was hilarious. Even seeing their act six nights a week, knowing most of their routines, I still never got tired of watching them.

Nothing is perfect, however, and I discovered we had a rather strange drinking/drug problem with our piano player, Henry Estelle. It seems he was hooked on a very powerful cough syrup and he used to drink it by the bottle, along with alcohol. One Sunday night he passed out on stage at the piano, sound asleep on the keyboard. Goodwin, Thomas and I stood in front of him for the rest of the set so management and the audience couldn't see him. This kind of behavior is not professional and totally unacceptable. We managed to wake him up so he could play the rest of the night, but the next week he still came to work with his bottles of cough medicine. I started looking around for another piano player and thank goodness there were plenty around Portland. Speaking of piano, Jim Goodwin taught himself how to play the piano and was quite good at playing traditional jazz. But I needed him on the cornet. I did find a piano player, Bobby Dyke, who was from the big bands and quite good. He was a character but he wasn't much of a drinker and very dependable.

One night an old friend of Monte Ballou's came in to hear us. He played trombone with Monte's Castle Jazz Band and went on to California to work for Walt Disney as a composer and musical director. He was famous for his composition of "The Ballad of Davy Crockett", a tune he wrote for the weekly television show of the same name. He also wrote "Yo Ho A Pirate's Life for Me," which became famous in the Disneyland *Pirates of the Caribbean* ride. His name was George Bruns. He later became tired of California, moved to Sandy, Oregon, building a mansion there with a music film studio where he could compose and arrange all the music for the Walt Disney movies. George and I became friends and we worked together often in later years.

Monte Ballou gave me a call and hired me for a recording date that sounded very interesting. We were going to record "Old Green River" and "Storybook Ball" with clarinetist Bob Helm from San Francisco, Ray Skjelbred from Seattle on piano, Jim Goodwin, cornet, Hank Wales on bass and Monte on banjo. My good friend Don Kennedy was producing the project. I was excited about this because I was being paired up with clarinetist Bob Helm. He was one of my favorite players and I had listened to him play on recordings with Turk Murphy when I was a teenager just getting interested in this type of jazz.

So a lot was going on, and on top of all that I got a call from the Democratic Party asking me to play some political rallies. I also got a call from the Bob Kennedy election committee and that really got my attention because not only was I a Roosevelt Democrat, like Frank Sinatra I was a big fan of the Kennedys. I made arrangements to come talk with them immediately.

So much was happening musically for me that I hadn't paid too much attention to the political scene, which was unusual because I always found politics fascinating. When I got a call from the Oregon Democratic Party and then from Bob Kennedy's election headquarters, I started to pay attention. So much had been going on this spring; starting with the assassination of Martin Luther King in Memphis, Tennessee on April 4th and then President Johnson's surprise announcement that he would not be a candidate for reelection. This caught everyone off guard, but LBJ's poll numbers looked very grim and he would have had a tough time in the primaries, let alone the general election. The Vietnam War was responsible for his loss of confidence of the voters.

So with LBJ out of the picture that gave the primaries a whole new look and the Oregon primary was coming on May 28th. It was a race between Herbert Humphrey, Eugene McCarthy and Bobby Kennedy, and with Oregon being the liberal state that it was, it became a tight race between McCarthy and Kennedy.

I gathered Jame and Bob up and we drove to downtown Portland for my appointment with the campaign staff for Bobby Kennedy. The boys and I walked in to the Kennedy's campaign headquarters and there were just a few people milling around. To my surprise among them was the candidate himself, Bob Kennedy. I had no idea that he was going to be there and by the looks of things I don't think anybody else did either. Kennedy approached me and the boys, shook their little hands and asked them if they were registered to vote in the Democratic primary. Everyone had a good laugh out of that because it looked like Kennedy was after any vote he could get. The campaign people introduced me to Kennedy and I explained to him that my band would be playing his events when he was in town. I was a little taken back and surprised at his presence and couldn't figure out what to call him. I finally blurted out Senator Kennedy, which was correct thank goodness, as he was a senator from New York State.

It was strange being so close after seeing him on TV for so many years. He was about my height, lots of hair that he kept pushing back and

I noticed he had freckled hands. He was dressed well with a gray pinstripe suit, light blue shirt with a red tie and shiny Boston style businessman shoes. I thought him very personable and sincere and I got the feeling that he really cared about people and the United States. His campaign staff hustled him off to some event and as they left I was already looking forward to playing my first political event with him.

I finished my business with the campaign people, which would involve a couple of whistle-stop train events through Oregon plus a few political events at the Sheraton Hotel. I then took my two little Democrats and went home.

The Kennedy campaign had two train trips planned through Oregon. One was Portland to Medford and the other a shorter run from Portland to Eugene. I couldn't do the long trip because of my nightclub obligation at the Flame Supper Club, but the trip to Eugene was doable. The campaign car was actually the caboose of the train and was decorated with all kinds of patriotic ribbons and flags. It wasn't the kind of caboose you would see on a freight train, but one more luxurious and possibly from a private train of some sort.

With everyone on board, the train started rolling south and our conversations were subdued because RFK was going over his speech with a few of his staff. It didn't take long to get to the first stop in Oregon City. When the train came to a halt the band jumped off and started playing some happy campaign music. Then RFK was introduced to a wild, enthusiastic crowd. At that point the band boarded the train and waited for the speech to finish and we would immediately be on our way to the next stop, which was Salem, the state capital. Kennedy came back into the car and acted very happy and relaxed, now that he had given his first speech of the trip. He looked at me and said "Great music, but where are your boys?" This took me totally by surprise because bringing Jame and Bob with me to a job of this kind was the last thing on my mind. Then he said - they would have really enjoyed the train ride. I soon found out that if you worked for the Kennedys you automatically were considered part of the family. Now I was kicking myself because I hadn't brought them along, but who knew? The trip ended in Eugene, where a bus drove us back to Portland. It was a fun, relaxed train ride was with lots of sandwiches and soft drinks, not to mention some pretty cool company. My next event with Bob Kennedy was going to be at the Sheraton Hotel.

The Sheraton was a large, classy hotel several floors high with a number of ballrooms and a large lounge with a piano bar that was a very popular hangout. The Kennedy functions were always held at the far ballroom at the end of the hotel. These rallies were always filled with very nicely dressed people, probably big financial donors to the Kennedy campaign. There was always nice *hors d'oeuvres* that were passed around and a BYOB bar. As a rule we played on the ground floor and the guests mingled around us. One time a lady walked up to me wearing a beautiful mink coat and lots of gold bracelets and diamond rings. She pressed a $100 bill into the palm of my hand and requested that I play "September Song." She said, "That was Jack's favorite song, you know." I never did find out this lady's name, but she was obviously a member of the Kennedy entourage.

On another occasion we were playing on stage and I made a horrible professional blunder. The band was playing away when I noticed a guy walk on stage with a guitar, wearing beat-up blue jeans with a matching blue jean jacket, sneakers, and an unruly beard. He was strumming away on the guitar and I walked over and asked him what he thought he was doing.

He said that he was joining in with the band. I told him that I didn't think it appropriate because: 1 - he wasn't dressed properly and 2 - he didn't know our material and arrangements. With that he turned around and left with no trouble. Shortly after that RFK appeared on stage, ready to address the crowd. I went back stage to put my clarinet away when a Kennedy staffer came up to me and said, "Bobby wasn't very happy with you!" I thought he meant Bobby Kennedy, but he said no - Bobby Darin - he came out to play with you and you kicked him off the stage. That was Bobby Darin? It couldn't have been, because Bobby Darin was a clean-cut young singer and always dressed to the hilt, usually in a tux.

Well, I found out that Bobby Darin was often in Kennedy's entourage. He was a huge star and at one time was married to actress Sandra Dee. Besides having a terrific swinging voice he also played the piano, guitar and drums and probably several other instruments that might have been put in front of him. He made several "top ten" recordings including "Mack the Knife," "Beyond the Sea," and "If I were a Carpenter." His first big hit was a tune that he wrote called "Splish Splash." He also was in several movies, most notably, *Hell Is For Heroes*. Darin, had he lived, would have given Frank Sinatra a run for his money. Unfortunately he died young at age thirty-seven, after open heart surgery. He had suffered with a bad heart ever since he was a young boy.

Sometime in the mid-60s he became disillusioned with big-time show business and became somewhat of a hippie, selling his house and moving into a mobile home. He evidently stopped wearing dressy clothes and grew somewhat of a beard and mustache. That's why I didn't recognize him, and I've been banging my head against the wall ever since. I asked backstage where he was because I wanted to apologize to him, but they said he had already gone back to his room. After Bob Kennedy's speech I told him about what had happened. He said he would talk to Darin the next morning and was sure he would get over it. In my defense, had the Kennedy campaign staff told me in the first place that Darin would be there, that whole unfortunate incident could have been avoided. Actor

Kevin Spacey is a great fan of Bobby Darin and made a marvelous movie about him and his life called *Beyond The Sea*.

It was getting pretty close to Election Day and RFK did his last campaign stop at the Sheraton Hotel. As usual the band and I entertained the crowd from the stage waiting for Bob Kennedy to arrive. He was late, as usual, but when he did walk into the room everyone went wild. For some reason or another I didn't see Kennedy's usual entourage. As a rule former LA Rams football star, Roosevelt Grier, was constantly nearby acting as a bodyguard. But this time there were just two staffers backstage and I assumed that they were his transportation. After the speech, as a rule, people came backstage to shake his hand and hope to get an autograph. So, when he finished his speech he walked backstage, looked at me, and said – "Jim, I need a double scotch and I think you're the guy that can lead me to the closest bar." Now I always stashed a ½ pint bottle of scotch in my clarinet case and everyone backstage knew it was there, including RFK. I wasn't sure if he was just too bashful to ask for a plastic glass or he was concerned that someone might take a picture of him drinking from Jim Beatty's clarinet case. At any rate, I didn't pursue it and besides that I knew he'd get a much better brand of scotch at the bar. The guys in the band had already packed up and gone home, so it was just Bob Kennedy, his two staffers, and me. There was no Secret Service protection for presidential candidates at that time.

I grabbed my clarinet and soprano sax and said - follow me. We had a little walk down a corridor past other ballrooms. We passed one ballroom and noticed there was a wedding reception going on. Well, Kennedy could not resist that and the four of us crashed the party. At first when they saw RFK there was dead silence because people couldn't believe what they were seeing. But then the crowd went wild, including a very surprised bride and groom. They gave us each a glass of champagne and Kennedy gave a toast before we went back out into the hallway to finish our journey to the lounge. When we walked into the lounge the same thing happened there - pandemonium. Then RFK surprised everyone, including me, when he jumped up on top of the bar, getting his double scotch and toasting the crowd. I didn't know it at the time, but this would be the last time I would see him. I had just figured that he would go on to be the Democratic nominee for president and I would be working for him again on that campaign.

Unfortunately, RFK lost the Oregon primary to Eugene McCarthy by a very narrow margin, but he did go on to win the California primary and it was important. I was playing at the Flame on California's primary night, Tuesday, June 4. On my intermissions I would run out to my car and listen to the radio. After the announcement was made that he had won, the announcer said they expected him to address his well-wishers at midnight. That was great because it was intermission time for me and time for Mike and Brian to do their show. So at midnight I grabbed a scotch and went out and sat in the car listening to RFK's victory speech. I sat in the car listening to the speech and wishing I could be there. I was just ready to turn the radio off and go back in to play when I heard a lot of commotion and someone said, "The Senators been shot!" Oh my God! That can't be happening. But it was. Information was sketchy and I didn't know if he was alive or dead. I went back to work as Mike and Brian just finished their show. Should I tell them? Should I tell anybody? No, I just couldn't say a word. It wasn't too long after we started playing when customers came in that had heard the news and it spread like wildfire around the club. They turned the television on above the bar, something that was never done during show time, and the whole terrible thing was being shown. Everyone surrounded the bar watching television and that was the end of the evening for us. It's still difficult for me to remember those days with RFK as he was a wonderful, warm, caring man and had he lived would probably have gone on to be one of the great presidents of the United States.

After Bobby Kennedy was shot, America waited in hopes that he would survive. He didn't, of course, and passed away the next day on June 6· 1968. The next number of days was painful to watch on television, yet we did. My birthday was June 9th and we let that pass with very little celebration. It certainly wasn't much fun to go to work on those days, yet we all have to get on with our lives, including the entertainment business. I felt sorry for comedians Mike and Brian trying to put on a happy face and do their show that they had done for RFK and his family many times at the ski resort in Aspen, Colorado. I never expected the Kennedy campaign headquarters to open again and I dismissed the idea of getting paid for the work I had done for them. So I was very surprised when I got a call from a Kennedy staffer, asking me if I was going to stop by and pick up my check or did I want them to mail it to me? I had it mailed because it would have been difficult to walk in the campaign headquarters again.

Herbert Humphrey won the Democratic primary and went on to campaign for the presidency against Richard Nixon. I got a call from the Hubert Humphrey campaign people asking me to play for a rally of his, at Civic Auditorium in Portland. After agreeing on my fee, I accepted the job, and then they asked me to send them the names and addresses of all the members of the band, because we would be going in the stage door and they would be checking our names.

We arrived at the Civic Auditorium about an hour before we were to play so we could get set up. When we walked in the stage door there were four or five very unfriendly men standing there asking for our names and identification. What is this all about? It turns out that they were Secret Service men and with the recent assassination of Bobby Kennedy, they were in no mood for formalities. They then opened my clarinet case, took the clarinet out and looked through the barrels of my clarinet, piece by piece. Of course my bottle of scotch was there as well and they took that, telling me I could pick it up on my way out. It was quite a production getting backstage and when we did get there, there were many more Secret Service men milling around.

We went out on stage and did our thing, keeping the audience entertained until it was speech time. We got the signal to quit playing and they introduced VP Humphrey. I went back stage and put my clarinet away and like I did with Bobby Kennedy so many times before, I grabbed a chair and sat down to listen to his speech. I just got myself seated when there was a tap on my shoulder. What do you think you're doing? It was one of the Secret Service guys. I said I was just listening to the VP's speech. The Secret Service man said, "The hell you are - you have to leave now!" These were not very nice people and I thought of asking him where he was when we really needed him - but wisely - I didn't. On my way out the door I retrieved my bottle of scotch and just to be funny I held it up to the light to see if there was any missing from my bottle. This didn't even get a smile out of them so I thought I'd better leave while I was ahead. That was my first experience with the Secret Service. I didn't think they were so secret, because you could spot them a mile away as they wore little American flags in their lapel and had a wire running down the back of their ear so they could talk with one another. This whole incident came back to me years later when I was followed around Beijing, China by the Communist Secret Police.

Things settled down after the elections and we got back into our normal routine. Six nights a week at the Flame Supper Club and Sunday's at the Longhorn Steakhouse. Pauline was still nursing away at Good Samaritan. Jim Goodwin had been living in an apartment not far from us but was dissatisfied and moved out. We worked so much together that I told him that he could crash at our house until he found a place that he found suitable. He said he often stayed up late into the night playing jazz records and drinking wine and didn't want to bother us or keep us and the kids awake. But he did ask if it would be okay to move into our station wagon. I know this sounds ridiculous, but you had to know Jim Goodwin to understand. We ran an electrical cord from inside the house out to the station wagon so he could have a light and run his record player. We also gave him a key to the house in case he needed to use the bathroom. Jim was in business. He set up a beautiful little apartment in the back of our Ford station wagon after folding the backseats down. In the mornings children on their way to school were quite amused as they passed our car and saw him sound asleep in his little apartment. Pauline and I would take the boys and go grocery shopping with him in the back and he would often wake up wondering where he was. But that was Jim, one of the happiest guys that I ever met, and a brilliant musician as well. Jim was also a big hit with Jame and Bob and kept them entertained for hours at a time.

My cousin Sandy was also a frequent visitor at our house and she loved Jame and Bob as well. Sandy drove a little Volkswagen Beetle that the two of them loved to ride in. Sandy still worked for the daily paper, the *Oregonian*, but was thinking about moving back East again. We were hoping that she wouldn't because she was such a great person and wonderful company. We thought that maybe Jim Goodwin and Sandy would be a match, but that was not to be, as music was the first thing on Jim's mind.

Pauline and I realized that sooner or later we would have to try and find a house to either rent or buy because the boys were starting to get bigger and going to need some space to run around. Pauline became in charge of finding a house and it didn't take long before she found one that she thought might fit the bill. It was in a suburb, Lake Oswego, about ten miles from Portland. We took a drive out to see the house and it was beautiful, but I thought way beyond our means. It was on about one acre of property and had a family room, laundry room, kitchen dining room, living room, two bedrooms and a bathroom on the main floor with the master bedroom, another bedroom and a bathroom with shower on the second floor. It also had a huge attic. The asking price was $18,000, a considerable amount of money in those days, especially for us. We decided to apply for a mortgage. Nothing ventured, nothing gained, and I'll be damned if we didn't get it. We couldn't have been happier and that house on 16666 Roosevelt Drive was going to see a lot of activity for the next 28 years.

Our contract at the Flame came to an end after a nice long run. We were picked up immediately by the Copperstone Restaurant and Lounge in Hillsboro, the fifth-largest city in Oregon and fifteen miles west of Portland. The Copperstone was a very popular hangout and it had a nice restaurant on one side and a bar and lounge, with a stage, on the other. We signed on for four nights a week, Wednesdays through Saturdays. On Sundays we still played our session at the Longhorn Steakhouse in Portland. This new schedule gave me a little more free time to do other things and spend more time with Pauline and the boys.

I had many requests from a restaurant in Jamestown to come back and play a couple of concerts with my old band. This was doable now and I accepted two nights at a place called Gordy's in Jamestown. It was fun getting back together with the Dixielads and renewing friendships in the Jamestown area. We had packed houses both nights and I was also surprised to find a guy named Art Weiland in the audience. He was the bass player that worked with my father and wrote the words to my dad's tune "The Girl with the Golden Hair." I even got him to come up and play bass with us on a couple of tunes.

One of our good customers at the Copperstone was a fellow named George Gaylick, a bartender at the Hoyt Hotel in Portland. He was so impressed with the band he told me that he was going to bring Harvey Dick, the Hoyt Hotel's owner, in to hear us. Harvey Dick also owned another bar in Portland, Zircon Jim's. Harvey Dick had bought the Hoyt

Hotel in 1941 and it was a real fleabag. Over the years he began to jam the hotel full of antique's, such as Tiffany shades, mahogany bars full of bullet holes, stained glass, luminescent paintings of curvaceous nudes, and a huge antique player piano with bells and whistles. It was truly a magnificent place and you couldn't see it all in one night. For anybody going out on the town or visiting Portland, it was "thee" place to go.

I had brought Bobby Dyke, my piano player from the Flame, with me to the Copperstone. He left the band because he didn't drive and Hillsboro was just too far for him to go from Portland. I heard of a good piano player, Norm Domreis, I gave him a call, and fortunately, he was available. Norm was fantastic and fit in with the band perfectly. He knew all the tunes and could play his own solo feature songs. It started another musical friendship that lasted 20 years.

I soon found out that Norm was a heavy-duty drinker, but he could hold it and it never affected his playing. I often wondered how he made it home some nights. He had a day job teaching English at a Portland grade school. He told me that to get through the day he had a bottle of vodka in his desk drawer and a bottle of 7 UP mixer. He became so busy playing with my band that he was able to give up his teaching position. He was also a womanizer and through years I saw him go through some wild situations with his love life. The big problem was he was married.

One evening, being true to his word, George Gaylick arrived at the Copperstone with Harvey Dick and his hotel manager, Joanne Kolin. They all sat and listened to the band, and by the look on their faces, they seemed to enjoy it. Harvey Dick was a big jovial guy, dressed immaculately in a tailored suit. He was probably in his early 60s at the time. Joanne, his hotel manager, was much younger and businesslike, but pleasant.

Harvey Dick didn't beat around the bush. He came right out and said "Jim, I like what I see and hear and I'd like to offer you a job in Portland at my nightclub, Zircon Jim's." We settled on my salary, shook hands, and it was a done deal. I told him that I had to give two weeks' notice to the Copperstone. That worked out fine because the owner of the Copperstone, Lloyd Jameson, had decided to sell it and move elsewhere.

This was all great, because Zircon Jim's was in downtown Portland on First Street near the Civic Auditorium. It was an easy drive from my home in Lake Oswego and I would have a whole new downtown Portland audience. Norm Domreis had previous commitments that he could not get out of and could not play Zircon Jim's with me. However, my bass player, Ed Fontaine had a good friend that played piano and assured me that he would fit in nicely. So we played our last two weeks at the Copperstone and got ready to settle into Zircon Jim's.

Recording Session. Jim Goodwin, Monte Ballou,
Bob Helm, Jim, Ray Skjelbred, Hank Whales, 1968

Muddy River Jazz Band, 1968. (back row) Paul Sabrowski,
Nat Pope, Bill Stauffer, Axel Tyle, Don Kennedy
(front row John North, Jim Goodwin, Jim.

## CHAPTER 18

# Jim Goodwin

I MET JIM GOODWIN AT the Orleans Ally jazz club in 1967 and that start-ed a friendship that was to last over 40 years, until his death. We both liked hot jazz and we both enjoyed playing it. We also had a grand time partying together and in general, we enjoyed each other's company. We would stay up for hours on end listening to jazz records along with drink-ing beer, wine and whatever else we could find. I smoked lots of cigarettes, however, something Jim never got into.

Jim would come out to our house and we would watch a spooky soap opera called *Dark Shadows*. It was a daily afternoon show about a vampire and we rarely missed an episode. Our television set was in the family room and we would shut the window blinds and close the curtains to make it as dark as possible. Anyone walking in on us, I'm sure, would think we were totally out of our minds. There was another show that we watched with my boys: *Batman*. It featured a different villain every episode, trying to escape the ever-pursuing Batman and Robin. One of the villains was called the Penguin, played by Burgess Meredith. He ran around in a tux and top hat smoking a cigarette in a cigarette holder mumbling, "Quack Quack." It didn't take too long for Goodwin to pick up on that and we all ran around the house squeezing our fingers back and forth yelling "Quack Quack" and driving Pauline crazy. There was another villain on the show named Lord Fog, and that became our code word for marijuana.

Despite what people say about Jim not doing drugs, at least in those days the two of us did our share of smoking Lord Fog.

Jim and I loved Alaskan king crab and at that time it was quite affordable compared to the price it sells for now. We decided to have a giant crab feast one afternoon and I had ordered one entire Alaskan king crab. Before Jim got to the house I put the crab on the front lawn, dressing it up with a hat, a pair of sunglasses and a pipe. So when Jim pulled in the driveway, there it was waiting for him. He got out of his car with two huge Hershey candy bars and gave one each to Jame and Bob. I said "Jim! What are you doing, that's going to ruin their appetite." Jim said, "Now you get the picture!" The two of us had the entire Alaskan king crab to ourselves.

At that time Jim drove a beautiful 1954 British Jaguar convertible. Boy, what a car that was. He was a real classy dresser in those days and looked like the all-American boy. His father, Bob, was a stockbroker and Jim started out working at his firm as a "board boy." He went on to a New York stockbroker's school and after graduation came back to Portland and started work. Jim loved music and taught himself how to play the cornet and piano. He decided that music was for him and he left the stock brokerage business forever. He always joked that he was the country's youngest stockbroker, and it's youngest retired stockbroker. You can see just a hint of the beginning of his independence and freedom in a photo I have of the Muddy River Jazz band with Jim and I in it. We're all dressed up with shirts and ties and looking very formal. Jim's tie is slightly askew and he is the only one in the picture with his leg crossed.

At one point Jim left Portland and started playing around the Bay Area with some good local musicians. For some reason or other those California musicians thought they were pretty cool, drinking beer like mad and looking rather unkempt. Of course Jim fell into this lifestyle very easily and I was shocked to see him when he came home to Portland for his father's funeral. He walked into the service, with his mother, needing a shave, haircut, and a cleaning-up in general. Jim's mom and dad were wonderful people and dressed immaculately, so I don't know where in the world Jim picked up on that terrible dress code of his. But there again, that was Jim Goodwin and you couldn't help but like him despite his sometimes bizarre appearance.

He stayed at our house often and was just considered part of the family. He loved Pauline's cooking, especially Chinese, and called her Chinese Pauline. When he was staying at our house, which he did off and on for several years, he very seldom slept in the house, but preferred to sleep in a shed at the back of our house. He even made a plaque out of an old piece of wood and it read "Preservation Hall," after the old jazz nightclub in New Orleans. After he eventually abandoned the shed, the sign stayed up and the shed was forever known as "Preservation Hall."

Jim and I loved to put people on and so we would start a conversation back and forth to each other within earshot of other people with totally unrehearsed nonsense. One time on an intermission we were having drinks with a group of people when Jim told them that he was invited to my house after we were through playing and I was going to cook my specialty for him, Kentucky Baked Owl. Now the ball was in my court, as all the curious people at the table asked me how I prepared it. I said – Well, first of all you have to catch the owl with a live mouse and then gut the owl and stuff it with wild rice and spices. Then the secret is baking it with the feathers on. Jim would then speak up and say something like – it's the greatest tasting bird I've ever had! With that we would get up, grab our horns and start playing the next set, leaving everyone at the table in amazement. We had these types of conversations often and loved to watch the expression on people's faces.

Jazz societies would often ask Jim and me to be featured guest musicians and come play as a team. We did this often for jazz clubs in Eugene,

Salem, and Portland. One time we played for the Puget Sound Jazz Club in Seattle. It was an afternoon show and we were through playing at 5 p.m.. The two of us were just getting fired up at that time and looked at each other wondering what to do next. We went to the nearest store, bought a six pack of beer and headed for Vancouver to visit Pauline's parents. They were very happy to see us and another party started, after I called Pauline and told her that we had taken a slight detour. We stayed in Vancouver a day extra so we could have a sit-in with Lance Harrison and his band.

One year we played the Vancouver Jazz Festival as a team and got carried away after our session and partied into the next morning. Unfortunately, we had an early session to play and when we got up things were a little shaky. I remembered an old remedy for a bad hangover, which was mashed potatoes and gravy. Jim and I headed for the nearest buffet and filled up on our new miracle cure. That did the trick. We felt much better and played our part of the show and were ready for whatever came our way. I always regretted the fact that of all the times Jim and I spent playing in the Vancouver area, we never got up to Sakinaw Lake together. Jim loved hiking through the woods and would do so for hours. Perhaps if he had visited the lake he might not have wanted to ever come back.

Jim was in and out of town often. He might be playing in the Bay Area, crisscrossing the United States or touring Europe. He knew that whenever he wanted to come home to Portland, whether it be a week or a month, I always made room for him in my band, either on cornet or piano.

When Jim came back permanently, for the last few years, his teeth went to hell and the dentist would not help him until his blood pressure was down. And to get his blood pressure down meant to quit drinking - and that was out of the question. So when Jim couldn't blow the horn anymore I switched him over to permanent piano player with my band. He was great!

People loved him. But here again the alcohol started to affect his piano playing and we had a few embarrassing episodes in public. Jim and I talked about it and he said he was going to try to cut down, but that didn't happen, and one night he called me, highly intoxicated, and said that he wouldn't be to work because his car wouldn't start. I didn't want him to drive to work anyway, in that condition, so just for the heck of it I called my old piano player, Harold Koster, and I asked him to come play on one hour's notice. He did me a favor and made the job and saved the night. But I couldn't go through this any longer and had a talk with Jim telling him that I could not use him anymore under the circumstances. Jim said – "I Understand" - it broke my heart.

I could go on and on about Jim, a wonderful friend and fantastic musician. He was right up there with Louis, Wild Bill and Bix. He did have his opinions, although he kept them to himself, except with me. He knew that he could trust me with his deepest secrets and I became a rare confident. For instance, he had impersonations of many local Portland musicians, and they were hilarious. He also had nicknames for a lot of the guys. Most of these musicians are still around and would be amazed if they found out the content. No one will ever know about Goodwin's secrets because I'd never betray our confidential trust.

Jim was married once, in 1983, to a gal he met in Holland, Machteld Van Buren. Her lifestyle was much like Jim's and I never could figure out why it didn't work. He also spent time with Aretta Christie, in sort of an on and off relationship. She was wonderful for him and even after they separated she watched over him like a mother hen right up until he passed away. Jim's love for good beer got him involved with his old friend, Fred Bowman and along with Art Lawrence they formed the Portland Brewing Company. When Jim realized the responsibilities and work this would entail he asked for his investment money back and was satisfied with playing piano at the company's Flanders Street Pub.

It affects me emotionally to write about Jim and know that he is gone.

### Jame Beatty on Jim Goodwin

My first memories of Jim were that of a cool uncle. Jim loved sports, especially baseball and he would enthusiastically talk with Bob and me for hours about the great players of today and years past. At some point Jim was storing some things in our attic on Roosevelt Drive and Bob and I would sneak into his whole collection of baseball cards. We would sit up in the attic and stare at his cards and marvel at the likes of Yogi Berra, Roy Campanella, Sandy Koufax, Hank Aaron and hundreds of other Hall of Famers. Bob and I spent many hours together in the attic dreaming about baseball and the careers of these great players and wishing that we could have such amazing cards in our own collection. Well, one day Jim did give Bob and me his baseball card collection. The joy and excitement that we both felt about receiving such an incredible gift cannot be overstated.

Jim played in several competitive softball leagues in Portland and also in the Bay Area when he lived in Oakland. He would tell Bob and me many stories of his exploits on the softball field. He did this not a boastful way, rather in an "I can't believe I did this" way.

Jim was a switch hitter and I remember him telling me how he hit this towering home run in Oakland, left-handed. This was amazing to him because he hit left-handed for contact and not power. If you told me this left-handed home run story once he told me ten times. Every once in a while he would play catch with Bob and me in the front yard. He would always encourage us with a bright smile.

Jim also enjoyed camping in the woods and the pursuit of the legendary Bigfoot. One time Jim joined the family on a weekend trip to Mt. Hood. Bob and I got up early and planted a Sasquatch footprint in the woods. We then ran into the cabin to tell Jim. He followed us out to the woods and was amazed at what we had found. He never let on that this was a ridiculous attempt by two young boys to pull one over on Uncle Jim.

Jim was an amazing musician. His cornet playing was some of the best. He could hear and feel things instrumentally that few humans could. His harmonies and solos came from places such so that I would sit with amazement and wonder how anyone could produce such music. He was one-of-a-kind. He was equally gifted at the piano. I used to love to sit on the piano bench next to Jim while he was playing. Often this would be a jam session at Roosevelt. Jim would sit on the bench with his eyes closed, both legs pumping to the beat, humming/grunting a tune that only he could understand, and pound out strides of silent jazz that left me mesmerized.

In my youth I admired Jim for his many talents and the attention that he gave to me and Bob. As I got older I began to understand what alcohol was and what it did to people. My perception of Jim changed and he eventually became a disappointment to me because of this. But not so much that I won't always remember him with great affection.

## Bob Beatty on Jim Goodwin

Jim Goodwin was one of the singular personalities I have ever known, and really his like is only to be found in fiction. I came to know him when I was very young, so he made a strong impression on me, and also was important in shaping elements of my own personality because his own life was so uniquely free. He was a living example of, as the cliché goes, living for the day and for his music, and being open to anyone who also wanted to join him in doing so.

He was a "free spirit," but much more than that…a brilliant musician on cornet and piano. Like Bix Beiderbecke, the relatively few recordings Goodwin made can't come close to the unbelievable jam sessions that I was witness to when Goodwin, Jim Beatty, and whoever else was in the house would start playing in the family room. Usually Goodwin was at the piano in those sessions. He played piano as if he were blind; closing his eyes and humming as if he was in a trance as the music pulsed through him. Can you imagine a jam session that included Jim Goodwin and Bob Helm on a houseboat in Sausalito in which there was an audience of one: me! To hear Goodwin at his best, musically, was a true joy.

Jim was great with kids because in all things except music he was a kid. He didn't worry about bills or responsibilities like adults were supposed to. He loved kid's stuff, such as baseball cards, and he talked like a hipster from the 60s, which for a kid growing up in the 1970s and 1980s, was unbelievably cool.

I love Goodwin in the way you can love something that can't be possessed or owned. It took me a long time to figure that out. I remember coming home from college one year, being with some friends and arranging a baseball game and talking to Goodwin, and him saying he would be there, and me and my friends standing on the field, so excited because they loved Goodwin too, and then him never showed up. I was angry, but later realized that it was silly to have expected him to show up in the first place. The very thing that must have enabled him to close his eyes and produce ineffable music did not allow him to be a conventional, functioning member of society, at least by the rules of a functional society. I know he frustrated, and even angered, a lot of people with that behavior, which they saw as shades of disloyalty or venality.

I saw Goodwin much in the vein of a Bix or an Orson Welles. He was possessed of a genius and a childlike approach to the world that made him so cool, but lacked the capacity to know where, or even how, to take that genius beyond its most elemental expression. It could be he drank so much for that reason, or maybe he drank so much because it was as simple as him being an alcoholic. It doesn't matter now; he was the ultimate cool cat.

**The two Jims - Goodwin and Beatty**

CHAPTER 19

# Hoyt Hotel

IT WAS GETTING NEAR THE opening night for my band at Zircon Jim's and I had a get-together with my new piano player, O.T. Smith. Bassist Ed Fontaine recommended him and he was a very good musician and piano player. He wasn't, however, a New Orleans style player, but leaned more into the middle of the road swing style. This was good because it gave me a chance to play some different jazz tunes. Because O.T. and Ed were black and my drummer, John Picardi, and I were white, Harvey Dick suggested we call ourselves the Café au Lait Four, which means "coffee with milk" in French. The name was fine with me; in fact it was a little catchy.

Opening week was huge because Harvey Dick had put good-sized ads in the two Portland papers, and I had built up a following from my days at the Flame Supper club. Despite Zircon Jim's location in downtown Portland at the labor Center building, it wasn't all that convenient to get to. You had to enter the Labor center Building, take an elevator to the second floor, go through a small lobby and then into Zircon Jim's. When you entered you walked into the bar area and then to your left was the lounge and stage. And if you were unlucky enough to have to use the bathroom while you were there it was quite a distance. In fact, there was a flyer on every table in the lounge giving you directions to the restrooms. But, it was a fun place to go once you got there. There was also another bar downstairs in the basement. It was used by union people during and after their meetings. The downstairs bartender was a neat guy and we would often take the elevator down to the basement and have an intermission drink.

O.T. Smith was a riot because at first all he did was complain about the stage lights blinding him. His complaints went on night after night until finally I went to a ski shop and bought him a pair of the darkest sunglasses I could find. I knew that when he put them on he could hardly see anything, but he didn't complain. O.T and Ed Fontaine both had wonderful voices and were tremendous assets to the band.

Our time at Zircon Jim's was to be short-lived because Harvey Dick had other plans for me. One night he came in to Zircon Jim's with Joan and they told me they would like to offer me a better position at his Hoyt Hotel, fronting the band in the Roaring 20s Room. I immediately accepted because this was a big step up, performing in the most popular entertainment establishment in Portland.

Playing at the Hoyt hotel was like going back in time every night. Harvey Dick bought it in 1941 at the peak of Portland's war time shipyard business. It was a rundown railroad hotel and he turned it in to an antique filled extravaganza. During the World War II era Harvey owned two steel foundries in Portland and he needed people to work in them. Henry J. Kaiser was building ships in Portland at that time and was importing workers from the East Coast via the railway. When they got off the train at Union Station, the first thing they saw was a sign on the Hoyt Hotel: Workers Wanted - Rooms! Since rooms were at a premium - Harvey got the workers.

After the war Harvey began filling his hotel with his passion - antiques. It's impossible to describe each and every antique in the hotel, but the Barbary Coast lounge, for instance, was completely illuminated by seventy-seven, custom-made gas lamps. The Tiffany Dining and Banquet Room featured several colored glass Tiffany shades, personally selected by Harvey Dick. There was also the Roaring 20's Room where there was a large stage with a gay 90's review. This room was also used for big band concerts for bands such as Duke Ellington and Woody Herman. The ladies room featured a harp player performing while the ladies were doing their business. The harpists would play such tunes as "Every little Movement has a Meaning all its Own," "Whistle while you Work," and "Give Me Five Minutes More." In the men's room there was a huge communal urinal that had a replica of the Manneken Boy who would tinkle back at you while you were doing your thing. In addition to that, if you hit a certain target, bells and whistles would go off. The Manneken Boy was made by the famous sculptor, Francois Duquesnoy, as a reward to the finder of his lost son.

There was also a small piano bar in the hotel, usually with a pretty lady behind the keyboard. The hotel also featured a men's bar for men only, spittoons and all. And there was a full jar of pickled eggs for five cents each at the end of the bar. You would get one hell of a strong drink there. For a time while I was playing at the hotel, a woman's lib group came into the men's bar to make a statement. Everyone ignored them and they finally gave up and went away. In total there were three huge mahogany bars in the hotel, all from the Wild West days and all with bullet holes in them at some place or another. One was located in the men's bar, another in the Barbary Coast room, where I played, and the other in the Roaring 20's showroom. So it was pretty hard to go without a drink while you are in the hotel. The funny thing is was that Harvey Dick never drank or smoked. In the parking lot there was a beautiful 1936 Rolls-Royce for people to gape at. There was also Harvey's Hooterville railroad steam engine from the television series *Petticoat Junction*. If you watch a rerun of that show you will see at the end: "Train Courtesy- Hoyt Hotel, Portland, Oregon."

I opened with my band at the Barbary Coast Lounge with a different group than I had at Zircon Jim's. Because of the antique decor of the hotel we had to play the early New Orleans style of jazz, and for that I was lucky to get Norm Domreis back on piano, along with Hal Hoyt on bass and John Picardi on drums. The piano we used was one heck of a contraption. It was called a Fotoplayer piano that could be used as a regular piano or as an old-fashioned player piano.

The Fotoplayer, Style 45, was built in 1912 in Berkeley, California to provide music and sound effects for the silent movies. It was in use in the Arcade Theater in Hoquiam, Washington until the theater closed in 1925. Harvey Dick found it and had it restored to its original condition in 1963, and at the time it was valued at $40,000. There are only a few of these playable Fotoplayers left today and one of them sold at an auction in 2012 for $414,000. When you played a piano roll you could accompany it with 30 different instruments that you controlled by pushing buttons, pulling ropes with symbols, pushing foot pedals and by pulling on levers. There was also a pipe organ, snare drum, bass drum, Chinese gong, cowbell, doorbell, pistol shot, papist diesel horn, and more. I also had all kinds of piano rolls to play, including songs like the "Twelfth Street Rag," "William Tell Overture" and "Beer Barrel Polka." I always loved it when somebody would request I play the Fotoplayer, and they usually bought me a drink as well.

The entrance to the Barbary Coast Lounge was on Hoyt Street and when you entered, the Fotoplayer and the band were on your immediate left. The men's bar was on your immediate right, swinging doors and all. There was a stand-up bar surrounding the Fotoplayer with enough room behind it for my quartet. No matter where in the hotel customers were going, they usually entered via the Barbary Coast entrance and walked past my band. Therefore, while I was playing, I saw everyone coming and going. The Gay 90's showroom was a big attraction and many celebrities would stop by and listen to the band or the Fotoplayer on their way there. Television late night host, Johnny Carson, came in one night, as did Eddie Albert, the star of the popular TV series *Green Acres*, and radio/television personality, Art Linkletter. Also, Mel Blanc, the voice of Bugs Bunny, Captain Caveman, and many other comic characters, was in often because he was originally from Portland. He was known as the man with 1000 voices. Fred Meyer, the founder of Oregon's Fred Meyer stores, was also a frequent visitor because he was a good friend of Harvey Dick.

The band was sounding great and the customers were really enjoying us. They would often buy us a round of drinks. John Picardi didn't drink so I would get his as well. In other words for every round of drinks, I would get two. So, those days at the Barbary Coast Lounge were happy ones for me.

Wherever I played, people would ask me where they could buy some of my recordings. I didn't have any and clearly I was losing money. There were recording companies around that I'm sure would have been happy to sign me to a contract, but the royalties were small. I decided to eliminate the middleman and finance my own records. Doing this took money because recording studio time was expensive and on top of that I had to pay the salaries of the musicians and put out more money for the printing and packaging of the album and shipping costs. You had to order at least 1000 records at a time to keep the costs down. I didn't have that kind of money so I went to my local Lake Oswego bank and applied for a loan. They must've thought that I was a good investment because I got the loan very easily.

I used my Barbary Coast Quartet for the recording: Norm Domreis on piano, Hal Hoyt, bass, John Picardi, drums, and myself on clarinet. We recorded eight selections, which included "Honeysuckle Rose," "Closer Walk with Thee," "Sweet Georgia Brown," "Burgundy Street Blues," "I Can't Believe You're in Love with Me," "Blue Prelude," "Little Rock Getaway," and "I Surrender Dear." The name of the new album was *Jim Beatty in Portland.*

We recorded at Northwestern Studios in downtown Portland, a company that I still deal with to this day. The records were 12 inch vinyl disks, recorded in stereo. It turned out to be a great business venture for me because we sold out of the first pressing quickly and I had to put in an order for a second one. The bank was very happy.

An amusing story happened because of this recording. The president of the gas company in Portland was a good customer at the Barbary Coast and he loved the band. When I told him that we had a new record album available he said he would not buy one from me, but would make a trade. If I gave him the new album he would trade me for a new gas barbecue. I told him that was a great trade but that I lived in the country area of Lake Oswego and we did not have a gas line out there. He said –No Problem – I'll take care of it. He took my address and new record album and said "You'll have your new gas barbecue in operation in a few days." The both of us had been drinking and I thought there was a good chance of him forgetting about the whole thing. Wrong!

A few days later I woke up to a lot of commotion in the front of the house. Pauline said that the gas company had been working on our road all morning; they had dug our entire street up, right to our house. There were all kinds of gas company work trucks and workers with picks and shovels, along with traffic directors - it was a madhouse out there. Our house was on an acre of property and it sat way back from the road. They had to dig up our entire front lawn and then work their way around the side of the house in back to where I wanted the barbecue to be located. This was an all-day project for the gas company, but they got it done and did a good job of putting the lawn back together. After they were all done, a nicely dressed gas company representative showed up with our new barbecue and hooked it up for us.

This has to be the most expensive LP album in the world. I can't imagine how many thousands of dollars it cost in labor and materials for that one gas barbecue. Of course, this called for a party, and my bass player, Ed Fontaine, barbecued the best ribs around and we ended up having a big jam session and barbecued rib party on our next day off.

The gas company executives loved the band and followed me around for years whenever I played in downtown Portland, because it was close to their offices. I asked one of my gas company friends where I could find a propane refrigerator. We didn't have electricity at our Sakinaw Lake cabin in Canada and had been using an old propane refrigerator that was starting to poop out on us. My friend said he would look into it and get back to me. Well, it turned out that propane refrigerators at that time were made in Brazil and he took the liberty of ordering one for me. About a month later I got a call from the gas company warehouse, telling me there was a refrigerator there for me. We took that refrigerator up to the lake, where it ran like a charm for many years. Eventually we got electricity in the cabin along with an electric refrigerator and we gave our Brazilian propane refrigerator to a neighbor across the lake, where it's still working.

As my name was starting to get popular around the music circles in Portland, I got a call from KOIN TV, Channel 6, asking me if I would be interested in appearing on their new variety show, *Northwest Illustrated*, on a once a month basis. At that time KOIN had its own studio orchestra for both its television and radio stations. Trouble was, they taped the show at 7:30 a.m., which was a ridiculous hour for me to be roaming around, let alone playing. I accepted the job, despite the hours, because television was something I had not had much experience in and besides that it would be tremendous exposure for both me and the Hoyt Hotel.

I arrived at KOIN about 6:30 a.m. to meet with the studio orchestra and discuss what tune I would play. After we settled on a song, we went over it quickly and I was ready to do the taping at 7:30 a.m. I usually didn't get home from playing at the Hoyt Hotel until around 3:30 a.m. I'd then have a couple of drinks to wind down and then jump in to bed for about two hours of sleep, at the most. I could have never have done this on a daily basis, but I thought, what the heck, once a month is doable. I arrived at the television studio looking and feeling remarkably well and ready to play.

The studio crew at KOIN was amazing and wonderful to work with. They went over my part of the show with me, telling me where to look and were to stand and other tricks of the trade. The only thing that bugged me was that one of the cameramen loved to zoom in on my fingers while I was playing and sometimes they could be a little shaky. Pauline and I would watch the show when it re-ran at noon and she'd always look at me when they zoomed in on my fingers, but never said anything. All in all, considering what I had gone through to do the show, I thought I looked halfway decent on TV and sounded good with the studio orchestra too.

One morning I arrived at KOIN for my show and as I entered the studio no one was there except an attractive blonde lady, probably in her late 50s. As I was putting my clarinet together she came over to me and introduced herself. "Hi, I'm Ginger," she said, "and I'm pedaling pantyhose for the JC Penny Company." I shook her hand and told her that I was Jim Beatty, the featured clarinetist on the show. I said that it was nice to meet her and good luck with the pantyhose. And with that, I excused myself telling her that I was going out to the lobby and get a coffee from the coffee machine.

It sounded just like a normal show to me. They always had news and then local personalities of sorts, such as the police chief, fire chief, city councilman or the mayor. Then there would be a back and forth chit chats from the program's two hosts. There would also be the musical portion of the show featuring a vocalist or an instrumentalist playing with the studio orchestra. So, in this case it looked like we were going to have a representative from the JC Penney Company.

As I was getting my drink from the coffee machine I looked out the window and saw a big Cadillac limousine parked outside. A cameramen walked by and I asked him if the limousine belonged to the owner of the station. Oh no - he said - That belongs to Miss Rogers! For a moment I thought "Who in hell is Ms. Rogers?" And then my foggy, early morning brain put two and two together and came up with "Ginger Rogers!" Oh my God I did it again, just like Bobby Darin. But at least this time I didn't kick her out of the studio.

I was mortified. Ginger Rogers, of course, was Fred Astaire's dancing partner in ten films from 1933 to 1939. They did such musical hits as "Top Hat," "Swing Time," and "Shall We Dance." She also won the Academy award for best actress in the motion picture *Kitty Foyle*. She was great friends with Lucille Ball, which would have given us a lot to talk about. Ginger Rogers had a summer ranch on the Rogue River in Oregon. It was called The 4 R's – Rogers Rouge River Ranch. She kept the ranch until 1990 when she moved to Medford, Oregon. Ginger passed away at her winter home in Rancho Mirage, California in 1993 at the age of 83.

I rushed back into the studio to apologize and make amends, but it was too late, she was already surrounded by the show's hosts, producer, director and cameramen. We began taping the show, I played "Sweet Georgia Brown" and sure enough, Ginger Rogers was recommending her brand of pantyhose for the JC Penney Company to the television audience. After that ridiculous blunder I always made sure that I took the time to know who I was talking to, and it has paid off over the years.

Sundays at the Longhorn came to an end, as did the Muddy River Jazz Band. Don Kennedy, the co-leader of the band, was the spark plug and promoter of the group. He bought the uniforms, monogrammed shirts, ties and even cuff links. I did, however, talk him into losing the spats - they were ridiculous. Kennedy would jump from one hobby to another and he just got tired of playing music. I had told him that I had learned how to fly airplanes back in New York. He thought that was exciting and made that his next project, buying a single engine airplane and learning how to fly. He was also very busy with his Portland Auto Auction, which was very successful and financially rewarding. Over the years I've had many interesting adventures with Don.

Now that I was not playing at the Longhorn on Sundays I was able to start accepting other job offers that I had been turning down. Having the band at the Barbary Coast in the Hoyt Hotel made my name familiar to music venues all over Oregon and Washington. I was always getting calls for my band to play on Sundays, even as far away as Pendleton. We had many calls from Elks lodges that we accepted and they would advertise - Jim Beatty – "Direct from the Hoyt Hotel in Portland." When we played far out of town, I would ask for a larger fee and hotel rooms. This was all great but on the downside it took away from family time.

Now that I was driving more I felt I needed a better car. I found a beautiful, one-owner, 1963 Cadillac four-door sedan. It was in showroom condition and had all the bells and whistles, including power seats, power windows, whitewall tires, tinted glass windows, door locks, cruise control, automatic headlight dimmers and fog lamps. It was unusual for a car to be loaded with extras in those days. I felt good about driving this car and I wasn't even in the mob anymore, or so I thought.

Jim Goodwin was back and forth between Portland and San Francisco, and when he was in town he knew that Preservation Hall was there for him to stay. Jim and I loved pizza and we would take Jame and Bob to a nearby pizza place for lunch. We noticed that when groups of people came in for lunch and ordered large pizzas that they would always leave a few slices. When we saw this we would send the boys over to the table to retrieve them. And then we realized why bother to order our pizza at all! So from then on we just ordered drinks and sent the boys around the room retrieving leftover pizza. Pauline was not at all happy about this, but I figured it was teaching the boys the art of survival. Hopefully they are not doing this anymore, but that doesn't mean to say they're not!

Drinking and driving wasn't much of an issue in my early days behind the wheel. To get a ticket for drunken driving you almost had to swerve from one side of the road to the other. More than often I would have a bottle of beer in the car with me, much the same as you do with water now. If you did have to be cautious it was mostly at night when the police were not very busy and they knew that probably people had been nightclubbing and they were easy prey for a ticket and a fine for the city treasury. I always drove carefully at night after drinking and always within the speed limit. Fortunately, I rode back and forth to the job with my drummer, John Picardi. John lived close to me in Lake Oswego and would drive to my house and pick me up. We took turns taking each other's car and he especially loved to drive my Cadillac. John drank nothing but coffee, so it was a perfect arrangement.

One night John Picardi was ill and I got a substitute drummer to take his place. That meant that I had to drive to work on my own. When I got to the job, Hal Hoyt told me that his wife had dropped him off at work and he wondered if I would give him a lift home at the end of the night. I told him - no problem - although he did live a bit out of the way in Beaverton. After work I drove him to his house and we arrived around 3:30 a.m. He asked me in to have a nightcap with him, as if we hadn't had enough, and of course I said - sure. One drink led to another and I left his house to go home at about 5 a.m. I wasn't familiar with his neighborhood in Beaverton and got lost trying to find the freeway home. A sheriff noticed me driving slow, looking at street signs and pulled me over. Well, the party was over. As soon as I opened my window he must've gotten a big blast of alcohol and cigarette breath. He put me through the sobriety test and of course I failed and was under arrest. He took me to the county jail in Hillsboro, the city where I had so many enjoyable nights playing at the Copperstone Lounge.

After they booked me I called Pauline and told her what happened. Of course she was worried because I never came home that night. Later that morning I had a court hearing and Pauline came down and bailed me out. My case was set to come before the court in about one month's time. I had to hire a lawyer and hope for the best. To make things worse the judge I was to face was especially hard on drinking and driving arrests.

We told no one about this and fortunately it never got into the news-papers, which wouldn't have been to cool for my job at the Hoyt Hotel. The only person that knew other than Pauline and me was John Picardi because of our driving arrangement. My day in court came and the judge declared me guilty as charged. I was fined and my sentence was two weeks in jail under the work release program. This meant that they would let me out of jail each night so I could go play my job. The judge said "Mr. Beatty - if I hear that you return to jail after work with alcohol on your breath - I'll put you in jail for a year!" This was not fun. I had a two week jail sentence, a fine, a lawyer to pay, and a very unhappy wife. I don't know which one was the worst.

I reported for my jail time and was searched and put in a fairly large cell with six or seven other guys. They were in for minor convictions such as DUI's, embezzlement and things of that nature, although one guy was there for beating on his wife. He seemed like a nice man and, as Wild Bill once said under similar circumstances, he must've had a good reason. They gave me a prison uniform (no stripes), and the food was surprisingly good. It was boring laying around all day, but we did have plenty to read and a small TV set. At 5 o'clock each night they unlocked the cell and let me out to drive back to Portland and to work. I had plenty of time to stop by the house and change into my dress clothes.

The first night at the Hoyt Hotel after my sentence, I knew that when work was over I had to report back to the county jail in Hillsboro sober. I knew that this would be a challenge because playing for five hours and turning down free drinks was impossible for me. So for starters I switched from scotch to vodka. Vodka has no smell and that was a step in the right direction. I held my liquor very well from my early training back in my Jamestown days. I didn't forget what the judge told me about if I was caught drinking coming back to jail at night...he'd change my sentence to one year! So there was only one thing I could think of, and that was to bribe the jail guards, not with money but with food.

The Hoyt Hotel had a 24-hour restaurant that had wonderful comfort food late at night. So the first night before I returned to jail I stopped at the restaurant and got a big bag of takeout chicken, nice juicy thighs, legs and wings. When I reported to the jail I was immediately searched and asked what was in the bag. Chicken, I said, they like me in the restaurant and I think they gave me extra pieces, have one if you like. Well, who turns down a nice piece of chicken? The guards absolutely loved it! So I said - if you like, I'll bring extra chicken back every night, plus they also make pizzas that are out of this world and the baby back ribs are not bad either.

Well gee-whiz, this was great! Now I could go back to my scotch and my regular routine at night and the only difference would be sleeping in a jail bed each evening. When I got back to jail every night I would have a variety of chicken, ribs and pizza to share. I even ate with the guards in their little lunchroom. Fortunately, nobody escaped during my time there, because there wasn't much security going on. As the guards got to know me better, they got interested in my music, so I passed out my new record album as well. All this didn't cost me that much because I had an employee discount at the Hoyt Hotel restaurant and the albums were at my cost. I'm sure that when my two weeks were up the guards hated to see me leave and probably hoped I'd be arrested again soon.

I had a few days left on my jail sentence when one of the day guards came by my cell and said if I wanted to get some fresh air I could go out and wash police cars. It was a beautiful day and I was getting, as the old saying goes, stir crazy. The only trouble was when I got outside; the convicts were washing the police cars on the main drag of Hillsboro in front of the county court house. This was a busy street with all kinds of cars driving by, staring at us. My face was a familiar one in Hillsboro because of all the Copperstone Lounge ads in the local paper. But I'm sure if anybody thought that they saw me that they would think they were imagining things.

This whole ordeal taught me a lesson, and I never have had a drink out of an open bottle of alcohol while driving since then, with the exception of my travels with Wild Bill Davison and Jim Goodwin. I certainly don't recommend mixing alcohol with driving a car. Of course now, when we're out on the road driving our cars, we not only have to look out for drunken drivers but we have to be careful of other drivers with their iPhones and texting.

After completing my two weeks in jail I got a letter from the DMV informing me that my driver's license was revoked for six months. Then I got another letter from my insurance company telling me that because of my DUI that my rates would be going up. This was very inconvenient but fortunately I could ride to work with John Picardi. Around this time my neighbor, Meryl Conger, informed me he knew of a beautiful 1963 Lincoln Continental for sale. Meryl had a Lincoln Continental himself, and I always had admired it. The Lincoln that was for sale belonged to the former manager of the Portland Sears Roebuck store. He bought it new, drove it to work every day, and parked it in the Sears service garage where it was washed, serviced and pampered daily. I went and took a look at it and bought it immediately. Now I had a Cadillac and a Lincoln Continental parked in my driveway and I couldn't drive either one of them. John Picardi was elated because he had the pick of two luxury cars to drive me to work in every night. He eventually bought my Cadillac, so that was off my hands. Fortunately, I was so busy playing at the Hoyt Hotel, doing my TV shows and playing casual engagement on Sundays so the time went by quickly and I was behind the wheel once again, although John Picardi did the driving after I had a few drinks.

I also got some good news at that time. Anne Davison called me and said that she and Wild Bill were back in the United States after a very lengthy time living in Copenhagen, Denmark. They had bought a home in Santa Barbara, California and Wild Bill was anxious to renew our musical friendship again. I thought that was great and told Anne all about my engagement at the Hoyt Hotel and that I would talk to Harvey Dick about possibly bringing Bill in for a guest appearance with my band.

Although the crowds that came to hear us were very good at the Barbary Coast Lounge, the rest of the hotel, including the Roaring 20s Showroom, was experiencing a slowdown in business. So, when I approached Harvey Dick about bringing in Wild Bill, he was all for it because he thought perhaps it would bring in a bigger crowd. I called Anne and we set a date. She said that she would be unable to come along with Bill on this trip but perhaps the next one, if I could put it together. I knew what this meant; we hadn't seen Wild Bill since we were in Jamestown and we were in for a wild time since he was on his own. When the word got out that Wild Bill was coming to Portland it was the buzz of the jazz community and everyone was looking forward to coming to see and hear him, as he had never played Portland before. They had no idea what they were getting into.

Pauline, the boys and I met Wild Bill at the Portland airport. It had been some time and we were all happy to see each other once again and he was amazed at how much Jame and Bob had grown. When we got home and Wild Bill was all settled in, he informed us that the Barnum & Bailey Circus was in town and the vice president of the Circus, Rudy Bundy, was an old friend of his. Rudy Bundy was a clarinet player and worked with Bill back in the early 1930s with the Benny Meroff Orchestra. The two of them had been talking on the phone and agreed to meet on Bundy's private railroad car that evening. Bill also wanted to see the Hoyt Hotel and meet Harvey Dick. This was all great because the Circus railroad cars were pulled into Union Station, not far from the Hoyt Hotel.

Bill and I went down to Union station, wandering around the railroad tracks until we found the Circus train and Rudy Bundy's private car. Rudy Bundy turned out to be a fun guy and he and Wild Bill had lots to talk about after not seeing each other for so many years. His railroad car was absolutely beautiful, a home away from home. He had a living room, dining room, kitchen, a large well-stocked bar and a large master bedroom. We sat and chatted for the longest time drinking scotch and having *hors d'oeuvres*. Before we left to walk over to the Hoyt Hotel, I told Rudy that he was welcome to bring his clarinet and play with Wild Bill and me at the Hoyt anytime he wanted. We then wandered over to the Hoyt Hotel and found Harvey Dick in the Gay 90's Showroom. Harvey Dick and Wild Bill got along famously and Bill was introduced to the crowd and played a tune with the show band. It was a fun night and it was going to be fun working with Wild Bill again, although I was going to have to watch him very carefully with all those antiques all over the hotel.

Opening night was a smashing success and Wild Bill was his usual brilliant, musical genius. Rudy Bundy showed up with his clarinet and sat in with us as did Jim Goodwin, playing the valve trombone. Then it happened; evidently it got around to the Circus performers that the vice president, Rudy Bundy, would be playing with the band at the Hoyt Hotel. After the Circus was over, a parade of characters started appearing in the crowd. The bearded lady, the tallest man in the world, little people, the lizard man, the ringmaster; you name it, they were all there. Anybody walking in off the street probably thought that they were in the Twilight Zone. This went on every night the Circus was in town. Everybody was in there except the elephants.

It was a wild week with a wild guy. During the day, musicians were stopping by our house just to meet him. He was also running around chatting with the neighborhood ladies and having coffee in his famous shorty pajamas and bedroom slippers. Wild Bill would be coming back to play many more times and fortunately Anne Davison would be with him to keep him in line.

The Roaring 20's Showroom would often feature music of the big bands. Before I started working at the Hoyt Hotel, Harvey Dick had such bands as Wayne King, Count Basie, Les Brown and Harry James. After I started playing in the Barbary Coast Lounge, several other big bands were scheduled to come in. One Sunday on my night off I came down to the Hoyt on some business and when Harvey Dick saw me he excitedly said – Jim, Duke Ellington has arrived and is having lunch in the coffee shop! Would you like to meet him? I said – Hell yes! - It would be special to meet one of the greatest jazz musicians of my time, and followed Harvey into the coffee shop. When we walked in, Harvey pointed him out sitting at a booth at the end of the room eating a big fat juicy steak. I said - Harvey, I'm sorry to tell you this but that is not Duke Ellington! Well, evidently some black gentleman came in off the street and passed himself off as the great Duke Ellington himself. Harvey laughed and said - "Let him finish his steak - he deserves it for pulling the wool over my eyes". That's the way Harvey Dick was, and now he had another interesting story to tell. Duke Ellington drew a big crowd that evening and the admission at that time was only $5.00 a person.

Another big band due to come in to the Hoyt Hotel was Buddy Rich. He was a famous drummer and was known to be very difficult to work with. I was asked to play the warm-up session before his band came on. After our part of the program was over I had the opportunity to meet Buddy Rich back stage and take in his personality. All the things I heard about him were correct - he was a jerk!

The next big band to appear was Woody Herman's 16 piece "Thundering Herd." This was the band I was really looking forward to because I knew Woody Herman from back in my New York days. For some reason or another we were playing in the Barbary Coast Lounge on the same Sunday as Woody was playing in the Roaring 20's Showroom and the same hours as well. I caught up with Woody Herman as he was setting up with his band and he was surprised to see me in Portland, of all places. We agreed to meet after we were through playing for the evening and go out on the town, catching up and having a few drinks. I picked Woody up when he was through at the Roaring 20's and we hopped in his rental car and went to a jazz club called the Prima Donna, where Jim Goodwin was playing in Monte Ballou's band. Of course Jim and the band got a kick out of me bringing Herman in and we had a good time on their intermission.

Woody Herman was a wonderful person, a great clarinetist and bandleader. Unfortunately, he evidently had a bad manager and got in serious trouble with the IRS. They were about to take his house when old friends like Frank Sinatra came to his rescue and bailed him out. I never saw Woody Herman again after that evening, but I will always treasure our friendship together.

We had purchased a new Ford Fairlane station wagon and for some reason or another I was driving it that night. Why - I don't know, because I had my Lincoln Continental to drive. At any rate, I got on Interstate 5 and headed home to Lake Oswego. I guess I wasn't familiar with driving the Ford, or maybe it had something to do with having too much to drink, but I drove all the way home in the low gear. As I pulled into our driveway I noticed the engine going "clickety clank, clickety clank." It was also smoking a bit. I shut the car off and thought – OK - it will cool down and be fine in the morning. Well, it wasn't.

The next day I started it up and it went – "clickety click, clickety clank." Looks like I screwed up again - big time. I took the car to the Ford garage and acted dumb (which wasn't too hard to do) and the service manager said "Mr. Beatty - your engine is toast!" But then he looked at the odometer on the car and said – "fortunately you're still under warranty." They rebuilt the engine, courtesy of the Ford Motor Company. I didn't feel so bad later on after I bought so many of their Lincolns.

With the financially successful week with Wild Bill, Harvey Dick evidently saw the possibilities of pumping new life into the Barbary Coast Lounge and Hoyt Hotel. He approached me one evening and asked me what I thought of enlarging the band and moving it from playing in front of the Fotoplayer to a new stage on the other side of the room. In addition to that he would also include a dance floor. I was all for this, of course, and I could give Jim Goodwin a job with the band too. I mentioned to Harvey about the possibility of bringing in Pete Pepke as a guest, like we did with Wild Bill. Harvey was all for it and said that he would get his carpenters to work on the stage immediately.

I alerted Pete Pepke about doing a week with me and the band at the Hoyt Hotel and he was excited to do it. He just had to get time off from his job at the bank in Warren. Jim Goodwin was happy as well, as he had not had full-time work for some time. So, besides Pepke, Goodwin and me, we had Norm Domreis on piano, Bob Pettengill, bass and John Picardi playing the drums. At the suggestion of Harvey Dick I added a vocalist as well, Gussie Hartney, a red-hot mama with a great voice. This had the makings of a great band.

On opening night, with guest Pete Pepke, we played to a full house and the customers loved the new bandstand and dance floor. We also had a great sound system and stage lighting. Pete Pepke's playing and stage personality came across to the audience and this was one of the many of his appearances with my band on the West Coast and other locations around the United States. Gussie Hartney, like many of the red-hot mamas, had a large gay following in Portland and that added to our already capacity crowds.

Portland was a fun town with a variety of music available. Besides my band at the Hoyt, there was also the hotel's Roaring 20's Showroom and a piano bar at the Old Ore House. There was the Golliwog Room at the Sheraton Hotel, Pat O'Neil's quartet at the Top of the Park, Andy's, Smitty's, the Frontier Room, the Piccadilly Room at the Benson Hotel, the Cosmo Dugout Lounge and many other places of entertainment scattered around Portland and its suburbs.

For our intermissions, Harvey had a new gal run the Fotoplayer. The sign on her piano said Foto Roller Jockey, but we all referred to her as Foto Roller Fanny. She was a piece of work but a very nice person. Honestly, I think I was jealous of her because I really enjoyed running the Fotoplayer.

There had been whispers amongst the employees of the Hoyt Hotel for some time about the drastic slowdown in business, especially in the Roaring 20's Showroom and the 24-hour restaurant. Flamboyant entertainer and hostess of the Roaring 20's, Gracie Hansen, had been there since the showroom opened in July, 1965. Monte Ballou and his Castle Jazz Band was the original music for the showroom, but as Gracie Hansen began putting on more elaborate Broadway type shows; Monte was replaced by Johnny Reitz and his big band. The shows were spectacular and drew capacity crowds nightly for a number of years. Gracie even put on special Sunday events, and bringing in the big bands was always a crowd pleaser.

They would also rent out the Roaring 20's Showroom on Sundays to various organizations in town that wanted to have a special private affair. One Sunday, while I was there, it was rented out to the gay community having a Halloween party. It was a wild party night with all the guys dressed in drag in hopes to be named "Queen of The Ball." I think that became an annual event until the Roaring 20's closed.

Gracie Hansen left the Hoyt Hotel in early 1971 and that perhaps was the demise of the Roaring 20's Showroom because Gracie had been there from the very beginning, and when you thought of the Hoyt Hotel and Harvey Dick, you also thought of Gracie Hansen.

To keep the Hoyt running required a payroll that was enormous. The hotel had 175 rooms to rent, but none of them had their own toilets and bath tubs; if you were lucky you had a wall sink in your room. If we had a surprise ice or snow storm while we were playing, we could always spend the night at the hotel - I did this twice. There were also around 100 employees to pay, such as bartenders, waitresses, hotel clerks, musicians and everyone else it took to run an operation of that size.

When I got to work at the Barbary Coast the night of July 15, 1972, a chill went up my spine when I got the word that the Roaring 20's Showroom had been closed. I guess I knew it was coming but I had put it out of my mind. Gracie Hansen undoubtedly had seen the handwriting on the wall and exited while she was ahead of the game. Now the big show in the hotel was my band, along with the Fotoplayer. This was all well and good except our little room couldn't support the whole hotel, and I knew it. The band was a good one, with all swinging musicians on top of their game. Gussie Hartney was a big favorite and belted out all the great red-hot mama songs. We had good crowds during the week and we were packed full on the weekends. The Fotoplayer was always fun for people to listen to on our intermissions and it looked like this was a party that would never end. But it did.

On August 2nd, 1972, just three weeks after the Roaring 20's closed I went to work, only to find out that the Barbary Coast Lounge was closing as well, along with the entire hotel. It was all over and I never saw so many sad faces and in my life. We all just looked at each other - dumbfounded. How could this be? Probably one of the most unique entertainment emporiums to be found anywhere in the world was no more.

Harvey Dick was interviewed by the press and he blamed the decline of railroad travel, the poor economy and a gas shortage for the Hoyt's business slowdown. But that was just part of it, as far as I was concerned. For one thing, I imagine he took a big financial hit after being caught up with by ASCAP (American Society of Composers, Authors and Publishers) for not paying royalties on all the music performances at the Roaring 20's Showroom. I never heard what it cost him but I can imagine it was a considerable amount of money. The hotel also did not accept credit cards or checks; it was a cash only operation. Credit cards were just catching on back then but there was no excuse for not accepting a check. On top of that, Harvey had some old fashioned ideas about a dress code. Men had to wear jackets, which was at that time, the norm anyway. But ladies apparel was changing and ladies pant suits were becoming quite popular. The hotel would not serve any lady not wearing a dress. Talk about turning people away! One night Pauline's mother came in wearing a pantsuit, I had warned her not to, but she did anyway. They turned her away at the door and told her that she could not come in wearing pants - so what did she do? She took her pants off and came in wearing her panties! Thank goodness she had on a long jacket! This seemed to be OK and she spent the rest of the night enjoying the music.

We packed up the bandstand taking our music, music stands and drums and loading them in our cars. I then invited all the employees of the Barbary Coast Lounge out to my house for a farewell party. We went behind the bar and all grabbed an assortment of our favorite liquors and taking one last look around, locked the doors behind us. The party at my house that night went until wee hours of the morning and we all shared stories of all those enjoyable nights in The Barbary Coast Lounge.

Café au Lait Four – Zircon Jim's, Portland. OT
Smith, Ed Fontaine, Jim, John Picardi

Hoyt Hotel, Portland. John Picardi, Hal
Hoyt, Jim, Norm Domreis, 1971

CHAPTER 20

# Hoyt Auction

IT WAS SUMMERTIME WHEN THE Hoyt Hotel closed, so we took advantage of a bad situation and took the boys to our place at Sakinaw Lake in Canada. It had been some time since I had had the chance to get away for a couple of weeks with the family and we had a great relaxing time.

Labor Day came along and it was time to come back to Portland, as school would soon be starting. When we got back I started getting all kinds of calls for work because the word had gotten out about the closing of the Hoyt Hotel and other club owners figured that my band was available for work. I had so many interesting offers for casual engagements that I decided to do that for a while instead of jumping right back into the nightclub scene.

I got a very interesting call from my old friend, Don Kennedy, telling me that Harvey Dick was selling off all his antiques from the Hoyt Hotel and he wanted Don to be the auctioneer. Don said that he no longer had the Muddy River Jazz Band because he wanted to concentrate entirely on his auction business. He owned the Portland Auto Auction along with his business partner, Roger Sheik. Don Kennedy, with his booming voice and personality, was also the auctioneer for many private auctions and charity events throughout the United States. Don said that he would like my band to play during the auction to keep things lively and also demonstrate the Foto-player when it came up on the auction block. Of course I said yes, so it looked like I wasn't done with the Hoyt Hotel after all.

The dates for the auction were November 16-19, 1972. It broke my heart to go back to the hotel and see all of Harvey's treasures being taken away to the Roaring 20s Showroom, where everyone could look them over before bidding on them. I just used my regular Barbary Coast rhythm section to play background music for the event, while customers were roaming around looking at paintings, statues, stained-glass windows, Tiffany shades and all the other hundreds of items up for auction. The auction attracted people from all over the United States and I even spotted Frank Baker in the crowd. He owned the nightclub in Vancouver where Lance Harrison played. I don't know what items he bought but I'm sure they are floating around Vancouver somewhere.

The auction advertisement read: "every antique, original oil paintings, art objects, antique furnishings and items of hotel equipment will be sold." Also to be auctioned off was one of the largest collections of Tiffany lamp shades in the world. Plus, the complete furnishings of the renowned Barbary Coast Room and the Roaring 20's Showroom. One of the big items to go was Harvey's train – The *Hooterville Express* from the *Petticoat Junction.*

Most of Harvey Dick's wonderful antique collection was auctioned off way below its true value. But that's what the auction advertisement said – "Everything sells to the highest bidder - no limits - no minimums." The majority of the antiques and the art were going for less than $1000. The big items like the Petticoat Junction train sold for $8000 and Harvey's 1936 Rolls-Royce went for a mere $4700. One of the large bars was auctioned at $7000 and the bar in the Roaring 20's showroom went for $10,000. A beautiful, baby grand Steinway piano bar sold for the giveaway price of $2000.

The one item up for sale that I was really interested in was the Fotoplayer piano. At auction time I came out and played it for all the interested bidders. Don Kennedy auctioned it off for just $8600. After all the entertainment the Fotoplayer gave the public all those years at the Barbary Coast Room, I played the "Maple Leaf Rag" on it, for the final tune.

I did get to say a final goodbye to the Fotoplayer. The gentleman bought it under the condition that it was shipped to him in Phoenix, Arizona. In order to do this it had to be completely taken apart, piece by piece. Don Kennedy asked me if I would like the job of disassembling the photo player, marking and numbering the parts and entering them in the ledger for reassemble, then fly to Phoenix and put it all back together again. Only a crazy person would offer to take this job on! Of course, I said yes. After the auction was over I returned to the hotel, got myself in back of the Fotoplayer with a set of tools, a pencil and ledger, and started disassembling. I had no idea what I was doing, but then I thought probably nobody else did either. After it was disassembled and shipped to Phoenix, I waited for a call to reassemble, but that never came. I have no idea what happened to it, but wherever it is, it's now worth over $400,000. I remember during the auction I thought that if I had the money it would be fun to buy the Fotoplayer and put it in our family room. Wouldn't that have been nice?

There is quite an interesting ending to the auction story. When I played Harvey Dick's Zircon Jim's Bar in the Labor Center, there was a working man's bar in the basement that was used mostly by union people before and after their meetings. Harvey had a collection of stuffed animals, and that is where he kept them and showed them off. Early in 1973 Harvey Dick decided to auction off this collection as well. Don Kennedy was the auctioneer, so I decided to go and see what it was all about. Kennedy was dressed in a safari outfit for the affair and he did a great job auctioning off lions, tigers and all kinds of wild animals. I bought a mounted coyote skin, head and all, and it hung in our family room for years, until it completely disintegrated. That was the last time I saw Harvey Dick, who passed away, at 72 years old, in 1977. He was one of a kind and I'm sure that I'll never work for another more interesting person again in my life. One of the most bizarre facts about Harvey Dick was that he wheeled around Portland constantly in his Cadillac and never had a driver's license.

We spent the Christmas season of 1972 in Vancouver with Pauline's family. It was always enjoyable to go up there as Vancouver is a great town to visit. I spent a few nights sitting in with Lance Harrison's band at the Attic. The nightclub was owned by Frank Baker, a well-known Vancouver business man, and it was a fun place to go to have a good time listening to Lance and his band. Frank Baker, like Harvey Dick, was a collector of sorts himself and had one of the James Bond 007 cars parked in the front lobby. Lance and I always loved getting together and playing the old traditional jazz tunes and the intermissions were often spent in his Cadillac drinking out of his big bottle of gin. I actually never cared for straight gin, but never complained.

We had to get back to Portland so I could play a big New Year's Eve party at the Portland Elks Club. It seemed nice, for a change, to get back to playing casual engagements again around the Portland area. I also took a few jobs out of town that required an overnight stay, but that didn't happen too often. The casual engagement situation didn't last all that long because in late summer I got a call from my vocalist from the Hoyt Hotel, Gussie Hartney. She told me that she had a friend that was opening a new nightclub in downtown Portland that she would be singing at, and that she had recommended me and my band for the music.

I made an appointment with the owner of the new nightclub and it didn't take him long to figure out that my band would be the best fit for his new restaurant. His name was Phil Talbert and was a local business-man, but had never been in the restaurant end of it. He assured me that he was hiring good people that were experts in their line of restaurant/nightclub work. He planned to call his new adventure, "The Godfathers Retreat," and take advantage of the *Godfather* movies that were so popular at the time. It was going to look like an old Chicago speakeasy from the 1920's, and this seemed like it was just perfect for me and the band.

Phil and I agreed on the price, shook hands and he planned to open at the end of the summer or early fall. I didn't realize it then but I was getting myself into one of the strangest situations of my musical career.

We opened at the Godfather's Retreat on September 18th, 1973. The club was located in the cellar of a building on 6th and Alder Street, right smack in the middle of downtown Portland. It was very similar to some of the old jazz clubs on 52nd Street in New York City. When you walked in the front door the first thing you saw was several pistols mounted behind a glass enclosure. You then walked down a flight of stairs and into a very plush 1920's modern day speakeasy.

I was very excited about the new lineup in the band. I was able to get Harold Koster on piano. Harold was in the Leroy Anderson big-band that played at the Hoyt Hotel's Roaring 20's Showroom and he often came in to listen to us play in the Barbary Coast Room on his intermissions. Harold was brilliant and I called him Professor Koster because he was absent-minded. He had wonderful credentials in the field of traditional jazz as he worked with both Jack Teagarden and Red Nichols and the Five Pennies.

I got George Baker on banjo and guitar and he was another musician that was highly regarded throughout the West Coast. George was a roly-poly guy, rather short and stocky. But he played the banjo like you wouldn't believe. He had one feature song called "Three Banjo's" and if you closed your eyes, you would swear that you were listening to three banjo players. He also did the popular banjo tune from "Deliverance," playing both banjo parts. George Baker had also spent a number of years playing with Turk Murphy's band in San Francisco and the Spike Jones band.

I had a new drummer, Chick Coburn, who was thought of as one of the top percussionists in Portland, and he also sang. The remaining members of the band were with me at the Hoyt Hotel and included Bob Pettengill playing base, Gussie Hartney, vocals, and myself on clarinet and soprano sax. This was a very versatile group and we not only played jazz but we also kept up with the latest pop tunes of the day.

Philip Talbert was the owner of the club and had another very good business in Portland. He was the president of Philip H. Talbert and Associates, Actuarial Consultants, and this was probably where he was able to come up with enough money to go into the nightclub business. He had a club manager and a girlfriend that were around most every night. Everyone was very nice to me, in fact I thought overly nice. For the first time ever, I was given signing privileges, which meant I could have food or drink anytime I wanted and all I had to do was sign for it, and along with that I could comp any of our customers as well. As I said, this was all very nice, but it just isn't done. You don't give free drinks and food to your bandleader, especially drinks! It was certainly a privilege that I didn't turn down. I also noticed the club manager was comping certain customer friends quite often. This was a practice that was certainly not good for the cash register, but then again it wasn't any of my business, and I told myself to concentrate on the music end of things. All in all this was a great job and business was booming.

Not too long after we opened at the club, Philip thought it might be a good idea for the band to record "The Theme from the Godfather" to capitalize on the *Godfather* movies that were so popular at the time and to promote the club. I thought that was a great idea as well, and brought the band into a studio one afternoon and we recorded "Theme from the Godfather" on one side and Duke Ellington's "C-Jam Blues" and the other. It was just a single 45 RPM vinyl disc that was very popular at the time. The band sounded great and on "Theme from the Godfather," George Baker starts the song playing mandolin and sounding very Italian. Those two recordings have gone from 45 RPM to cassette and finally transferred to CD.

Unfortunately, this whole Godfather thing got out of hand rapidly. The events that happened after this were bizarre and I honestly don't understand it all to this day. I did make the mistake of telling Philip and the club manager, over drinks one night, about the coincidence of me playing at the Godfather club after my times with Johnny DeVita back in New York. At any rate, one night before work the club manager called me aside in his office and gave me a loaded pistol and ammunition. He said Jim - Philip has some problems and we could very well have trouble in the club some night. He told me to have the pistol on the bandstand just in case gunplay erupted. I thought it very strange, but I took the pistol and put it in my clarinet case where it sat every night while we played, and fortunately never used, even though I kept my eye on the front door constantly. I also came to realize that the club manager really didn't know a damn thing about running a bar or restaurant business, but there again, that wasn't my concern and I told myself just to pay attention to the music.

The club advertised a special Sunday brunch featuring roast beef and Yorkshire pudding. Wow! I couldn't believe it because that's a hell of a dinner to pull off in a restaurant because the Yorkshire pudding has to be taken straight out of the oven and on to the plate to be served. I thought this chef must be one hell of a cook. Sunday was my day off so Pauline, the boys and I went for a roast beef and Yorkshire pudding treat. Well, when I got to the buffet table and to the Yorkshire pudding, I just about fainted. The Yorkshire pudding was not even close to being what it was supposed to be. It was more like a lemon cake that the chef cut up, put on your plate and poured gravy over. I was dumbfounded on how he had pulled the wool over Phillip's eyes to get the job. This was the worst excuse for a buffet I've ever seen. So now we had a Portland businessman owning a business that he knew nothing about, a club manager that didn't know what the hell he was doing and a chef that was a complete phony. All this and I'm running around with a pistol in my clarinet case. What's next?

Up to this point I had never tried any drugs other than marijuana. One of the guys in the band brought some cocaine to work with him one night and offered to turn us on during an intermission in a back room at the club. Well, wouldn't you know, I was the only one to take him up on the offer. So there I was, on an intermission, sniffing a white powder up my nose. It didn't take long for me to get the most wonderful feeling I ever had in my life and I went to the bandstand and played unbelievably well, or at least I thought I did. Wow - that was a great trip and I thought I might like to do it again until the next night I inquired about the price. Well, that did it for me. Using cocaine was a very expensive habit and fortunately that was the first and last time I used it. My God, I had a family to support and at least that time I had enough brains to make the right decision.

I got a call from Philip one morning asking me to do him a favor. He wanted me to drive his car to Battlefield, Washington, early that afternoon. I didn't know all the details but I did know the Philip had a new Lincoln Mark IV and I would love to drive it. I met him at his manager's girlfriend's apartment and got my instructions to drive through

Battleground and go past a house there several times - back and forth. He also said there was a slight possibility of trouble and I was to take a shotgun in the car with me. And with that the club manager came out with a loaded shotgun and before he could give it to me - BOOM! - The damn thing went off, blowing a hole in the ceiling into the apartment above us. Holy Crap! Not only does the club manager know nothing about the restaurant business, he's also a poor excuse for a gangster if he can't even handle a shotgun. Philip told me to forget the gun and gave me his car keys along with the address of the house in Battlefield that I was to cruise by. I drove to Battlefield and passed the house several times before being tailed by a police car and I immediately turned back out of town towards Interstate 5 until the Battlefield police car quit following me. I don't know what the whole thing was all about and I don't know what happened about the shotgun going through the ceiling of the apartment. All I knew is that I was safely back in Portland and gave Philip his car keys back. Other than all that, it was fun to drive that new Lincoln Mark IV.

We were still getting good crowds at the club and thanks to Gussie the gay community was a big part of our business. Portland has a large gay population (second only to San Francisco), and if you can tap into that business you're a winner, because the gay crowd are fun, like to party and spend lots of money.

One morning I got a call from the club manager telling me that Philip Talbert was in bad trouble because he shot and killed a man early that morning. He told me he was going to stop by my house and get the pistol that I had, and was I glad to get rid of it. He came by the house and picked up the pistol and filled me in on the shooting. Evidently Philip and his girlfriend went for breakfast at Denny's after we closed the bar that morning and got in a confrontation with a bartender that worked next door at the Ramada Inn. It was a stupid argument over dirty dishes on his table, but nevertheless it got ugly.

When Philip and his girlfriend left Denny's at 4a.m. the bartender followed them out into the parking lot and started a fight. Philip took out his gun and shot and killed him in self-defense. Philip was a very nice easy-going guy that would never look for trouble and it looked to me like everyone was at the wrong place at the wrong time. Philip was held at the Rocky Butte jail with no bail. I was happy to get rid of my gun but it dawned on me that my fingerprints were all over it and I should have wiped them off. Fortunately, I never heard any more about the pistol, but the Godfather Club was now in a big turmoil with Philip in the Rocky Butte jail.

Following a hearing in the Multnomah County Circuit Court, the judge ruled that the evidence was not strong enough to hold Philip without bail and he was released on his own recognizance and a trial was set for January 24, 1974. In the meantime, things were not going well at the nightclub because the shooting was all over the Portland papers and I suppose that people thought twice about coming to the Godfather's Retreat, in fear of more gunplay. Besides that, there was talk about the OLCC shutting the place down. Philip did hire a new manager in hopes of turning things around. His name was Burt Lee and was an old pro around Portland.

We spent Christmas in Vancouver again and we really had a fine time. On Christmas Eve Lance Harrison and his group played at the Attic, so we all went there and I sat in with Lance. We didn't get to bed until 4 a.m. and Jame and Bobby were up at 6 a.m. to open presents from Santa. Help! On Christmas Day, Pauline's dad took the whole family out for dinner (sixteen of us) and it was very enjoyable. A trio played and a good time was had by all.

After Christmas we went back home to Portland as I had to finish out the year at Godfather's Retreat and New Year's Eve.

There was an ad in the paper that said, *Jim Beatty - King of Swing: Gussie Hartney - Queen of Hearts: Burt Lee - King of Hosts.* Advertising usually does wonders, but our New Year's Eve crowd was still not good. And it didn't get any better after the first of the year. There was some good news, however. Philip Talbert's court trial came up and he was found not guilty for reasons of self-defense. But there was just too much bad publicity in the newspapers, radio and TV that the club was never able to overcome. Philip put the place up for sale and the music ended the first part of February, 1974. Godfather's Retreat had the potential to be a very successful nightclub had it been managed professionally. Even with all its shortcomings it probably had the best entertainment in the city of Portland at the time.

**Wild Bill and Jim in front of fotoplayer – Hoyt Hotel, Portland, OR**

Hoyt Hotel Auction Day, November '72

## CHAPTER 21

# Oregon City

Now THAT I WAS FREE from my nightclub work again I could start accepting some casual engagements. The first call I got was from a guitar/banjo player, Dick Monsey, who went by the nickname "Moon." He had a weekend job playing at a tavern in Oregon City called McAnulty and Barry, probably one of the most popular and oldest pubs in the area. The tavern was now operated by Dick Hing, who was the brother of Kenny Hing, who played tenor sax with the Count Basie Orchestra. So it was a musical family. Moon had been playing there as a trio with, of all people, my old piano player from the Hoyt Hotel, Norm Domreis, as well as Delane Guild. Moon asked me if I would like to join them and see how it went. It was a step down from the Hoyt Hotel and the Godfather Retreat, but what the heck, nothing ventured nothing gained.

The McAnulty and Barry Tavern was known in the community as just Barry's and was on Main Street in downtown Oregon City, just across the street from the Clackamas County Courthouse. When you walked in the tavern, immediately to your right, there was a very long, beautiful English walnut bar, with a beveled glass mirror. It came over to this country around the 1870s and somehow found its way to Oregon. The tavern had a small menu and was filled with tables and chairs. There was a long room and had at the far end three pool tables and a small bandstand in the corner. When the music started, a piece of plywood covered the pool tables and they were converted into nice-looking dinner tables. The tavern served a variety of good beers and wine.

Moon Monsey was short, stocky and very overweight, and had a full beard. At first sight he looked like a redneck, but you soon found out that he was a very gentle, friendly guy. His main instrument was the guitar and he doubled on banjo after taking lessons from my banjo player at the Godfather - George Baker. Moon had a very pleasant voice and a special talent for composing his own songs and lyrics.

I played the first weekend and it was good to be working with pianist Norm Domreis again. I was very impressed with the new drummer, Delane Guild, and thought it would be great to record with him. He was a tall young man who was married, but had a wandering eye for the girls. I agreed to continue on with this band at least for a few weeks, until I knew in which direction I was going in. I'm glad I did because it took me into some wonderful musical experiences that I would otherwise have missed.

I couldn't believe it! I went to work at Barry's and on my second week I found myself in another mess, this time no gunplay, but even worse, it was the government. It seems that Moon was an unemployed machinist by trade and was collecting unemployment insurance and working at Barry's and getting paid under the table. The State Unemployment Department considers this a serious issue and subpoenaed Moon for a court hearing, along with the rest of the band for our testimony. They also wanted to question the proprietor of Barry's, Dick Hing, for not filing the proper employment papers for the band members, who were considered employees. To top it all off, Norm Domreis had not filed his earnings from Barry's on his income tax form and was shaking in his boots in hopes that they would not find him out. All in all it was a big mess and I was right in the middle of it.

Moon never came back to Barry's after the controversy. I think Dick Hing paid a small fine and the federal government never did find out about Norm Domreis' failure to declare his wages at Barry's. Dick Hing came to me and asked me to take over the band. I agreed, providing that I would handle the government tax requirements and have a free reign with the music, which included bringing in special guests now and then and adding one other musician to the band. He was fine with all of that and I got to work immediately making my changes.

First of all, I had received a call from a very well-known cornetist that had moved to the Portland area to get away from the hustle bustle of Los Angeles. His name was Ruben "Danny" Alguire and he was a veteran of the Bob Wills and His Texas Playboy's, a very famous Texas swing band of the time. He also played with T. Texas Tyler's Western Band and later the Firehouse Five +2, a group made up of employees from Walt Disney Studios. Danny went to work for the Disney studios as assistant director for animation in 1955. He worked on such great Disney movies as, the *Aristocats, Lady and the Tramp, Sleeping Beauty, The Jungle Book, Robin Hood* and a good deal of the Winnie the Pooh features. I invited Danny over to my house and I could see immediately that he would be a great asset to the band and hired him. I did notice that Danny loved his cigarettes and had a heavy appetite for the hard stuff. But what else is new?

I needed a banjo player to replace Moon, and luckily a good banjo man had just moved into Portland who was also from Los Angeles. His name was Dave Wierbach. He had some nice credentials and had worked with Turk Murphy at one time. He also had owned a small jazz club in Los Angeles called the 23 Skidoo. He called me for work and I invited him over to the house for an interview. I thought him to be sort of an odd duck, but harmless, and I hired him. He smoked cigarettes and drank beer like it was going out of style - but again - what else is new?

Pauline and I wanted to make a trip to Vancouver before the boys returned to school after their summer vacation. I had a few days where I could get away, so we all hopped in the car and headed north. The boys always enjoyed getting away for a visit with grandma and grandpa because they were spoiled so much and got most anything they asked for. The trip to Vancouver in those days was an easy one, you could figure on a 4 ½ to 5 hour drive, easily. Nowadays with the increase in traffic it's not what you'd call a pleasant drive, especially going through the Tacoma and Seattle area.

I wanted to catch up with Lance Harrison and his band at the Attic. Pauline didn't come along because she and the boys were doing family things. It was great getting together with Lance and his band and we had a ball playing a bunch of good jazz tunes. Lance told me that the Mills Brothers were performing at the Cave, in downtown Vancouver, and that after we were through playing we could catch part of their last show for the evening. I was excited about this because I hadn't seen the Mills Brothers since I worked the convention show with them at the Emerald Beach Hotel in Nassau.

The Mills Brothers were about the smoothest entertainers I had ever seen. They had started out as a quartet but now they performed as a trio with Harry, Herbert, Donald, and a guitar player. They were the first African American group to perform before the British Royalty in 1934. They made several hit recordings, the biggest being "Paper Doll" that took them fifteen minutes to record and sold 6 million copies. In later years their hits were "Glow Worm" and "Cab Driver." In 1976 they celebrated their 50th year in show business and Harry, nearly blind from diabetes, died in 1982.

Lance and I went back stage and watched their last few numbers of the show. He was an old friend of theirs and they remembered me. We waited until they changed out of their tuxes, then went to an after-hours speakeasy-type bar that Lance knew about. It was illegal as hell, but business was booming and the booze was flowing, along with a little trio playing in the background. We must've stuck out like a sore thumb, with Lance being 6 foot five inches, four black guys, and me starting to grow my hair long with a beard for the upcoming United States Bicentennial. The six of us got our drinks and relaxed at a table talking about music and old times. Harry remembered me getting him some marijuana when he was in Nassau. A lot of things had happened to all of us since those days.

We were having a great time and then it happened just like in the movies, somebody shouted – IT'S A RAID! The Vancouver police stormed in the front entrance so quickly that it took everyone by surprise. Lance Harrison yelled at me and the Mills Brothers – Follow me! Fortunately Lance was a regular at this after-hours club and knew of a back way out. Because of his height, Lance was easy to follow through the crowd of frightened customers and we found ourselves running through the door and into a dark alley. It was so dark that I had a hard time seeing the Mills Brothers. We knew it wouldn't take long for the police to find the back door, so one at a time we reemerged on the main street and made our way to Lance Harrison's car to regroup. All our hearts were pounding so fast that we had to take a few sips from Lance Harrison's gin bottle to calm down. I thought for sure that I was going to jail that night, but thanks to Harrison's quick thinking we all made it through to tell the tale.

After all that happened, the six of us decided that we were hungry. Harry Mills knew of a great Chili House that he had gone to on a previous Vancouver engagement. That sounded great to the rest of us, and off we went. Before going into the restaurant Harry told Lance to bring the bottle of gin with him. When our chili was served Harry told us that you can make a good chili better by mixing gin in with it. And that we did! I must say, at least that night, it tasted fantastic.

I didn't get back to the house until around 5 a.m. and probably wasn't too popular the next day, but when I told the family about my adventure the night before, all was forgiven. After a few days our visit was over. Jame and Bob had to get ready for the fall season of school and I was starting a new Sunday job at the Greenwood Inn, a plush restaurant/lounge in Beaverton, Oregon. On top of that, my old friend Don Kennedy wanted to talk to me about the possibility of putting on a jazz concert at Civic Auditorium in downtown Portland. Don always had big ideas but this was his biggest yet because Civic Auditorium seated around 3000 people.

So it looked like I had a full plate of work to finish off the year with the Civic Auditorium project, Sundays at the Greenwood Inn, Barry's and the pet project I was working on, a new album called A Musical Salute to the Bicentennial. On top of that I had been contacted by Young Audiences, a national organization that put on educational programs about the arts in schools. I would have to come up with a jazz program that was educational and musically entertaining. This was something we would have to audition for and paid very well. The downside of this, of course, was that I would have to get up early in the morning after playing late at night, to do the school concerts. But I thought it was doable.

To go along with the bicentennial celebration, I let my hair grow and grew a mustache and beard. Looking back at the photos of me, I look pretty far out, but right in with the 1970s fashions. It was fun and I felt like I was being a part of something happening in the culture.

Don Kennedy had talked to the manager of Civic Auditorium (now Keller Auditorium) about the possibility of putting on a jazz concert there. The rent was very expensive, plus there would be a huge advertising budget on top of hiring a name jazz band for the event, along with local groups. Don would take care of promotion, his partner, Roger Sheik would take care of the bookkeeping, I would handle the music end of it, and we would split the profits three ways. Don and I looked at each other and said – "Let's Do It!

Walt Disney's musical director, George Bruns, was originally from the Portland area and had retired from Disney, moving back to his hometown in Sandy, Oregon. I knew George from when he came in to hear us play at the Flame Supper Club. Besides being an arranger and conductor, George played the trombone, string bass and tuba. He let it be known to me that he'd love to work in my band if ever the occasion arose, and I planned to make that happen.

George was born in Sandy in 1914 and went to Oregon State University. He played in different bands in the Portland area, including Monte Ballou's Castle Jazz Band. He moved to California in the late 40s, working with Turk Murphy, before going to Disney Studios and ending up as Walt Disney's musical director.

His big hit for Walt Disney was the song "The Ballad of Davy Crockett," which George told me he composed in about fifteen minutes. He was ready to leave his office for a vacation when Walt Disney stopped by and asked him to write a song about Davy Crockett and George was in a hurry! Bruns wrote the film scores for many of Walt Disney's movies, including *Sleeping Beauty, One Thousand and One Dalmatians, The Absent Minded Professor, Jungle Book, Love Bug* and *Robin Hood*. He was also nominated for four Academy Awards. He also produced and directed the famous *Country Bear Jamboree* animatronic musical attraction at the Disneyland resort.

George built a beautiful home in Sandy and Pauline, the boys, and I were frequent guests. I played several years with him at the annual Sandy

Jazz Festival and George worked with me on many of my jobs when I needed a trombone player. George even had a movie studio in his house so he could work on the occasional movie for Walt Disney.

Sadly, George's health deteriorated badly and of course his heavy drinking didn't help. It got so bad that at one of my Christmas parties during a jam session he lost control of his bladder while he was sitting on our couch. I felt so embarrassed for him. He passed away at a very young age in 1983 from a heart attack and his wife, Dottie, died shortly after with cancer.

Another Portland musician that went on to fame in California was Don Kinch. Don had also played around the Portland area with local bands, including Monte Ballou's Castle Jazz Band. He then went on to play with Turk Murphy in California along with George Bruns on tuba. Following in George Bruns' footsteps, he got a job at Disney Studios and went on to play with the Firehouse Five +2. Kinch had come back to Portland and opened his own string instrument repair shop and formed his own group, the Conductors Ragtime Band. Later on I took advantage of his musicianship and had him play on a number of my recordings, playing string bass and trumpet.

Things were rolling along well at Barry's Tavern and the crowds were still standing room only. But I thought we should try and keep things fresh by bringing in a guest musician now and then. I talked to Dick Hing about it and he agreed. To cover the extra expense of bringing in guest artists we charged a modest cover at the door and people were happy to pay it.

Our first guest was New Orleans clarinetist Joe Darensbourg. He was semiretired at the time, being choosy about where and who he worked with. Joe was a small, good-looking, light-skinned Creole from Baton Rouge, Louisiana and he had lots of musical credentials. He was born in 1906 and in the early days played with Jelly Roll Morton. He even got involved playing with Circus bands when he was younger. During his touring days he fell in love with Seattle, settled and bought a house there, playing music around the area for sixteen years.

He then moved to Los Angeles joining the Kid Ory Jazz Band before forming his own group and recording the "Yellowdog Blues." It became a hit and sold one million copies, which was very unusual for a jazz record. He was known for playing "slap tongue" clarinet, which is an art in itself that very few musicians can do, including me. He went on to work with Louis Armstrong and the All Stars, touring with him for three years. During that time he recorded "Hello Dolly" with Armstrong and it became one of Armstrong's biggest hits and most requested songs.

I felt very fortunate to be able to work with Darensbourg and get to know him via long, late-night chats before he fully retired. He was a soft-spoken, easy-going guy that never let his success go to his head. We had a wonderful time playing with Joe and the crowd loved him. I can't remember how many requests he had for "Yellowdog Blues," but he happily played them all.

I also thought it was time to bring Pete Pepke back to play with the band. People had often asked me about Pete, after hearing him play with me at the Hoyt Hotel. He was still back in Pennsylvania working at the bank and playing music at night. Pete had worked his way up in the banking business and was doing very well. He jumped at the chance when I called him to come play at Barry's. Business was so good at Barry's Tavern that I was able to add a bass man by the name of Dave Gentry, a tall, lanky guy with a big smile on his face. He fit in with the band perfectly because he drank like a fish!

Having Pepke back and playing with me again was like a breath of fresh air. We knew what each other was going to do before we did it. We always considered Pete a member of the family and Jame and Bob always looked forward to his visits. Pete was still single at that time and more often than not at the end of the nights playing, he would run off with one of the girls in the crowd and wouldn't get back to our house until the wee hours of the morning, making Pauline none too happy. There are many Pete Pepke episodes to tell.

We had a wild New Year's Eve party at Barry's. The band was hot and we were especially enjoying our new bass player. The New Year was looking unbelievably busy. Don Kennedy and I were working on the jazz concert at civic auditorium and decided that the featured band would be Turk Murphy, if we could get him. So Don and I flew to San Francisco and spent the night listening to Turk and his band. I had brought my clarinet with me and sat in for a few tunes. I talked with Turk about coming to Portland for the concert, we settled on his fee for the band, and I agreed to pay for their air fare and accommodations in Portland. I also hired Don Kinch and the Conductors, and as an added attraction, appearances by Monte Ballou and Gussie Hartney. We had one hell of lot of musicians to pay, not to mention the rent on the civic auditorium. This better work or I'm going to have to skip town.

The Portland Symphony contacted me and wanted my band to do a jazz show with the Symphony. This is something that would require a lot of musical thought, but I was looking forward to it for the New Year. I also scheduled an audition with Young Audiences, playing in the schools for the next year. On top of all that, the Sacramento Jazz Festival called and wanted to book me for their big show in 1976. All this, plus the casual engagements that I had booked, was overwhelming. In seven short years I had the most popular band, not only in Portland, but in the Pacific

Northwest. Life was good, but when do I sleep? Last but not least, I scheduled a recording session the very first part of the year for my Bicentennial album – *The Battle Hymn of The Republic.*

One night on an intermission at Barry's Tavern I was approached by a group of fans asking me my thoughts about starting a jazz club in Oregon City. I told them that I thought that it was a good idea and I would be glad to help in the formation of the new club in any way I could. I agreed to be the music consultant to start with, and we had our first meeting at Bill and Corrine Bertrand's home, with my band kicking things off. There was no money in the treasury so the band and I donated our services for the first meeting. Dick Hing was elected president, Betty Zuiches, vice president, Corinne Bertrand, secretary and Jo Simms, treasurer.

This was the start of a jazz club that has lasted for nearly 40 years and still going strong, with a membership of 175 fans. We had a few more meetings at Betty and Bill Zuiches' home in Estacada and from there, with membership growing, we started meeting at the VFW Club in Oregon City. This was good because we now had food service and a bar for anyone wanting a cocktail. From the VFW we moved to the downtown Oregon City Elks Club and from there to the Milwaukie Elks Club, where we have our meetings to this day.

Traditional jazz was catching fire up and down the West Coast, with clubs springing up in Eugene, Salem and Oregon City. The Eugene Society had over 600 members. A jazz club also sprung up in Seattle and Vancouver, BC. All this plus the Sacramento Jazz Festival just exploded with traditional jazz. There was a new interest in all the early jazz greats such as King Oliver, Louis Armstrong, Sidney Bechet and Jelly Roll Morton - and I was right on top of it.

Most of the bands that sprung up in the 70s were of the West Coast traditional jazz style and they followed the pattern of Turk Murphy's band, with banjo and tuba. This style of traditional jazz can be very exciting but after listening for a while I found it repetitious and predictable. More than anything, I think the tuba drove me crazy after a while and it was anything but delicate. The standup bass was the answer for me and I got a lot of criticism from traditional fans for using it. It wasn't that I was getting modern or anything like that, because that's what I grew up listening to on the East Coast. Wild Bill, Bechet and those idols of mine all used the standup bass. At any rate I stood my ground and won out in the end.

The Oregon City Traditional Jazz Society (now the Portland Dixieland Jazz Society) was off to a good start and over the years brought in many great jazz artists and jazz bands. I became much too busy to stay involved with the club, but I was happy that I helped to get it started and off in the right direction. I still play a Christmas Show for them every year and as I look over the crowd many fans have grown older along with me.

The day of our big jazz concert at Civic Auditorium arrived, with advanced ticket sales and reservations at the door looking good. We had done plenty of advertising in the newspaper and on radio, along with posters and flyers scattered around the Portland area. The Eugene Jazz Society had their meeting that afternoon with guest artist, soprano saxophonist, George Probert. Their show broke up at five in the afternoon and there was a large group of them coming up to Portland for our show, along with George Probert and the band. So we wouldn't know how big a house we would have until curtain call and all the last minute ticket buyers were accounted for. The lights dimmed, curtains opened, and it was show time, beginning with my band with Gussie Hartney on vocals. We were followed by Don Kinch and the Conductors, Monte Ballou, and then the featured band from San Francisco, Turk Murphy. The show was terrific and everybody loved it. Guess what? It was a full house! After all was said and done and all the bills were paid we made a profit of $3000. That was $1000 apiece for Don Kennedy, Roger Sheik and me. That was a lot of money in those days and needless to say, I was very happy.

Don Kennedy used his $1000 and hosted a big after-show party for all the entertainers at a banquet room in a nearby hotel. Don had deep pockets and could do things like that. After that party broke up I invited a bunch of musicians out to my house for more drinks and food. George Probert came out to the house because he didn't book himself into a hotel for the night, which didn't matter because we partied all night anyway and his airplane left at 6:30 a.m. We had a big jam session in our family room that night along with a feature of four of us playing our soprano saxophones! God it must have been awful and I'm glad it wasn't recorded. Anyway, a good time was had by all and poor Pauline ended up driving George Probert to the airport in the early a.m. My mother was visiting us at this time and she kept up with all of us. Jame and Bob were so accustomed to these kind of affairs that they slept through the whole crazy party, jam session and all.

Our next appearance at Civic Auditorium was with the Portland Symphony, under the direction of Norman Leyden. Norman was an excellent, well respected, musician who on top of arranging and conducting played the clarinet. During World War II he was an arranger for the Glenn Miller Orchestra. The show was a big deal for me and the band, and it took a lot of time for me to put it together along with Norman Leyden. We had two shows to do, one on Sunday evening and a repeat performance on Monday evening. We had an afternoon rehearsal with the Symphony on Sunday. After the rehearsal we all went home and relaxed before the show. Danny Alguire was to stop by my house and ride to the auditorium with Pauline, the boys and me. When he arrived at the house he was absolutely falling down drunk! I couldn't believe it! How could he do this to me and the band...especially for a big event like this? I got him down to Civic Auditorium and into a dressing room, out of sight of Norman Leyden and the Symphony players. I was beside myself trying to figure out how to pull this all off with a drunken cornet player.

We arrived for the show plenty early and did have some time to try and get Danny straightened around. I started with giving him a few cups of coffee, but of course all he was then was a wide-awake drunk! The rest of the band started to arrive one by one and were horrified when they saw the condition Danny was in. I had hired George Bruns to play trombone for this concert and he had a fit when he took a look at Danny. George, of course, worked with Danny at Disney Studios and played with him with the Firehouse Five +2, so they were old friends and I think George had gone through something like this with Danny before. George called Danny every name in the book and just raised hell with him.

Curtain call came and it was do-or-die. Fortunately, some of the alcohol had time to wear off a little bit. Danny was able to play his part for the show but the stage was crowded with Symphony musicians so we had to stand right in front of the orchestra pit. I was just horrified thinking that Danny might fall into the pit! If he did I planned to jump in right behind him, never to be seen again. We got through the concert, although it seemed like an eternity. Danny knew that he was not only in trouble with me, but the whole band. He disappointed us all. We got through the concert without anyone knowing our handicap, but this was not going to happen again for our appearance on Monday night.

For Monday night's show, Danny showed up at my house very sober and ashamed. I felt sorry for him and I did give him a drink to calm his nerves. We also had a few drinks in our dressing room before the show and on intermission. The show went well and everybody was happy. It was a ball playing jazz with a beautiful symphony behind me, something I'll never forget it. After the show we all went back to our house for a band party. Jame and Bob were able to sleep through this one as well but no matter how long the parties lasted into the a.m. Pauline had to get up and give the boys their breakfast and send them off on the school bus. A woman's work is never done.

I got a notice in the mail from Young Audiences to report for my audition, along with my band, at the Musicians Union Hall, followed by a luncheon. If we were selected we would be performing school concerts, so I put together a program of the history of early jazz that started with Ragtime, went into the New Orleans jazz era, and finally swing. It had to be understandable for young people, along with being entertaining enough to keep their attention. For instance, my banjo man Dave Wierbach, doubled on the huge baritone saxophone. I brought out my tiny curved soprano saxophone telling the kids that Dave's sax had a baby and the children loved it. We also had a question and answer period and talked about some of the jazz greats.

I was understandably nervous about the audition because the judges consisted of top notch musicians from Los Angeles and New York City. One of them was violin great, Yehudi Menuhin. I had concentrated on early jazz all my life and knew little about classical music or its superstars.

Yehudi Menuhin was born in the United States in 1916. He started playing violin at four years old and by the age of seven he was a soloist with the San Francisco Symphony. And now he was regarded as one of the greatest violinist of the 20th century. During World War II he performed over 500

concerts for the Allied troops. And after the war he brought his music into the concentration camps.

He became very involved with young musicians and would organize concerts for them to play in prisons and in hospitals. He lived and breathed music and saw it as a way of making peace in the world. Yehudi, by the way, means Jew in Hebrew.

He also got involved playing jazz with another superb violinist, Stephan Grappelli. After all was said and done he held the record for the longest recording career in the history of music, almost 70 years. In 1965 he was knighted but it didn't go into effect officially until 1985, when he became a British citizen. In 1987 he received the Order of Merit and in 1993 he was made a life peer. After a long and illustrious career he passed away in Berlin, Germany in March 1999.

After our audition we waited in another room while they were making their decision, and after a short while we were congratulated for being part of the Young Audience program. I was thrilled and looked forward for this new daytime life I had ahead of me. We all went to lunch, and for some reason or another, Yehudi Menuhin took a liking to me and insisted that we sit next to each other. I was just scared to death that he was going to start talking to me about classical music, of which I knew very little. But to my surprise he couldn't stop complimenting me about the way I dressed. I was wearing a very 70ish outfit, a plaid green sport coat with a vest and tan pants, along with a shiny pair of black shoes. Other than my dress we chatted about my music, my life and my family. Here I am having lunch with a musical genius of the violin and we're talking about me. He was probably the most soft spoken, kindest and gentle person I have ever met in my life.

Looking back at the luncheon I had with Yehudi Menuhin, I would like to go back in time and do it all over again, because now I would have steered the conversation into something more interesting than my plaid green sport coat. I really feel fortunate to have had the opportunity to spend time with that wonderful man as he made me feel warm all over and he must have been very close to God.

I spent the next several years performing in schools for young audiences, in fact over 400 of them all over the state of Oregon and Washington. In later years Young Audiences extended their concerts to nursing homes as well. These concerts I found very depressing because of the conditions of some of the homes we went into. It was a great experience playing for Young Audiences and something I'm happy that came my way.

I've met two musical geniuses in my life, Jazzman Sidney Bechet and classical violinist Yehudi Menuhin. They both were the same, kind, gentle and gave me lots of encouragement. I found this true through the years. The greater they are the more humble they are, because I don't think when you do reach the top, you really never know it.

Things were still rolling along great at Barry's and I felt that it was time to record a new album. I used the regular bunch of guys and added Don Kinch to play standup bass and double on trumpet. I also planned to have Dave Wierbach play his banjo and double on bass saxophone. For this recording I used the Tri-Ad Recording Studio in Eugene because I heard good things about them.

We recorded "The Battle Hymn of The Republic," "Buddy Bolden Blues," "Black and White Rag" (featuring Domreis on piano, "Temptation

Rag," "Banjorama," "When You and I Where Young Maggie Blues," "Little Orphan Annie," "LOUISIANA," "Weary Blues," "Dr. Jazz," and "Canal Street Blues."

I named the new album *The Battle Hymn of the Republic*, to go along with all the promotional activities for the big year of 1976. The tune "Battle Hymn of The Republic" fit right in with the celebration and it was a big requested number to play around that time. Of all the requests my band got, undoubtedly the number one favorite was Danny Alguire's rendition of "Little Orphan Annie." Danny's vocal recalls those nostalgic days in the late 30's and early 40's of gathering around the radio after school for some real adventures with Annie and her dog, Sandy. Dave Wierbach and I collaborated on a vocal for "When You and I Where Young Maggie Blues" and it became one of my favorites on the album. "LOUISIANA" was written by our recent, featured guest at Barry's, Joe Darensbourg. Joe gave me a copy of the music and I decided to record it featuring Dave Wierbach on vocal.

When this album was released it sold like hotcakes. I don't think people were disappointed in it because listening to it now after all these years, it still sounds like we were having plenty of fun. I enjoyed the Bicentennial and all its activities, including letting my hair grow along with a mustache and beard. All this along with the 1970s clothing style, and I guess I looked pretty far out. It's as close to being a hippie as I ever got.

As far as the recording goes it was a miracle that I could keep this gang sober enough to get through it, but we made it. We had the Sacramento Jazz Festival coming up and I asked Pete Pepke to play with us. That sounded like the makings of another album.

Memorial Day weekend of 1976 was my band's first appearance at the Old Sacramento Dixieland Jubilee. This festival started out in 1974 and took off like a rocket, attracting jazz stars and fans from all over the United States and Canada. In later years it brought in musicians from all over the world.

For our first engagement there I brought in Pepke. He played a perfect New Orleans style trombone and we had many vocals that featured him. Along with Pete we had the regular Barry's band – Norm Domreis, Danny Alguire, Dave Wierbach, Delane Guild and me. The motel rooms were paid for by the jazz society and we stayed at a place called the Pony Express.

The Jubilee was very well organized and when I got there I picked up an envelope at Jubilee headquarters. The envelope contained our admission badges, programs, drink tickets for the band and any last minute directions or changes in our schedule. Each band performance was limited to 30 minutes and we had five minutes to set up and five minutes to tear down and leave the stage for the next band. It was an audience-oriented, fast-paced show and you had to keep on your scheduled time. The shuttle buses were on a 10 minute schedule from almost any point and any time, so it was easy to get from job to job. Each stage had a drum set and all our drummer had to bring were his cymbals and sticks. I was given 500 drink tickets for the band but I didn't give them to the guys all at once because I knew them too well! I gave them a few at a time to spread their drinking out as much as I could.

It was a fun, but tiring Memorial Day weekend, because it wasn't unusual to be playing our first concert for the day at noon and the last concert at midnight. But the band got through it with no major catastrophes and we went over very well and were asked to come back the next year. We were paid so much for each set we played and of course the more we played the more money we made. After all was said and done the Jubilee figured out their profits and gave a certain percent of it to each of the participating bands as a bonus, which was a great thing to do.

I was very pleased to run into my old original drummer in Portland, John Picardi. He had moved to Sacramento and opened a porno store that had several little movie booths you could go into, drop a quarter into a slot and watch a very interesting movie. I dropped by to see his new business one afternoon and could see where it would be a very intriguing place to hang out, but unfortunately I had to get back to work. He was doing very well with his new business but still liked to play occasional music jobs. He was playing with a Sacramento group and sounding great on the drums. John told me that although he was doing well in Sacramento, he missed Portland very much. We said goodbye to Sacramento and the Dixieland Jubilee, looking forward to next year when I had ideas of enlarging the band somewhat and also bringing Pauline, Jame and Bob with me.

While I was at the Sacramento Dixieland Jubilee a tall, lanky Texan came over to me and introduced himself as Sam Johnson. He told me that he was the manager of the Max Collie Rhythm Aces, a British jazz band. Sam explained to me that he was on a vacation in London, England and heard them playing at a club called The Trafalgar and was so taken by their talent that he offered them a tour in the United States.

It turns out that Sam Johnson was President Lyndon Johnson's nephew. Sam's father, the president's brother, Sam Houston Johnson, was an alcoholic and embarrassment to the president and was kept a virtual prisoner in the White House. They kept him tucked away in some rooms that were well stocked with alcohol to keep him happy. During Lyndon Johnson's presidency, Sam Johnson Jr. spent a lot of time at the White House with his father.

With Sam's Washington connections, he was able to get the band the proper papers to tour the United States. I had heard a few things about Max Collie's Rhythm Aces and it was all good. I understood that they played very traditional New Orleans jazz along the lines of George Lewis, which sounded fine to me. Sam told me that he had the band booked in Eastern Oregon and wanted to know if I would be interested in bringing them into the Portland area. We agreed to talk it over that night after I was through playing in the early a.m. Sam suggested we go to his motel room and talk and that he had plenty to drink there.

He was waiting for me when I finished my early morning concert and we went over to his motel room. His room had two single beds with a little table between them. He sat on one bed and I sat on the other bed facing him, with a bottle of whiskey and a couple of glasses on the table and several packs of cigarettes. We talked and talked about his life in the White House and his interest in New Orleans jazz. I found him very interesting with his broad Texas accent and enthusiasm for promoting his band. So I agreed to get to work on booking the Max Collie band in the Portland area. I had a number of months to do it and knew it wouldn't be a problem.

To my surprise it started to get light out and I had a noon performance to play. So I excused myself and Sam showed me to the door. Well, when I opened the door, the motel manager was standing outside and he looked at Sam and said "Ah Ha," you are only paying for one person and sneaking an extra guy in the room for free! We told him to take a look at the beds and he would see that they hadn't been slept in, but he just said that we probably made them up ourselves. And then he told us that he was going to the office and call the police. I looked at Sam and said - What are we going to do? Sam looked back at me and said - Run!

So now I am running through the streets of Sacramento with President Lyndon Johnson's nephew, eluding the Sacramento Police

Department. How do I get in these situations? I'll never know. That's all I needed, my first year playing Sacramento's Dixieland Jubilee and I end up being arrested. We ducked into a restaurant and sat down and ordered breakfast, watching police cars driving back and forth. After the coast was clear I went and played my first concert of the day and I guess Sam somehow fixed things at the motel because I saw him later in the day and he said everything was cool.

I was happy that I made those arrangements with Sam Johnson because I became very good friends with Max Collie and his band and it started a friendship and musical association that was to last over 30 years. In fact, Max and that particular group of sidemen he had, generated more excitement than any other band I had heard at the Jubilee.

On top of all this work I did find family time. Following the Sacramento Jazz Festival, Pauline, the boys and I took the month of June and headed east for a vacation. We visited Philadelphia, New York City, and Washington, DC, finishing up at a vacation rental on Chautauqua Lake with my mother and Pop. Pete Pepke booked a few jobs for me while I was there and we visited him at his home in Warren. Pete had a huge backyard with a small river running through it. Jame and Bob spotted a mother Muscovy duck with several little ducklings and asked if they could bring the baby ducks home with them. We couldn't turn them down and drove coast-to-coast with these baby Muscovy ducks, sneaking them into our motel bathtubs on the way home. These ducks grew up and provided us with eggs for years to come.

Lance Harrison and Jim – The Attic, Vancouver, BC

Barry's Tavern, Oregon City, Delaine Guild, Danny
Alguire, Dave Weirbach, Norm Domreis, Jim

CHAPTER 22

# Busy Times

ALL HELL WAS BREAKING LOOSE with requests for the band's appearance. In addition to playing at Barry's, we now had Young Audiences to take care of, and that meant playing night and day. On top of that we found ourselves playing Sunday sessions for the Eugene, Salem, and Oregon City jazz societies, plus the jazz clubs in Washington, including Olympia and Seattle along with crossing the border and playing for the Vancouver Jazz Club. We also played one nighters at various jazz nightclubs in the Portland area. It got to the point where we had to leave Barry's Tavern because taverns didn't pay that much money and I was just turning down to many good paying jobs, and that wasn't fair to the guys in the band. We left Barry's on good terms with the agreement that we would come back and play now and then when our schedule permitted.

The time rolled around for my visit from the Max Collie band. Sam Johnson and I decided that we would do a battle of the bands between my group and the Collie band. I booked the event for two nights at a very nice nightclub called the Cinnamon Tree, just outside of Portland.

Sam Johnson called me and asked directions to my house in Lake Oswego. They had just finished playing their tour in Eastern Oregon and were on their way to my place. They pulled into my driveway in a huge motor home with a bewildered driver behind the wheel. They had picked up a hitchhiker and somehow talked him into being their chauffeur for the rest of the tour. I went out to greet them and never saw such a bunch of characters come off a bus in my life. They all looked like they just came from skid row and I had no idea that they would actually be playing in the same outfits, but they did. One by one they introduced themselves - Max Collie - trombone, Phil Mason – cornet, Jack Gilbert –clarinet, Trevor "Fingers" Williams – bass, Gentleman Jim McIntosh – banjo, and Ron McKay - drums and vocals. Although their motor home was quite large, it certainly wasn't big enough for all of them to live in, so we divided them between the motor home and our house.

What a great bunch of guys they were, and super characters as well. They were great musicians in the New Orleans tradition and I could see where we were going to have one hell of a time. Jame and Bob were excited to have these crazy guys from England living with us and it didn't take them long to have a ballgame going out on the front yard. And on top of all the craziness going on, who shows up but Jim Goodwin. He was just back from a tour of Holland and knew the entire Max Collie group from when he played in England.

We played our two nights at the Cinnamon Tree to packed houses, with both bands playing, and on the last set we all joined together for a giant jam session, which brought which brought raucous calls for encores. Jack and I brought the house down by trading solos on the last tune for over ten minutes! Max Collie and the gang stuck around a few days after our job and we partied with them day and night. One night I went to bed and found Ron McKay mistakenly in my bed with Pauline. I woke him, pointed him in the right direction and Pauline slept through the whole thing. After they left and the dust settled, we found empty beer caps and bottles all over the house for weeks, a reminder of a great time. Fortunately, a few years later I was to reunite with these guys, but this time in England.

If enough wasn't going on, I had Wild Bill Davison coming in for a couple of concerts. The two of us played in Coos Bay, Oregon and then on the way home we played for the Eugene Jazz Society. It was just a short trip this time and we made plans to do more in the next couple of years.

While Max Collie and the Rhythm Aces were with me Sam Johnson explained to me his idea for the World Championship of Jazz. It was to be held in Indianapolis and was to feature bands from all over the United States. At the end of the event one of the bands would win the world championship, decided by a combination of judges and audience voting. Although the idea seemed novel to me, I really didn't like the idea of it because I never thought of jazz as a contest. I felt that Sam was feeling me out to play the event but gave up when he realized that I didn't seem very interested. I bumped into Turk Murphy at the Sacramento Festival and he was planning on playing The World Championship, but pulled his band out after I told him that it was a competition. Wild Bill Davison was even flying in from Copenhagen, Denmark for the event.

Personally, I thought that Sam Johnson was pushing the envelope too far by putting on this type of jazz show. He was a promoter, yes, but he should have stuck to his management duties and keeping the Max Collie band busy. I got to know all of Collie's sidemen when they stayed at our house and they were all wonderful guys that had fun on and off the bandstand. Max himself looked like an aborigine or someone you wouldn't want to jump out at you from behind a tree in the middle of the night. He was tall with unruly hair and a beard so full that all you could see were his eyes, nose and cheeks. When he ate, he spit and dropped parcels of food all over his beard while he talked very loudly in his Australian accent. Another thing that made him different was he was a left handed trombone player and he just looked awkward when he played. But boy could he play! What made his band really different from most other jazz bands was that they had no piano, but after listening to them, you never missed it.

I'll never forget Collie's bass player, Fingers Williams, who could play the slap bass just like the old New Orleans bass men. It was a technique where the bass player slapped the base while pulling the strings - that's the best way I can explain it. Like Max Collie, Trevor had lots of facial hair and long hair on his head, but what made him different was that he was very small and sometimes it was even difficult to see him standing behind the bass. Trevor fell in love with my Lincoln Continental and I offered to let him drive it - big mistake! He got behind the wheel (thank God I went with him) and he was all over the road like he had never driven before. The fact of the matter was he *hadn't* driven before! He not only had no license but he had never driven a car before, let alone a Lincoln Continental on the right side of the road! We just drove around the block and got back to my house safely, although I was a nervous wreck.

Phil Mason played the cornet and was the good-looking sex symbol of the band, even with his long hair and facial hair. He was from Scotland, lived on the Isle of Bute, and was proud of it. The banjoist was my favorite person in the group. His name was Gentleman Jim McIntosh and was originally a trombone player but of course he couldn't play the trombone in Collie's band, so he took up the banjo and probably became the most popular banjo player in England. Jim had a great sense of humor and was always hitting me up for cigarettes, because he said he didn't buy any as he didn't smoke. He always had a mischievous twinkle in his eye. The clarinetist was Jack Gilbert and probably was the most clean cut musician in the group, along with being a first-class clarinetist. Ron McKay played the drums and did most of the vocals. He played and sang with such excitement that he brought the audience right along with him. Like Jack Gilbert, he too was fairly clean-cut and being the oldest and wisest in the band was more laid-back and sensible.

As for the World Championship of Jazz, it turned out to be a catastrophe for Sam Johnson. First of all it started out with a fistfight between Bill Basin, a jazz writer, and Sam Johnson, with Basin ending up in the hospital. Most of the music was great because there were so many wonderful bands playing the event. The winner of the championship was none other than the Max Collie Band. Of course Sam Johnson was their manager and also head of The Championship of Jazz, which you might say was a conflict of interest. Rumors also started circulating that Max Collie himself was a partner with Sam Johnson for the event. Anyway, the rumor circulated that the whole thing was rigged and dishonest and on top of that a good many of the musicians never got paid, including Wild Bill.

So what can I say - I wasn't there but I got many reports from my musician friends that did play, including Wild Bill. It was supposed to be an annual event and I think most people would have forgotten about the thing being rigged, because after all the Max Collie Band was a good one and could easily have won anyway. However, not paying musicians was a kiss of death for anyone in the nightclub business or running a jazz festival because the word would get out, which it did, and Sam Johnson and the Championship of Jazz lost all credibility. It's too bad, because I liked Sam Johnson and he was doing a good job promoting jazz music along with the Max Collie Band, but now it was all over.

A few years later, Sam Johnson called me and said he was bringing Max Collie back for a US tour, and would I be interested in promoting it in Oregon again, along with my band. I told him – absolutely - just give me some dates. I got the dates and was starting to get ready to put things together, when he called again and said the whole thing was off. That's the last time I ever heard from Sam Johnson.

Writing about my adventures and memories of Ernie Carson is something that I would have just as soon skipped, but he became such a big part of my musical life it's something that I just can't ignore. I watched him transform from a pleasant, charming person to a very scary, evil man who seemed to love making people's lives miserable. I started to see two people in him, the charming and kind Ernie and the frightening evil person, who I called Bernie. As time went by you saw less and less of Ernie and more and more of Bernie.

This took a number of years to come about and when I met him we became instant friends and enjoyed playing music together. I had heard that he could be difficult but I saw nothing personally to indicate that. He was a top notch musician, playing the cornet and piano, sometimes at the same time. For recording sessions he could quickly write arrangements for the band with beautiful handwriting.

Ernie was born in Portland in December, 1937, and passed away in January, 2012. My friend and trombonist, Pat O'Neil, told me that he grew up with Ernie and played music with him when they were just teenagers. Pat told me that in those early days, Ernie was fun to be around and easy to work with. In fact, they were so young that when they were playing nightclubs they had to leave the room on intermissions. They were playing one such nightclub and on their break they used to go across the street to where Monte Ballou and his Castle Jazz Band were playing and sit outside and listen.

Ernie went on to play with the Castle Jazz Band when he was 15 years old. He later spent two years in the US Marine Corps. After his military service he went to Los Angeles and played with Dave Wierbach, Jig Adams and Ray Bauduc. Following that he went to San Francisco and joined the Turk Murphy Jazz Band. He finally settled in Atlanta, Georgia, forming his own band and became quite successful. At that time George Buck's Jazzology record company was located in Atlanta and Ernie recorded several albums with them, including an album with me, titled – *Just A Little*.

Ernie was a very small man, probably around 5'4" tall at the most. When I knew him in the early days he had a receding hairline, was always clean-shaven, and very neatly dressed. He had a great sense of humor, although sometimes it was rather bizarre. I met him when he was in Portland visiting his parents, who were also small people and very pleasant. I could see where Ernie would fit in with my band easily, because he loved to drink and smoke and party all night.

Ernie told me that he was going to be on tour with the Dixieland
Rhythm Kings and they were going to be in the Washington and Oregon
area the first part of 1977. Together, we thought it would be a good idea
for me to book the Rhythm Kings for a concert show with my band,
much the same as I did with Max Collie. I told Ernie that I would get
right to work and put it together with their leader Gene Mayl.

After finishing off a very busy 1976 Bicentennial year, it was time to move
on to new things and a new year. First of all I had Gene Mayl's Dixieland
Rhythm Kings coming to Portland to do a show with me and my band.
For this concert I booked the Terrace Room on SW. 11ᵗʰ Street in downtown Portland and scheduled the event for January 22, 1977. The Terrace
Room was operated by George Reinmiller, a Portland attorney who also
had a very well-known and popular big-band. He used the Terrace Room
for some of his big-band dances and also rented it out to other groups, like
in my case, a jazz show. It was a big old-fashioned ballroom that had bar
service and also served small snacks.

The Rhythm Kings, along with Ernie Carson, arrived and I put them
all up at a Motel 6 in Lake Oswego. Gene Mayl had toured with his
Dixieland Rhythm Kings since 1948. His group was probably one of the
world's most traveled jazz bands, as they logged around an average of
40,000 miles a year. They covered the Midwest and much of the East and
South like a blanket, ranging west to the Rockies and north to Canada.
They did numerous concerts, nightclub and college appearances each
year, and recorded extensively since the 1940s. Now they were in Portland
and we had pretty much a full house to listen to them.

The Rhythm Kings sounded great, especially with Ernie Carson
punching out the lead notes on his cornet. They had mostly all East Coast
players and they all had great credentials. I had my regular band and

added Jim Goodwin to join Danny Alguire on cornet and I also hired George Bruns to play trombone. So the crowd had two excellent bands to listen to and for the last few numbers we all joined together for a big finale. It was a great ending for the evening and the audience loved it.

Following the concert we had a big party at our house with the two bands. I made the drinks and Pauline was very busy preparing food. At the end of the night when everyone left, Pauline and I went over the figures for the concert. Pauline discovered there was one envelope missing, full of cash; and when we worked the numbers we discovered we were off by $200. The next day I called down to the Terrace Room and asked George Reinmiller if anyone had turned in an envelope full of money. He talked to a few of his employees and nothing was found. So that was that and we just marked it down to experience.

Now fast-forward 27 years to 2004! I got a call from George Reinmiller and evidently much had happened in his life and he told me that he was making amends for things in his past life that he was not happy about. George told me that he was writing me a check for $200 because he, in fact, did find the missing cash- filled envelope, and kept it. I guess God does work in mysterious ways.

Reuniting with George Reinmiller opened up new doors and I ended up being a feature soloist with his big-band. He had two special arrangements made for me on clarinet and soprano saxophone. One was Sidney Bechet's *"Petite Fleur"* and the other was, "It Had to Be You." I also backed his singer, Shirley Nanette, on a few of her tunes.

So I guess things have a way of working out in the end. The missing money was recovered and I was able to reach one of my goals, which was, my solos being backed by a big-band. And for icing on the cake, my son Jame had a big event for his client's and hired the George Reinmiller Big Band, along with me and Shirley Nanette to play. I also had my band there, with Pete Pepke on trombone, to add to the show. It turned out to be one fun party.

With the next Sacramento Jazz Festival staring me in the face, I had to start thinking about putting together a bigger band than I had the previous year. All the other bands there consisted of seven or eight players so I thought that I should up the number in my group. Jim Goodwin was in town again and I signed him to play the cornet along with Danny Alguire. I liked the idea of two cornets and Jim and Danny worked together well. I also had Pete Pepke on trombone, Dave Wierbach, banjo, Norm Domreis, piano, Don Kinch, bass, and Delane Guild on drums. To top it off, I asked my old Canadian buddy, Lance Harrison, to join the band playing tenor sax.

I thought with this group of musicians it would be a shame not to make a recording. So, I called Pete Pepke and asked him to come to Portland early before the Sacramento Festival. We recorded again at TRI-AD in Eugene and cut twelve tunes. The recording session went very well and I did a fairly good job keeping the guys sober, although you'd never know it by all of the empty beer cans lying around the studio. The name of the new album was to be called *The Joys of Jazz* and it became very popular, later being released on cassette and then CD. I asked my son Jame to come along on the session because I thought it would be a good learning experience for him, especially since he was taking cornet lessons. Later in life, Jame became a successful businessman and that day at the recording studio was probably his first big business adventure. He collected all the empty beer cans and took them over to a nearby supermarket to cash in on the deposits. I think Jame did very well financially that day. I was in a big hurry to get this album out, so while we were recording, Pauline was in another room behind a typewriter, banging out the liner notes.

Jim Goodwin, Dave Wierbach, Pete Pepke and I left for the Sacramento Festival a day early because we were going to meet Ernie Carson in San

Francisco and go to hear Turk Murphy and his band. We all went to see Turk and he avoided us like the plague. I learned that Ernie had left Turk's band on bad terms and Turk didn't want to be anywhere near him. This was the first warning signal I got in regards to Ernie Carson, and it was by no means going to be the last.

We arrived in Sacramento and I met up with Pauline, Jame and Bob at the Sandman Motel. They had driven to Sacramento with Danny Alguire and his wife. I also greeted Lance Harrison for the start of a very successful Memorial Day weekend of Jazz. The band consisted of nine pieces now and we just blew everyone away. On top of that, Ernie Carson had started a rumor around the festival that movie star Warren Beatty was my brother and was coming to hear me play. Well, it didn't take very long for that false rumor to spread and we had huge crowds with everybody looking around all over the place trying to spot my brother Warren.

One afternoon Pauline, the boys and I were lounging around the motel swimming pool, along with several other musician and fans. We noticed that Bob Haggart came out of his room and jumped into the pool to relax with the rest of us.

Bob Haggart was a bass player and composer and played with Bob Crosby and the Bobcats during the 1930s and 40s. While with Crosby he became well known for a recording where he whistled with drummer Ray Bauduc, "Big Noise from Winnetka." After Crosby he settled in New York City doing radio and made a series of Dixieland albums with Yank Lawson in the early 50s. He was the co-writer for many hits, including "What's New" and "The South Rampart Street Parade." He and Yank Lawson organized The World's Greatest Jazz Band and traveled extensively with that band.

Evidently Pauline and the boys heard Bob Haggart whistling "Big Noise from Winnetka" earlier in the day on one of his shows and were quite fascinated with him. I was half asleep in my lounge chair when I heard Bob say to Jame – "I think I'll swim over to Bob Haggart and ask him to whistle "Big Noise from Winnetka" for me. Before I could jump out of my lounge and stop him he was over at the other end of the pool talking with Haggart. I thought, Oh My God! No! He's really not going to do that - I hope. But I'll be damned, out of the blue standing in the water with Bob at the end of the pool, Haggart started whistling "Big Noise from Winnetka" for him. Everyone at the pool loved it and applauded wildly - it was the big surprise hit of the afternoon and in the swimming pool, no less. I had a talk with Bob and told him that perhaps once was enough.

We just had one more little incident, this time involving Jame. After one of my concerts Pauline told me that she had lost Jame in the crowd and she was very upset. Now, it's pretty hard to pick out a young boy in a crowd of over 50,000 people. So I tried to be calm and told Pauline not to worry because he would tell someone his name and who he belonged to and I was sure he would be returned to our motel. And sure enough, we went back to the motel and within minutes some nice lady returned him to us. I think I gave her one of my albums as a reward.

The Sacramento Jazz Festival ran like a well-oiled machine. It was amazing how well it was put together, shuffling all those musicians around for four days, let alone keeping track of their transportation and salaries. My band was given $700 in addition to our salary for transportation and housing. This doesn't seem like a lot now but we drove from Portland to Sacramento and gas was very cheap then. Pauline, and the boys and I had a very nice room at the motel, with two double beds, for only $12 per night. 55,000 jazz fans attended the four-day event and the festival paid $46,000 for musicians. Each band member was paid by how many sets or concerts they played and as I recall we received $25 each per set. And, for the 1977 Festival each musician received a percentage of the profits, which was $90 each. I was asked to bring the band back again in

1978 and I agreed immediately. The extra good news was that Wild Bill Davison was going to be one of the stars, and already I was planning an after-Sacramento tour for the two of us and possibly a recording session. This gave us all something to look forward to for the next year.

Following the Sacramento Jazz Festival, my brain was stuffed full of jazz, after listening to so many bands and especially all those banjo/tuba combos. When I got home I played nothing but classical music on the stereo for a week. But it was time to get back to my regular schedule of playing the schools for Young Audiences and my casual engagements, including Sundays at the Wannigan Lounge at the Greenwood Inn, located in Beaverton.

I got a call from the Jazz Quarry, a popular downtown Portland jazz lounge, asking me if I would be interested in being a guest performer every Wednesday evening with the Sky Trio. I took the job because Eddie Wied, the piano player of the group, was excellent and I always had wanted to work with him. He was called "the professor" and was a very good teacher and an excellent piano player. In the 40s and 50s he played with a lot of bebop groups, but was able to go both ways and play great mainstream jazz as well. He was with the Navy Band during World War II and after the war he moved to Portland and became a very successful piano teacher. He was even classically trained, studying with Katherine George, who played piano with the Oregon Symphony.

Eddie earned his Bachelor's degree from Lewis and Clark College in 1959 and had received his Master's degree in art from the University of Nevada in 1974. He played piano with The Modernaires, a jazz vocal group, for six years and appeared with them on the Johnny Carson late show. He ended up spending time in Las Vegas and working with Bob Crosby and the Bobcats.

In 1972, trombonist Pat O'Neil convinced Eddie to return to Portland and run the Sunday jam sessions at the Top of The Park. He stayed in Portland for the rest of his life, playing various jazz clubs around town, including the Jazz Quarry. That was the start of a musical relationship I had with him and we worked together on many occasions during the following years. Wied was a character, to say the least. He wasn't very tall and he seemed to have a hell of a time getting his clothes to fit. He also had a hairpiece that he must've bought off the rack, because it was way too big for him. One time he was playing a Young Audience job with me and while we were unloading the car with our musical equipment a gust of wind came up and blew his hairpiece off, and it went tumbling down the middle of the street with everyone in the band chasing it. Another time he came to work wearing two pairs of glasses! I asked for the reason for the double pair of glasses and he said he could see twice as good! Eddie drove a Chevrolet Malibu and it was a complete disaster. I never saw a car so banged up and dented in my life. It was so bad they wouldn't let him go through the car wash with it. But that was Eddie and everyone loved him and his music.

The drummer in the Sky Trio was Dave Dickey. For obvious reasons, he took the stage name of David Elliott. He was a small guy about the same size as Eddie Wied and always had a very bewildered look on his face. I noticed right away that he was a big-time chain smoker and drank horrendous amounts of white wine. Dave turned out to be a great guy, with fabulous sense of humor, besides being a swinging drummer. At the end of the night after the job Dave would always come up to me and tell me how great I played and how wonderful the evening went. He would be absolutely hammered on white wine!

Brad Harrett was the bass player in the group. He was tall, good-looking with a thick head of curly hair. He almost seemed too happy, and I suspected right from the beginning that he was either a heavy drinker or into drugs. I later found out it was both. Brad was known around town as a superb, schooled bassist and always in demand.

So that was the Sky Trio, and it was three guys that I enjoyed playing with every Wednesday night. The Jazz Quarry was located at SW 11th and Jefferson Street in Portland. It was a very friendly and fun place to go and always featured good jazz. It certainly wasn't anything fancy, but clean and comfortable. It was simply laid out so when you walked in there was a long bar on your right with lots of table seating on your left. I became good friends with Eddie, Dave, and Brad, and all of them became members of my band in the following years to come.

The nice thing about playing casual engagements, as opposed to steady nightclub work, was that you're much more flexible organizing time away with the family for vacations or short trips. I took advantage of this as much as possible and even bought a small trailer for camping trips. I sold my Lincoln Continental to drummer John Picardi, who had moved back to Portland after tiring of the adult bookstore business. I bought a fairly new Lincoln Town Car and had a hitch put on the back bumper to tow the trailer, attached our little boat to a rack above the car, put the boat motor in the trunk, and off we'd go to Detroit Lake, a great vacation spot about two hours away from our home. When we got to the lake the boys would have fun with the boat along with fishing with me. Pauline would cook most of the meals outside and we would just generally relax. We also took advantage of our place at Sakinaw Lake in Canada and spent time in Vancouver as well. It also gave me a chance to hang out with my friend Lance Harrison and play a few sessions with him.

Pete Pepke had booked the Warren County Pennsylvania Fair and asked me to come and play with him. The fairgrounds were just 20 minutes away from Jamestown, across the state line, so I could visit with family and friends while I was there. It also gave me a chance to go to some of my old haunts and eat Western New York's delicious Beef on Weck, not to mention Johnny's Texas Hot's hot dogs. The Texas Hot's often gave you the runs, but boy, it was worth it. I could never figure out why the Beef on Weck never caught on around the rest of the country, like Buffalo Wings did. I often have mentioned the beef on wecks to Portland businesspeople - and they give me that look of - what does he know - he's just a musician!

My drummer, Delane Guild, gave me his two weeks' notice, because he had some things going on and was going in a different direction. Delane was an excellent drummer, as you can hear from all the tunes he recorded with me. As luck would have it John Picardi was more than happy to come back with the band.

The band was busier than ever and we were playing our Young Audience engagements, along with a host of different casuals that were coming along, such as weddings, conventions and private parties. The holidays were especially busy, playing the Christmas office parties that were so popular at the time and we were also booked at the Salem Elks club for New Year's Eve.

Pauline and I always had a huge Christmas party at our house with close to 100 people showing up. Many musicians came to the party and we had one giant jam session all night long. Sheriff Brooks was always one of our guests, so we never had to worry about the noise complaint. And besides that, we invited all the neighbors anyway.

In 1978 I would be getting together with Wild Bill Davison again. He had been so busy touring Europe that I hadn't seen him in a while, so it would be a great reunion with Bill and Anne.

A new nightclub in Vancouver, Washington opened its doors and they planned on featuring a variety of music. They wanted to schedule my band one night a week on different nights. I went over to Vancouver and checked it out; they called it The Main Street Station and did a great job of remodeling and it looked like they might make ago out of it. We went over very well and drew the more adult crowd that came in and drank, had dinner, danced and spent money. Management was happy and so were the employees because they were keeping busy and getting good tips. Every time I went to work, the waitresses greeted me warmly and told me how happy they were to see me back. That made me feel good, and one night after we were through playing I passed a couple of waitresses at a table, counting their tips. I didn't want to be nosy but I quickly glanced at the $20, $10 and $5 bills stacked on the table and came to the conclusion that the waitresses were making more money than me! Talk about a bad career choice!

Anne and Wild Bill had been making their home in Copenhagen, Denmark for the past few years because Bill was in such demand in that part of the world, and flying back and forth from the United States was very tiring. After hearing Wild Bill would be a feature artist at the Sacramento Jazz Festival I told Anne that I could organize a few jobs in Portland after the festival and would also like Bill on my next recording. Anne and Bill thought that this was a great idea and we could all ride back to Portland together after the Sacramento Jazz Festival ended.

Pauline accompanied me to the festival and the band went over great again. It was exhausting because our jobs were so spread out during the day that we might be playing at 11 a.m. and finishing up at midnight. However, we were young and didn't complain, at least most of the time. With the spread-out hours, of course, I was constantly keeping my eye on the boys in the band and hoping that they would stay at least halfway sober for the jobs. Wild Bill went over very well with the fans and of course everyone, including the musicians, were anxious to hear him play. Bill had slowed down on his drinking a bit and told me that for the most part, he only drank when he worked.

At the end of the festival Pauline and I picked up Anne and Bill at their motel and took off for Portland. The day before, Bill asked me to buy a pint of Scotch and have it stashed in the glove compartment. For the drive back to Portland Bill sat in the front passenger seat and Pauline and Anne sat comfortably in the back seat. So as we were driving, Bill would take a swig of Scotch and pass it to me for a taste. The bottle passed back and forth for quite a few miles until the girls started realizing that we were having a party in the front seat. So our little plan didn't work but we all did get a big laugh out of it.

We got home from Sacramento, safely on Tuesday night and had Wednesday and Thursday to rest up and recuperate until we played Friday night at The Old Town Strutter's Hall in old town Portland. Strutter's Hall was just a Tavern serving beer and wine, so a table was set up in the balcony with a bottle of scotch on it for Wild Bill. It was a different club for entertainment because the band played in the front window. It wasn't in the best section of town and often there would be street people looking in at us playing, through the window. There was no dancing but lots of seating in front of the bandstand with a good-sized bar on the left hand side of the room. Besides Bill and me, we had Rip Robinson on trombone, Norm Domreis on piano, Dave Gentry playing bass and John Picardi on drums. We also had a vocalist, Jan Harmon, who had many good credentials in the business and had worked with Wild Bill a few years before in California. I planned to use Jan Harmon on the upcoming recording session. We got a fantastic review the next day in the Oregonian. John Wendeborn wrote:

*The highlights came with Davison and Beatty. It was obvious they had spent much time together playing in the past. Harmonies were always on the money and they "read" each other well.*

A couple of years later Strutter's Hall was sold, enlarged and remodeled, and was turned into a bar. They renamed it "Hobo's," obtained a full liquor license and still serve excellent food to this day. A few years later I ended up playing several nights there and still do to this day. If you should walk by or go in for a drink you will see the front window where we played

Our next job was a very hot Sunday afternoon for the Oregon City Jazz Society at Oaks Park. Wild Bill, of course, had a fifth of Scotch with him, but was behaving well and having a great time at the picnic. Jame and Bob were with us and enjoying the picnic and all the rides at Oaks Park. After an intermission we all went back to the bandstand, but Wild Bill was nowhere to be seen. I asked around and someone told me that they had just seen him with Jame and Bob over by the rides. I wandered over and I'll be damned if Wild Bill, Jame and Bob weren't riding through the park on the little children's train. I talked to the train operator and asked him to please stop the train the next time it came by and let Wild Bill off, so he could come play some music. I asked the boys not to run off with their Uncle Bill again that afternoon, because he wasn't responsible. I did see him with Jame sitting in a rocket ship later in the afternoon, but I just looked the other way. I was just thankful that we got through the day without him stealing something. Pauline and Anne drove over to hear our last set of the afternoon and I was glad they did because the heat and the Scotch finally got to Wild Bill and for the first time I saw him exhausted and unsteady on his feet.

The next day we drove to Eugene to the TRI-AD recording studios to record our tunes. Wild Bill was a workhorse in the recording studio and we kept going over our songs until he was satisfied with them. We recorded nine tunes, with Jan Harmon singing two of them. Naturally a lot of drinking was going on during the recording session and on the drive back to Portland. When we got back to my house we all sat at our kitchen table, winding down from the recording session. Our kitchen table had a glass top, so you could see everybody's legs and feet below. Domreis had too much to drink and just couldn't control his wandering eye and hands.

I just about died when I saw his hand reach over to Anne Davison's leg. We all saw it, including Wild Bill, and all he said was, Get your hand off my wife's leg! That's about all he could say because that's something he wouldn't think twice about doing himself.

Anne and Bill left a couple days later to play in New York City and then they were going back to Denmark. All in all it was a good trip and we made a lot of good music, plus it was so much fun getting together with them again after so long a time. Later, they would be moving back to the United States and we would have a chance to get together again for a big West Coast tour.

I didn't do many jazz festivals because we were so busy playing around Portland and the surrounding area. I liked to do a few a year, however, because it kept the band's name out there and we sold quite a few albums. The Denver Jazz Club was planning a festival on August 25th, 26th and 27th and wanted my band to perform. They were having the festival in Central City, about 40 miles west of Denver, up in the mountains. It sounded interesting to me and I accepted the job.

Central City is an old, gold rush type town, and when I got there it reminded me of being back at the Hoyt Hotel. Everything was just the way it was back in the late 1800s, including the house they gave me to live in, which was built in 1878. Denver, of course, is known as the mile high city and Central City was higher yet, and it was difficult to breathe, especially when I was playing my clarinet or walking up a hill.

The name of the festival was The Central City Jazz and Ragtime Jamboree, and it featured 18 bands and six Ragtime piano players. A three-day ticket to the event was only $20. I took most of my regular band from Portland with the exception of my friend Pete Pepke, who flew in from

Pennsylvania. I was short a banjo player and at the suggestion of Jim Goodwin I called banjoist Lueder Ohlwein from Three Rivers, California who had his own group called the Jazzberry Jam Band. Lueder was a German who came to the United States via Ireland.

One of the other bands featured was Ernie Carson's All Stars, a group of musicians he assembled from Atlanta, Chicago, and Denver. Jim Goodwin and I looked Ernie Carson up and we all had a few drinks together and talked about old times. One day I met Ernie just as he was finishing one of his jobs and we were going to another place to catch one of the bands. As we were walking out the door a nice young man said "hi" to Ernie. Ernie looked at him and told him what a lousy musician he was and that he should stick his horn up his ass. Then Ernie called him all the dirty four letter words he could think of. The fellow he was dressing down stood there in shock, as did I. And then, before you knew it, Ernie looked at me and said "OK Jim, let's get going," as if nothing had happened.

It was a very good festival with excellent bands performing from all over the United States. Ernie and I met for farewell drinks after the festival was over. As Ernie and I were walking to our rooms, there was a friendly stray dog that came over to us and wanted to be petted. We then got a great idea, picked the dog up and walked over to the house Goodwin was staying at. He was sleeping in a first-floor bedroom with the window wide open for air. We dropped the dog into his room and shut the window and all hell broke loose. Ernie and I got a big laugh out of our prank and Goodwin did too. When we boarded the airplane to come back to Portland, Goodwin reeked of garlic! He had purchased some cloves of garlic and chewed on them before getting on the plane. He absolutely stunk and it wasn't much fun sitting next to him and smelling garlic on the whole flight back to Portland. Goodwin got the last laugh!

I got a call from Bill Oakley, promoter of the Ragtime Festival in St. Louis. The festival was held aboard Oakley's moored ship on the St. Louis levee, the Goldenrod Showboat. It was a large ship with lots of room to feature several bands around the vessel at the same time. Oakley wanted my band to play and I accepted immediately. The festival was a popular one and went on for one week, and I was asked to perform the full seven days. They treated us well and we flew to St. Louis, only to be greeted by a representative of the Anheuser Busch Brewery, the brewers of the popular Budweiser beer. The Budweiser people had been making beer in St. Louis since 1876 and of course it was one of the most famous beers in the United States. The Budweiser representative helped us retrieve our luggage and led us outside to an awaiting Budweiser bus. The bus had a full bar, along with a bartender, and of course we could have all the fresh draft beer we wanted. I told the bus driver to take his time and not break any speed limits on the way to our hotel.

For this festival I brought along Harold Koster on piano, Dave Gentry - bass, John Picardi - drums, John McKinley, banjo - Bert Barr (leader of Seattle's Uptown Lowdown Jazz Band) on cornet and of course Pete Pepke. Banjos are always crowd pleasers so I knew that John McKinley would go over very well, as did Pete Pepke's antics. The whole band was very well received and we got lots of enthusiastic applause and standing ovations.

There was a record sales table where bandleaders left their records and were sold at your price, minus a small percentage for handling the sales. It wasn't easy lugging those big boxes of heavy LPs around to different festivals, but we all did it. It got much easier in later years with the cassettes and CDs. I was surprised to learn that one of my records was a big hit in the St. Louis area. For some reason or another they were playing my version of the "Apex Blues" on the radio stations. I have no idea how that happened, but I wasn't complaining because it was great for my record sales.

Turk Murphy and his band were there from San Francisco and it was great to see him again. I was surprised to see George Rock playing the trumpet with Turk's band because I had heard him play so many times with Spike Jones when I was a kid. Murray Field, a fan and friend of Turk Murphy's, had an afternoon luncheon at his house and me and my band were invited. It was a very private affair with just Turk's band and mine. I had met Murray in San Francisco at the bar at Earthquake McGoon's, Turk's well known jazz club. We became fast friends and I guess he didn't forget me.

Ernie Carson also had a band playing the festival and I was happy to see that he had one of my favorite piano players, Don Ewell, working with him. It was fun to see Ernie again after Central City and we managed to find some time to get together and talk along with a few drinks. But then it happened again! At the end of one night's playing Ernie invited me back to his hotel room as he said he and his band were having a get-together with some snacks and drinks. When we got to his room, his band guys were already there waiting for us. We walked into his room and everyone happily welcomed us to the party, when out of the blue, Ernie went into a terrible, angry tirade! He called his band members terrible names and told them they were all lousy musicians and to get the hell out of his room and out of his sight. Ernie looked at me and said "Everybody but you Jim." His band members scurried out of the room as fast as they could, with Ernie swearing and cussing them each as they left. Ernie slammed the door, smiled at me and said, "Let's have a drink Jim," just like nothing unusual had just happened. I was beginning to see this behavior more and more and wondered if and when he would turn on me. As it turned out it was a long time later before it happened.

Jazz writer and promoter Bill Basin was at the festival and it was always great to see him. He was a friendly guy to talk to and an expert on Scotch. He would often take me to his hotel room and give me samples. Bill made it a point to attend most of the jazz festivals and I saw a lot of him down the road. He was the one, by the way, who got into the fistfight with Sam Johnson at the Championship of Jazz fiasco.

It was a very successful jazz festival and it was amazing how they could have all those bands on that one ship, the Goldenrod Showboat. And best of all, the Jim Beatty Jazz Band went over very well and I was asked to come back for the next festival in 1980. That's one of those festivals you don't want to miss. When I got back to Portland, I had a musical surprise waiting for me - totally unexpected.

**Jack Gilbert (Max Collie Band) and Jim –
getting hot. Cinnamon Tree, Portland**

Turk Murphy and Jim - after Civic Auditorium
Jazz Concert with sellout crowd.

CHAPTER 23

# Harvey's

AFTER GETTING BACK FROM THE St. Louis jazz Festival I got a call from an old friend that I hadn't seen since the closing of the Hoyt Hotel. It was Barry Colin, the son of Joanne Colin, who was the manager in charge of the several bars in the Hoyt Hotel. Barry told me that he and his mother were opening a new nightclub/restaurant, kitty-corner from the old Hoyt Hotel, at Sixth Avenue and Glisan, and calling it Harvey's, in honor of the late Harvey Dick. It would be like bringing the old Hoyt Hotel back to life again, only on a smaller scale. Barry said that he'd love to have my band play at the new club and it would be just like old times.

This was an offer that I'd have to think long and hard about because I was doing so well just playing casual engagements around Portland and jazz clubs up and down the West Coast, including a few jazz festivals around the country. On the other hand, having a steady job to go to every night was a very entertaining thought, although it would tie me down and give me less time to spend with the family. However, the boys were grow-ing up and had their own friends and were very involved in sports and not as anxious for family trips as they used to be. I talked to the guys in the band about what their thoughts were. I also was aware that nightclubs in Portland were beginning to struggle. This could very well be the last of full-time employment in a nightclub for me.

We all decided it would be a good move for everyone because playing casual, one night engagements could be exhausting. I set up a meeting with Barry and Joanne and told them I would take the job, providing I could have time off for the St. Louis Jazz Festival and a week-long vacation at our place in Canada. It was a deal and I was back in the nightclub business.

Harvey's was not due to open until late summer or early fall of 1979. The place was still under construction and Barry wanted my advice about the bandstand and the dance floor. We put the bandstand at the far end of the room and the dance floor on the left-hand side of the band so that people could sit, watch, and listen to the band without dancers in front of them. We had a wonderful sound system put in, along with excellent stage lighting, and we were in business.

Harvey's was split in two, the restaurant entrance was on Sixth Avenue and you entered the bar on Glisan. The restaurant was elegant and well-lit, but many people complained that it was too bright. They had a good menu and you could always get food on the bar side as well. The lounge was a comfortable room with an old-time bar that was reminiscent of the Hoyt Hotel. It turned out that I was going to spend quite some time playing there and meet many interesting people along the way.

I was looking forward to working with Joanne and Barry again. Barry was just a young man when I met him at Zircon Jim's tending bar, and I would see him often at the Hoyt Hotel. He was good looking and was always happy, with a smile on his face. His mother and I had a very good relationship and I liked her very much. She was a true professional in the restaurant business and when a waitress came to work, they reported to Joanne first as she always inspected their uniforms, fingernails and looked them over in general, and then would always tell them how nice they looked. Joanne had another son, Michael, who she brought in as a bartender. He was tall, trim, good looking with a mustache and in very good shape. It was obvious that he worked out a lot and if there was any trouble at the bar, I knew he could handle it. Michael, like his brother, had a great personality and was very friendly.

Opening night and Harvey's was a madhouse. It was standing room only with a long line outside the door with people waiting to get in. With my band playing tunes like "That's A Plenty," and "Muskrat Ramble". The joint was jumping! I used a quartet for my band at Harvey's and it consisted of Harold Koster on piano, Ed Fontaine, bass, John Picardi playing drums and myself on clarinet and soprano. I was happy that I'd suggested we have the dance floor on one side of the bandstand because many customers loved to sit and watch and listen to the band in those front row seats. We played from 9 p.m. until 2 a.m. Monday through Saturday. It was a long haul, but the time just flew by.

Some of our customers were amazing. Executives from large companies would stop by after work for happy hour and would still be there when I arrived to work at 9 p.m. Many times they were still there at closing time. The early 1980's...gotta love 'em. It seemed like everyone had an endless supply of money and the good times would never end. Customers bought the band drinks quite frequently; in fact, rarely did I have to ever buy myself a drink. There was a group from the shipyard that used to come in and six-pack the band, which meant I got six Scotch and waters, and because John Picardi didn't drink I got his six too. One night one of our good customers came in and said "Beatty – I'm buying twenty shots of tequila," ten for you and ten for me and after you're through playing for the night I'll be waiting for you at the bar. I think I only had one set to play and then went to the bar and drank my ten tequilas, one by one. Fortunately, John Picardi drove me home and when we got to my driveway I opened the car door and fell out, flat on my face. John Picardi took me into the house, sat me on a kitchen chair and ran, before Pauline discovered me. The waitresses at Harvey's figured that I drank between twenty and twenty-five Scotch and waters a night, and then I would go home and have a few more drinks just to wind down. Looking back, I don't know how the hell I did it and played my clarinet at the same time. I guess that I was just in "condition." Many people didn't want to go home when the bar closed at 2 a.m. They had a half hour to finish their drinks and had to be out of the door at 2:30 a.m. Even then they were mad as hell because you were making them leave. Those were the days.

I should clarify that finishing off the night with 10 tequila shots was a one-time only adventure, stupid as it was. And, my Scotch drinking was stretched out over a five or six hour job at the nightclub. I was always in control of my performance and if I did feel that I was going over the line, I would stop the drinking. I found that if I showed up for work 100% sober that it was impossible to get so intoxicated that I couldn't play my horn. I also expected this behavior from all my band members. I never watched or counted their drinks just as long as they could handle themselves professionally on the job. Whenever I had a day off with the family, I never drank or smoked. I just did those things when I worked.

Night life was fascinating to me because it was a whole new world with very interesting people roaming around, as opposed to the daytime way of life. I met people from all walks of life and became good friends with many of them. The Harvey's crowd was very diverse and on any given night you could see popular local television personalities, CEOs of large companies, doctors, lawyers, union leaders, off-duty police, judges, car dealers, priests and even a nighttime burglar, who could get me anything I wanted. I never bought much from him except when he had a good supply of boxed CDs. There was also a hit man that loved to come listen to the band. He was out of town at great lengths of time on business but when he came back to town he would bring in his entourage and they would drink and eat the night away like there was no tomorrow. When he did plan to come down for the evening, he'd call me in advance so I could arrange a private waitress for him. Once he called me from Hawaii and wanted to fly me over for a party. That was out of the question, of course, because I had work and had my family here.

There were also celebrities that I always enjoyed seeing. One was movie star, Sam Elliott, who grew up in Portland as a child after moving there from Sacramento, California with his family. His was born in 1944 and graduated from David Douglas High School in Portland. He went to Clark College in Vancouver, Washington and became interested in acting and from there moved to Hollywood and broke into the movie business. His first big movie was *Butch Cassidy and the Sundance Kid*, with Paul Newman and Robert Redford, along with Katharine Ross, who he later married in 1984. When I met Sam Elliott he was a young, tall, slim, good-looking guy with a mustache, around 6' 2" who accompanied his mother into Harvey's. He was a good guy to his mother and came to see her often as the both of them enjoyed listening to the band. The waitresses also melted when he came to spend the evening.

One night on an intermission, Sam and I were talking and he mentioned a new movie he was in that was being released. It was called *Lifeguard* and he told me that I might like it and find it interesting. So, one Saturday afternoon Pauline and I took Jame and Bob to the movie theater to watch Sam in *Lifeguard*. Well, he was a lifeguard all right. He was running up and down the beach with a skimpy bathing suit, looking for sex with all the girls on the beach. We had to get the boys out of the theater and leave early, much to their disappointment. The next time Sam Elliott came in to hear the band, I looked at him, and said –Thanks A Lot!

Andre the Giant was a very interesting, well known professional wrestling champion that frequented Harvey's when he was in Portland. He was associated with The World Wrestling Federation and was undefeated from 1973-1987. When he walked in the door the whole lounge went quiet as he was 7' 4" and weighed 520 pounds. He was born in France in 1946 and when he grew up, boy he did grow up. He became a professional wrestler, one of the All-time greats.

Portland was a big wrestling town and consequently he visited often, and we became friends. I was sitting at the bar with him one night while he drank cans of beers, one after another. It was known that he could drink over 100 cans of beers at one sitting. His hand was so big the can of beer disappeared in his grip.

One time I went into the men's room on my intermission and as I was standing by the urinal and heard a deep voice say – Hi Jim. I thought I was the only one in the restroom. I looked around at the toilet in back of me and there was Andre's head above the toilet door, looking down at me. He was actually sitting on the toilet and was so big he could see over the door of the toilet. He knew he startled me and just laughed like hell. Once he asked me if he could sit in with the band - of course I said yes - what do you want to sing? He said you just play anything and I will sing. It didn't sound like a good plan to me but I wasn't about to argue with Andre the Giant. When he got on stage he announced he was going to sing, "The Fish Song." I think we just played a blues behind him and he moved his lips and cheeks around and looked like a fish. It wasn't much of a show, but the crowd went wild. I liked Andre very much; he was very friendly with a nice smile and was ever so careful not to squeeze when somebody shook his hand. He later went on to have a big part in the movie *The Princess Bride*. Andre died from heart failure in 1993 while in Paris, France.

Just across the street from Harvey's and down a half a block was a bar called the Jazz Nest. After I got to work every night and set my horns up, I'd like to get out of the place until show time because I knew I'd be there for five or six hours straight. The Jazz Nest looked like a cute little bar where I could go relax with a cigarette and a beer. Well, the first night I went in, as soon as I walked in the door, everything went silent and the patrons all looked around at me - the place was totally black. I was welcome, but they were all just surprised to see a well-dressed white guy wander in to their watering hole. I introduced myself to the bartender, who was the owner of the place, and explained to him that I was playing at Harvey's. The owner's name was Vern and was a very nice, friendly guy. Over time when we all got to know each other I became one of the guys and they all looked forward to seeing me every night before I went to work. Actually, it reminded me of a black version of *Cheers*.

I was happy to go back and play the St. Louis Ragtime Festival after having such a great reception the last time. I brought Bob Pettingell on base and replaced banjoist John McKinley with his son, Craig. Craig was brilliant and was taught how to play by his father. The rest of the band was the same as the year before. The Festival scheduled me to play a special opening dinner at a downtown St. Louis hotel. It was quite an event and there was a big story about it in the St. Louis newspaper, along with a picture of me. We played for a festive crowd who were amped up for a full week of jazz and ragtime music. While I was on an intermission I was given a note that there was someone out in the hotel lobby that wished to speak to me. I went to the lobby and a young man walked up to me and said – Hi Jim - My name is George Beatty, I saw your picture in the paper and have come to talk with you!

Well, I had a cousin, Wally Beatty, who lived on Long Island, New York. He had two boys, George and Harry. Back in 1968, while I was playing at the Flame Supper Club, Wally flew the whole family to Portland to visit with us and hear me play. So, I knew George when he was a young boy. When George grew up he joined the Navy and served for four years and after he was discharged he never came home and seemingly disappeared from the face of the earth. His family, of course, was frantic, and Wally spent several years trying to find out what had happened to his son, but to no avail. After Wally had tried everything, including private detectives, we all thought something terrible had happened to him after his discharge and he was assumed dead.

And now, there he was, standing right in front of me! I was dumbfounded, and temporarily speechless. I said, "George! What happened? Where have you been all these years? Your family has been searching all over the country for you!" There were tears flowing down George's cheeks when he told me that while he was in the Navy he got into drugs - big time. When he was discharged he really went off the deep end and was ashamed to come home and have his family see him in that condition. He said that he met a nice girl along the way, who helped him break the habit, and now he was totally clean and had a job. After he got the monkey off his back, it had been so long, and he was so ashamed, that he was frightened to go home. He had a nice young lady with him and I took them into the party so we could talk after I was through playing.

At the end of the night we sat and talked and I had to tell him that his father had passed away recently. I told him that his family would be overjoyed to know that he was alive and well. He agreed to come to my hotel room the next morning and I called his Uncle Frank (Wally's brother) and put George on the phone to him. All this got him back with his mother and brother and all those terrible years were behind them. It was just too bad that Wally wasn't around to see this happy ending. This certainly was a surprise beginning of the Jazz Festival for me.

When we arrived in St. Louis we were told that there was a convention in town and a shortage of hotel rooms, so they had to split my band between two hotels, one block from each other. Bob Pettingell wasn't happy with his hotel and thought mine was better, but that's the way it was. The next morning I was walking through the lobby of my hotel and who did I bump into? None other than Bob Pettingell. I asked him what he was doing over at my hotel and he told me that he had called and there was a room available and he took it. I told Bob that he just couldn't do those things and that was up to the festival promoters. As soon as I got back to my hotel room the phone was ringing and it was the producer of the festival, Bill Oakley. He said "Jim - what in hell is going on? Your bass player booked another room for himself at your hotel and now I'm paying for two rooms for one guy!" He wasn't a happy camper, but the damage was done and Bob got to stay in his room at my hotel. We were off to a bad start here, because when you play these festivals, you try to stay under the radar and not ruffle any feathers along the way.

The next evening when I went to work on the boat, Bill Oakley was waiting for me with a couple of security guards and Bob Pettingell in tow. Oakley angrily said – "Beatty! Does this guy belong to you?" Evidently, Bob forgot his pass to get on the ship and decided to sneak on by a galley at the back of the ship, and was arrested by security. I was in trouble again, and all because of this Pettingell idiot. I apologized to Bill Oakley and promised that nothing like this would happen again. I knew then that I had to vet my musicians more closely when I played concerts as important as this. I should point out, however, that Bob Pettingell was one of the best bass players around, and he also played excellent tuba. He was with me at the Godfather's Retreat and I never had any problems with him, but I guess he was just one of those guys that you couldn't take anywhere.

Just when I thought the dust had settled and all was forgiven, I went to work one night and there again, Bill Oakley was waiting for me at the door, and he didn't look happy at all. We all had passes to get on and off the ship and if we had a wife or girlfriend we wanted to bring on with us, that was okay, but you had to go to the office and get them a pass. Well, it seems that one member of my band met up with a companion that he wanted to take with him, but he didn't go to the office and get an extra pass. So when he went to get on the ship they wouldn't let him bring his companion with him. Unfortunately, tempers flared and my guy called the admission man a N*****. Needless to say, this is horrible word for a white guy to say, especially in St. Louis, where there was such a large black population.

Bill Oakley told me that we had a very serious situation on our hands. I had to get the musician involved to come and apologize to the ticket-taker and hope for the best. So, I went to my guy and said – Please - go and apologize and get down on your knees if you have to - otherwise we could have a real racial situation here. Well, he gave his apology and it was accepted, and all was well but certainly not forgotten.

When we finally get up to the stage to play, I had another surprise waiting for me. Pete Pepke was drunk as a skunk! Pete loved to drink, but I had never seen him show up to the job soused. We got through our concert without anybody noticing because there were enough guys in the band to cover for him, but I'm sure that Bill Oakley observed Pete's inebriation.

All in all, the band went over very well again and deserved to be asked back the next year, but I knew that after everything that had happened, there would be no next year in St. Louis for the Jim Beatty Jazz Band. Of course something like this spreads around to other festivals and was by no means a good recommendation for me.

The festival was over and we headed back to the St. Louis airport. When we got there, Harold Koster, discovered that he left his plane ticket back at his hotel room. Just what I needed, more stress! I called the hotel, and fortunately they went to Harold's room and found the ticket. I had them put the ticket in a taxicab and it got out to the airport in time for Harold to get on the plane with us, back to Portland. I was starting to have second thoughts about babysitting six or seven guys at jazz festivals, and sometimes they brought their wives with them; babysitting a dozen people was pretty difficult.

It was back to Portland and more music at Harvey's. Besides my band playing some good music in St. Louis, I also found my long-lost little cousin. Or did he find me? At any rate, getting George Beatty back with the family was well worth the trip.

To keep the show fresh at Harvey's, it was decided to bring in a guest performer now and then. I got my old friend, Gussie, from Godfather's Retreat, to come and do a show with us. She did a great job and packed the place with a standing room only crowd. She had her usual gay following and that helped fill the room as well.

I also brought in comedian Brian Bressler, for a change of pace. Brian, you'll remember, was the other half of the Mike and Brian show from the Flame Supper Club, back in the late 60s. Mike and Brian went their separate ways and did very well. Brian went on to be a regular on Rowan and Martin's *Laugh-In*, a very popular weekly television show in the 60s and early 70s. Brian was also on Johnny Carson's late night show and played the grandfather in the movie, the *Roome's*. Brian had not lost his touch and had the audience in stitches.

But our most popular guest was a gal named Diamond Lil. She was a big lady with a big voice, and boy, could she belt those songs out. Lil fit in with our band perfectly, because she sang the same vintage tunes that we liked to play. She performed tunes like "Won't You Come Home Bill Bailey" and "Alexander's Ragtime Band," along with her specialty songs, such as, "He's got the Cutest Little Dingy in the Navy." She became a regular performer with my band on the weekends.

I also got Craig McKinley to play banjo with us on the weekends. He was still in high school when he worked for me and could only be in the lounge on stage while he performed. On intermissions he had to leave the lounge and sit in a little anti-room, just off stage. It was pretty boring for the poor guy to sit in that room for five intermissions every night, but I think a band member might have slipped him a drink or two to help him pass the time.

Dan Robin was a new cornet player in town and he seemed to have some good credentials. He would come down and sit in with us quite often. He sounded very good and knew all the tunes, and he played on one of Wild Bill Davison's old cornets. He had a rather different personality, but with a good sense of humor, although he did not drink, and that was always a red flag for me. For instance, Bob Pettingell didn't drink! However, good cornet players were hard to come by and I always used him whenever the occasion arose.

Right next door to Harvey's, in fact right behind the bandstand, there was a recording studio – Vector Records. I got the bright idea that if we drilled a couple holes through the wall into the recording studio we could make a live recording of our performance at Harvey's. I talked it over with Barry and the people at Vector Records and they agreed to give it a try. So they drilled holes in the wall and pushed through the recording wires to microphones on the bandstand. We did some experimenting with the band and I'll be damned if it didn't work. So, I set up a big weekend for recording *Live at Harvey's,* with a live audience and all the excitement and applause. I brought in Pete Pepke and had Dan Robin on cornet, along with Diamond Lil. We were all set for a new album.

I set the recording date for *Live at Harvey's* for April 11th, 1981. We talked it up around the club for a couple of weeks beforehand to be assured of a big, enthusiastic crowd that was needed for a live recording. Vector Records pulled their wires through the holes in the wall and with our large receptive audience, we were all set to go. My band had the same personnel, with one exception; my bass man, Ed Fontaine, had retired, and I hired a young fellow named Mark Sobolik to fill his spot. The only trouble was he played electric bass, but what the heck, I thought I'd give it a try.

The amazing part of recording this new album was that Diamond Lil was well enough to do it with us. She had a stroke about a year previously and had forgotten the words to many of her tunes. However, by coming in now and then and singing with the band, the words slowly came back to her and she was back in business. Unfortunately, a while later, a couple of doctors talked her into having some sort of brain surgery and she was never the same again. On top of all that, John Picardi had been having severe chest pains that turned out to be very serious and he needed open heart surgery. After the recording John went to a hospital in Seattle for the surgery and made it through with flying colors. Except, immediately following surgery, he went back to his old habit of drinking lots of coffee and smoking pack after pack of cigarettes.

We recorded the whole evening and then I went back into the studio and picked out what I thought were the best eight numbers. This wasn't easy because there was so much good material to choose from. This process took several days, and then the music had to be balanced before a final master copy was made. The eight tunes we ended up with were: "Bill Bailey" – "Royal Garden Blues" – "Petite Fleur" – "Margie" – "Harvey's Blues" – "Alexander's Ragtime Band" – "Sugar Blues" – and "Muskrat Ramble." The album came out quite well and to this day, I still enjoy listening to it.

Business at Harvey's, for the most part, had been very good, but eventually I started to notice a slowdown. It wasn't just Harvey's, but all the nightclubs in the Portland area were feeling it as well. I'm not an economist and can't pretend to tell you why there was such a decline in the nightclub business, but it didn't take too many brains to look into the future and see most nightclubs being a weekend adventure. It helped if you were a small group, but in my case I had a quartet and sometimes more. To help the situation, we cut our nights down from six nights a week to five.

Roger Sheik and his buddy Tom Garcia were two loyal fans that came in to hear the band frequently. Roger was my partner, along with Don Kennedy, when we produced the jazz concert at civic auditorium. He told me that he had a son, Chris, who played the drums in a local rock band. Roger asked me if I would come with him some evening on my night off and listen to Chris play the drums and give him my professional opinion of his playing. On my next night off, Roger, Tom, and I went to a place called, The Earth Tavern, to listen to Chris perform. When we got there, Chris was on a break and came over to our table. I couldn't believe it! Chris was wearing a skimpy pair of shorts, a raggedy beat up tank top, and a grubby pair of sneakers with no socks. He was a nice-looking young man and had a great personality. When he went back to play with the band he was full of energy and had lots of spirit. Although I didn't know a lot about rock, I was impressed with Chris's musicianship and I told Roger so. It was the farthest thing from my mind at the time, but I was looking and listening to one of my future drummers.

Jim Goodwin had been playing off and on in Holland for a number of years and had been after me to come over for the Breda Jazz Festival. Jame just had one more year of high school and Bob was a year behind him. They both played in the Lake Oswego High School Band – Jame playing the cornet and Bob, the trombone. Jame also played piano. They both loved sports and played high school basketball, along with other school activities. In other words, they were both getting close to graduating from high school and moving on. With this in mind, and the fact that the nightclub business was going to hell, Pauline and I decided that I should go to Holland and across the channel for a visit to England, while I was at it. If I was going to start traveling and doing guest spots, why not across the pond?

One of the last big events that I did at Harvey's before leaving, was my friends, Pat and Terry O'Neal's wedding reception on March 16th, 1982. It was a grand affair and even Diamond Lil was there after recovering from her brain surgery. It was sad to see her in such bad shape but she was a good sport and even sang "It Had to Be You" with Pat O'Neal. Pat had retired from music some years before and was now in the car sales business. He planned on getting back into music on a part-time basis, playing with the Stumptown Jazz Band.

After we left Harvey's, they had a bad fire and were closed for quite some time before reopening. Barry added a new room and opened up what was to become a very successful comedy club, which is still thriving to this day. I'm happy that Harvey's is doing well, because the Colin's were a great family and a big part of my life for several years.

You would think that at 48 years-old I had learned a little bit about drinking sensibly, but evidently I hadn't. It was time to go on my big trip to Holland and I found a great deal on Air Canada, from Vancouver, BC, to Amsterdam, Holland. It was the band's last night at Harvey's and Pauline and the boys picked me up after work at 2:30 a.m. Pauline drove and I sipped on a six-pack of beer on the way to Vancouver. I intended to take a nap when we arrived at Pauline's folk's house because my plane didn't leave until late afternoon. Pauline's dad, however, had other plans and was in the mood for a little drinking party for the two of us. So, I never did get my nap, but I thought that would be okay because I could sleep all the way over to Holland. When I boarded the airplane I sat next to a nice Dutch fellow that was a captain of a cruise ship and on a two-week leave back to his home in Holland. Needless to say, he was very interesting to talk to and I also found out that his hobby was octopus hunting - or is it fishing? He was all excited about his vacation and we ended up partying the whole flight over to Holland.

Once we landed in Amsterdam Jim Goodwin was waiting for me and we went immediately to the nearest bar for some Dutch beer and to catch up. After a few beers, Jim and I caught a train to Breda, where Jim was staying with his girlfriend and her family, and it also was the city that held the jazz festival. When we got to Breda, all of Jim's friends were anxious to meet me and it was one party after another. At one party I was introduced to a young man, who looked at me in amazement and said - Are you Jim Beatty - the American clarinetist? Well, I was just as amazed as he was because I couldn't believe that anybody knew of me in Holland! The young man said – My father is a big fan of yours and I'm going to call him and tell him you're here. His dad did come over to the party and we had a nice chat and then I realized that recordings have a way of creating fans all over the world.

I learned how to drink like a Dutchman, very quickly. Their national drink is called *Jenever*, and you drink it with beer, somewhat like a German schnapps. *Jange Jenever* has sort of a neutral taste, somewhat like vodka, with the breath of Juniper and malt wine. *Oude Jenever* is aged in wood and has a whiskey taste, made of barley, wheat or rye. At any rate, *Jenever* was pleasant to drink and very powerful.

After all the parties and jam sessions, I started to realize that I was fading fast and needed some rest. It was going on four days without sleep and I was ready. Jim had arranged for me to stay at a friend's house and I went there and slept and slept and slept. Fortunately for me, I lived through it all, but it was a very ridiculous thing to do and it never happened again.

After I recovered from all the parties, I went on to enjoy the Jazz Festival and I got to play music with many wonderful musicians. I was on my way to England for a week and I told Jim Goodwin to gather up some good musicians from the Festival and when I got back to Holland we would have a recording session. The exchange rate was one Dutch *Gilder* to $.35 American. I figured it wouldn't cost very much to finance the recording session and it would be well worth it.

I had a great time in Breda and the food was wonderful. A humorous thing happened to me at lunch time one day when I walked into a Dutch deli and looked into the window at all their meats and cheeses. I looked around and they were making beautiful big sandwiches, so I ordered a ham and cheese sandwich. The waitress looked strangely at me and soon delivered one ham sandwich and one cheese sandwich to my table.

I took a train to the coast to catch my ship over to England. Somehow I got my wires crossed and ended up at the wrong dock. But it was the same cruise line and they had a ship leaving about the same time, so they felt sorry for me and let me on. To my surprise, after boarding, I found out that it was a gambling ship, with no sleeping accommodations. So it was no sleep for me once again.

Pauline's father had a cousin, Roy Vickerstaff, who lived in Bude, Cornwall, England. I planned to visit him and his family after I first made a pit stop in London. London was as exciting as I thought it would be, and watching the changing of the guard at Buckingham Palace gave me goose pimples all over my body, as it does every time I visit. At my hotel I had a typical English breakfast, which is out of this world. They brought me warm milk, and I just thought that's what the British put on their dry cereal – so that's what I did. It was for my tea of course - dumb American!

I arrived in Bude and the Vickerstaff family was wonderful. Bude is a small, seaside resort town and about as British as you can get. Cousin Roy and family owned a large amount of property in Bude, including a liquor store. After we got to know each other over a few drinks, he gave me a key to the liquor store, which I have to this day. It also turned out cousin Roy was quite a drinker, and he took me to his private Social Club every day at noon for drinks - my God! Is anybody sober? After our afternoon drinking we would go back to the house and have a mid-afternoon dinner of roast beef and Yorkshire pudding, prepared by his wife, Bertie. I was home! It was like being back at 11 Shaw Avenue all over again. Roy and Bertie had a wonderful family of two boys, James and Roger, and a girl, Judith.

On my return voyage to Holland I managed to get on the right ship and had a very enjoyable trip back to the Netherlands. I got on a train to Breda and met up with Jim Goodwin again. He had everything all arranged for the recording session and had signed up some good musicians that were left over from the jazz festival. In addition to Jim and me, we had a popular American drummer, Jeff Hamilton, and we rounded out the band with Dutch musicians Joep Peters, on piano, Peter Kanters, guitar, and John Rynen on the bass.

The recording session was set for May 31st, 1982, at the Roaring 20's club in Breda. The club was closed that night and we had the place to ourselves, thanks to Jim Goodwin, who was a good friend of the owners. An American jazz fan, Ralph Parsons, had a tape recorder that he set up in the middle of the room along with one microphone. A select group of friends were invited for the taping and I bought large amounts of Dutch beer, along with some whiskey and Scotch to keep everybody in a happy mood.

We recorded: "How Come You Do Me Like You Do" – "Out Of The Galleon" – "I Would Do Anything For You" – "Blue Skies" – "Wait Till The Sun Shines Nellie" – "I Left My Sugar Standing In The Rain" – "What Is This Thing Called Love" – "Memories Of You" – "Sweet Lorraine," and "After You've Gone." With just one microphone in a near empty jazz club, the recordings came out extremely well. It was issued on cassette tape, which were becoming very popular and slowly replacing LP records. The cassette was small and more convenient and portable. You could buy pre-recorded cassettes and if you wanted to record yourself you could buy blanks. I had my brother-in-law, Brian Hemingway, design the front cover of the cassette case. We called it, *Jim Beatty in Holland.*

Then it was back to the United States, where I was now out of the nightclub business and back to playing casuals and whatever may come my way. And as it turned out I was in for a lot of different and unusual musical experiences.

## CHAPTER 24

# Portland Trailblazers

I WAS BEGINNING TO FIND out that Dan Robin wasn't going to fit into my musical plans. For one thing, he was so hard to find because he had obtained a Ford Econovan from Pat O'Neal and had made it his home. He would move from one rest area to another and if a job came up, it was a nightmare trying to find out where he was parked. He had no telephone and never checked in with me. The first time he came to my house he looked at the address above the door and saw that it read 16666 Roosevelt Drive. He was telling people that was bad karma and the sign of the devil. Another time he was at my house, a fruit fly was flying around the kitchen, and I smacked it between my hands. He had a fit, telling me that was bad karma and I would pay for it in another life. He was also telling people that I was a Nazi because my hobby was the Second World War and collecting German memorabilia, which I had been doing since I was a kid after befriending the German prisoners of war. It got to be too much, so I quit calling him, which wasn't too hard to do because he didn't have a phone. He went on to play jazz festivals with the Stumptown Jazz Band and I understand that he self-destructed with them, as well.

Lose one – win one. A brilliant musician had just moved into the Portland area. His name was Jim Maihack and he played the piano, trombone, banjo and tuba. Jim was a wonderful guy and married to a very nice lady, Wendy. He was born in Rock Island, Illinois, in 1935 and started music by playing the accordion. He later switched to piano, trombone and tuba. In his early professional career he worked with the popular Clyde McCoy and in 1963, he moved to Sacramento California, and then he joined the Turk Murphy Band in San Francisco in 1969. He had been playing with Turk off and on ever since. In 1975, he moved to Orlando, Florida for a few years and then back to the West Coast. Jim recorded an album called *Never Mind I'll do it Myself,* in which he played piano, banjo, clarinet, trombone, tuba and vocals. Brilliant!

Jim was about my age and it was great to have him around. He worked with me quite often playing the piano, trombone or tuba. I had him play the trombone with my band later on when I brought in Ernie Carson and also Wild Bill Davison as guests.

After so many years of being a bandleader and all its responsibilities, the thought of being a side man was sounding better and better. As a side man, all you had to do was show up for the job and play your instrument. No negotiating with club owners, no responsibility of figuring out the set list every night, no looking for substitutes if one of your musicians was sick, and no payroll to meet every week. Those are just a few of the responsibilities of a bandleader, and there are many more.

I had been getting calls from Bill Borcher, the leader of the Oregon Jazz Band, from Coos Bay, asking me if I would be interested in filling the clarinet spot in his band. It sounded like a nice change of pace for me and I decided to do it. It certainly wasn't going to be convenient because of the distance from Portland to Coos Bay, but I thought I'd give it a try.

Bill Borcher had an interesting background in education. From 1945 to 1951 he was the head basketball coach at Marshfield High in Coos Bay, and from 1951 until 1956 he was the head coach at Oregon State. While he was at Mansfield High he founded the Oregon Jazz Band in 1947, playing the trumpet. In 1972, he founded the Sacramento Jazz Festival, which became the largest of its kind in the world. So he was an organizer, and a very good one at that.

The only trouble was, Borcher didn't play the trumpet, he just owned one. I was shocked the first time I played with the band and saw and heard what an amateur he was. Although the band was made up of amateurs, there were some good players in it, such as Bud Baird on the piano and Walt Hill on tenor sax. There was also an older member of the band, Neil Hart on drums, who Bill always introduced as the Mayor of Dixonville, Oregon. Borcher had a very lovely wife, Pat, and I often wondered which one was really the boss.

I was also surprised, and dismayed, when I found out about all the different uniforms the band wore. One was all white - shirt, pants and shoes, and it was a nightmare trying to keep it clean and neat looking. There was also pink and white striped vests that made us look like ice cream salesman. There were a few other ridiculous outfits, but the worst of all was the logger uniform. It was a heavy red wool shirt with jeans and hiking boots, not to mention the red handkerchief tied around your neck. I was embarrassed when I stepped onto the bandstand, and this was before we even started playing.

The band was run just like one of Borcher's basketball teams. He expected everyone to stick together all day, even when we weren't playing. At a jazz festival we would start out around 11 a.m. in Borcher's room for a pep talk and Bloody Mary's. This was a band that had a hard enough time playing sober, let alone starting to drink first thing in the morning. I was there for the pep talk but didn't partake in the Bloody Mary's, and of course I was looked at like I wasn't part of the group. When I got paid the first time, I noticed there was some money missing from my check. I went to Bill and asked about it and he said that it was a deduction that was put into a slush fund for the beer and pizza parties after the jobs. Well for one thing. I didn't drink beer and eat pizza after playing. If anything, I would find a cocktail lounge and enjoy a nice glass of Scotch. There again, I wasn't a "go-along guy," and I knew they thought that I was some kind of a loner.

I had another surprise coming when we went to Phoenix, Arizona, to play a weekend jazz party. We flew to Phoenix out of Portland and stayed in a pleasant hotel outside of Phoenix. We played the jazz party and it went as well as could be expected. On the way back on the airplane, Borcher handed me a check in an envelope. I discreetly opened it up and found the check to be for $50. I thought, this might be to cover meal expenses or something like that, so I asked Bill what it was for. He told me that that was my pay for the Phoenix job. I couldn't believe it - I flew all the way to Phoenix, Arizona and played for the weekend for $50.

It was then that I realized I certainly was in the wrong place with these guys, and it was my fault for not figuring it out in the first place. They were all nice people, but because most of them were amateurs and had day jobs, they looked on the Oregon Jazz Band as a way to have fun playing music, drinking early morning Bloody Mary's, and having late-night beer and pizza parties. I didn't belong and I am sure that they were happy to get rid of me.

The Village Jazz in Lake Oswego was always a great place to play. The band played there often, as well as having Wild Bill Davison as a guest with us a couple of times. Ernie Carson was coming to town, I suggested that he play with us as a guest, management was all for it, and we set a date.

Ernie preferred two-beat jazz with tuba and banjo, so I put together that type of band for him. I had Bill Baird on piano, Bill Stauffer on tuba, with Moon Monsey on banjo. Along with Ernie on cornet, I had Jim Maihack playing trombone and myself on clarinet. Ernie was at his best with that type of band and the crowd loved it.

Following the job at The Village Jazz, Ernie came back to the house with me to have a drink and relax. Well, there was no having just one drink with Ernie Carson, and before I knew it the boys were stirring upstairs, getting ready for school. It also dawned on me I had school as well, as I had two young audience shows to play, the first one at 8 a.m. I told Ernie I had to get going and he said – I'll go with you!

We must have smelled like cigarettes and alcohol that morning at school, but thank goodness for the teachers smoking room where we could cover it up with some hot coffee. In other words - we were wide awake drunks; but the children and teachers probably heard one of the hottest jazz concerts ever that day!

Although the jazz nightclub scene was slowing down, there still were many places featuring jazz music in Portland. There was Harvey's, the Benson lounge, Brasserie Montmartre, Chuck's Steakhouse, Bogart's, Cousin's, The Prima Donna, Hobo's, Jazz De Opus, Jazz Quarry, Tuck Lung and Geneva's. There was also a few places in the outskirts of Portland like the Village Jazz in Lake Oswego. I could keep busy just playing around town in the clubs, casuals, jazz societies, and the occasional jazz festival. I also had some projects to look forward to in the future, such as a west coast tour with Wild Bill and an engagement in Jamestown, and I intended to bring the family along.

So much had happened in the last few years that I didn't know where the time went. The majority of my playing had been in the Portland area, but there was a of lot work where I was away from home more than I wanted to be. So Pauline and I decided that on spring break we would take a trip back to Jamestown.

It was the 1982–83 school year and Jame was already a senior in high school. He played varsity football as a wide/receiver/defensive back at 6' 2," 160 pounds. He was in the stage band and marching band, along with working weekends at North's Chuckwagon Buffet. Jame broke his wrist playing football and was put on injured reserve. After football season we got his cast off and he played varsity basketball. Jame didn't feel he was ready for college after high school and decided to join the US Army. Pauline and I had to sign for him because he was under eighteen. Bob was one year behind Jame and was playing JV basketball along with playing trombone in the marching and concert band and a cast member of the high school musicals. He was also school newspaper editor along with being yearbook assistant editor. So we had two busy boys who had lots of friends that enjoyed hanging out at our house.

We had our trip planned and were anxious to get going, when Pauline got into a fender bender on the way to work one afternoon and broke her fibula and was put in a cast. She insisted on going on our trip and we were pushing her around airports in a wheelchair. She was a good sport and didn't let it bother her for the whole vacation.

We flew into Cleveland, Ohio, so we could spend some time visiting my sister Linda, who lived not far away in Norwalk. We then drove to Jamestown, about 3 1/2 hours away. When we left Ohio it started to snow and the more we drove, the more it snowed, and when we got near Jamestown we were in a huge whiteout snowstorm. Welcome to Western New York!

It was great to see family and friends again and everyone was surprised to see how the boys had grown. I had jobs lined up to play and one of them was at the Elks Club in Warren, Pennsylvania with Pete Pepke.

My whole family came along to the job. Bob had an impersonation of Pete Pepke singing, "Into Each Life Some Rain Must Fall," that was just hilarious. I got Bob to come on stage and do it - he was the hit of the evening. We all had a wonderful visit and took advantage of the Jamestown fish fry, along with the beef on weck. It was time for the boys to get back and finish up at school.

Jame went to the senior prom with is high school girlfriend, Cherie, and graduated in June. He asked me which school he should attend in the Army, and I suggested military police school, after thinking about the nice job they had in Fort Eustis. In August, he left for basic training in Fort McClellan, Alabama, and later MP training. Bob went on to his senior year of high school and it became a busy one. Pauline's leg healed and then it was back to business as usual.

I had one great fan that followed me around wherever I was playing, including jazz clubs and festivals: Lorna Coffel. She had a boyfriend, Clyde Bittner, who was with her all of the time. Lorna had a fitness center in Lake Oswego called the Rivers Edge. It was a first-class operation with a swimming pool, gym, racquetball court, and workout room, with all the machines and equipment. The club was located near the Tualatin River and had a full size track in the back. Lorna and Clyde were a lot of fun and were probably ten or fifteen years older than me.

Lorna approached me and asked me what I was doing to keep fit. I said that I was doing nothing except lifting a glass of Scotch up to my mouth several times a night. She said – What would you think about working out? I realized that required exercise and I hadn't had any exercise since Army basic training. Lorna wanted to give me a free membership to her fitness club because evidently they liked having a few members with familiar names around town. I never considered myself a familiar name, but evidently she thought differently. I thought about it and realized that I probably could use some exercise because I was 50 years old now and I should start taking care of myself.

I started to go to the club every other day, and Laura's son, Lance, was in charge of the body shop and was a personal trainer as well. Lance took me around to the various weightlifting machines and put me on a program, starting out easy and slowly progressing to heavier weights. Several members of the Portland Trailblazer basketball team worked out there and I became good friends with Mychal Thompson. There were other Blazers working out there, like Terry Porter, Clyde Drexler and Sam Bowie. Sam was drafted into the Trailblazers and was supposed to be their big star; they picked him before Michael Jordan. Sam, unfortunately, became injury prone and was benched a good deal of the time. Mychal Thompson and I went in for our workouts about the same time and we must've looked hilarious together. I was 5'10" and weighed about 175 pounds and Mychal was 6'10" and weighed 275 pounds. Mychal was born in the Bahamas in 1955, so we had a lot to talk about because of my playing there years before. He was the first foreign-born, NBA number one draft pick and played for the Blazers for eight years. He then went on to the LA Lakers and won two championships with them. He is now a sports analyst in Los Angeles and a talk show host. He has three sons, two of them in the NBA (one is all-star Klay Thompson), and his youngest son, Trayce, is a professional baseball player with the White Sox.

I had another Blazer connection, but he wasn't a player. It was the radio announcer who talked you through all the games, Bill Schonely. He had been the voice of the Trailblazers since their beginning, in 1970, and broadcast for them nearly three decades, until 1998. He was famous for his saying "Rip City!" and became one of the most popular personalities in the Portland area. I knew Bill because he used to come in to the

Village Jazz to hear my band and he loved to sing, and he had a good voice. He still comes to hear me play occasionally and I always ask him up to sing a few tunes. He's an amazing guy and is going strong as the goodwill ambassador for the Blazers. Bill is five years older than I am and still keeps busy in broadcasting. You often see him on television doing commercials for Standard TV and Appliances, advertising anything from mattresses to refrigerators. He's probably got the most recognizable voice in the Portland area.

I stuck with my exercising routine for some time until I was on the road and gone so much I got out of the habit. But I still continued jogging and did so wherever I went. Perhaps the working out and jogging did do me some good, because amazingly, I'm still around.

San Francisco's Turk Murphy was looking for a new clarinet player and he called me to see if I might be interested. I talked it over with Pauline and we decided that since Jame was in the Army and Bob was now studying at Carleton College in Minnesota, I should go and give it a try. It really didn't make a lot of sense financially because I had so much work in the Portland area, but what the heck, it was an adventure and an opportunity that might not come along again. So I packed my car up with all my belongings (I had a beautiful Lincoln Mark V) and headed to San Francisco on a Sunday and arriving early Monday afternoon, in plenty of time to start with Turk's band at the Fairmount Hotel on Tuesday evening.

Jim Maihack had rejoined Turk's band playing piano. He had moved back to the San Francisco bay area with his wife Wendy. The two of them were wonderful people and invited me to stay in their guest room while I was playing with Turk. That made it very nice because I didn't have to be alone in some apartment. We got along great and it worked well because I babysat their dog on our days off when they weren't home.

Jim and I went to work together each night and got to the Fairmont Hotel early so we could have a great dinner in the employees dining room. The food was delicious because it was leftovers from all the big banquets at the hotel. Trouble was, it was also a good way to put on weight. Turk was happy to see me and bought me a drink as soon as I walked into the lounge for work. The guys in the band were wonderful and had been with him for quite some time. Along with Turk on trombone and me on clarinet, there was Bob Schultz, cornet, Jim Maihack, piano, Bill Armstrong, banjo and Bill Carroll on tuba.

See's Candy sponsored a live radio broadcast from the Fairmount Hotel featuring Turk's band every Tuesday evening. This was a little nerve-racking because my first night on the job playing with Turk was heard all over the San Francisco area. I knew Turk's band was heavily arranged and required reading parts, but I never knew to what extent the arrangements were. Everyone else in the band had been with him long enough to memorize their parts, but I had to have the music in front of me since I had never played the arrangements before. So, I stood uncomfortably on the bandstand, the only one in the band with a music stand in front of me. On top of that, Turk had terminal bone cancer and was in the last days of his life. As his condition worsened he had trouble playing the trombone and often just strummed on the washboard. Although I loved listening to Turk's band, I just didn't have my heart into reading that style of music night after night.

After a few weeks Turk and I both knew that it wasn't working out and I went back to Portland and picked up where I left off. There was a big tribute to Turk at Carnegie Hall in January, 1987. I called him shortly after and asked permission to record a tune he wrote, called "Little

Enough." He gave me his permission and then said "Jim - I hope you have some good news for me." Unfortunately I didn't, and he passed away in May, 1987, at just 72 years old. I'm glad I made that trip because it was a thrill to play with such a legend of traditional jazz.

Just when I thought that the band couldn't get busier, we got busier. Sundays, for instance, started out at 10:30 in the morning playing the brunch at Cal's. It was a rather large restaurant with a bar area on the right as you walked in. There were lots of tables for dining, with a beautiful view of the river. On Sundays, tables were moved to make room for a large buffet. There was a great selection of food and lots of it, including fresh fruits, assorted salads, assorted cheese, raw vegetables, salmon, scrambled eggs and Eggs Benedict, Potatoes Au Gratin, pork sausage, chicken livers, baron of beef and all kinds of desserts and pastries, and even champagne. At the time, the buffet was only $11.95, and believe me everyone was stuffed when they left.

Every Sunday there was always some kind of ice sculpture in the middle of the buffet. It was always different; one week it might be an animal of some sort, or a bird, or whatever the sculpture artist was asked to do. The band was set up just behind the buffet on a riser and we had a good view of the whole room and everything that was going on. Well, this one Sunday it must have been warmer in the room than usual because the sculpture started to melt quite rapidly and as it melted it lost its original shape and little by little it started to look like a giant penis. The band was right in back of it and we saw it take shape and slowly, one by one, the diners begin to notice, and before we knew it the whole room was dying from laughter. The manager came running out and ordered the waiters to cart it away and he looked up at me like I had something to do with it. I always kept my eye on the ice sculptures from then on, but it never happened again.

When we were through with our job at Cal's at 2:30 in the afternoon, I went home and relaxed or took a nap and then headed for Portland to play at the Brasserie Montmartre. The Brasserie was a very popular downtown French restaurant and was the place to be seen in those days. It was a rather narrow but long room, with a large bar running along the right-hand side, and the band was situated at the very end of the room. It was unique because all the dining tables had paper tablecloths, along with a pack of crayons, so you could doodle while you are having your cocktails or dinner. The music was mostly for background and people actually didn't pay much attention; until we started playing there. For one thing they mostly featured modern type jazz, which can get rather repetitious and annoying. Since our style of jazz included melodies that people knew, all of a sudden the patrons started to applaud after each tune and the Sunday crowds began to get larger and larger. The manager couldn't believe it and was happier than hell because the cash register was ringing all night. Most of the bands were booked in there just for a few weeks at a time, but our job turned into a steady Sunday engagement.

It was very important and less stressful for me to have the same musicians in the band as much as possible. I was lucky because I had two piano players, Norm Domreis and Harold Koster, and they went back and forth playing with me for many years. I never used music on the bandstand and that eliminated many of the musicians around town. On top of that, many of the good players were working with several different bands and weren't always available to play with me. There was also the issue of musicians with day jobs, and in most cases that didn't work out with my band because of our busy schedule. But my main problem was finding a good drummer because John Picardi had moved out of town.

I remembered the young drummer I heard back in 1982 with a rock 'n roll band, Chris Sheik, the son of my friend, Roger Sheik. I told Roger to ask

Chris if he might be interested in playing jazz with my band and if so, have him give me a call. Chris called me shortly after and said he would be very interested, although he didn't know a lot about the style of music I played.

Chris came out to my house and for several days we listened to the many jazz drummers that I had in my record collection. Chris had a lot of rhythm in his soul and I knew that all he had to do was to absorb the style of jazz I played and he'd be fine. He was a natural percussionist, and looked good behind a set of drums. I was happy to find a new, young, drummer and probably the only one happier was his father, Roger, who was thrilled to see him work with me.

Learning the music was one thing, but now I had to get him cleaned up. I told Chris that he had to burn the short shorts, torn tank top, and dirty sneakers and get some grown up clothes. He had to buy a blue blazer, grey slacks, white shirt and tie, and dark shoes, quite a change from his rock 'n roll getup, and I suppose the young girls didn't think he was as cute and sexy now, but that's the way it goes in show business.

Chris started with the band and he worked out beautifully. He was given the nickname, "Kid," and officially became one of the group. He was a busy boy because he also joined his dad's car auction business as an auctioneer. Roger was still a partner with my friend Don Kennedy and they ran a real first class auction business.

When Chris joined the band, we had our doubleheader every Sunday, playing the Sunday brunch at Cal's from 10:30 a.m. until 2:30 p.m. After we were through playing we pigged out on the brunch and then went home, rested, and drove to Portland and performed at the Brasserie Montmartre from 8 p.m. until 12:30 a.m. - making it a very busy day.

Kid Sheik was funny. One morning he showed up for work for the brunch at Cal's wearing his new blue blazer and grey slacks, but with a pair of sneakers. I asked him what the sneakers we're all about and he said that nobody could see his feet sitting behind the drums, so it didn't matter what shoes he had on. I explained to him that he couldn't hide behind the drums for four hours, eventually he would have to get up and go to the bathroom or something. He also enjoyed having brunch with the band, and I told him that he wasn't going to sit with us wearing a pair of sneakers. So, I sent him home to change shoes. He was a good sport about it and the two of us still laugh about it to this day.

Later that evening when we were playing at the Brasserie Montmartre, the band was swinging along when I happened to turn around and saw Chris happily playing his drums and reading a book at the same time. I couldn't believe it! In all my years of playing I had never even seen any of my drummers reading music, let alone a book. I explained to Chris that this just wasn't done on the job and wasn't professional. I think that he was just so relaxed playing with my band that he thought that it would be a cool way of getting some reading in. I've often wondered if he finished that book.

It was a delight to have Chris in the band, but after about three years he had to leave because he became busy as an auctioneer. He later start-ed his own business, got married, and became a well-known auctioneer around the country. But over the years, whenever I needed a substitute drummer, I always called Chris first. We did a fun thing together on many of my jobs, having Chris auction off one of my CDs. People loved it when we did this and he would often get as much as five times the money that the CD was worth, and we split the profits. By the way, if you ever attend an auction and see a good-looking young man in a beautiful tux and a shiny pair of black patent leather shoes, that very well might be Chris Sheik.

Getting back to the business of playing casuals or freelancing is a matter of getting the word out, and it didn't take that long. We played a few weekends in a restaurant in downtown Portland called the Cinnamon Tree. It was a so-so restaurant and didn't have the character that Harvey's did, and on top of that they didn't advertise the band. I had a mailing list but it takes more than that to get a crowd out. We had one young man that became a fan of the band, and was there practically every night we played. Trouble was it was a sad case because he drank himself into oblivion every night. He could afford to do it because his last name was Phillips and his grandfather invented the Phillips screwdriver. He was in his 20's and would party every night, buying the band drinks as fast as we could drink them. I often wondered what happened to that young man. I hope that he straightened up and got his drinking under control because if he didn't, I'm sure he's not around anymore.

I went back to Jamestown, played a few engagements and visited with my mother. My Jamestown trips were more frequent and I would play there at least once a year. Nothing had really changed much in Jamestown except a lot of the old furniture factories had disappeared. Chautauqua Lake was as beautiful as ever and it was fun visiting my old haunts, including the Rod and Gun Club on the lake.

I got a call from the Vancouver, BC, Hot Jazz Society asking me to be their featured guest artist at their annual jazz festival the first part of November. I accepted the invitation because that gave Pauline and I a chance to visit with our Canadian side of the family. I suggested to the Jazz Society that along with me they also include Jim Goodwin, who would be home from Holland about that time. Jim always came home broke and I knew he would be able to use the money. The Festival committee thought that was a great idea and we rounded out the band with local Vancouver musicians, calling ourselves the Beatty/Goodwin All-Stars.

Goodwin, Pauline and I drove to Vancouver together for the Festival. Pauline dropped me and Jim off at our hotel and continued on to her parent's home. The Festival had three sites with continuous music all day and night. The music was held at the Anza club, Biltmore Hotel, and the Hot Jazz Society, all within a few blocks of each other. Besides me and Goodwin, the other bands were Lance Harrison, Phoenix Jazzers, Dixieland Express, Roy Reynold's Quartet, Rainier Jazz Band, Razzmajazz, Island City Jazz Band, and the Dave Roberts Jassband. It was a good show and the "two Jims" were having one heck of a good time.

In the band schedule, the last set was from 1 a.m. until whenever. This wasn't good news, especially for Goodwin and me, because we were scheduled to play at 12 o'clock every afternoon. That was always the trouble with jazz festivals, because you might be playing your first set at noon and your last set at 1 a.m., which was the case for Jim and Jim. The only thing that kept us going was that wonderful Canadian beer and whiskey.

The very first night of the festival ended up around 3 a.m. for us. We shared a room with two single beds and I was looking forward to getting some sleep so we'd be in shape for our noon concert. Well, it seems that one young lady who was an officer in the jazz society had the hots for Goodwin and followed us to our room. Because she had a lot to say in the jazz society, Goodwin and I felt we had to be nice to her and asked her in for a nightcap. One drink led to another and we were getting tired, to say the least. All of a sudden Goodwin stripped his suit off and hopped into bed. Then I'll be damned if his young lady friend went and took her clothes off and hopped in bed with him. Now I was sitting there by myself, so I hopped in my bed as well.

As I said, she was hot for Goodwin and wanted to be with him in the worst way. But as soon as Goodwin hit the bed he was out like a light and she was doing everything she could to revive him. This went on for some time and I finally told her that she was wasting her time and should try again the next day. In the meantime, I told her that we had to play at noon and I needed some sleep, so I would appreciate it if she left. She got up and started putting on her duds and glanced over at me. I said, don't look at me, I've had as much to drink as he has and besides that, I'm married - please leave. She did leave and I hope for her sake that she did catch up with Goodwin in the afternoon; after all that, she deserved it.

You have to remember one thing about Jim Goodwin and that is jazz music and alcohol were the most important things in the world to him. He also really loved the outdoors and taking long hikes in the woods. He could take or leave anything else. For instance, when his father passed away, Jim could have had his dad's new Ford Mustang. He didn't want it; he preferred his old beat-up jalopy instead, so I ended up buying the Mustang from his mother.

When Goodwin and I did get up late the next morning we felt terrible and were a bit shaky. Of course we had to play at noon, and that's the last thing we felt like doing. I remembered an old cure for a hangover. I always liked to listen to the newspaper and radio gossip commentator, Walter Winchell, and heard him say that a great cure for a hangover was mashed potatoes and gravy. There was a Kentucky Fried Chicken restaurant nearby so we got some delicious mashed potatoes, smothered with gravy. Thanks Walter and Colonel Sanders! That did the trick and we went and played one heck of a jazz show at noon.

After the festival was over, Pauline picked Jim and me up and we went over to her folk's house. Pauline's father was anxiously waiting for our arrival, all rested up and ready to party. We didn't want to let him down so we joined in and had a heck of a good time visiting for a couple of days. Pauline had a piano at her folk's house and we rented a U-Haul and brought it back to Portland with us. It's an old upright piano and besides

Pauline's playing, it has served us well for many band rehearsals and jam sessions over the years.

Moon Monsey was one-of-a-kind. I worked with him in the early 70s at McNulty at Barry's in Oregon City. As busy as I had been with all my nightclub work, I hadn't seen that much of him in the 80s. But he had still been busy around town playing his guitar, banjo and singing. He was heavy when I first met him, but over the years he had put on even more weight. Moon loved to eat and if you put any food in front of him it was gone quickly.

One day my phone rang and it was Moon on the other end of the line. Jim, he said, I've always wanted to go to New Orleans, but I want someone to go with me who knows their way around - would you go with me if I paid all expenses? Evidently, his mother had passed away and left him her house and a little money. He sold his mother's house, bought himself a trailer in a trailer park, and had money left over and it was burning a hole in his pocket. I looked at my calendar and found a few free days and told Moon that I would be happy to be his tour guide.

So, off to New Orleans we went, and what a trip it was. Moon insisted that we eat in all of the most expensive restaurants in town. We went to all the old, famous eateries in the French Quarter, such as Arnauds's, Antoine's, Tujaque's, Broussard's, and many more for breakfast, lunch, and dinner, and money was no object. At night we went up and down Bourbon Street, listening to jazz bands, concluding the evening with an early morning snack. I've never been so full of such fine food in my life, and Moon was in seventh heaven.

One night we went to Preservation Hall to listen to some good, old New Orleans Jazz. I knew all the players because they were well known in the traditional jazz world. Moon had a big booming voice and after the clarinet player's solo, he looked at me and said – "Jim - You're better than that!" I could've crawled under the table, and everybody turned around and stared at us. Moon wasn't at his best in social situations. Then he looked at me and said that he had heard enough New Orleans jazz and ate enough New Orleans food and wanted to know if I'd like to go to San Francisco and listen to Turk Murphy's Band? Now, this meant changing our airplane tickets at the last minute, which was always expensive to do, but it was his money and I agreed to go. On our last night, I brought my clarinet into the Famous Door and sat in with my old bandleader from many years ago, Murphy Compo. It was a treat, and we had a great reunion that night on Bourbon Street.

We flew to San Francisco the next morning, checked into the Hyatt Regency Hotel, went out to a very fancy steakhouse for dinner, and then went and listened to Turk and his band to finish out the evening. It was great to see Turk and the guys again and it gave me a chance to sit in and play a few tunes with them. We spent one more day in San Francisco and flew back to Portland. A few days later the phone rang and it was Moon. Jim! I've always wanted to go to Mexico - Will you go with me? I didn't.

George Buck Junior was president of Jazzology and GHB Records of New Orleans. He had been headquartered in Atlanta originally, but in later years moved his company to the Mecca of jazz. It was a very successful recording company, recording only traditional jazz, and the first album he released was none other than Wild Bill Davison, his favorite musician. I met George at the St. Louis Jazz Festival. He was very impressed with my band and expressed interest in recording it. George ran a first-class and honest business treating his musicians very fairly and paying them very well.

My band was booked to play The Oregon Dixieland Jubilee for 1987, so I thought that would be the perfect time to record the Jazzology album. Both Ernie Carson and Pete Pepke would be in town to play the Festival with me, and along with the rest of my band, it would make for a good recording group. I had booked two nights at the Village Jazz, which would be a good warm-up for a recording session to get the cobwebs out of our horns.

As if I didn't have enough on my mind, I started getting warning signals about Brad Harrett and his drinking. He was such a wonderful young bass player and I hated to see him go down that road, like so many others that I'd known. On top of that, I knew he liked to smoke marijuana, and the two didn't mix. I also had alarms about Ernie Carson, but so far he hadn't given me any grief over the drinking situation. I wasn't a teetotaler myself, but I did draw the line when it came to business and making good music.

Before going to the Seaside Jazz Festival we went to the recording studio and spent an afternoon and early evening recording ten tunes. We recorded "Going To New Orleans," "Lonesome," "Peg o' My Heart," "Sweet And Lovely," "You Were Only Fooling," "Knee Drops," "Just A Little Loving," "The Pearls," "My Gay Paree," and "Just A Little While To Stay Here." We had, besides myself on clarinet, Ernie Carson, cornet, Pete Pepke, trombone, Harold Koster, piano, Moon Monsey, banjo, Brad Harrett, bass, and Kid Sheik on the drums. "My Gay Paree" was Moon Monsey's composition and it involved a bit of band vocal. For some reason or another, Ernie Carson's mother stopped by the recording studio, and if you listen closely you can hear her singing along with the guys in the band. Pauline took a great photo of the band on the beach, and it was used for the cover. It captures a fantastic group of musicians enjoying what they're doing and at that moment, seemingly carefree. The record came out very nicely and was titled, *Just a Little, Jim Beatty*. It was the last one I recorded in an LP format. Unfortunately, it was never released on CD.

We headed for the Seaside Jazz Festival in mid-October with the band in good shape, fresh from our recording session. On the way down in the car I found out that Brad Harrett was a real baseball fan and all he could talk about was the Minnesota Twins and the St. Louis Cardinals, then playing in the World Series. Our first performance was at a dance hall and we were expected to play danceable music, which was no problem. After the first couple of tunes the band was swinging along nicely, but I thought I heard a radio announcer and after listening more closely I realized that it was the World Series. I turned around and I'll be damned if Brad didn't have a little portable radio sitting by his bass, with the World Series on. I went over to him and explained that we didn't listen to the radio on the job and to please put it away. He wasn't very happy about it, but he'd just have to wait until the end of the set to find out the score. What in the world this going on? My thoughts went back to Chris Sheik reading a book while he was playing his drums. It looked like I would have to make a list of the do's and don'ts of the music business and pass it out to each one of my side men.

We took an intermission and I suppose Brad got the score of the game, plus a few drinks and God only knows what else. We went into our second set, when I felt that the bottom drop out of the rhythm section, and I couldn't figure out why, until I looked out onto the dance floor and saw Brad dancing around with the audience cuddling his base. I couldn't believe it! Is this how the entire jazz festival is going to go? Do I have to be a babysitter on every job I go out on?

I went to Brad's room that night and read him the riot act and got him to get into a cold shower and straighten up. The rest of the band and I kept a close guard on him for the remainder of the festival and managed to keep him out of too much trouble. I got through the festival, but it was nerve-racking. Playing the Seaside Fest was enjoyable, it paid well, and it was close to home. Would I be invited back to play next year...or would it go the way of the St. Louis Jazz Festival?

It looked like it was going to be another busy year in 1988. I had met a couple of interesting musicians at a Christmas party given by a doctor friend of Pauline's from the hospital. He lived in a huge house with his partner. The house was decorated beautifully and fit in perfectly with the Christmas music being played very tastefully by Jim Blackburn on piano and Dave Duthie on bass. On their intermission, I introduced myself and found that they had a steady weekend job at a place called Hobo's, a gay bar/restaurant in the old town section of Portland. I then realized that it was in the same location as Old Town Strutter's Hall, the bar I played with Wild Bill Davison a couple of years before. The first of the year I made it a point to go sit in with them at Hobo's, and was pleasantly surprised to see the place remodeled and doubled in size, with a beautiful bar and restaurant. This started a musical friendship with Jim and Dave that exists to this day.

The Jim Beatty Jazz Band had its usual weekly schedule playing at Cal's, Brasserie Montmartre, Village Jazz, Julep's, The Whaler (a restaurant in Lake Oswego), weddings, birthday parties, anniversary celebrations, along with the jazz clubs and jazz festivals. Ernie Carson called me early in the year and asked me to play with his band at the Helena, Montana, Jazz Festival, and he asked Kid Sheik to play it as well. Ernie also hired Pete Pepke to play trombone; it was starting to look like my band! Kid and I flew to Helena and met up with Ernie, Pete and the rest of the band. Ernie rounded out the rest of the group with his banjo player, Debbie Schreier, and a tuba player from Seattle, Tom Jacobus. The band consisted of excellent musicians and I was sure that we would be greeted warmly by the festival fans.

Well, I was wrong. Evidently, Ernie decided to go on a binge, and I found out that when he did this he could get nasty and would take it out on a few of the musicians in his band. This time he aimed his venom at the tuba player, Tom Jacobus. Tom was a big guy and could've taken care of Ernie very handily. But Tom held his cool like a true professional and took all the various insults without blowing up. Ernie yelled at him for playing wrong notes and chords, which of course he wasn't doing at all. Tom was a good musician and was playing perfectly. I was embarrassed, but it wasn't my band and I minded my own business. I later found out that the festival manager had a cornet player follow the band around to all our performances in case Ernie became so intoxicated that he couldn't play. The payoff came when we were to play a jazz mass on Sunday morning, and Ernie hadn't been to bed as he was drinking all night. We got a ride to the church and Ernie walked in drinking a can of beer and smoking a cigarette. A Catholic priest grabbed him right away and ushered him out the back door with orders not to come back until he had ditched the beer and cigarette. Ernie came back and we somehow managed to get through the service.

My God! I was never so happy to see a jazz festival come to an end in my life. This should have been a huge wakeup call for me and my musical relationship with Ernie. But, I was forgiving, and it was his band and his reputation, so I let it go. These were the things I had been hearing about from other musicians over the years, and now I saw it firsthand. What a shame and waste of talent to see this happen to such a brilliant musician. Ernie was without a doubt one of the top jazz cornetists in the country, if not the world. I think that when he drank, he had this evil demon in him that he could not control. I had experienced so many happy times with Ernie that I couldn't believe it when he turned into this other person.

Besides being a top-notch musician, Ernie had great social skills; he was always immaculately dressed, very intelligent, and polite. He did have a stuttering problem, but that only showed up after too many drinks. This was always the first clue when there was trouble ahead.

I had a surprise phone call from the Oregon Dixieland Jubilee asking me if I would like to bring my band back again for the next Festival. I guess the incident with my bass player was overlooked and I was getting a second chance. The Festival director, Obie O' Bryant, did ask me one favor: They had hired Ernie Carson to be a featured guest artist of the Jubilee, and instead of having him play with different bands at the event, they wanted to assign him permanently to my band, because we had played together so often. I agreed to the deal because Ernie had never given me any trouble when he played with my band and I had no reason to believe that he ever would give me grief.

Shortly after my call from the Jubilee I got another call from George Buck at GHB Jazzology Records. George had heard that I was playing the Jubilee again with Ernie and asked me if I would be interested in making another recording for him. He liked the first recording that we did the year before so much that he wanted me to make another, only this one would be released on the CD format. That sounded great to me, and I told him I would arrange for a studio and do it before we went to the Jubilee, just as we did before.

Ernie Carson and Pete Pepke flew in a few days early for the Jubilee because I had booked the band into the Village Jazz for two nights before the recording. I had to make some changes in the rhythm section because Moon Monsey was on the sick list and Kid Sheik had just married and was auctioneering. I got Chick Colburn back on the drums and hired Brian Darby to play the guitar. Brian was an excellent guitarist and fronted his own Gypsy jazz style band called Everything's Jake. Harold Koster was back in Los Angeles, but luckily I was able to get Norm Domreis to play the piano. For frosting on the cake, I hired Kathy Smith for a couple of vocals. Because the session was going to be released on CD we were able to record many more tunes then we would normally do on an LP. We recorded "Mighty Oregon," "Gone Fishing," "*Si tu vois Ma Mere*," "Hard Hearted Hanna," "Down South," "Wrap Your Troubles in Dreams," "The Girl With the Golden Hair," "Dill Pickles," "All Raccoons Look Alike To Me," and a medley of six tunes ending with the ensemble playing "Nevertheless." The session went great and the playbacks I heard were excellent. We spent most of the afternoon and well into the evening recording this CD. I always permitted drinks during recording sessions to relax everyone, as long as it didn't affect their playing. Everyone performed beautifully at the session, but I did notice that Carson and Domreis managed to polish off a fifth of vodka between them. But to be fair, I also had my share of Scotch.

The Oregon Dixieland Jubilee was held in Seaside and Astoria. It was a little awkward driving back and forth between the two cities to play, but it was doable and it seemed to work out fine for everyone, musicians and fans alike. Since it was close to Portland and on a weekend, Pauline decided to accompany me. At our first show I thought Ernie had a few drinks, but he was playing his usual beautiful cornet style. As the night went on I overheard him order a drink from the bartender - a triple rum and Coke! My God! That's enough to get Andre the Giant loaded. Fortunately, it was Friday evening and we didn't have long to play. The next day, our first set was early afternoon, and once again I heard Ernie ordering a triple rum and Coke. This is not good! If he keeps this up, he's just not going to make it through the day. The trouble was that he was not technically in my band, but assigned to my band as a Jubilee guest star. So, I had no real authority to reprimand him about his drinking. Well, sure enough, it happened. We were playing in the banquet room of a restaurant in Seaside and the place was standing room only, waiting to hear some hot jazz. Ernie showed up absolutely polluted, and I knew that we were going to have a rough time playing the show. To make matters worse, we had an upright piano that had a loose top and it was very wobbly. I told everyone about it and to be careful, although there were a couple of ashtrays and a drink or two on it as well. Ernie put his drink on top of the piano, along with his cigarette in the ashtray, while he was playing. Then it happened. Ernie leaned on the piano top and it went flying through the air with the ashtrays, lit cigarettes, cigarette butts, and drinks all over the floor, all landing on the nearby audience. Ernie ended up on the floor as well, and the band's performance came to a crashing finale.

Fortunately, no one was hurt from the flying debris. Ernie, rather than being apologetic, raised hell with the management about having a dangerous piano on the bandstand, and he became very nasty with anybody within earshot. We were the last band playing at that site for the evening and that was our last job for the night as well. I was very embarrassed, and I knew that no matter how much I explained the situation to the Jubilee officials, I would end up taking the blame.

The next day we started out playing again and I was praying for a better day ahead. Thank goodness, Ernie was licking his wounds from the night before and was drinking only beer. At least I knew that we were going to be playing some good music and everyone could regroup and try and gain our respect back.

The jazz festivals often featured an old swing-era electric guitarist, Alvino Ray. He was a guitar legend because he had invented the first electric amplifier for a guitar when he was fifteen years old, but unfortunately never had it patented. However, he went on and made a name for himself in music and married one of the King Sisters, a popular singing group of the 50s and 60s. Alvino was in many movies and made several recording hits through the years. My favorites were, "The Third Man Theme" and "Bumble Boogie."

Alvino and I became friends over time; he especially took a liking to me and followed my band around the festivals whenever he could. He loved to sit in with us with his banjo and we loved having him because he was a neat guy and obviously very talented. Alvino was a Mormon and worked out of Salt Lake City. But, I guess that when he left Salt Lake City to play on a road trip he was free from all the Mormon rules and regulations. Mormons, of course, do not drink, but Alvino drank like there was no tomorrow. So, when he sat in with our band, he was in good company. I believe it was our last set on Saturday night in Seaside when he caught up with us with his banjo. It was late at night and he had had plenty to drink, but he seemed to be playing fine. When he sat in with us that night he didn't take a chair, but sat on the end of Norm Domreis' piano bench. During our performance, Norm stood up for some reason or another and unbalanced the piano bench, sending Alvino and his banjo flying through the air and onto the stage floor… another Jim Beatty Jazz Band performance with a spectacular ending. Fortunately, Alvino and his banjo were not hurt, only the reputation of The Jim Beatty Jazz Band. I could just hear people saying "We can't wait until their next show!"

I got back to my hotel room that night praying once again for things to go better on Sunday. Sundays were a short day because the Jubilee ended mid-afternoon. Pauline and I were ready to call it a night when there was a knock on the door. Pauline answered it, and there was Norm Domreis standing outside, bleeding profusely from his forehead. He evidently had too much to drink and got lost and fell onto some gravel. We brought him in and Pauline cleaned and dressed his wound with some bandages that she carried around with her. Why did she carry bandages with her? Well, I suppose, just for that reason.

The next day we played our last show. It had been quite a weekend and we all survived, although Norm Domreis looked like he just returned from "The Battle of the Bulge." I saw Alvino Ray in the audience and we waved to each other, although he never made any attempt to come up and sit in with us. As Pauline and I were driving home, I was thinking that perhaps God had his hands full of taking care of drunks, and he assigned me to take care of his overload, starting way back with my dad.

**Seaside Jazz Festival, Oregon, 1988. Ernie Carson, Pete Pepke, Brad Herrett, Chris Sheik, Jim, Moon Monsey, Harold Koster.**

**Long Island with Dick Henzel**

## CHAPTER 25

# Eastern Band Tour 1989

I HAD TALKED FOR YEARS about taking the Jim Beatty Jazz Band back East for a New York and Pennsylvania tour. I thought that the time was right, and put out my feelers to my good friend Ray Anderson in Jamestown and Pete Pepke in Pennsylvania. It would mean a lot of organizational work putting this whole thing together with airfares, hotels and ground transportation for the tour. The last thing I needed was a drinking problem from any of the musicians, so I had to make two major changes in the band lineup. When Jim Goodwin was playing overseas, I had been using a Portland trumpet player by the name of Roger Amato, who was a dependable guy and played well. I also had started using a new bass player, Steve Dickinson, who was also very good and eager to join the band.

Pete Pepke got busy and booked us into Bradford, Kane, and Warren, Pennsylvania. Ray Anderson arranged a show for us at the Red Coach Inn's large banquet room because the Jamestown area crowds would be huge and we needed plenty of space to accommodate them. The Red Coach Inn is where I featured Wild Bill so often back in the 1960s. So we had a pretty good tour lined up and decided on the first week of April as the date.

I had one other band problem for the tour, and it wasn't a drinking problem. It was Moon Monsey's weight. Moon loved to eat and did plenty of it. I got him aside and explained that if he wanted to go on the tour with the band he would have to lose 25 or 30 pounds in order to fit into one of the airplane seats. I told Moon that if he lost the weight I would include him on the tour. On top of that, I would buy him a new blue blazer, dress shirt, gray slacks, and shoes. His eyes lit up immediately and he told me that he would start a diet and promised that in three months the weight would be gone. I knew that this was going to be a big job for him but I thought that he'd pull it off, because he really wanted to go on the tour.

Along with myself on clarinet, I had Roger Amato on trumpet, Moon playing banjo and guitar, Norm Domreis, piano, Steve Dickinson, bass and Chic Colburn on drums; a good group to take back East. Of course, Pete Pepke would be waiting for us with his trombone. With the dates set, engagements booked, and musicians lined up, I had to get to work on all of the final traveling arrangements and so forth.

I arranged for the round-trip airplane tickets and cartons for the bass and drums, to make sure they made the trip without any damage. The Red Coach Inn gave me a special rate on the motel rooms, because we would be doing a show there. I had a good relationship with the Teamsters Unions on both the East Coast and West Coast and they were happy to pick the band up at the Buffalo airport, along with our luggage and band equipment, and also take care of us on the return trip to Portland. Ray Anderson also put his large Oldsmobile 98 station wagon at my disposal, so we could get to and from our engagements in Pennsylvania.

When it got close to go, Moon Monsey had lost his weight, and boy, did he look good. I took him out and bought him a new wardrobe, as promised, and he looked like he was just out of *Esquire* magazine. Only one problem: I found out that Moon was frightened to death about flying. That was something that he would have to overcome. I knew he'd be happy once he got to Jamestown because our recording of "Dixieland Doris" was popular in the Western New York area, and played on the jukeboxes there. Moon wrote "Dixieland Doris" and was also on the vocal, so he would be getting a lot of extra attention from the fans.

On our flight to Buffalo, Moon slipped into his seat very easily after his weight loss, but it was a white-knuckle flight for him; he was scared to death. When we landed in Buffalo the Teamsters were there and Ray was there as well, with the Oldsmobile station wagon. On our way from Buffalo to Jamestown all Moon could talk about was buying some New York State cheese that he had heard was the best cheese in the country. When we pulled into the Red Coach Inn, Moon spotted a supermarket across the street and he bolted out of the car heading for the supermarket for his New York State cheese, even before we had even checked in to the motel. Poor guy, he had been on a starvation diet for several weeks and now he could eat again.

Our concerts went over very well in Pennsylvania and we finished the tour playing at the Red Coach Inn. It was a mob scene, with standing room only, and it seemed like half of Jamestown showed up. Michael Zabrodsky from the *Jamestown Post-Journal*, wrote the next day:

> *The concert was great because of Beatty's big hometown following. I noticed that most of the audience knew him on a first name basis, and he knew everybody by their first names, too. It was a very friendly atmosphere, where worries were set aside and friends got together and enjoyed some wonderful music.*

There were so many of my old friends at the concert, along with my mother, who was so proud to have me back in town. My sister came down from Ohio for the event and it was great to see her again. It was a wonderful way to end the tour. In between all our shows I managed to get the band to Johnny's Texas Hots, a Beef on Weck restaurant, and a trip to Lake Erie to buy some smoked fish. We also managed to sit down to a big dinner of Jamestown fish and chips - none better in the country.

When we were getting packed and ready to leave for the Buffalo air-port, Moon announced to me that he was cashing in his return plane ticket to Portland and going home via the Greyhound bus. I guess flying was just too much for him and he rode that bus with his luggage, guitar and banjo all the way back to Portland.

Back in Oregon, Bob was a senior in high school when he came home one afternoon and told me about a friend at school who was a German exchange student. He evidently had lost his home with his host family and needed to find another family to take him in, or they would send him back to Germany. Pauline and I talked it over and told Bob to go ahead and tell his German friend to come over and meet us and we would con-sider taking him in. After all, we did have a vacant bedroom since Jame was gone in the Army.

The next day, Bob came home from school with his German friend in tow. His name was Tim Dabringhaus. He was a tall, blond, good-looking German, and would have been a perfect candidate for the German SS had it been in the 1930s or early 1940s. He was nicely dressed, spoke English quite well and was obviously from a nice home in Germany. He must've been quite a nice boy, because Bob wouldn't have been friends with him, otherwise. Bob had three other friends, Joel Johnson, Dave Thompson and Mike Peebles, that were around the house constantly, so why not one more? We told him that we would give it a try and showed him Jame's va-cant bedroom. We now had a new member of the family and it felt good because it seemed lonely without Jame around.

There were minor adjustments to get used to, having a new member of the family. In Germany, the children start drinking beer with the fam-ily meals at an early age, so it's no big deal. They also get served beer and wine in bars, after they turn 16, and after that at 18 they can start drinking hard liquor as well. When I played in Holland I thought many of the customers looked rather young, and I asked the bartender how old you had to be to have a beer - and the bartender replied to me - you have to look 14. So, drinking customs are different in other countries around the world. If Tim's German parents were okay with him drinking, I wasn't about to make it a big issue. Even when Pauline found a bottle of vodka in his bedroom while she was cleaning, I told her just to put it back where she found it and not let him know that we knew. What we didn't know was that Tim was kicked out of two other American families because they couldn't adjust to his behavior.

Tim was great to have around the house and he was quite popular at school, as well. He was a big movie buff, especially the James Bond films. If he saw that there would be a James Bond film showing during the day, he would at always ask if it was okay to stay home from school. I marked the experience down to education and said okay. Tim wanted to work in the film industry someday and years later his wish came true and he brought me along on a few of his film adventures.

When I was playing the Village Jazz Club, Bob and his friends would come down and sit by an open door near the bandstand and listen to the music. It reminded me of when I was young and sat on the curb outside of Jimmy Ryan's in New York City. Bob graduated from high school that year and went off to Carleton College in Minnesota. Tim went back to Germany and the rest of Bob's friends went their separate ways to other colleges.

Jame had made a six year deal with the U.S. Army, signing up for two years active duty and four years in the reserves. In September of 1983 he took his basic training at Fort McClellan, Alabama. He was able to come home on Christmas leave in December of that year before going back to duty at Military Police school and graduating in March, 1984.

After MP graduation, Jame was stationed at Fort Clayton in the Panama Canal Zone and later that year deployed to Honduras. He returned to Panama and then in August of 1984 he took a 10 day leave, came home to Portland, and became engaged to Cherie Brambilla, his high school sweetheart. Jame then returned to Panama after his leave to finish the rest of his two year enlistment in the Army.

Pauline was still plugging away at Good Samaritan Hospital. She was now evening supervisor and thinking about the possibility of going into the administrative end of medical care. We were still taking our holiday trips to Sakinaw Lake in Canada and trips to the Oregon Coast. It was strange around the house with Jame in the Army and Bob off to college. Where did the time go?

After playing the Helena, Montana Jazz Festival, I returned to Portland in time to celebrate our 25th wedding anniversary. So much had happened to Pauline and me over those 25 years, it was hard to believe. Pauline started as a nurse with good Samaritan Hospital in 1967 and went on to be the evening nurse supervisor, and then took a full time day position as the nurse recruiter, a big job, interviewing and hiring all the nurses for the hospital. Her job was also a lifesaver for our family because it provided us all with health insurance.

We had our 25th anniversary celebration party at Cal's Restaurant and Lounge. Because I played there, they gave me a big discount on the banquet room, food and drinks. It was a wonderful night with all our friends and family there. All of our Canadian relatives showed up for the event as well, and after the evening ended the party spilled over to our house and went on to all hours of the night.

Jame finished up his service in the Army with duty in Honduras and Panama and received an honorable discharge in September, 1985.

He returned home and was married to Cherie in November, 1985. The wedding was celebrated at the Lady of the Lake Catholic Church in Lake Oswego, Oregon, and there was a large reception at the Lake Oswego Country Club. My band played for the reception and as things loosened up many of the wedding party came onstage and sang "Auntie Skinners Chicken Dinners." Those were the days when there was enjoyable music at weddings and you didn't have to wear earplugs.

In December, 1988, Cherie gave birth to a beautiful baby girl and they named her Brittney. Brittney grew up, graduated from college, and married Nick Salisbury and made Pauline and me great grandparents to a baby boy, named Jameson. Cherie gave birth to another beautiful baby girl in 1992 and they named her Reagan. Reagan was married to Ethan Bays in the summer of 2016 with a beautiful wedding at our place on Sakinaw Lake in Canada

Bob completed his four year education at Carleton College with a bachelor's degree. I spent a lot of time playing music at his college and also in the Minneapolis/Saint Paul area. Bob was a good promoter and through the college activity director I played college events quite often, including Parents Weekend. I didn't bring my band, but instead I hired musicians from the Minneapolis/Saint Paul jazz community. There were a lot of good traditional musicians in the area, such as cornetist Charlie DeVore and the superb pianist/clarinetist Butch Thompson, who played for Garrison Keillor. The college couldn't have been nicer to me; they sent a chauffeur-driven car to the airport to pick me up and gave me very nice accommodations in the faculty dorm.

Because I got to know so many of the local musicians, they started hiring me for their jobs when they knew I would be in the area. I was hired to play with one band at a mall in Minneapolis Saint Paul, but I needed a ride into town. Bob said – "no problem" - he had a friend who had a Volkswagen Beetle that we could borrow for the night. That was great - but there was only one problem - it had no brakes! So when you drove the damn thing you had to use the hand emergency brake to stop it. Well, Bob and I didn't let a little thing like that get in the way of our trip to the big city. It was around a 40 mile drive into town on the freeway and it went fairly well. The city driving was a bit tricky but we made it to our destination in one piece. On top of working the emergency brake I also had to shift gears, not an easy job! After a few drinks during the engagement, the drive back went like a breeze, because Bob drove!

On the outskirts of Minneapolis/Saint Paul there is a tiny town called Mendota, and oddly enough it had one of the most popular jazz clubs in the United States. The proprietors were Stan and Russ Hall, they had the Hall Brothers Jazz Band and they called their club The Emporium of Jazz. The brothers brought in some of the top-notch traditional jazz artists in the country to guest with their band. I had heard a lot about this jazz club from Wild Bill Davison, who appeared there several times a year when he was available. Evidently they had heard a lot about me and called to see if I would be interested in being a guest artist at their club. I accepted the invitation and we set up a date that would coincide with one of my appearances at Carleton College. After four years of playing music and partying with the college students, I became quite well known on campus. So on the night of my appearance at the Emporium of Jazz there was a huge crowd of Carleton students in the audience, along with Bob. The place was full, thanks to Bob and his friends; the band was swinging with the audience joining in on the fun.

At the end of the night, I packed up my clarinet and soprano to get ready to ride back to the college with Bob and his friends. I was looking around for one of the Hall Brothers so I could get paid for my evenings work, but no one in sight. I waited and waited and looked around to no avail. So I gave up and figured the Hall Brothers would probably send me a check in the mail. When we went out to the parking lot to get in the car to go back to Carleton, I spotted the Hall Brothers hiding behind another car in the lot! I couldn't believe it! It looked like they didn't have the money to pay me and I wasn't about to go chasing them around the parking lot for it. The Hall Brothers opened their club in 1966 until it ran into hard times and closed in 1991. It was a sign of the times and the old established jazz clubs around the nation were running into financial problems because the audience was shrinking. Stan and Russ Hall didn't know me very well, of course, and all they would have had to do is explain their financial situation to me and I would've understood. I really felt sorry for them hiding behind that car in the parking lot.

Bob came home from college with his bachelor's degree and went off on his own adventures in life. Jame went after his own degree, now that he was out of the Army, married, and onto a new career. Pauline was climbing the corporate ladder in health care. As for me, I found out that there was going to be a lot more music to be played.

A new restaurant/lounge opened in Lake Oswego, right on the lake, and they wanted my band to play Sunday afternoons. It was called The Whaler. That was a perfect job because it was in such a beautiful setting, by the lake, where you could arrive by car or boat. Since Chris Sheik had left the band I had to use different drummers at different times. For the Whaler job I was lucky to get Dave Elliott, the drummer at the Jazz Quarry in Portland, where I often played. He was a terrific musician to have for the job, because he was a fussbudget and had the whole bandstand arranged for me by the time I came to work. When I walked in the door he always walked up to me and said "Jim - I would like to report that I have the bandstand set up along with the microphones and stands, for your approval." Of course, everything was set up perfectly, and all we had to do was start playing.

Our German exchange student, Tim, had gone back to Germany following high school graduation, but he missed us so much he came back to see us at least twice. He also enjoyed getting together with Bob and friends and when Sundays rolled around you could always count on him to say "Are we going to Za Vailur?" The Whaler became a popular hangout for young and old alike during our time there. One fellow came in without fail, every Sunday, and danced his heart out with any woman that would cut a rug with him. His name was Jack Dick, and he became a huge fan of the band and never missed one of our public appearances. He was a local barber and not only became my number one fan but my newfound barber.

One Sunday a very popular car dealer friend of mine, Bud Meadows, came into the Whaler and said that he wanted to hire the band to play a private party, just a short distance away on the lake. When? I said. On your next intermission, Bud replied! Well, it seems that he was invited to a private party and thought it would be funny to bring his own band with him. I said okay, and on our intermission, Bud had a couple of cars waiting in the parking lot that drove us the short distance to the party. We played while we marched into the house, to the surprise of the party's hosts and all their guests. We had time to play one tune for them and then we were driven back to the Whaler in time to play the next set. Needless to say, Bud paid us very well to do this stunt for him. He was a wild and crazy guy and I ended up having a lot more ridiculous episodes with him. Bud was always on television selling his cars, and he was probably the most popular car dealer in Portland at that time.

The 80s finished on a sad note, however. My good friend and musical partner of so many years, Wild Bill Davison, passed away at 84 years old. He didn't survive an aneurysm operation. It was in November, 1989 and I was back in Jamestown, New York, playing a few jobs there. Before he died I got a message to call Anne. When I did, she said she wanted me to come to Bill's bedside and play my clarinet for him, hoping that that would bring him out of his coma. Anne and Bill were in Santa Barbara, California and I was on the East Coast and it was impossible for me to get there in time.

It's amazing to think that I was just a teenager when I met Bill, and I more or less grew up with him through the years. We sure had some crazy times with him and he taught me so much about being a professional musician. I'll never forget him.

I finished the late 1980s and early 1990s playing jazz festivals with Dr. Jon's Jazz Band, a group from Albany, Oregon. Pete Pepke had joined the band and when they needed a clarinet player, Pete talked me into joining so we could work and spend some time together. I was reluctant to do it because it was just another one of those banjo-tuba groups that I didn't especially enjoy playing with. However, it would get me out of the responsibility of leadership on the festivals and I wouldn't have to be a babysitter to the musicians. So I took the job and it turned out to be a fun group of people to work with. Jon Balschweid, the leader and cornet player, was a very nice guy with a wild sense of humor and played a nice, straight melody lead on his horn, which is so important in a traditional jazz band. I also got a kick out of the piano player, Dee Rickey, who was a bookkeeper for a trucking firm and played a fun, old-style type of piano. She was a short, middle-aged lady, but she really spanked the hell out of the ivories. The rest of the group was rounded out with Bob Tarrant, banjo, Dick Miller, tuba, Herb Brennan on drums, and Dr. Jon's wife Deni, doing the vocals.

We had a rehearsal shortly after I started and I found out that Dr. Jon had hired a new drummer who would be rehearsing with us that evening. His name was Jack Dawes, a tall, lanky guy, around my age. He was new to traditional jazz and in the past had been a rock 'n roll drummer, much like Chris Sheik. Jack was a very pleasant and friendly person, who, come to find out, lived in Lake Oswego, not too far from me, and was in business for himself as a real estate appraiser. We agreed that we should try and carpool to future jobs and rehearsals. Tragically, Jack's son, James, had recently been killed in a traffic accident caused by an impaired driver. I can't think of anything worse than losing one of your own children and my heart went out to him. I think that getting back into music and learning the traditional jazz style was probably the best therapy for both Jack and his wife, Earline.

I played a number of jazz festivals with Dr. Jon, including Seaside, and Albany, Oregon, and Ocean Shores, Oak Harbor and Aberdeen, Washington. We even made a cassette tape that didn't come out all that bad. We recorded "Just a Little While to Stay Here," "Make Me Know It," "Someday Sweetheart," "Chicago," "Just a Closer Walk With Thee," "Second Hand Rose," "Move the Body Over ," "Dusky Stevedore," "Daddy Do," "Old Fashioned Love," "*Si Tu Vois Ma Mere*," "If I Had You," "I've Got What It Takes," and "Bedella."

I had to leave Dr. Jon's band because I was just getting too busy with my own work in Portland and around the country. But listening to these recordings, you can't help but think that all the musicians in the band were having one heck of a good time.

The last recording I made in the 1980s was February 22nd, 1989; it was titled, *Sweet and Lovely*, and released on cassette tape. I used my quartet, with Norm Domreis on piano, Steve Dickinson, bass, Chic Colburn, drums, and me playing clarinet. We recorded sixteen songs, along with the title song, "Sweet and Lovely."

Back in 1957, Wild Bill Davison recorded an LP with the Percy Faith Orchestra for Columbia records, called *Pretty Wild*. It was a big hit and could be heard on the radio frequently. Many years later in Oregon, Wild Bill and I were going through some of his music and we came across the tune "Sweet and Lovely." It was the arrangement he did with Percy Faith, and Bill gave it to me to use on one of my own recordings in the future. I put it aside and forgot about it until early 1989 and decided it was time for a new recording and that would be a great one to record. I was glad I did because Wild Bill passed away later that year and he had a chance to listen to my version of it.

I released it on cassette tape because that was the fad of the day. Everybody had a cassette player and recorder and all the new cars were equipped with cassette players as well. I never cared for the cassette tape because if you wanted to hear a particular tune in the middle or end of the tape, you had to fast forward until you got to where the tune was. They were also very small, and consequently the liner notes and pictures had to be small, too. One advantage, however, was that they were very lightweight and easy to cart around to sell at jazz festivals and other jobs. People were still buying the vinyl LPs, so I was still carting them around on my jobs. Many of the festivals sold your LPs and cassettes for you, which was very handy, because it was a pain in the neck to try to sell them off the bandstand.

I did have an unfortunate event happen to me when I played my last time at the Saint Louis Ragtime Festival. The Festival had a fellow selling recordings for the bands and taking a small percentage of the sale for himself. I thought that was fair, as he had sold them for me the year before. He had a huge table set up with all the recordings on it and I checked every day and saw that he was selling a bunch of mine.

After I played my last show at the Festival I packed my horns away and went out to the recording sales table, only to find the table void of any recordings and the salesman gone. He flew the coop with my money and any leftover recordings there may have been. I tried to track him down, but to no avail and it looked like JWB was screwed. After that, Pauline did the sales or I only dealt with festival accredited salespeople.

Fortunately, my recordings sold very well and the fans were always asking when we would be making a new one. Recording in those days wasn't as easy as it is now, with the sophisticated recording equipment and computers. It's funny, every now and then someone will come up to me with one of my LPs recorded way back in the 70s and 80s, and show me that I autographed it for them, way back then. And if you ever go into an old record store you're very likely to find some beat-up old LP of mine.

The new drummer with Dr. Jon's Band, Jack Dawes, impressed me because he was really serious about playing classic traditional jazz and had been taking drum lessons for several months from a local percussion teacher. Not only that, he was sensible, very easy to get along with and believe it or not - sober. I decided to give Jack a try and asked him to play a job with me to see if he liked it. It was an odd job to start out with the band for the first time, because we played in the men's department at the Meier and Frank store in the Clackamas Town Center Mall. He fit in with the band very well and I offered him the job permanently. Once again I had a permanent drummer and didn't have to worry about substitutes all the time. Jack also went far beyond the call of duty and was there to help out in any way he could. He had a very pleasant wife, Earline, and Pauline and I became very good friends with them. What Jack didn't know was that he was getting involved with all the crazy jobs and escapades of the Jim Beatty Jazz Band, but I knew that he could handle it.

I had one big project I wanted to get done early in the year and that was releasing a new recording that was made back in April. It was a live recording of my quartet playing a concert at the Portland Art Museum on April 12th, 1989. The art museum featured a band in concert once a week, and we always played it at least once a year.

Besides myself on clarinet and soprano sax, I had Norm Domreis on piano, Steve Dickinson, bass, and Neil Masson on drums. We recorded "Sweet Georgia Brown," "*Si Tu Vois Ma Mere*," "Little Rock Getaway," "*Petite Fleur*," "St. James Infirmary," "That's A Plenty," "In The Mood," "Don't get Around Much Anymore," "Sugar," "I Remember You," "Birth Of The Blues," and "When The Saints Go Marching In."

My musical relationship with the two piano players, Domreis and Koster, was still going smoothly. It just seemed to work out perfectly; if one could not do a job the other could. They were both great pianists with distinct personalities. Norm was the quiet type and loved his vodka, but no matter how much he drank, his piano playing never faltered, it was almost like he was on remote control. There was a time that he must have been bugged with me and didn't speak to me on the job for a month. It was rather awkward playing four-hour jobs and not communicating with your piano player, but we got through it; he never told me what the problem was and I didn't ask. That's the only time in our long musical relationship that anything of that nature happened. It was hilarious some nights when Norm had too much to drink, I'd be talking to him and he would be standing in front of me with a drink in his hand, listing from one side to the other. He was hilarious. Koster on the other hand was quite talkative, but blunt and to the point, and certainly not diplomatic. He was very intelligent and knew his music inside and out. He wanted to be a music teacher and passed his college tests, but when it came to the final test of classroom teaching - they failed him. That might give you a clue of his communication skills.

One time we were playing a job at the Schnitzer Concert Hall in downtown Portland and Harold showed up on his bicycle in the pouring rain. Another time, playing the Benson Hotel, right in the middle of a tune and during my clarinet solo, he started tuning the piano with his tuning wrench. It seems that he had taken a course on piano tuning by mail and he decided to bring a tuning wrench with him to his jobs and tune the pianos if he thought they needed it. There's nothing worse than listening to a piano being tuned up, and I explained to him that if he wanted to tune a piano to come to the job early when the room was empty and do his tuning. I never saw the tuning wrench again.

Randy Keller, a tuba player from Seattle, had formed a new and unique type of band called the Wild Cards. I had known Randy for quite some time when he played with the Rainier Jazz Band and the Uptown Lowdown Jazz Band. He was a jolly, happy-go-lucky young man, originally from the Bay Area in California. His mom and dad were big jazz fans and very active in the jazz scene in that part of the state. Randy had been a lieutenant in the Navy and he loved the water and being near it. He also was devoted to traditional jazz and was very enthusiastic about all aspects of it. I got to know him better when I bumped into him at the Central City Jazz Festival in Colorado. He was playing with Uptown Lowdown at the time and disliked his accommodations. It seems that the Festival put the Uptown Lowdown band in a large dorm-like room and they were sleeping on cots with sleeping bags. He was on his way to bed and wasn't too happy about it. On the other hand, the Festival and given me a nice, two bedroom apartment. They obviously, had the misconception that I was somebody important. So, Randy and I went to his sleeping quarters, grabbed his belongings and sleeping bag, and he moved in to the other bedroom in my apartment. We talked a lot about music that night and I told him that it would be to his advantage to learn how to play the string bass, because he would be much more versatile and could play more of a variety of jazz. I also said that I would be happy to use him on some of my jobs.

Randy took up the string bass and learned to play it very well. The change of instrument also fit in with his new concept of "Wild Card Jazz." I was asked to be one of his Wild Card musicians and of course I took him up on the offer immediately. The band was made up of his ever-growing list of interested friends and musicians from around the country. A wide range of styles of vintage jazz could then be terminated or blended on the mix of "Wild Cards," as appropriate for each occasion. The best part of the concept of this band was the idea that there are no rules, no charts, no limits, no pre-determined structure or organization. All Randy asked of his musicians was to show up on time and be fully clothed.

It was fun for me to play with the band because every time I worked with a bunch of different musicians it made it more interesting. Other Portland musicians that became a member of the deck of cards were, Jim Goodwin, Ernie Carson and Jack Dawes. Most of the jobs were near Seattle and north, with the occasional weekend jazz party. With Randy playing the string bass now, I was using him on some of my jobs in the Portland area and a few jazz festivals. He also recorded the CD, *Song of Songs,* with me in the late 90s.

Over the years I have made many trips to play in Seattle, not only with my band but guesting or substituting with other bands such as Uptown Lowdown. I had watched the Uptown Lowdown and its leader, Bert Barr, from its beginning, and had played with them often, but just as a substitute because of the long drive from Portland. Bert was a hard-driving cornet player and his band kept getting better and better. They became a favorite in the jazz festival circuit. They occasionally would need a substitute clarinet player and would call me. I enjoyed playing with them and would always try to make their jobs.

The last job I was asked to play with them, however, was a disaster that I never saw coming. The job was on a cruise ship that traveled from Seattle's Puget Sound, through the Ballard Locks, and into the fresh water of Lake Washington. In Lake Washington we docked at an authentic Indian village where a big salmon feast was waiting for us. I was told to wear all white for this job to fit in with the cruise theme. So, I wore a white shirt, white pants, white socks, and white shoes. The cruise was booked by bankers from all over the United States and was quite the event. *Hors d'oeuvres* were served and there were all kinds of cocktails, wine and beer. It was a beautiful summer day, so I decided and that I would stick to drinking beer. When we arrived at the Indian village there were more snacks and more beer. A great party, indeed.

Finally they announced that the salmon dinner was ready and everyone started lining up for it. I realized that before I could eat that I had to go to the bathroom - big time. There was only one outdoor toilet and when I got to it there was a long waiting line. I couldn't wait that long - I thought - but right behind the outdoor toilet there was a woodsy area and I nonchalantly walked behind the toilet into the woods and discovered that I was in a swamp/quicksand and immediately sunk down to my kneecaps in muck! The more I struggled to get out, the more I sank. Finally, after a lot of effort I managed to get out on some dry footage, but I was covered with filthy muck, up over my knees. To make things worse, of course, I was dressed in all white.

Well, the ending of this story is quite obvious. I had to get back on ship covered in mud and play clarinet all the way back to Seattle, looking like an idiot. I knew how Bert Barr was feeling, because I had gone through so many of these kinds of things with my own band. That was the last time I played with the Uptown Lowdown Band and the last time I wore white on a job.

I was asked to bring my band to play for the first Salt Lake City Jazz Festival in 1991. It was called The Wasatch Dixieland Festival and held on a landlocked cruise ship that was used as a restaurant and had a number of banquet rooms. For this festival I used, besides myself on clarinet, Pete Pepke, trombone, Norm Domreis, piano, Randy Keller, bass, Jack Dawes, drums, and a new banjo player who had just moved to Portland, Bob Beck. I also used Dick Williams, a cornet player from California. The Festival flew the band to Salt Lake City and put us up in very comfortable accommodations downtown.

Salt Lake City has a huge Mormon population and Pete Pepke told me, being a non-Mormon, some strange situations he got into with them. One was that he lived in an all- Mormon neighborhood and at Christmas time the Mormon children would go around the neighborhood decorating mailboxes. Everyone's mailbox, that is, but his! But the main thing that bothered me was that the Mormons were death on drinking alcohol and trying to get a drink in Salt Lake City wasn't easy - at least back then. I was interested to see how a jazz festival would go over without alcohol, because that's big revenue for the festival itself.

I saw on the band schedule that my old buddy, Alvino Ray and his band were playing the Festival. I hadn't seen him since he and his banjo crashed on the stage while we were playing in Seaside. I was interested to see how he would handle the alcohol situation in his hometown. I looked him up the first day I was there and he was getting ready to play his show, sipping on a soft drink of some kind. Instead of being happy to see me, like he usually was, he was very distant and acted very uncomfortable around me. I guess he was in his home territory and had to be a good boy, and hanging around me was probably not the best thing to do.

The Festival went quite well and there were some good groups playing exciting, old-time jazz. The boat (that didn't go anywhere) was a nice venue and at least we didn't get seasick. It did seem strange that there was no way that you could get an adult beverage, there was just an eerie feeling about the whole thing. I had managed to find a liquor store, and believe me, that wasn't easy, but at least I had a small bottle of Scotch in my clarinet case.

The band didn't play that late into the night so after our last show, we all sort of looked at each other and said - now what the hell do we do? As a rule, after a long day at a festival we all might find a little pub and sit around, have a few drinks and talk about our day. But, we couldn't do that here, except go to our room like a bunch of underage teenagers and have a drink. I had heard that they could serve liquor at private clubs in Salt Lake City and I suggested that we go out and grab a taxicab and have him take us to the nearest private club. I knew that we were not members of any private club, but we'd cross that bridge when we got to it. We went out on the street and hailed a cab and told the driver to take us to the nearest private club. When we got there, I pressed the buzzer and a man came to the door and asked for membership cards. I explained the very serious situation that we were in, and charmed our way into the club. When he let us in the door it was like finding paradise – Utopia - full bar with beer, wine, and assorted liquors. We quickly became friends with all the patrons and they made us feel more than welcome and gave us an open invitation to come back again.

I don't mean to be disrespectful of the Mormons because they are entitled to their own beliefs, and I respect that. But being one who had grown up around drinking, smoking, and wild women, it was like being in some foreign land within the United States. I was, however, going to see the beauty of Mormonism the next afternoon when I planned to visit the Mormon Tabernacle and Mormon Temple.

I had seen the Mormon Tabernacle Choir many times on television, especially at Christmas time, and they are absolutely astounding. I had heard the acoustics were so perfect in the tabernacle that you could hear a pin drop. I doubted that very much because it was so large; my God, it had a pipe organ with 11,623 pipes. However, on my tour of the tabernacle the tour director asked everyone for silence, and he dropped a pin from 170 feet away - and I'll be damned if I didn't hear it - absolutely amazing. I would love to play there, just once. The Mormon Temple was incredible. It was absolutely breathtaking and beautiful. I must admit, when you walked away from that experience, you had a very good feeling about life and God.

They were offering free Mormon Bibles to anyone that wanted them. They wouldn't give them to you there but they explained that someone would deliver one to your door if you gave them your address. Sure enough, after I got home a couple of nice-looking young boys, on a mission, came to my house with my Bible. I invited them in and they talked to me about Jesus and God - and I listened.

When the Festival was over it didn't take too many brain cells to figure out that they didn't make any money. However, the promoter insisted that it was the first year and they would do better, next year. I was also invited back to play. The next year rolled around and I brought the same band except I switched the cornet player for a clarinet/saxophone man, fairly new in Portland, Cal Abbott. Carson and Goodwin were not available to play Salt Lake with me on cornet and I was just spoiled. So I thought why not try a two reed frontline with the trombone, because it was something different and would set us aside from the other bands.

This time around the Festival was held at the Little America Hotel in downtown Salt Lake City and we also stayed there, which was very convenient for all the bands. Artistically, it was a great success, but it was another financial disappointment for the Festival promoter. He announced at the end of the Festival that that would be the last and final Salt Lake City Jazz Festival. Let's face it - Salt Lake City just isn't a jazz town, which is ironic because the name of the professional basketball team in Salt Lake is the "Utah Jazz."

Another jazz event was scheduled the latter part of 1991 for December 6th through the 8th. December seemed like a bad time for a jazz festival, but it was being held in Santa Rosa, California, where the weather was fairly nice, even that time of the year. An old friend of mine, Jan Scobey, was the promoter and organizer. Jan was the widow of the late, great, bandleader and trumpet player, Bob Scobey. Bob Scobey went way back to the early jazz revival days in San Francisco, along with Lou Waters and Turk Murphy. He became very popular through the years and in the late 50s he opened his own jazz nightclub in Chicago called Club Bourbon Street. He married Jan and unfortunately passed away from cancer in 1963. Jan wrote a very good biography about Bob Scobey called, *He Rambled Until Cancer Cut Him Down.* Jan moved on and married a real great guy, Gene Paleno, and the two of them started a business selling jazz records and promoting her book. They traveled across the country in a huge van, selling jazz recordings at the various festivals across the United States, and there were lots of them. On top of selling their merchandise they would also sell recordings of the bands playing the festivals, which made it very convenient for all the musicians. Jan and I became very good friends and she knew that I always had a bottle of Scotch in my hotel room. So when I arrived at a festival I always looked her up and we went to my room for a couple of drinks and got caught up on all the musician gossip around the country.

Jan wanted me to bring my band to her festival and of course I told her that would be one festival that I wouldn't miss. Santa Rosa was drivable from Portland and our new banjo player, Bob Beck, had a huge, luxurious, Chevrolet van. So, to save Jan airplane fares, we agreed to drive to Santa

Rosa in the van. The main venues for Jan's event were held at the luxurious DoubleTree Hotel along Highway 101 in Santa Rosa, and the bands stayed there as well. Another venue was the Luther Burbank Performing Arts Center Complex, only a mile away from the hotel. Another site was set up for professional video recordings, while the musicians played their show. This definitely was the best organized and professional jazz festival that I had ever seen. It was a "Who's Who" of West Coast jazz, a traditional jazz lover's dream. But, very few people came. The jazz venues were practically empty; it was obvious that we were looking at a professional, artistic, success but a financial disaster.

I don't know why such a wonderful event like this crashed. I had heard that the Santa Rosa Jazz Club wasn't too fond of Jan and didn't give her any support. It also could have been lack of promotion and advertising. This I have seen time and time again - you can have the greatest show in the world - but if you don't tell people about it - you're not going to have a crowd. It could have been too close to the Christmas holidays. Who knows?

At the end of the Festival I went to Jan's room to pick up my check for the band. Of course, I figured that there would probably be no check. I went into Jan's room and she and Gene were sitting there upset and devastated. Jan said, Jim, I have no money to pay you tonight but I promise you, as I have all the other bandleaders, that they will get their money in the near future. I believed her, because she would never let musicians go unpaid. I probably felt just as bad as she did, because Jan and Gene were such wonderful people and had done so much for jazz and the musicians, that it was heartbreaking to see them going through this. Before I left the room I noticed that they had several very large bags of unsold popcorn. So I said, Jan - I'll tell you what. Since you don't have any money, I will accept payment in popcorn! So on our way home the band drank beer and devoured popcorn all the way back to Portland.

It was just a matter of a few weeks later when I got a check in the mail from Jan Scobey for the full amount that we had coming for playing her festival. Evidently they mortgaged their house and everything else they had that was valuable, and paid each and every musician that performed. Jan and Gene didn't let that get them down because they kept showing up at all the festivals around the country, selling their merchandise and promoting all the bands.

In the early 90s, CD recordings became the rage and not many people were interested in cassettes anymore, nor LP recordings. I simply took the recordings from my LP records and cassettes and had them transferred onto CD. The first one was called *West Coast Years* and included 25 years of recordings, from 1968 through 1993. To get it up to date, I brought the band into the recording studio and we cut three new tunes. Included on the CD were: "Old Green River," "Just a Closer Walk with Thee," "Theme From The Godfather," "Sweet Substitute," "Apex Blues," "Dippermouth Blues," "Corrine Carrina," "Margie," "Out of The Galleon," "Just a Little While To Stay Here," "Dixieland Doris," " Sweet and Lovely," "*Petite Fleur*," "Sugar," and three new recordings, "Sweet Sue," "That Da Da Strain" and "Tin Roof Blues." Besides myself on clarinet and soprano Sax, I used Cal Abbott on clarinet and alto sax, Jim Blackburn on piano, Dave Duthie, bass, Jack Dawes, drums, Bob Beck, banjo and Brian Darby doing the vocal on "Sweet Sue." This is an interesting recording to listen to, especially with Cal and me both playing clarinet and saxophone. At the end of the CD I thanked my fans for their support over that 25 years and I jokingly said, "Now let's go for another 25 years. Oh boy!" I'll be damned if we didn't come pretty close to doing it.

The second CD that was released was called *Clarinet and Rhythm*, and it was just that. As I did on the *West Coast Years*, I went back into my LP and cassette recordings and transferred them onto the CD format. To keep it fresh and current, I brought pianist, Jim Blackburn into the studio with me to record "Ain't Misbehavin" and "Over the Rainbow." The tunes on this CD also include "Sweet Georgia Brown," "Burgundy Street Blues," "I Can't Believe That You're In Love with Me," "I Surrender Dear," "C Jam Blues," "Temptation Rag," "New Orleans," "Makin' Whoopee," "Wrap Your Troubles In Dreams," "Just A Gigolo", "Hello Dolly," "But Beautiful," "Here's That Rainy Day," "*Si Tu Vois Ma Mere*," and "Little Enough." After listening to these recordings again, I think I hear a clarinet player torn between playing hell bent for election hot jazz, and pretty melodies. As time went on I became to blend the two together, very easily.

There was to be very little recording activity for a while because unexpected musical events took me away from Portland and when I was in town, my band was busy playing a variety of jobs. And, with the changes in the band personnel over the past few years, there wasn't much of a drinking problem, and my stress level was way down. Probably the only heavy drinker left in the band was me, but with age and maturity, even my drinking had become much more sensible. Sort of!

As if the early 90's weren't busy enough, we also had a wedding to look forward to. Bob was engaged to a young lady, Stacey Beak, who he had met while he was at Carleton College. The wedding was set for July 27th, 1991, in Champaign/Urbana, Illinois, where Stacey's parents, Sandy and Peter Beak, resided. Pauline and I visited the Beaks earlier in the year and ironically, the students and faculty of the University of Illinois were putting on a jazz concert. Peter Beak, who was a professor at the University, had asked me to help him out with the selection of the band to play for the wedding reception, and this was the perfect opportunity to scout the talent. I also needed to find a good piano player for the rehearsal dinner party. We all went to the concert and I was able to hear some excellent musicians that would work out well for the occasion. I contacted them and secured their services for both the rehearsal dinner and the wedding reception. For icing on the cake, Pete Pepke agreed to come to the wedding and play the reception as his wedding gift to Bob and Stacey. This was going to be a great band and the wedding couldn't come fast enough for me.

There were a lot of hurdles to jump over before there was any music played. Friends flooded into Champaign/Urbana from all over the world, including Canada, Japan, and Germany. Tim and his brother Stephan Dabringhaus, came to Portland, bought a car and drove to Illinois. Tim was as crazy as ever and Stephan wasn't very far behind. My kind of people!

Jame and I organized a "stag day," which consisted of a softball game, a pool and pizza party at the motel, a golf tournament, and a house party that lasted well into the night. Pete Beak was the designated driver and rented a bus to haul us all around. Everyone came through it in one piece, except there were a few tired looking guys at the wedding rehearsal and dinner afterwards. We wanted to feature Oregon wine at the rehearsal dinner so we gave every Oregonian going to the wedding a bottle of Oregon Oak Knoll Pinot Noir to deliver to us when they arrived in Illinois. Amazingly, all the bottles arrived safely and not a one of them opened, not even Tim and Stephan's.

The wedding and wedding reception was great. And the Illinois musicians were superb. I don't think that the Illinois guys knew what to think about Pete Pepke and me, along with the tunes we played, but they all joined in on the fun and it turned out to be not only a wonderful reception but a terrific musical evening, as well.

The only casualty of that whole crazy weekend, other than the police being called to the motel a couple of times, because everyone was swimming naked, was that Pete Pepke had a terrible itching on the back of his neck. Pauline looked at it and discovered it was a giant tick that had dug his way into the skin of the back of his neck. Pauline, Pete and I ended up in the emergency room while the doctor dug the tick out. The motel was later closed down, by the way, after there were several murders there. Now that play time was over we had to get back to Portland where there was lots of work ahead for me and many unexpected musical surprises.

Back in Portland, my friends, Jim Blackburn and Dave Duthie, were still playing at Hobo's on 3rd Street in downtown Portland. They had a nice job there, Jim Blackburn played the piano during the week and Dave Duthie joined him on bass on Friday and Saturday nights. If I had a night off during the week I would often go down and sit in with Jim, just for the fun of it. Quite often, Harriet, the owner and manager, would hire me for special occasions and holidays. It was a very pleasant place to be and definitely the most elegant of all the gay bars in Portland. Plus, they had an excellent menu and tasty food at reasonable prices.

Jim and Dave had a large repertoire of music that they played, but they had never got into traditional jazz until I introduced them to it. For instance, Blackburn was not familiar with Willie "The Lion" Smith and the Harlem stride piano style. And, they were completely oblivious to the names of the early players, like Sidney Bechet. That all changed very quickly, however, and we were soon playing a variety of the old traditional jazz tunes. I loaned Blackburn a Willie The Lion record and he quickly caught on to the style and even taught himself how to play one of Willie's great and difficult compositions, "Echoes' Of Spring." I included Blackburn and Duthie on several of my recordings and they had me on their recordings as well. I enjoyed playing with them and did so as often as possible.

I also discovered a whole new world and life that I didn't know existed. When I walked into Hobo's to play, it seemed like I came from the cruel world outside and inside to a bunch of happy carefree guys and gals with a great attitude about life and a wonderful sense of humor. The ones that paired up and became partners were called "DINKS", which meant double income - no kids. They had money to spend and loved to go out for a good time with friends for drinks and to enjoy a nice meal. I had a good laugh one night when I came to work, because usually I just brought my clarinet in to play, but this particular night I decided to bring my soprano sax, as well. So I walked in with my clarinet case and my soprano case and I heard someone at a table near the piano bar say, "Look! She brought two purses in with her tonight!"

It was a fun crowd to play for because no matter what we played or what tempo we played it in, we always got a wonderful round of applause. Jim Blackburn played on a beautiful baby grand piano and on top of it sat a rather large tip bowl, which was usually pretty much full at the end of the night. During intermission they played soft, pretty music in the background. Hobo's was just a great place to come and spend an evening, whether you were gay, straight, or whatever.

A favorite customer at the piano bar was a very wealthy and well-known businessman, not only in Portland but the entire state of Oregon. He lived with his wife and children in a very comfortable home in Portland and also had property and a winter home in Palm Springs, California. He also had a young male lover in Portland, who always accompanied him to Hobo's. When it was time to go south to Palm Springs for the winter, he and his family went and he brought his young lover along (separately of course) and put him up in a hotel. A rather bizarre situation, but it seemed to work for him.

He was a great fan of Blackburn and Duthie, and on the occasions that I played at Hobo's he enjoyed my music too, and bought several of my recordings. He told me that I could be very successful in Palm Springs if I ever wanted to pursue it. He also told me that he had two musician friends there that he would love to introduce me to. I always enjoyed the sun and warm weather and thought it wouldn't be a bad idea to just go and look around and see what the musical situation was really like. Oddly enough, Pauline and I had just bought a Mustang convertible - the perfect car for the desert. I had also recently received a letter from the Musicland Hotel in Palm Springs for a 50% discount on rooms for musicians. I could get a room for one or two people for $29 per night - what a deal! So I figured nothing ventured nothing gained, and I told my new found friend that I would love to come to Palm Springs and meet his musician friends. He gave me his telephone number and said to call any time and he would set up a luncheon so that we all could get acquainted. This would be a decision that would be the first in a series of events that would affect my career in music for the next 20 years.

In July, 1992, I received a letter from my old Army friend, Dick Henzel, who I hadn't seen or heard from in thirty years. Dick hadn't lost his crazy sense of humor and his letter was his update on the many years that had gone by since I had last seen him. He said he had been to West Africa and married a local chief's daughter in Uganda. The letter got worse when he said he bought a French lottery ticket and won $100,000. He went on to say he took the money and bought a Mexican hat shop. The trouble was, old gullible me believed him and I began to think what a dull life I had led in comparison. At the conclusion of the letter he did get to the truth and tell me he married a wonderful girl from Tarrytown, New York, and raised four children. He said he also took up a legitimate occupation and went into labor relations. Coincidentally, I was playing a concert in Jamestown, New York, later in the month and I wrote and told him my plans. He and his wife, Adrienne, said they would drive up from Ossining, New York and meet me.

We did meet in Jamestown at the end of the month, before my job at the Casino in Bemis Point, New York. There was a lot to catch up on and yes, in fact, Dick had married, raised three boys, a girl, and worked in labor relations. Dick had been trying to find me for several years but didn't know my mother's married name of Nelson and therefore was unable to track me down in Jamestown because I had moved to the West Coast. So it wasn't until he was reading a jazz magazine, the *Mississippi Rag*, and saw an ad about me playing at the Casino, that he was he able to track me down. It was enjoyable talking over old times and we agreed to meet again. That meeting turned out to be not far off in the future because Dick had labor relation business in Salem, Oregon, later in the year. He was still playing the piano and we had fun going over a few tunes together at my house while he was visiting.

Dick told me that his retirement was coming up soon and that he would be having plenty of free time. His thought was that he would start playing the piano again, promote some music engagements in the New York and New Jersey area, and get into the music business on a part-time basis. He asked me if I would be willing to play jobs with him and of course, I happily accepted his offer.

Dick and his family loved vacationing on Long Island, where Dick had a very good friend, Ed Kelly, who was a resident of Riverhead, New York, and had all kinds of good connections in the business world and politically. So, with Dick's promotional abilities and an inside track in the Riverhead area, along with the summer tourist trade, it would be a good place to promote some music events. The nice part about it was that Dick and Ed would do all the groundwork, including hiring the musicians, and all I would have to do was show up and play my clarinet. I was ready for Long Island, anytime I got the call.

## CHAPTER 26

# Frequent Flyer

IN MARCH 1993 I LOADED my clarinet and suitcase into the bright red Mustang convertible and headed south on I-5 to Palm Springs, California. Luckily, there wasn't very much snow going through Mt. Shasta, which made the trip quite enjoyable. After I got over the peak of the mountain, I pulled into a rest stop and shed my winter clothes and slipped into a pair of shorts - and boy did that feel good. I stayed overnight in Bakersfield, California, and the next day drove through the Mojave Desert and then down to Highway 111 and into Palm Springs. When I got into the city limits, the first thing I did was to pull the car over and put the convertible top down - what a way to live.

I arrived at the Musicland Hotel, which I found was not a hotel, but a motel. I checked in and met the owner, who was a retired pilot from United Airlines who bought the motel for his retirement investment. He was mad about jazz and that was the reason for the name of his motel and giving special rates to jazz musicians. He had speakers by the pool and played jazz music all day long. I contributed a couple of my cassettes, which made him very happy. The Musicland was right on Highway 111 and very handy to convenience stores and restaurants and an easy walk into downtown Palm Springs. There was an Italian restaurant right next door and a large restaurant/lounge across the street, featuring music nightly. So far so good; I liked the place, especially the weather.

I had a lot of exploring to do because Palm Springs and its neighboring communities were spread all along Highway 111, and there were restaurant/lounges all along the way. Driving down Highway 111 from Palm Springs you go through Cathedral City, Rancho Mirage, Palm Desert, Indian Wells, La Quinta and Indio. All those little communities are connected and if you're not watching carefully you don't know which one you're in along the way. When I checked around Palm Springs I found several piano bars with, surprisingly, mediocre piano players. I also found a few jazz clubs, but for the most part featuring modern jazz.

It was time to get down to business and I called my Portland friend to set up our luncheon meeting with his two musician buddies. He set up the meeting for the very next day and said he would pick me up at my motel. He and his boyfriend picked me up in a beautiful Mercedes Benz convertible and we drove down into Rancho Mirage for lunch at a gay resort. It was a beautiful place and we had a table by the swimming pool where I found out that wearing a swimming suit was optional. It looked like it was going to be a very interesting afternoon, to say the least. His musician friends arrived and they couldn't have been more friendly and welcoming to me. Their names were Dale Garber and Terry Thomas and they worked as a duo at the Desert Horizons Country Club in Indian Wells. They evidently were very close to my newfound Portland friend and trusted his judgment about my musicianship.

They both were partners in music and I gathered were partners in life as well. Terry was the outgoing one with a smile on his face and he could charm the hell out of you. He was also obviously in charge and made all the decisions. Dale was very friendly too, but on the quiet side and looked probably about the same age as me, except both dyed their hair coal black and it was hard to tell. They were obviously old pros in show business and very professional.

Terry said that he would very much like it if I came to the country club and sit in with them the following Saturday evening. But there was one problem: They wore tuxes at the country club and I didn't have mine with me. No big deal, Terry said, Dale has an extra at the house that he can't fit into any more and Terry was sure that it would fit me. So, after lunch we agreed that I come out to their house the next day and pick up the tuxedo. They lived in Palm Desert in a beautiful home with a swimming pool and Dale had a big grand piano in the living room. They also had a new Mercedes-Benz sedan in the garage that they only drove on special occasions. I tried the tux on and it fit perfectly. I told the guys I'd see them Saturday night. The only thing left I had to do was to find a shiny pair of dress shoes to go with the tux and I was set to go.

For the first time in ages I was nervous about going to a job. Everything was overwhelming and I didn't have a clue what the hell Dale and Terry were going to play. Nevertheless, after getting into my tux and new shoes, I grabbed my clarinet and soprano saxophone, got behind the wheel of the Mustang convertible and headed down Highway 111 to the Desert Horizons Country Club. At least I looked good.

I pulled into the Desert Horizons Country Club off of Highway 111 in Indian Wells. I first came to a guardhouse and gate where a very friendly guard came out and asked me the reason for my visit. I told him my name and that I would be performing at the country club lounge with Dale and Terry. He checked his clipboard and my name was on a list, so the gate was opened and I drove down the road to the parking lot in front of the country club restaurant and lounge. I could see that if you didn't have a good reason to be there, that it probably would be harder to get into than the White House.

Dale and Terry were waiting for me with big smiles on their faces. We were off to a good start when I found out that we could have a drink whenever we wanted, we just had to ask. The job turned out to be an easy and pleasant one. For our first set we mostly played soft ballads for the dinner crowd. After the crowd finished dinner we played more up-tempo swing tunes along with Dale and Terry's occasional vocals. We only played until 10 o'clock in the evening and our last few numbers of tunes were on the rock 'n roll side, after people had a considerable amount to drink. There was also a bass player, Hal Brain, who was very good and filled the band out nicely, with Dale on the piano and Terry on drums. It amazed me that during the course of the evening, Terry knew the names of just about everyone in the crowd; he was one of the most personable guys I had ever met in my life. He should have been a politician. At intermissions Terry brought me around to different tables and introduced me to people from Oregon, especially the Portland area. As it turned out I already knew a couple of car dealers, Ron Tonkin and Vic Alfonso, along with Howard Dietrich, the owner of Portland's Red Lion Hotel.

After the job was over the band sat down at a table and relaxed with a couple of drinks. The lounge was very comfortable with a large bar serviced by two bartenders. If we wanted we could go out a side door to the patio looking out to a beautiful golf course and have our drinks. I liked that, because I could smoke outside and in those days I was still puffing away, big time. Before the kitchen closed we all ordered what we wanted for dinner, which was also a nice perk for the job because the dinners there were top-of-the-line, sort of like going to the Ruth's Chris for a steak. Dale and Terry always liked to have their dinners boxed up, and they had a relaxing meal when they got home. That night I was invited to go back home with them for dinner. I did, and it was a great opportunity for us to get to know each other better.

In their home, we sat around a bar in their living room and had a few cocktails before dinner.

I found out that Dale was originally from Ohio, just outside of Akron. He attended the University of Akron and also Florida Southern College in Lakeland, Florida. He traveled to the West Coast and became the music director of Sea World in San Diego from 1965 through 1968. He was also the organist for the San Diego Sports Arena and their hockey team, the San Diego Gulls. On top of those activities he found time to do nightclub work in the San Diego area. I also found out that Dale did not like to talk about his age and I could see he was uncomfortable when I brought up the subject. It probably had something to do with him being so much older than Terry.

Terry, on the other hand, had no trouble telling me that he was 43 and born in the San Diego area in 1950. Along with his parents, he was an active member of the Mission Bay Yacht Club where he became an excellent sailor. He won the junior Sabot national championship in 1967. He was also a snow skier and surfer. He loved music and was well known for his drumming and vocals. He met Dale in 1970 playing in a night club and they became attracted to each other and formed a musical partnership as well, called the Dale and Terry Duo.

The following year they had a two-week engagement in Palm Springs, and loved it so much that they stayed in the desert and never went back to San Diego. Dale and Terry also toured the United States with the very popular accordionist, Dick Contino, along with being featured with him at the Tropicana Hotel in Las Vegas, Nevada. They played at the Gene Autry Hotel in Palm Springs for 11 years and spent 27 years at the Desert Horizons Country Club. In between all that musical activity, they opened their own Mexican restaurant right on Highway 111 in Palm Springs. Over the years, Terry had taught himself how to cook and he became an accomplished chef. Their restaurant became very popular and was the place to go and be seen. The two of them missed music, however, and went back to entertaining. In the summer months when it got unbearably hot in Palm Springs and most everything shut down, Dale and Terry worked on the Holland America Cruise Line, playing their music and traveling the world.

We had our dinner that night and it was delicious, especially after Terry fixed it up a bit. I returned my tuxedo and got into my street clothes, as it was getting into the wee hours of the morning. Before I left, Terry offered me a job. They loved the way I played and evidently the entertainment committee at the Country Club liked me as well. So, I was offered the job starting the next New Year's Eve and playing weekends and special events. Terry was the entertainment director of the Country Club and I guess that he just added me into his budget. Now I could keep warm in the wintertime, and I didn't even dream it at the time, but it became a yearly routine for 20 years. Dale and Terry also became like the two brothers I never had.

After a gap in our friendship of 33 years, Dick Henzel put together a summertime tour of Long Island engagements that would be the first in a series we would play for the next 10 seasons. Long Island in New York State is the longest, largest, and most populated island in the United States, with a population of around 7 million people. With Dick's affiliation with the New Jersey Jazz Club, we also played engagements there as well. Not only that, but being so near to Jamestown, New York, I could fit that yearly trip in too. Dick turned out to be a great promoter and he could really sell a band and get top dollar for it. I don't know what he told people about me, but he built me up like a superstar and paid me extremely well. God bless him. Dick and Adrienne were great hosts and for the most part of our tours rented a large home on the bay that would accommodate Pauline and me, along with the rest of the musicians in the band.

On our first year we ran into musician problems, mainly because Dick wasn't really familiar with the Long Island musicians and didn't know who he was hiring some of the time. For instance, we had a trumpet player who was with us the first night. We found out he couldn't even blow his nose. After fumbling through the first tune he blamed his false teeth. We also had a trombone player with a chip on his shoulder; he played okay, but so what! Thank God that Dick was there on piano and we were able to get through the evening without anybody throwing tomatoes at us. The following year Dick found a good cornet player, Richard Sudhalter, who I had heard of because he had authored a book about Bix Beiderbecke, called *Bix - Man and Legend.* What I didn't know about him was that he was "different," and I mean "different"! Our first job with him was at the Southampton Golf Club where he was waiting for me on the bandstand with a band aid on the bridge of his nose. He explained that it was a new device to assist in breathing by opening up the nasal passages. He really was something else. He played well, that is, if he liked the tune that you called. If he didn't, he impolitely said he just didn't play that tune because he doesn't like it! We got through the night just fine thanks to the rest of the band, including a great trombone player from New York City, Bobby Pring.

I had one more night to go through with Dick Sudhalter and he was just as nutty as ever. First he tried to take over the band, starting calling tunes, playing double solos, and switching keys. But that was not the worst of it. In the second set, while playing his solo, he falls down on the stage floor and while on his back, continues to play his horn. At first we didn't know if he had passed out or was injured. But we soon realized he was just making a jerk of himself (and of the band). Where in the world did these musicians come from? I was beginning to miss my West Coast group. I did have one more trumpet player that drove me nuts when he asked me – "When are we going to take a break?" - when we had just finished the second tune of our first set of the evening.

Fortunately, by trial and error, we finally came up with a good crew of musicians to play the Long Island tours. We got some excellent musicians from New York City that were easy to work with and were happy to get the job. We found Paul Squire on trumpet, who happened to be alumni of The Salt City Six, the group I played with from Syracuse, New York. Russ Grimelot joined us on trombone and Percy Brice, a drummer with George Shearing fit in perfectly.

One of my favorite jobs was playing on the *Peconic River Lady*, an old-fashioned paddle wheeler that cruised on Peconic Bay. The cruise went from 6 p.m. until 10 p.m. and included the music, open bar and dinner, all for $50 a person. The food was great and the open bar, even better. Another nice place to play was The Pridwin Hotel on Shelter Island, New York, on Peconic Bay. We took a ferry to get there and the island was beautiful, along with a very old and elegant hotel. Dick Petry, the owner of the hotel, was a super guy and perfect gentleman. An example of this generosity occurred when he insisted on feeding the band during the first break. Not in the kitchen with a quick sandwich, but right in the middle of the guest dining room, with a table specifically reserved for the band. I didn't realize this until it was too late and on our first intermission I saw the band sitting down and ordering from the menu, drinks, appetizers, main course and dessert. What in hell were they thinking? But what could I say? The owner of the hotel was the boss, even though people were there to hear the band and the musicians were busy having a feast. Well, by the time the band finished their dinner, we had lost most of our crowd. What a night! We barely made it off the island to make that last ferry boat's departure at midnight. Dick Petry told us not to worry, if we miss the ferry he would take us back to the mainland on his yacht. We did make the ferry - just!

Dick scoured Long Island for engagements and he found plenty of them, including Claudio's Clam Bar in Greenport, Digger O'Dell's and The Birchwood Champagne Room in Riverhead, The Wine Garden Restaurant and Apple Tree in Mattatuck, and The Southampton Golf Club in Southampton. We also played the Westhampton Beach Summer Concert Series along with the annual show for the Riverhead Concert Series in the Town Park off the Peconic River. On top of all that, Dick booked me into Jack O'Connor's Beef House, a jazz club in Bridgewater, New Jersey. I was booked for three nights with New York musicians Jim Andrews on piano, Chuck Slate, drums, and Ed Cohen playing bass. That was a great three nights with big crowds and a lot of New York and New Jersey musicians showing up to check out the "hot shot" West Coast clarinet player. Dick and I stayed at his sister and brother-in-law's house, Nancy and Bud Clarke, while I played at O'Connor's. It was very relaxing after the job sitting in their living room with a cocktail looking out across the Hudson River to the bright lights of New York City.

On one of my Long Island concerts, a friend of Dick Henzel's was in the audience and he just went crazy over the band. He was from Chicago and was Commodore of the Wooden Boat Club on Lake Michigan. His name was Toby Lindo, a very interesting man and an amateur ragtime piano player. He told me that his club was putting on a big wooden boat show the next summer and would very much like me to provide the entertainment for it. It just so happened that it was right after the Long Island tour, so I could stop in Chicago on my way back to Portland. We agreed on the dates and price, I got Dick Henzel on piano, and filled out the rest of the band with Chicago musicians.

The early summer of 1995 was hot and muggy on Long Island. There were frequent power outages because everyone had their air conditioners on full blast. Consequently, the supermarkets were practically giving away perishable foods before they completely went bad. So the band ate well at the Henzel household with beautiful T-bone steaks on the barbecue and lots of lobster. We had the band personnel down to a science now with good New York City jazz musicians and all our jobs went over well and without any major incidents.

Following the Long Island engagements I flew to Chicago to play for the Wooden Boat Club and their annual big show on Lake Michigan. If I thought that Long Island was hot, I had a big surprise waiting for me when I arrived in Chicago. They were having their biggest heat wave ever! The temperature hovered around 106° and killed 739 people, mostly the elderly that did not have air conditioning in their homes or apartments.

I had a great band to perform with at the boat show, with Dick Henzel playing piano and the Chicago musicians filling in the rest. But it was so hot that when we played no one had the energy to dance. In fact, Henzel was so affected by the heat that he came close to passing out on the bandstand and we had to lay him down on the couch in a side room. However, after the sun went down and it cooled off a bit, the band and the audience started to come to life and it ended up being a successful party. I survived it all by drinking a lot of beer.

One of the benefits of this engagement was that I got to see many cool, beautiful old wooden boats. One there really blew my mind - it was *The African Queen* from the movie with Humphrey Bogart and Katharine Hepburn. The old boat was built in 1912 and there it was, sitting in Lake Michigan. Luckily they were giving rides on it and I jumped at the chance. We glided through Lake Michigan on the *African Queen* going ever so slowly – Put. Put. Put. The only thing that was missing was Bogart and Hepburn.

But the star of the Wooded Boat Show had to be a 62 foot sloop called the *Serenade*. It was the most beautiful sailing vessel that I have ever seen and was built in 1938 for the great violinist Jascha Heifetz. Oddly enough, Heifetz and Humphrey Bogart were great friends and they sailed together often on this beautiful vessel. Quite a jump for Humphrey Bogart, going from the *African Queen* to *The Serenade*. Heifetz eventually sold *The Serenade* to ocean explorer Jacques Cousteau, who later sold it to Zsa Gabor, who had it until selling it to a new owner on Lake Michigan.

There was a rather eccentric lady at the boat show who evidently loved to hang around with musicians. I understood that she was a very wealthy Chicago socialite who was very popular in the social circles of Chicago. She knew the owner of *The Serenade* and invited me, Adrienne, and Dick to accompany her on a private cruise. Of course we didn't turn that down and we went on a first class sailing voyage on Lake Michigan. It was a wonderful experience, along with a captain and the crew that spoiled you with drink and food. There was a very good wind that day and the ship was really moving. The captain invited me to take the wheel and when I did I never had felt such power in my life -absolutely amazing.

Our new socialite friend insisted on taking us out for dinner that evening to one of the most exclusive restaurants in Chicago. She wined and dined us until we were stuffed, but when the bill came she never went for her purse and offered to pay. So the rest of us had to scramble around and find enough money to pay the bill. So much for Chicago! After spending those days in that heat, it was nice getting off the plane in Portland to some cool weather and rain. I never thought I'd say that.

We had our usual schedule of weddings, anniversaries, birthdays and the Jazz Societies in Oregon and Washington. Every now and then we would be booked into the Tri-Cities Jazz Club in Kennewick, Washington. Although the fans in the Tri-Cities were very friendly and accommodating, I didn't like the long trip up the Columbia Gorge because we had to leave so early in the morning to play our first set at 1 p.m. I eventually worked out a contract with them where they put us up for the night, and we didn't have to face that long drive home after the job.

Pauline's nephew, John Vickerstaff, was getting married to his long-time girlfriend Lesley in Vancouver, Canada and they asked me if I would play for their wedding reception. It was too costly to bring my band up from Portland, so I teamed up with my old buddy Lance Harrison and his band to play the job. It was a beautiful, country club wedding and people came from all over, even Pauline's cousin, Judith Vickerstaff Smith from Bude, Cornwall, England. I knew Judith from when I visited the Vickerstaff family in Bude back in 1982. After listening to me play, Judith mentioned that they now had a week-long jazz festival in Bude, over what the British call the bank holiday, our Labor Day weekend. She went on to say that she was a friend of the promoter of the festival and would love to give him one of my CDs to listen to. She returned to England with my CD in hand and within two weeks I got a call from the British jazz promoter asking me to be a guest artist at their Bude Festival the following year. Gee -whiz! I had more or less forgotten about playing overseas, probably because I had been keeping so busy with work right here in the United States. But heck yes! We made a deal over the phone and I was booked to play England's Bude Jazz Festival in 1995.

I had another wedding to play in Canada that year and the money was good enough that I could bring my band from Portland. The wedding reception was held on a small island off the coast of British Columbia, near the border. We made the trip in Jack Dawes' big van that held all the band members and the musical equipment comfortably. We took a small ferry over to the island and drove to where the reception was to be held. It was a small, comfortable house, surrounded by lots of beautiful flowers in a wooded area. They had a bar set up along with a beautiful buffet with all kinds of delicious looking foods. I did have one thought when I went to the restroom. I noticed that it was the "one and only" restroom in the house, with no portable outdoor toilets to be seen. I then thought it was going to be one hell of a lineup for all the guys and gals when they had to go potty during the reception. I'll be damned if I was going to step into the woods again and sink up to my knees in quicksand, like I did on that Indian island on Lake Washington.

There was no bandstand to speak of, so we had to set the band up in a grassy area just off the woods. The guests started to arrive and the party began with the arrival of the bride and groom. Everyone was having an enjoyable time and taking advantage of the very generous liquor bar along with wine and a large keg of beer. As I predicted, the lineup to the toilet was getting longer and longer. I also felt the ground getting soggy beneath my feet and as time went on it went from soggy to just plain wet, and also started to smell. And then I saw the guests going through the buffet line sinking down to what looked like – shit! My God! The old reception house in the middle of the woods had a septic tank and it had overflowed - including the toilet. People were sloshing around in poop and it was starting to smell unbearably bad. And, if things weren't bad enough, the flies started swarming in from the woods. The poor bride, with the bottom of her wedding dress covered in poop, was horrified and crying her heart out. It was her big wedding day and she, her husband, and all their guests were standing in a field full of excrement.

I suggested that we move the band, buffet and the bar way over to the far side of the property away from the septic tank area. They got a crew of guys together and carted everything over to dry land and we continued the party and tried to put on a happy face - but it wasn't easy, especially for the bride on her wedding day.

I returned to Portland only to find a message on my answering machine from Ernie Carson. Ernie had been thinking about moving back to

Portland for some time, and I thought he called to tell me that he was going through with it. I returned his call and it was a job offer that I couldn't believe. A month in China...Wow! - I never expected that. Now that was an offer I just couldn't turn down because it was a part of the world that I never expected to see. Ernie said that he would send me all the details about travel, accommodations and pay and we also had to get busy with all the paperwork for our work permits, visas and all the other necessities needed for an engagement of that magnitude. It looked like a busy time ahead for me with my Portland band, Palm Springs engagements, Long Island, England and now China. I was 61 years old and starting to look at the end of my career - it didn't turn out that way because I had many more notes to play before I was finished.

The job was one month at the Kempinski Hotel in Beijing. Evidently the hotel was saluting a different country every month and featuring food from that country in their restaurant. So we were booked for a month in the hotel's restaurant promoting American foods and beverages, which included a chef from Boston, Massachusetts. Ernie's booking was from June 9th (my birthday) through July 9th and was for a quartet. Of course I was in 100%, but come to find out, Ernie didn't have a band to bring over to China and asked me to find him a banjo and a tuba player. I didn't figure it out at the time, but Ernie was having problems getting musicians to work with him because of his sometimes bizarre explosions on the job due to too much alcohol. For tuba, I recommended my friend Randy Keller, who jumped at the chance to go to China as I did, but for a banjo I was stymied because most of the good Portland banjo players had day jobs, or families, and could not get away for that length of time. Randy Keller, however, knew of a banjo player from the Tri-Cities in Washington, Carl Walterskerichen, who, like Randy, jumped at the chance for such an adventure. So Ernie had his quartet: himself on cornet, me playing clarinet and soprano sax, Carl on banjo and Randy playing the tuba. We were all set to go and just needed to get our passports and visas in order so they could issue our round-trip airplane tickets. When I got my airplane ticket, I couldn't believe it. The hotel paid $2500 to fly me over, and that meant $10,000 just for airfare for the whole band.

When the big day arrived to leave for China we all flew into Tokyo, Japan from different airports and met there to fly into Beijing together. We had some time at the Tokyo airport to have drinks at the bar and to get acquainted. Randy and I had planned to share a room together and that left Ernie to share his room with Carl. Before we boarded our plane to Beijing, we all took advantage of the duty-free store and I bought a half gallon of vodka, as did Ernie. I don't know what Randy and Carl purchased, but whatever they did, it must have lasted them a long time, because compared to Ernie and me, they were teetotalers.

The flight over to Beijing was very interesting for me because I sat with a bunch of Japanese bankers who were on their way over to China on business. They were very anxious to talk with me and we had drinks and laughs all the way to Beijing. They were very interested to hear of my playing and said they would come to the Kempinski Hotel, have dinner and listen to the band.

I don't know exactly what I was expecting when I arrived in Beijing, but I was surprised when we landed in near total darkness, with the exception of some large spotlights out on the runway. We didn't taxi up to the terminal but instead the plane stopped short of it and they pushed a portable stairway up to the doorway of the airplane. It was like going back in time several years, like the old world. It was confusing, but we managed to depart the plane, get our luggage and get through customs inspection very easily. All we were told was not to bring any American propaganda or Bibles.

The Kempinski Hotel had a van waiting for us at the airport. The ride to the hotel was on a very modern freeway and we passed several small dwellings that looked like they had been there for many years, along with very large new high-rises being built. The hotel was fairly new and quite modern with air-conditioning and a beautiful lobby area, including a lounge and bar with lots of seating. I was anxious to get checked into our rooms and come back down to one of the bars for a little celebration as it was my birthday eve. We were checked in, received our room assignments, and went to the elevator where there was a guard at the door. He asked what floor we wanted and then instructed another employee to take us up. I suspected that he was a secret policeman and I was under the impression that they knew who was where in that hotel at all times. My room was large and very luxurious, so Randy and I had a lot of breathing space. It wasn't too long before our phone rang and it was Ernie on the other end asking for me. He said "Jim, sharing a room with this Carl character just isn't going to work! Please! Please! Would you room with me and let Carl and Randy room together?" My God. We hadn't even played a note yet and there was tension in the band. To make things peaceful, I agreed, and traded places with Carl and became Ernie's roommate for a month. Oh boy!

After I transferred my belongings over to Ernie's room we all went downstairs to exchange our American dollars for some Chinese yuan and proceeded to have a Chinese birthday party for me. We were surprised to learn that the hotel had a German restaurant along with an authentic Oktoberfest type of band all the way from Germany. The German band was very original and even wore *lederhosen*. We all enjoyed the German beer and food and decided that this would be one of our hangouts. We also looked in to the restaurant where we would be playing starting the next evening. It was quite large and very plush, with fancy white tablecloths covering the tables. You could order dinner from the menu, including cocktails, or enjoy a very large and varied buffet and salad bar. After that we decided to call it a night because we were tired from the very long trip to Beijing, and the next day we had to get the bandstand set up and see what the ins and outs were in the life of a Kempinski Hotel employee.

The following morning we went down to the hotel offices and had our pictures taken for identification cards to gain us admission to the executive dining room. This meant that breakfast, lunch and dinner was courtesy of the hotel - a very nice perk. It also meant that all our laundry was taking care of by the hotel as well. All we had to do was take our dirty laundry to the laundry room, drop it off and it would be ready for us the next day. We had a maid that took care of our rooms every day, cleaning up and giving us fresh sheets and pillow cases for our beds. Life was good!

The only question I had was that why in hell did they pick a traditional, two beat jazz band with banjo and tuba to play during dinner hours in a very exclusive upscale restaurant? I knew that they wanted American jazz to go along with the theme of things, but a more subtle, softer type of swing jazz would have been much more appropriate. As an example, a cornet, clarinet, guitar or keyboard and bass would be much more suitable and enjoyable dining experience for the customers.

But there again, I had to remember that I was not the bandleader and I was just there to play my clarinet. It was none of my business what the instrumentation of the band was or the selections of tunes that we played. In fact, after I thought about it, I had all those bandleader responsibilities off my back and all I had to do was sit back, play my clarinet and enjoy the show.

The next day in the late afternoon we started to play the first song of the first set of the first day on the job. We sounded quite professional, considering that this was the first time we had actually worked together. Ernie was so great to work with because he played such a great melodic lead that carried the band right along with him. Randy was a wonderful tuba player and Carl was very proficient on the banjo. Unfortunately, just as I had figured, we were much too loud for the dining crowd and were told by the restaurant manager to tone the band down so the customers could converse with one another without having to shout. This request wasn't new to us in the music business and we adjusted the volume of the band very easily to fit in with the dining room. I did have one pleasant surprise on our opening night in the dining room. My Japanese banker friends that I met on the flight in from Tokyo came in for dinner and presented me with one dozen red roses.

We played Monday through Saturday in the dining room and had Sundays off. The hours were easy, just four hours a night from 5 p.m. until 9 p.m. with 20 to 30 minute breaks, nobody seemed to care. We had very few Chinese customers because it was simply too expensive for the average Beijing citizen to have dinner there. Most of our Chinese diners where high officials in the Communist Party and they just signed their check at the end of the night. Otherwise, most of our customers were guests at the hotel, flight attendants, employees of the many embassies in Beijing, or wealthy visitors from Hong Kong. We did, however, have people come in that were curious to hear an American jazz band. I think we were probably one of the first, if not the first, jazz band to play in China, as I think that before us our music was banned.

I found our intermissions very interesting because I was often invited to have a drink with our guests. They were from different parts of the world and it made for some fun conversations that made the evening go quickly. I was very careful not to talk about American democracy, politics or religion; because you never knew who you might be talking to. Sometimes on our breaks we would take our horns and walk over to the German restaurant to play a tune or two and often joined in jamming with the German "umpa" band. It was always a lot of fun and we were given all the good German beer that we could drink. Quite often we had so much fun that we lost track of time and were late getting back to the dining room, but no one said anything because it was good public relations for the hotel. When we were finished playing for the night, we could go through the buffet line and eat as much food as we wanted. I was careful about this because I could see where I could put on one heck of a lot of weight in one month.

I had plenty of time on my hands during the day. There was so much to do and see and I took advantage of it. The Kempinski Hotel was on the outskirts of Beijing and it was too long a walk to get to the downtown area. That was no problem because there were hundreds of unique taxis around (given the nickname of "meatloaf"), a van-type vehicle that ran on two cylinders. When Randy and I took a meatloaf downtown we could barely squeeze into the back seat. But it was cheap transportation because the exchange rate on our American money was fantastic and went a long way. For instance, a pack of cigarettes cost me $.10 and to buy a beer from a street vendor was only $.15. One thing that really blew my mind was the fact you could buy a beer and drink it while walking through downtown Beijing without being stopped by the police. That's something I would never dare to do in the United States, except maybe in Las Vegas or on Bourbon Street in New Orleans. And, to buy an excellent lunch with the best noodles you've ever tasted in your life was a mere $.50. I ate lunch out on the street every day after discovering the executive dining room food was a little iffy after I scooped a ladle of soup in my bowl only to find a small skull floating around. That was the end of my eating in the executive dining room, even if it was for free, except for boxed cereal and milk in the mornings.

During my downtown Beijing excursions I realized that I was being tailed by the Chinese secret police. There were very few Americans walking around Beijing and maybe they figured that I could've been a CIA agent disguised as a musician over in China to overthrow their government. Whatever those secret police were thinking, they soon figured out my schedule and followed me wherever I went. So, to make it interesting, I thought I'd make them work for their money and I started to act suspicious by very suddenly walking fast, ducking into the nearest alley. They would run and catch up with me and we would start all over again. Playing games like this after a week or so, I'm sure they finally caught on and thought it was quite humorous, as well. There was always one in back of me and one across the street walking along with me. They were easy to spot because they wore dark suits and carried umbrellas, which was ridiculous during the hot dry Beijing summer weather. They reminded me of the German Gestapo back in the 30s and 40s. Anyway, they had a job to do and I think they had fun playing cops and robbers with me. Ernie Carson, however, didn't have such good luck with the secret police, when he threw one of his cigarette butts on the street he was immediately apprehended and given a ticket and had to pay a fine of $1.10 in American money. So you can see that we were being watched every move we made.

Although I roomed with Ernie, I didn't see much of him, other than on the bandstand. He kept mostly to himself during the day; in fact I don't know where he was most of the time. But in the evening he drank himself to sleep every night. Carl, we called "Mr. Gadget," was off running around on his own every day, as well. That left Randy and me, hanging out together and exploring all the interesting aspects of this wonderful city.

Randy and I talked it over and realized that we only had about five or six full days off work while we were in Beijing. There were several things that we wanted to take in and first on the list was the Great Wall of China. So, on our first Sunday off we rented a car and driver for a day and split the cost between Randy, Carl and myself. Ernie wasn't interested in going with us and I don't know if he ever did do it on his own. We left fairly early in the morning and it wasn't a long a drive to get there. But when we did arrive I was shocked to see the sales vendors all over the place. I couldn't resist and bought a Chairman Mao cap with a red star and looked like a real authentic communist. The secret police would be happy with me next week when I walked through town.

As President Nixon said when he first viewed the Great Wall – "This truly is a Great Wall!" I must say, I agree with him. When I first saw the Great Wall it was mind-boggling the way it just went on and on over the countryside. It's over 13,000 miles long and goes from the East to West of China. It was built with mostly slave labor and two centuries were required to finish it. The construction was all by hand and started in the 1400s BC and it wasn't finished until the 1600s. It was built to keep out invaders from the north and it worked, except for the time Genghis Kahn and the Mongolians conquered a good share of China in the 13th century.

When I was there an actor taking the part of a samurai Mongolian swordsmen jumped out at people from time to time and scared the hell out of them - including me. I did get Randy to take a picture of us. Another picture I got was sitting on top of a horse with the Great Wall sprawling out behind me. We spent the greater part of the day at the Great Wall before driving back to our hotel in Beijing. On the way back we stopped for drinks and dinner and invited our driver to join us - he was elated! The whole feast didn't cost any more than five American dollars.

We also took a day and visited The Forbidden City; another sightseeing trip that would take the entire day to take in. 24 Chinese emperors lived there in the Imperial Palace from 1420 until 1912. It was located right in downtown Beijing and we all went sightseeing, including Ernie. Again, like the Great Wall, it was overwhelming and to do it justice one should visit several times. It was surrounded by a 171-foot Moat that was 20 feet deep. There was an outer court for ceremonial functions and an inner court that was the residence of the royal family. It was a fun day and we all took lots of pictures. When we left to go back to the hotel we all grabbed a rickshaw for the ride back. That was a kick!

Tiananmen Square was fascinating because of its size, stretching out for 109 acres. It became especially famous during the protests for democracy in 1989, where the government declared martial law and killed hundreds of protesters. Communist Chairman Mao's preserved body lies in state there in a huge mausoleum and there were huge lines to file past his open casket to view his body. Randy and I decided to see him one afternoon and we were rushed past his casket at a very quick pace. I could see why, because to me it looked like a waxed dummy. When we got to the exit door I tried to linger and take a good look at him until suddenly I saw around 10 Chinese soldiers coming to chase me away.

Randy and I also took in the Chinese Military Museum, which was very interesting and was not only full of military equipment but full of communist propaganda. In the front of the building there was a captured American PT boat. How and where they got it, I don't know, because all the written information was in Chinese. There were also American tanks of all sizes and other US military equipment, along with some of their military jets and fighter-bombers, and huge rockets, so you can imagine how large the building was. There was also a crashed US jet on display that I assume was a spy plane that they might have shot down or, perhaps the Russians. We saw many oversized portraits of Stalin, Lenin, and of course, Chairman Mao. There was also a limousine that obviously belonged to a high Chinese official at one time, which was very close to looking like an American Packard. All in all, it was an amazing day at the museum, even though we couldn't read the Chinese posters by the displays.

Back at the hotel, things were going very well and the band was sounding better each night. Ernie only had one stumble with his drinking, and that's when he came to work one night at 5 p.m. loaded to the gills. He was pretty bad and obviously couldn't play. I talked him into taking the night off and going back to his room before the manager saw him. So we played as a trio that night and I simply told the manager that Ernie wasn't feeling well. A few days later I remembered that I had a half a gallon of duty-free vodka in my closet and decided to mix myself a drink. I went into my closet and grabbed the bottle of vodka only to find it completely empty. I knew it hadn't evaporated in that short a time and there was only one other solution for my bottle being empty. Ernie was in the room and saw me with my empty bottle and confessed immediately. Evidently he had polished off his half-gallon and then started drinking mine when I wasn't around. In other words, he had consumed one full gallon of vodka in the room since we had arrived in Beijing. I didn't get upset because there was plenty to drink in the different bars around the hotel and besides, Ernie is the one responsible for me being on this wonderful trip and I didn't mind giving him my half-gallon of vodka.

I became friends with one of our Chinese waiters in the dining room. He spoke very broken English and explained to me that he wanted to learn the language so he could speak it fluently. Tured out that his Chinese name in "American" was Sam. I offered to help him, as much as I could, but we had a problem getting together, because the Chinese employees of the hotel lived in the sub-basement and were not allowed to be in the upstairs hotel unless they were working. So we decided to meet in front of our hotel and walk to a restaurant to have lunch and then go to another hotel lobby and have our English lessons…Now that drove the secret police completely crazy. What in hell was I doing having lunch with a Chinese waiter from the hotel? Was I trying to convert him to Christianity? Or was I telling him about American democracy! We always had one and sometimes two secret police following us and even coming in and sitting next to us in one of the hotel lobbies, listening to our conversation. They soon realized it was nothing more than an English lesson and gave up the chase. I often think about Sam and hope that he someday was able to speak fluent English and maybe even make it over to the United States.

It's amazing how time flies when you're having fun and enjoying yourself. It was the first of July and it was getting close to the end of our engagement at the Kempinski Hotel. We did have one big job coming up that the whole band was looking forward to. The American Embassy in Beijing was having a gigantic party on July 4th. Anyone who was anybody was invited, and that meant all the high officials in the Communist Party. Different businesses around Beijing were donating their services, food and beverages for free. Even AT& T were going to be offering free phone calls to anywhere in the world. The Kempinski Hotel's contribution to the affair was our band, playing four hours from noon to 4 p.m. But here is the unusual part of the day: all US Embassy employees, including the United States Marine guards, had the entire day off to celebrate the holiday with everyone else. So who was guarding the embassy? The Communist Chinese Army! They had the place surrounded and it probably had never been so safe. The Chinese military were really paranoid that day because of all days, they didn't want any incidents at the US Embassy.

It turned out to be a beautiful sunny day; thank goodness because the party was held on the grounds of the embassy. There was more food being given away than imaginable, including McDonald's and Kentucky fried chicken, along with the many delicious Chinese dishes. For drinks you could have beer, wine, Coca-Cola or anything else you could think of, and there was ice cream and desserts all over the place. I was looking forward to the free phone calls but was out of luck because when I called friends and relatives in the states they were sleeping and didn't answer. There was one strange incident when we took our first break. With all the free goodies around I decided to take a walk around the grounds. Now we always took at least a 15 minute break and you always assume that, unless you're told differently. Fortunately I didn't wander off too far. I looked around and saw Ernie calling the rest of the guys back to the bandstand to play. My God, Ernie was deliberately trying to make me late! I ran back to the bandstand just in time to play the first tune - and Ernie looked at me and said "Jim - you're not so perfect after all!" This was very strange to me but I found it just a preview of things to come.

Time had seemed to have gone by so quickly, it was hard to imagine that we were about to play the last night and the last four hours of our engagement. It was also the last night of the American menu and buffet and the restaurant was full with many of our steady customers coming in to get their last American meal and say goodbye to us. Because it was our last night, things were rather loose and we took longer breaks and mingled with our customers. We even ran over and played a tune in the German restaurant, had a beer, and said our goodbyes to our German musician friends. Ernie brought over several CDs to sell and told me to do the same, and we easily got rid of them all on our last night. There were some big time spenders from Hong Kong buying all the drinks we could consume, but I left the party fairly early because I had to pack and I knew the next day would be a long one. Ernie stayed out quite late and when he did get back to our room he had the band payroll with him in US currency and he paid me immediately.

We had an early flight to Tokyo the next morning and we all met in the hotel lobby to check out and settle any charges we may have occurred. I must have looked pretty silly, because in addition to my luggage, saxophone and clarinet cases I also had a giant teddy bear to bring back. My son, Bob, after graduating from Carleton College, taught English in China for a few months. He had made many friends and had alerted some of them that I was playing at the Kempinski Hotel. One of them showed up at my door, just before going to work one night, to pay his respects, and to give me this huge teddy bear to bring back to Bob and Stacy. I brought him down to the restaurant with me and bought him dinner. He had no idea what kind of American food he would like, so I suggested a cheeseburger and French fries. As I was playing they delivered his order and he just sat there, the whole time I was playing, just staring at his cheeseburger in bewilderment. When we took our first intermission I went to his table and asked why he hadn't eaten his cheeseburger. He looked at me and said "I don't know how to eat it!" So I explained to him that all he had to do was pick it up and start eating. At any rate, he had a great evening and a treat that most Chinese citizens could never afford. But I was still stuck with that mammoth teddy bear.

Randy, Carl and I were in the lobby waiting for Ernie to show up so we could leave for the airport. Ernie finally arrived, pretty well smashed, and looking like hell. He had the whole band payroll, minus my pay, in US cash in his jacket pocket. So it wouldn't fall out, he closed the pocket with a couple of safety pins. He also had a bottle of Chinese liquor with a lizard, dead and preserved, floating around in it. The Chinese believed that it was very healthy for you and good luck to drink it like that. I had bought a bottle, as well, but had it safely packed in my luggage. Perhaps Ernie had planned to drink it on the plane - I don't know. After we all got settled and checked out of the hotel we got into the Kempinski Hotel van and headed to the airport for the start of the long journey back to the United States.

At the airport we checked our luggage and got our seat assignments, when I heard a loud shriek from Ernie – My God! I've lost all my money! Ernie had carefully pinned the top of his pocket together but didn't realize that he had a hole in the bottom of his pocket, and the band payroll had slipped out. It probably didn't happen at the airport, or one of us would have spotted it on the floor. So we figured that it either had to be back at the Kempinski Hotel or in the hotel van that took us to the airport. Needless to say, Ernie was frantic, and justifiably so, because it was a considerable amount of money and all in US currency, which made it extremely valuable in Communist China. Ernie ran off to catch a cab back to the Kempinski hotel. I thought his chances of finding his money were not good and besides that our plane was boarding soon and I thought that he probably would miss that as well.

Boarding time came and Randy, Carl and I got in the plane thinking that we would probably be leaving Ernie behind. Randy and Carl started to worry about getting paid for their month of playing at the hotel. I told them, despite all the predicaments that Ernie gets himself into - he is as honest as the day is long and they had absolutely no fears of not getting paid. The plane was getting ready to leave and they were starting to pull the portable stairway away when the terminal door burst open with Ernie running out with his cornet case and bottle of Chinese liquor and lizard followed by two Communist Army guards that were anxious to get him on the plane and out of the country. The plane was parked sideways to the terminal so I had a window seat and watched Ernie's wild run across the tarmac, along with his two guards, and up the steps to the plane door. Unfortunately, in his haste, Ernie slipped coming up the steps and fell with his Chinese liquor bottle and lizard smashing into a million pieces on the stairway. He sifted through the glass and retrieved his lizard, shoving it in his pocket, and entering the plane, just like nothing had happened. Fortunately for him, a Kempinski Hotel employee found his envelope with the cash in it on the lobby floor and turned it in. The employee probably never looked inside the envelope, or it might have been a different story. On the way to Tokyo Ernie paid Randy and Carl with liquor-soaked US currency. Evidently he had stuck the lizard in his coat pocket along with the band payroll and the money was stinky and wet. So that's the way we left China - Randy and Carl with their liquor soaked money, Ernie with his lizard, and its tail sticking out of his pocket and me with my giant teddy bear. I think that China was happy to get rid of us that day.

When we arrived in Tokyo we went to the lounge and said our good-byes. And then, each of us left for our separate destinations. I got back to Portland to my usual band schedule and started to make plans for my first tour of England. The Chinese experience and music was something I'll never forget and will always be grateful to Ernie Carson for making it happen.

**Kempinski Hotel, Beijing, China. Carl Walterskerichen, Ernie Carson, Randy Keller, Jim.**

**The Great Wall of China, 1995**

CHAPTER 27

# United Kingdom

THE DIRECTOR OF THE BUDE Jazz Festival in England was John Minnion, and to my surprise, he was very helpful in getting me in touch with other jazz promoters and bandleaders in the UK. One such contact he gave me was Dave Moorwood, the leader of a band called The Big Bear Stompers, who immediately booked me for two nights as a guest with his band at the beginning of my British tour. Another bandleader, Taffy Lloyd, hired me to play one night with his band, The La Harpe Street Jazz Band, at the Gildersome Lodge in Huddersfield, Yorkshire. Another jazz promoter, Dudley Firth, arranged for me to play two nights, one of them in Melthan and the other (of all places, my father's hometown) in Wakefield, Yorkshire. Following those dates it was off to the Bude Jazz Festival. My gosh, suddenly I had all these jobs to play and they hadn't even heard me yet. I was starting to get a little nervous because I didn't want to disappoint anyone. The British jazz musicians were very good and knew their stuff, including the history of New Orleans Jazz and how it should be played. For instance, George Lewis played there often and was a big hero to all the British traditional jazz clarinetist's. So much, in fact, that a good share of them copied his style note for note. Anyway, all I could do was to go in and play like I played and that's what I intended to do.

Pauline and I arrived at Heathrow Airport in London and I was a little concerned about paying duty for the CDs and cassettes that I was bringing into the country to sell. I kept the recordings in a medium-size metal box and thought for sure that the customs officials would spot it and ask its contents, but to my surprise we went right through without being asked about the CDs, cassettes, clarinet or the soprano sax. We then rented a car and headed for Dave and Zelda's home in Wantage, just 15 miles outside of Oxford. They graciously invited Pauline and me to stay at their home while I was performing with Dave and his Big Bear Stompers. I wasn't quite ready for driving on the left hand side of the road and also I found the huge roundabouts in England very confusing, especially when I didn't really know my way around. The Moorwoods were wonderful, had a very lovely home and made us feel welcome.

The Big Bear Stompers were an eight-piece band along with a gal vocalist, Judy Eames. They used two cornets, trombone, clarinet, piano, banjo, sousaphone and drums. They liked to play in the old original style of King Oliver and Jelly Roll Morton. So, they were right up my alley! The band had held a residency at Lains Barn in Oxfordshire on the third Thursday of each month since January 1990, where they always played with a guest artist. The list of guest artists was quite impressive and included such British jazz stars as Aker Bilk, Kenny Ball, Humphrey Lyttelton and Monty Sunshine. I was the first guest from America - so I had better cut the mustard.

Lains Barn was sold out and we had a great enthusiastic crowd that came to check me out. The Big Bear Stompers were great and I fit in with them perfectly, starting with the first note. They played most of the jazz standards, such as "Canal Street Blues" and "That's a Plenty" without having any trouble accompanying me on my feature numbers, such as "Song Of Songs," "*Si Tu Vois Ma Mere*" and "Auntie Skinner's Chicken Dinners." The next night we had a job playing for a private jazz club. It was another huge crowd and the band really got with it. The Big Bear Stompers had a tuba player and amazingly this didn't bother me because he didn't "ump pa" all night long but instead seemed to roll along and fit in with the band. I liked his playing. This was our last job together for this session, but I found out that the Bears were playing the Bude Jazz Festival and I was scheduled to guest with them. So we didn't have to say goodbye – just – see you later down the road.

Our next stop was in Huddersfield, Yorkshire, where I was playing at The Gildersome Lodge with the La Harpe Street Jazz Band. After several nervous miles driving on the left hand side of the road we arrived at the lodge in the early afternoon. The agreement was that along with my playing, Pauline and I received meals and lodging. We were given a beautiful suite and the lodge was very elegant in its country setting. Because I had to play that evening, we rested in our room for the afternoon and then went down to the dining room for cocktails and an early dinner. What was on the menu? Roast Beef and Yorkshire Pudding! This was the start of a beautiful evening. During dinner, the owner of the lodge, Paul Lawson, came into the dining room and introduced himself to us. He seemed like a nice chap, was a big time jazz aficionado and did a lot to promote the music. I also noticed that he was driving a big new Rolls-Royce sedan. Business must be good at the Gildersome Lodge.

The pub was in the basement and that's where the bands played. They had a full jazz band every week, along with a guest. Again, as with the Big Bear Stompers, I was the first American guest and the place was filled with not only jazz fans but curiosity seekers. The guys in the band were very good and fun to work with. Dudley Firth and his wife Maureen were in the audience and I chatted with them on an intermission. Dudley was a big guy, to say the least; he had a broad Yorkshire accent that was even hard for me to understand after being brought up with a Yorkshire British family. It was obvious that they both loved their cigarettes and beer. Dudley invited us to stay with them during my engagements with him and gave me directions to their house. This was another thing I came to find out about the British. They enjoyed having house guests. Pauline and I appreciated it because it cut down on our expenses a great deal. Paul, the owner of the Gildersome, was very happy about the night being such a big success and he invited Pauline and me to join him for breakfast before we left in the morning. It was the usual large breakfast that the British are so famous for, with lots of sausages, bacon, eggs, tomatoes, potatoes, toast and you name it. We were stuffed when we left for Dudley's house, only to find out that there would be lots more food to come.

Dudley and Maureen had a small, but very nice home, with a large backyard and gardens. We arrived at their house early afternoon to find them waiting for us in the backyard, smoking cigarettes like crazy and drinking beer. Now I was beginning to see where all the drinking and smoking came from in my British family back in Jamestown. Dudley had a friend, John, who was also waiting for us to arrive. He was another big guy, quite a bit younger than Dudley, who seemed to be Dudley's right-hand man and best friend. John told us that he was "redundant," which meant of course, that he was out of work and collecting checks from the government. We all sat in the backyard the rest of the afternoon with our beers and cigarettes. I had been trying to quit smoking and was doing a pretty good job of it, but I could see that it was a lost cause and I could never make it out of England without a cigarette.

Dudley had his own jazz club and brought in featured artists and bands once a month. He just loved New Orleans jazz and was a great help to musicians in finding them work, with all his connections around the country. After getting to know him I began to understand his broad Yorkshire accent and found that he had not only a great taste in music but a fantastic sense of humor. He offered to be of any help musically, now or in the future. In other words he became my British agent.

Before going to play that night, Dudley ordered takeout fish and chips with mushy peas, a meal that I found I would be having many times while in England. I played with the Yorkshire Post Band at The

Shovel in Burley, Yorkshire, that first night. Thank God that Dudley was our chauffeur because I would never have found the place on my own. The band was a good one and I would soon find out that all the bands were outstanding and the musicians knew what New Orleans jazz was all about. The next night I played with a very excellent and popular group called The Savannah Jazz Band at The Station Tavern in Huddersfield, Yorkshire. They had a great clarinetist, Tom Fox, who was fun to work with, but unfortunately he fell ill with cancer and a short time later we lost him. It was another full house and I was getting along very well with the musicians and the audience alike. I felt much more relaxed and was ready for the Bude Jazz Festival.

The next day we said our goodbyes to Dudley and Maureen, as well as our new friend, John. They were wonderful, down to earth people and we decided that we would have to do it again. The next time I came, Dudley said that he would put together a band for me to play with at his jazz club. He mentioned "Phil Mason"! I told Dudley that I knew Phil very well from when he played with the Max Collie Band and we worked together in Portland - not only that, but he stayed at our house. Small world..now we had a plan for the following year.

There were a couple of days before we had to be at the Bude Festival. So, on the way Pauline and I decided to go to the old Beatty town, Wakefield, Yorkshire. It was quite a thrill to visit there after hearing so much about it from my British family. We played the American tourist and took it all in, including a visit to the cemetery to look for my grandparent's graves, but to no avail. I could still see in my mind my father running around the streets of Wakefield when he was a little boy and I wondered what he would have thought of me touring England playing my clarinet and actually being treated like I was someone important.

The next day we arrived in Bude and at last I was in recognizable territory, because of my visit there in 1982. Ordinarily the jazz Festival provided a hotel for visiting musicians, but in our case they were off the hook because we were invited to stay with Pauline's cousin, Judith Smith. She was the daughter of Roy and Bertie Vickerstaff, who I stayed with on my last visit. Roy had since passed away and Auntie Bertie (what Pauline called her) had more room in her house, so we ended up staying with her, just three houses away. I liked that idea because I remembered her roast beef and Yorkshire pudding.

I met up with the Festival director, John Minnion, and he gave me my schedule for the bands that I was to play with. I started out Saturday night with John Shillito and his band, but I was looking forward to the next afternoon when I had a reunion and played with my old friends, The Big Bear Stompers, at a venue called The Parkhouse Hall. It was great to see them again and we had a huge crowd, with people curious to see and hear "that clarinet player from America," especially when the Festival program said to "watch out and listen out" for something very special. I had to be on my toes and not have too many of those wonderful British beers – and that wasn't easy. At any rate, it turned out to be a wonderful session and a good time was had by all

A fellow came up to me after I had finished my performance with The Big Bear Stompers and introduced himself as Peter King, owner of the P.E.K. Record Company. He explained to me that he enjoyed the chemistry that I had with the Bears and would like to record us. I talked it over with Dave Moorwood and we agreed to record it live the next afternoon while we were doing an early concert at The Summerleaze Hotel, one of the more elegant hotels in Bude. After getting the details worked out about the recording, I had to run off to do a guest appearance with a group called The Arthur Brown Band. They turned out to be a good band to work with and had just returned from a US tour, including performing in New Orleans.

The next afternoon I was back with The Big Bear Stompers and Peter King, who had an elaborate set of recording equipment. We had another packed house and once again the band was really hot. The whole afternoon was recorded and 14 tunes were picked for the CD that was called *Jim Beatty and The Big Bear Stompers – Together Live.* Later that night I was scheduled to play what was called The International Stomp. It was a big event with bands from Australia, Ireland and of course yours truly from the USA. I played with the Apex Jazz Band from Belfast, Ireland. I found this the most disappointing band that I had played with on my tour. They had very little enthusiasm and were not very friendly - perhaps maybe they just didn't like Americans. At any rate, by this time in the evening I had had enough British beers, that it really didn't matter. That was the end of my scheduled performances for the Festival. Then Pauline and I had two days to be sightseers and listen to some of the other performers.

The day before we had to drive back to London and Heathrow Airport I had two bands that were very important for me to see. One was clarinetist Monty Sunshine, who made Sidney Bechet's *"Petite Fleur"* popular and had sold over 2 million copies, and Phil Mason's New Orleans All-Stars. Trevor "Fingers" Williams and "Gentleman Jim" McIntosh were in Phil's band and of course they had stayed with us in Portland all those years ago, along with Phil. I couldn't wait.

The next day I caught up with Monty Sunshine and we had a great talk. Later I went over to Parkhouse Hall and caught up with Phil Mason and his band during their intermission. We had a bunch of beers at the bar and then went back to the dressing room for shots of Scotch to celebrate our reunion. Phil insisted, as I had hoped he would, for me to come up and have a "blow" with his band. Wow! What a powerhouse group he had, with a young clarinetist, James Evans who was fantastic. Phil also had a gal vocalist, Christine Tyrrell, who had a wonderful voice and always carried a bottle of Scotch in her purse. What a band! That was a wonderful way to finish up the British tour. We left for London the next day and flew back to the United States with an open invitation to return the next year and do it all over again.

The Beatty family's relationship with Tim, our German exchange student, was wonderful and in time he was considered a member of our family. Tim had a passion for film, especially the James Bond movies, and hoped for a career someday in the movie business. In 1987, Pauline and Bob made a trip to Wuppertal, Germany to visit Tim and his family. They came home with tales of their enjoyable time and of Tim's younger brother, Stefan, who wanted to be in the funeral business and drove around in an old funeral hearse. It reminded me of my younger days when I wanted to do the same thing but didn't have money for college. Stefan later came to visit us and I arranged for him to tour some local Portland funeral homes. Embalming dead bodies was not popular in Germany and when somebody died they were buried quickly or cremated. Stefan was very interested in learning the art of embalming and was impressed with American funeral directors. His big plan was to go back to Germany, get a job at a funeral home and save money to go to an embalming school in England. You could see that Stefan was an ambitious young man and I knew he had a big future ahead of him.

Now we had two "adopted" German boys that enjoyed visiting us and did so as often as they could. They even bought a car and left it at our house so they would have their own transportation when they were here. On one of their trips to Portland they took their car and drove all over the United States, even visiting Al Capone's grave in Chicago. The two of them were something else and always ready to party with me whenever visiting our house.

I had been so busy with my music that I hadn't had the chance to visit the Dabringhaus family in Wuppertal. But an opportunity came when I got an invitation to Stefan's wedding. He had met a girl from Munich, and they planned to get married. They also asked me if I would play for the wedding, and I gladly accepted their invitation.

I flew into Düsseldorf airport. Pauline didn't come with me because she had to work, so Tim picked me up and tookt me to his family's home in Wuppertal. I met Tim's mom and dad, who spoke very little English, and Stefan and his fiancé, Sabine, were waiting there for me as well. Their house was beautiful, with plenty of room for company, and they were very hospitable, serving all kinds of schnapps and trays of delicious meats and cheeses, not to mention great German beer. The city of Wuppertal was very quaint and beautiful, a town of about 350,000, and famous for its suspension monorail.

Stefan had a job at a funeral home in Lubeck, and that's where they decided to have their wedding. Tim and I took a train to Lubeck and were put up in a very nice hotel there, courtesy of Tim's dad, Klaus Dabringhaus. There were several parties and celebrations going on prior to the wedding and guests arriving from all over Germany. We spent one interesting evening having a rehearsal dinner at a potato restaurant that served potatoes in more ways than I thought possible. There was a civil wedding at the town City Hall and the formal wedding was at a very beautiful church in Lubeck. The wedding was beautiful, followed by a huge reception and dinner at a local hotel. I was seated at the head of the table and on the other end of the table sat an elderly gentleman, who was a German industrialist and a big time Nazi during the war. Pauline's sister, Valerie, was also there as she was very good friends with Tim and Stefan's aunt. I played a few tunes with a gal piano player that had to have music for everything, but we got through it okay and everybody seemed to enjoy it.

Before the wedding activities started, Stephan found the time to show me around the funeral home he worked at and introduced me to the owners and some associates he worked with. Lubeck is famous for its *Marizipan*, a form of candy that I don't enjoy at all, but people very proudly kept on giving me. It is a very old town that was founded way back in the 1100s. It's located near Hamburg and not too far from Denmark in northern Germany. There are many churches there and one famous one, St. Mary's, was bombed by the British in World War II, just for target practice. After the war it was built back to its original condition, brick by brick. It was also amazing to think that John Sebastian Bach played the organ in Lubeck for three years and also Handel and Mattheson were frequent visitors.

While I was in Germany, because of my World War II interest, I wanted to go to Bavaria and visit Berchtesgaden, the town near where Hitler had his home, The Berghof, on the Obersalzberg. He had his house there for many years and consequently all of his Nazi military advisers did the same. Toward the end of World War II American bombers located its existence and completely destroyed all the homes. There was one, however, that they missed and that was Hitler's secret hideaway high above his Berghof, atop the mountain Kehlstein, called The Eagle's Nest.

Stefan's new bride, Sabine, had a friend in Munich who was at the wedding and she offered me her apartment for my stay in Bavaria because she had recently moved in with her boyfriend, Jorge. Her name was Marion and she wanted to be as much help as possible. She said that her boyfriend had a Mercedes motor home and they would be happy to take me to Berchtesgaden, as they would like to see Hitler's Eagle's Nest as well. Tim and I boarded the train and headed for Munich, sitting in the dining car drinking and eating all the way.

On the trip to Munich, Tim told me about a wonderful idea he had for a movie story. He had really been getting serious about getting into writing movie scripts and had had some success in making commercials for television. His idea for the movie involved me and his brother Stefan, and was about the friendship of an American musician and a German undertaker, to be called *Undertaker's Paradise*. Tim had a wild imagination, and as I listened to his story idea I encouraged him, but in the back of my mind thought that this probably would never happen.

I thought Munich was a fascinating city, going back to its origin in 1589 and growing to a population of over one million people. Tim and I enjoyed our "freebee" apartment and it came with lots of schnapps, wine and beers that we were told to help ourselves to. We did some sightseeing and naturally, Munich, being the home of the Oktoberfest; we visited a few of their famous beer halls, The Ratskeller and the Hofbrauhaus, built in 1589. I got a kick out of the men's room in the Hofbrauhaus; it had handlebars attached to the walls to hang onto in case you had to throw up after drinking too many beers. Fortunately, I never had to use them. Munich also has a history with the Nazis and it was there that Hitler had his famous Beer Hall Putsch, when he and his followers tried to take over the government and failed. Hitler went to trial for high treason and was imprisoned in a castle called Landsburg, for five years. By this time he became a hero to some and was treated as their honored guest instead of a prisoner and spent the time writing his book, *Mein Kampf*. He was released early after only nine months and as history tells us, he was more successful taking over the government the second time.

Marion and Jorge picked Tim and me up early one morning and we headed for Hitler's Eagle's Nest. They had the beautiful Mercedes-Benz motor home and it was stocked the same as Marion's apartment, with anything you could think of to drink, along with generous amounts of food. I was also interested in seeing King Ludwig's castle, Neuschwanstein. It was 2 miles from Munich on the way to the Eagle's Nest and everyone else was excited to stop and see it as well. They called him "Mad" King

Ludwig of Bavaria because at 19 years old he was not only extravagant and spent Bavaria's money wildly, he was also gay. The castle was built in 1869 and he was King for 23 years before he was declared insane in 1886 and a few days later committed suicide by drowning - or some think it might have been murder. The castle was immediately opened to tourists and has been a gold mine to Bavaria ever since. Neuschwanstein is unbelievable and is a site that you have to see for yourself. This is where Walt Disney got his idea for his castle in Disneyland.

After leaving Neuschwanstein we left for the Eagle's Nest and became hopelessly lost. We drove and drove until I finally insisted on stopping at a restaurant and asking for directions Young Germans know little about Hitler and the Nazis because not much is taught about it in school and people would rather forget it ever happened. So when we pulled in to the parking lot of the restaurant, Tim was hesitant to go in and ask how to get to Hitler's house. So I said – Tim - I'll go in with you for support. Tim and I entered the restaurant only to confront a waitress with a tray full of food. Tim whispered to her - How do we find Hitler's house? And the waitress said in a loud voice, "OH! YOU WANT DIRECTIONS TO THE FUHRER'S HOUSE!" At that point everyone in the restaurant looked at us and knew where we were going - Tim was beside himself. At any rate we had good directions and ended up at the mountain resort of Adolf Hitler, the Obersalzberg.

We wandered around the Obersalzberg until I figured out where Hitler's house, the Berghof, was - or had been. It was now just an empty field, but I looked around hoping that perhaps I would find some kind of an artifact - no such luck. I did come across a sign in German that I didn't understand- so I yelled down to Tim and asked him what the sign said. Tim yelled back to me – "POISON SNAKES"! And that ended my visit to the Berghof.

491

We then boarded a bus for the long four mile trip up the mountain to the Eagle's Nest. The road leads to a point on the mountainside when you approach a tunnel that goes into the mountain and right below the Eagle's Nest. You then enter an elevator that takes you up 400 feet to Hitler's secret retreat. Since the American bombers never found it, it sits exactly the way Hitler walked out of it for the last time. It wasn't meant to live in but to entertain diplomats from around the world and so it had an up to date kitchen and a large dining hall. Hitler had a study and his secret girlfriend, Eva Braun, had her own room. It had a large sitting room that looked out to the beautiful scenery below. Hitler's right-hand man, Martin Bormann, had the Eagle's nest built for Hitler's 50th birthday, at a great amount of labor time and expense. And, of all things, Hitler didn't like the place because he claimed it was so high up it was hard to breathe, and consequently he only visited the Eagle's Nest about 12 times. It wasn't used at all by Hitler once the war started and sat there empty, but guarded until the end. And now, like King Ludwig's Newschwanstein Castle, it's one of the big tourist attractions in Germany. To accommodate the tourists they have turned it into a tea house where you can also buy souvenirs of your visit.

With our Munich visit finished, we once again boarded a train and headed for Berlin and to Tim's apartment for a few days before I had to head back to the United States and get back to work. We stopped in Cologne to take a marijuana break and for me to see the famous Cologne Cathedral, Germany's most popular tourist attraction with 2000 visitors a day. We took our pot break on a bench on the Cathedral grounds and just down the street was Frank Sinatra's favorite hotel where he stayed no matter where he performed in Germany. He loved the chef and the food there even though it was known that he wasn't fond of the audiences in Germany. We then went back to the train station and caught the next train to Berlin, which was exactly on time, to the minute.

Tim's apartment was in downtown Berlin on the top floor of a building so we had to climb up several sets of stairs to get there. The apartment was very nice and quite large; he shared it with a writer friend who I very seldom saw. Tim's apartment was accessible to the roof of the building where he had a good size crop of marijuana plants.

The next day I wanted to be a tourist, so Tim and I roamed around Berlin until we found the location of Hitler's Bunker. The Russians had blown it up, and covered it with dirt and there was nothing but an empty field when I saw it. We did, however, retrace the path of Hitler's right-hand man, Martin Bormann, and his breakout from the bunker following Hitler's suicide. Since the Berlin wall was now gone - it was built in 1961 and torn down in 1998 - it was easy to trace his attempted route to freedom from the Russians. He didn't make it and his skeletal remains were found several years later.

We were invited that evening to M. X. Oberg's house for cocktails and dinner. Oberg was a movie director friend of Tim's and was Tim's pick to direct his movie *Undertaker's Paradise* when it was ready for filming. There were a number of artsy type people at the party and it was interesting listening to their tales of the film industry. For my benefit, they spoke English that night. They all seemed happy to meet me because I was to be one of the main characters in Tim's movie. I took the script to bed with me that night and read it through. It wasn't bad and had potential, even though it was a little "far out." But of course the big question was - could Tim sell it to a major film production company? Tim had plans for me to play some of the music in the movie and actually be in a scene at the end of the film. I liked that idea and wished him lots of luck on his project.

I played in Scotland in 1997 and 1998. My friend Phil Mason was the director of a festival and invited me to play at its 10th anniversary celebration in 1997. The festival was held in Phil's home territory, The Isle of Bute. It is a small island, just 47 miles long, 30 miles from Glasgow, and just a 30 minute ferry ride from the mainland.

Going to the festival the first year in 1997 was a bit of a panic. Dudley Firth's jazz club chartered a bus to go to Scotland and Pauline and I had reserved seats for the trip. We flew into England on May 1st and stayed overnight at Dudley's house in Bradford, Yorkshire. Early the next morning we all boarded the bus and headed for the Festival, only to have the bus break down halfway through the trip. We had to wait quite a while for mechanics to arrive and make repairs so we could get underway again. This put us behind and we didn't arrive in Bute until mid-evening.

We checked into the Glenburn Hotel and I quickly changed my clothes because I was scheduled to play at 10 p.m. with a band called the Hot Revival Stompers. On top of that they had teamed me up with a trumpet player from Denmark, John Knudsen, and we were supposed to get together before the show. I met John, he was a terrific guy, and together we figured out our show in time to play. I had another guest shot with the Second Line Jazz band at midnight. Needless to say, I was ready for bed at the end of the night, but guess what? - The hotel decided to have a fire drill at 4 a.m. and it was absolutely hysterical to see all the sleepy eyed musicians wandering around outside of the hotel in a daze - including me.

I was fortunate because my schedule for the rest of the festival was all late-night appearances, which gave Pauline and me ample time during the day to explore the island and visit the 13th century Rothesay Castle. I even found time to go to a putting green and knock a few balls around. Of course the highlight of the trip was being a guest musician with Phil Mason's New Orleans All-Stars. We were all old friends and that band probably will go down as the most exciting one that I ever played with. Dudley Firth said that our performance together that night was the most exciting session he ever heard - and coming from him, that's really saying something.

I did a repeat appearance the following year in 1998. This time the bus didn't break down and it wasn't so much of a panic getting there. My friend, Dick Henzel and his wife Adrienne had heard so much about the jazz in the UK that they showed up not only in England but followed me to The Isle of Bute. I finished off the Festival playing an early morning, 1 a.m. concert with Phil Mason and his band. A perfect way to end the Festival.

I must say that the Scottish people went overboard to be nice to me and I found them to be more than friendly. It goes without saying that I really enjoyed their Scotch. However, on the Festival program they insisted on spelling my name - Beattie!

The promoter of the Bude Jazz Festival in Cornwall, England, John Minnion, also ran a jazz Festival in Keswick, England, situated where many people say is the most beautiful part of the country - the Lake District. There are six lakes: Derwentwater, Bassenthwite, Buttermere, Crummock Water, Loweswater and Thirlmere. They are nestled in the Borrowdale and Berthermere valleys, surrounded by the Skiddaw, Catbells, Bleneatha, Scofell Pike and Helvellyn Mountains. It was truly a beautiful setting for a jazz festival and was a sellout every year. John told me that he would very much like to have me play his Keswick Festival in the early part of May in addition to his Bude Festival the beginning of September. Doing this would mean two tours of the United Kingdom every year and spending time away from Oregon in the spring and summer, my favorite times of the year. I talked it over with Pauline and although it meant a pretty tight schedule, we thought I should give it a try.

After arriving at the Keswick Festival I found that I would be playing with many of my favorite British musician friends, including Phil Mason's New Orleans All Stars along with Christine Tyrrell on vocal, the Chicago

Teddy Bears from Liverpool, and my old buddy George Huxley and his band. I always enjoyed working alongside of George Huxley and his soprano saxophone, because he captured the feeling of Sydney Bechet, better than anyone I have ever heard. I was also scheduled to play with the South Frisco Jazz Band from the United States along with Digby Fairweather, a very popular British trumpet player and entertainer. Actually they were working the hell out of me and I was playing from early afternoon until the last show of the evening, but I wasn't complaining because I was playing with some of the greatest New Orleans style musicians around, anywhere.

I had one very big surprise ahead and it was one of the craziest performances for me ever. John Minnion came to me early Saturday afternoon after I finished performing with Tommy Burton's Sport House Quartet and said – Jim - I know this is not on the schedule but would you please do a performance with Bent Persson and his band at 3 o'clock this afternoon? He said - I forgot to assign him a guest musician and I hoped you would do it for me. This was great! I looked forward to playing with a Swedish band, especially being one half Swedish myself. There wouldn't be any language barrier because I understood a little Swedish from living with my grandmother when I was a child, and if the Swedish musicians spoke a little English, we had it made. Besides that, I found out that Bent, the Swedish bandleader, ran his own festival in Sweden. This might give me a chance to play in Sweden and visit some of my distant relatives. What a stroke of luck!

I went over to meet with the Swedish band well before our scheduled performance to go over the tunes that we would like to play and the keys that we would all agree to play them in. I walked into an empty hall and the Swedish band was there waiting for me. To my surprise they weren't all that friendly, nor were they impressed that I was half Swedish. They also spoke very little English and looked puzzled at my attempt to speak Swedish. They then brought out a list of tunes that they were going to play and didn't seem to want any input from me. I looked at their list of tunes and just about crapped my pants. There wasn't one song on their list that I recognized or knew. Could it be that John Minnion was playing a big practical joke on me? Was I having some kind of a wild nightmare? No, this was really happening and the Swedes were going to play their strange tunes in their keys and that was that.

Pauline was there during this whole episode and knew the position I was in. The crowd showed up and it was time to play. The Swedish band went through their list of tunes and I followed along the best I could. It was impossible to do any of my feature numbers, but I got the feeling that the audience realized the position I was in and understood. After all, they had heard me play with all the other bands many times before and knew what I could do. As far as the Swedish band is concerned, it's still a mystery to me as to what they were playing and why they were there in the first place. Oh yes - and by the way - I wasn't asked to come to Sweden and play their jazz Festival! The old Swedes in Jamestown would often laughingly refer to themselves as "Dumb Swedes" - and after all these years I finally understood the reason why.

The Keswick Festival was well organized and they did a very good job of selling my CDs. When in England, my CDs sold very well and it was a very profitable situation because the exchange rate from pounds sterling to US currency was extremely good and in my favor. This affected my performance fees as well, because I was paid in pounds sterling.

For this tour, Pauline and I flew into the Leeds/Bradford Airport instead of Heathrow in London. The reason for this being that Bradford was fairly close to Keswick and my agent, Dudley Firth lived in Bradford and drove us to Keswick in his big comfortable Mercedes Benz. This was a short tour, but Dudley had lined up a few one-nighters for me along with the Keswick Festival. We had left Portland on April 30th and returned on May 20th. It's nice to be popular and wanted, but I decided that two tours of the United Kingdom every year would be a bit too much, especially since I had so much work back home in the United States.

It was hard to believe but our German exchange student; Tim Dabringhaus had followed his dream and written a screenplay about my friendship with his undertaker brother, Stefan. Tim always had a wild and bizarre imagination, and his story line for the film follows true to his personality.

In the story, Tim had Stefan and me meeting in a jazz club in Germany, where I was playing as a guest musician. A gentleman in the audience apparently got overly excited with the jazz music, had a heart attack and died. Stefan was called to pick up the body and became acquainted with Jim ("me"). As a young man I had wanted to be an undertaker but ended up as a musician instead, always wondering what would have happened to my life, had I followed my first dream. True to life, Tim wrote about Stefan and me striking up a very good friendship and me helping him out at the funeral home. From here on in, any truth to Stefan and my friendship is thrown out the window and the film turns into a very dark black comedy with a little romance added.

Tim's idea was for me to fly over and show the actor, who would be playing my part, the correct way to handle the clarinet to make it realistic that he was really playing. That sounded great to me because I would've loved to have been a part of Tim's movie. Tim had another idea about me having a small part at the end of the film as a musician friend playing at the wake at "my" funeral. Sound wild and crazy? It certainly was, but that's what made it an interesting film, as only Tim could dream up.

On my previous trip to Germany I had spent the night at a party with Tim and some of his movie industry friends. We were at the house of a German movie director, M. X. Oberg, who had some of the most delicious Italian wines I had ever tasted. During my visits to Germany, when

I would see Oberg, I never saw him without a baseball cap on, and I often wondered what was underneath. Tim picked Oberg to direct *Undertaker's Paradise* and he had some good credentials from directing a film called *Under the Milky Way*, which played the Toronto Film Festival in 1995. Earlier he had directed several short films, including *Dreaming Is a Private Thing* in 1986 and *Tag für Bananenfisch* in 1994.

Tim's *Undertaker's Paradise* was picked up by a Munich production company, Claussen+ Wobke Film Production – Jakob Claussen and Thomas Wobke, producers. The director of photography was Martin Kukula, production designer, Ulrika Anderson, editor, Barbara Giess, and sound, Raul Grass. The distributor was Buena Vista Germany.

It was decided that *Undertaker's Paradise* would be filmed in English and on location in the Welsh town of Aberystwyth. A young German actor, Thomas Schmauser, was cast for the leading role, as the undertaker, and it would be his first English-speaking film. He starred in the 1996 production of *It's a Jungle Out There*, which had brought him to the attention of the movie going public.

A big surprise was who they cast to take the part of the American musician, Jim. To make it realistic they found an American actor to take my part: film legend Ben Gazzara. He was around my age, born in Manhattan, New York in 1930, and had made numerous TV shows and movies. His movies included the 1959 film, *Anatomy of a Murder, Capone* from 1975, *Bloodline* in 1979, and *The Big Lebowski* in 1996. Gazzara also did many television productions, such as *Arrest and Trial, Name of the Game* and the *Trial of Lee Harvey Oswald*.

The shooting of *Undertaker's Paradise* wrapped up at the end of September 1999 and was released by Buena Vista International in the year 2000. Tim had been sending me pictures and updates about how the movie was progressing and I started to see some changes being made from his original script. I also noticed that M. X. Oberg, the director of the film, was also listed as a co-writer on the screenplay with Tim. I thought this was Tim's story and was hopeful that it would stay his story.

I soon found out that after you sell your story to a movie production company it then belongs to them and they can do anything they want with it. It brings to mind how Hollywood butchered the lives of Benny Goodman and Glenn Miller. In *Undertaker's Paradise* they now had the American musician, Jim, with a severe case of arthritis, making it very difficult for him to play the clarinet and frequently injecting himself with pain medication. He was now a "has been," and at the end of his musical career and guesting with mediocre bands.

The production company advertised the movie as "A black, but also romantic comedy about Hugo, a young German, who arrives brimming with optimism in a little Welsh coastal town to learn the traditional craft of undertaking. But soon, being repulsed by the boss's vile son and his treatment of the corpses, Hugo opens his own up market funeral parlor. Although practically only pensioners live in the wonderful little town, the market is nevertheless too small for two undertakers. Desperately struggling to get his business running, Hugo meets an old jazz musician who treats him like a son and gives a helping hand to Hugo's business - with dubious methods."

I finally got a copy of *Undertaker's Paradise* for viewing and although I was disappointed in the fact that they had me playing with terrible musicians (they sounded like a grade school band) and the story of Jim had deviated a lot from Tim's original treatment, all in all it was an interesting and entertaining film. I can understand what a challenge it must be to make a movie from start to finish and I was proud of Tim for this wonderful accomplishment.

I never did get to go to Aberystwyth to coach Ben Gazzara on the clarinet, nor did I get to be an "extra" at Jim's wake, as Tim had planned in his original script. The production company cut that scene out from the movie and they got a Welsh clarinet player to coach Gazzara. However, one of my jokes did make it in to the film, and Ben told it well, but probably not as good as I would have:

"A German fellow went to his local Catholic Church for confession. He said – Father - I have sinned. During the war I hid a Jew in the basement of my home! The confessional priest said –My Son - I don't consider that a sin because you were harboring a poor soul from certain death. The German fellow then said – Father – But I have another sin to confess. I charged the Jew rent for room and board! The priest said My Son - I don't consider that a sin either, because you did have to put out your own money to buy food for him. The German fellow was very relieved but told the priest he had one more confession. And the priest said - and what might that be my son? And the German fellow said – Father – Should I tell him that the war is over?"

I hope the film did well financially in Europe. To my knowledge it wasn't released in the United States. I also hope that Tim made some money, as well; God knows he deserved it because he spent a great deal of time on this project. I understand that Ben Gazzara was paid $300,000 plus expenses to make the film. I do know that the real life undertaker, Stefan, and the real-life jazz musician, Jim, were paid zero. But the real reward was watching the film come together from start to finish. It was all worth it. Oh yes. I threw in the joke for free.

Our little community of Lake Oswego had an Arts Festival every year in late June. Over the years they had asked me to play for different events on their Festival weekend. For instance, they had a lobster feast that I played for and that meant that I got to pig out on lobster at the end of the job – a great perk. They had a main stage where they featured local bands and vocalists, mostly modern and boring. I often thought they should put my band on the main stage to liven things up a bit, but then again, I'd lose out on my crab feed.

One afternoon I got a call from the Arts Festival manager, Joan Sappington, who asked me if I would be interested in putting the music together for the entire Festival. This was strictly a volunteer job but I was a member of the community and it would be my contribution to it. It would be very time-consuming, but then again, it would be a challenge hiring good bands to play on the main stage to keep the crowd around and happy. And of course, if I accepted the position, I would hire my own band to play on the main stage as well. I said I would do it and went right to work finding the right combination of musicians to get the job done.

For my first year, 1994, I had to fill the stage with music from noon on Saturday until 9 o'clock in the evening. On Sunday the music went from noon until 6 o'clock in the evening. For Saturday I featured my band, Jim Blackburn and Dave Duthie, Everything's Jake (a gypsy swing group), and the Black Swan Jazz Band (a traditional jazz band, playing arrangements), alternating sets with each other. I did the same thing on Sunday, except with different bands. I hired Rebecca Kilgore (a pleasant and popular local vocalist, who went on in later years to become a favorite nationally), Dill Pickles (led by Ragtime pianist, John Bennett), and finally we ended the afternoon with my band. The Festival committee was elated. The music had added excitement to the Festival and people were joining in, dancing and having fun. They wanted me to do it again.

So, for the next few years I took care of the music for the Arts Festival, hiring a variety of the best music available in the Portland area. Besides my group for New Orleans jazz and swing, I had MaryAnn Mayfield on vocals, doing the blues and mainstream jazz. Everything's Jake played gypsy swing, The Eddie Wied Combo performed modern jazz, John Bennett played Ragtime piano with his trio, pianist Jim Blackburn gave them contemporary jazz, The Capital City Jazz Band played Dixieland, the East side Jazz Band offered the crowd some old-fashioned Chicago Jazz and the Black Swan Jazz Band belted out their arranged version of traditional jazz. It was all fun and danceable music and it kept the crowds and the vendors happy. And, of course, the Arts Festival committee was pleased.

Things were going along smoothly until I had a meeting with the Arts Festival manager, Joan Sappington. Joan told me that the Festival committee had hired a paid general consultant and among her duties would be to help me as music chairman. Well, I really didn't need any help because I had this job down to a science after doing it the past several years. And what's this about paying this new gal to be the general chairman? What about me? Why wasn't I getting paid? Oh Yes, that's right, I was doing it as a contribution to my community.

Well, you probably know the rest of the story. I had a meeting with the new general chairman and the first thing she wanted to do was put her nose in the music part of the Festival. Now as far as I know, she had never been to the Festival in her life and didn't have a clue about the music that has been played for the past few years. Everyone loved the music and as the old saying goes – "If it's not broken, don't fix it." She handed me tapes of bands that she liked and wanted to hire for the Festival. I never listened to them because I knew where this whole thing was going, so I very diplomatically turned the whole thing over to her, because I knew that was what she wanted in the first place. The Festival committee asked me if I would play the Festival every year with my band, as before. Of course I agreed and did so for many years.

One amusing thing that did happen during my musical chairmanship of the Arts Festival was when they asked me to have the band to play some marches for the Teddy Bear Parade. Every year the little children would come to the Festival and march around in front of the bandstand with their teddy bears. The child with the cutest teddy bear was awarded first place, and of course there was the second and third place winner, as well.

I didn't think that my band would sound very good playing marches; we needed a real honest to goodness marching band. Unfortunately there was no money in the budget for a band of that size. I got the bright idea that I would go out to a record store and buy a tape of some Sousa marches that the children could march along with. I went to one record store after another and couldn't find a tape of a marching band. Now what do I do?

I remembered that in my World War II collection I had an old LP of Nazi marches. The Teddy Bear Parade was coming close and I was desperate. So I went home and transferred the Nazi marches from my LP onto cassette tape. I then rushed to the Arts Festival stage and gave the tape to the sound man just in time for the Teddy Bear Parade to begin. So for about 15 minutes, little Lake Oswego children were marching around to tunes like – "*Horst Wessel Lied*," "*Deutschland Erwache*," and "*Sieg Heil Viktoria*." There is a huge difference between German marches and our Sousa marches, but nobody picked up on it - Thank God.

So here I am settling in to my new musical rotation. Starting out every year on New Year's Eve with Terry and Dale playing at the Desert Horizons Country Club. That was always an interesting way to start out the New Year because we had three balloon drops during the evening starting with the New York New Year, then Chicago, and finally 12 midnight on the West Coast. I was exhausted at the end of the night, not to mention being joyfully intoxicated. I played at the country club most weekends and for special occasions, and in-between I made the 3 ½ hour drive to Phoenix for more work there and to visit with Bob and Stacy and our new grandson, Alec.

My former banjo player from Portland, Bob Beck, had moved to Phoenix and was in a band, led by Gary Church. Gary was a young, good-looking, multi-talented musician, playing the cornet, piano, trombone and guitar. During his career he not only played in Dixieland Jazz bands but was also well known on the country music circuit. He worked with such country stars as Roger Miller, Willie Nelson, Mel Tillis and Merle Haggard. He also had worked at Walt Disney World in Orlando Florida playing in a Dixieland group there. Gary Church and his band were playing at a very nice nightclub called The Jet Lag and he had arranged with the management for me to play with them whenever I was in town. The club was full every night, the drinks were great and the food was excellent and both were free for the musicians - a very nice arrangement. Gary played the piano and occasionally picked up his cornet. Dick Obermiller was on bass and Bob Beck put down his banjo to play drums.

The Arizona Classic Jazz Society sponsored a jazz festival every year in Phoenix. In August 1998 I got a letter from the jazz society asking me to be their featured guest for that year's jazz festival. They said that they would put me and Pauline up at the Crowne Plaza during the festival and offered passes for Bob and Stacey too. I accepted the invitation, and ended up playing the Festival with a lot of pretty good bands, including The Golden Eagles Jazz Band, Night Blooming Jazz Band, Queen City Jazz Band and my old buddies from Washington State, Uptown Lowdown Jazz Band. I also got to play with some of my friends in the local groups, including clarinetist Cal Abbott and Bob Beck. It was a very enjoyable festival and to my amazement there were not too many tubas around.

I played several of the jazz society's monthly Sunday meetings and they invited me back to play their annual jazz festival in 2000 with what they called The National All-Star Band. The band was put together by a special committee of the Jazz Society and along with me on clarinet and soprano saxophone, they included Tommy Loy on cornet, Alan Fredrickson, trombone, KO Ackland, piano, Roy Calhoun, drums, Matt Mooney, banjo, and Danny Shannon on the bass.

The All Star band had good players from different parts of the country. Cornetist Tommy Loy, for instance, was from Texas and was very well known for playing the national anthem for the Dallas Cowboy games for 22 consecutive years and also playing the National Anthem for Super Bowl

V in 1970. The only trouble was that Tommy appointed himself the leader and spokesman for the All Stars without talking it over with the rest of us. He called the tunes and the keys and treated us like his side men. He was a guy that was really into himself. The Festival committee noticed his behavior right away and had a talk to him about it, and that problem was fixed immediately. Our trombone player, Alan Fredrickson, played wonderful New Orleans style tailgate trombone and had a marvelous, far out sense of humor that kept the band and the audience in hysterics. He was also the founder of the very popular Queen City Jazz Band. Probably the most interesting musician in our group was K.O. Eklund from Paradise, California. As a musician he was at one time a member of Walt Disney's Firehouse Five Plus Two and active with many other Dixieland style bands in the Southern California area. He was a commercial artist and had worked for the *LA Times*. He was also an author and wrote several books, including two jazz books, *Jazz West* and *Jazz West 2*. He was a cartoonist in addition to his favorite hobby of flying airplanes and writing books on that subject. K.O. and I got along famously and it was a privilege to know a man with such amazing talents. He was seven years older than me and passed away in 2009.

The rest of the group, bass, banjo and drums were all from the Phoenix area. They rounded out the group very well except I never could figure out Danny Shannon's bass playing. Danny played the electric bass, which is sort of out of place in a traditional jazz band, and he got a sound out of it like I had never heard before. The nearest description I had was it sounded like a rubber band - but everybody liked it, it seemed to work, and that's what is important.

I was back and forth between Palm Springs and Phoenix more times than I can remember. I even took my Portland band with me one time after we played the Palm Springs Jazz Festival. But then Father Time caught up with me on one trip to Phoenix while playing with Bob Lynn's band. I wasn't feeling quite right and seemed to be having occasional dizzy spells, especially after lighting up a cigarette. One day I was at the supermarket to buy a carton of Marlboro's when I spotted a blood pressure machine. Just for the hell of it I decided to check my pressure. Well! The damn numbers on the machine went through the roof! According to the chart on the blood pressure machine, I was in dangerous territory. I called Pauline in Portland and told her the results of my test and she in turn called my doctor, who suggested that I go to the emergency room immediately! Bob drove me to a nearby emergency room and just before I opened the door to walk into the hospital I took a last puff from my cigarette. I didn't realize it at the time but that was to be my last cigarette for the rest of my life. The emergency room doctor gave me some medication that immediately lowered my blood pressure temporarily, but told me that I had to see a doctor right away and get some blood pressure medication. I didn't know any doctors in Phoenix so the emergency room doc wrote down a name for me to call – Doctor Husband.

The next day I called Dr. Husband's office and explained my situation and asked for an appointment. The receptionist said, "What time would you like to come in Mr. Beatty?" I thought I was hearing things - doctors don't operate that way - they will usually see you when they damn well feel like it. Anyway, I told the receptionist that I could come in right away - and she said - well come on down. When I got to his office the receptionist ushered me in to a small room and it wasn't too long before the one and only Dr. Husband walked in and introduced himself. He was a good-looking young man of average height and probably just out of medical school. I told him my story and that I was due back to perform in Palm Springs in five days. He said – "Jim - I know the spot you are in being from out of town and without a regular doctor. So I tell you what I'll do – I'm going to start you out on some blood pressure medication and will adjust it day to day until your blood pressure levels out and have you on your way back to work in Palm Springs." He told me to come in any time, every day, until he had me good to go. In addition to all this he told me that there would be no charge - and that he was just happy to help me out of a bad situation. My God - I thought: Am I talking to a real doctor? I quickly glanced at his graduation certificate on the wall just to make sure. During the next few days we became good friends and I gave him a few of my recordings. As promised he had me fixed up and ready to go to Palm Springs in five days. I played the Phoenix Jazz Festival the following year and sent some passes for him and his family. I've had many dealings with many doctors since then, but nothing like him.

All this happened in the year 2000. Bob received his PhD and got a job at Washburn University in Topeka, Kansas and moved there with Stacey, grandson Alec and my new granddaughter Keira in July of that year. I still continued to play my usual amount of jobs in the Phoenix area, but I missed the company of my family. On doctor's orders I quit smoking cold turkey. In order to do this I had to quit drinking because the two went together. So for a few weeks the Portland Jazz audience got to hear and see a smokeless, sober Jim Beatty. A rare sight indeed!

**With Dave Moorwood's Big Bear Stompers, Bude
Jazz Festival, Cornwall, England, 1995**

**Monty Sunshine at Bude Jazz Festival, England**

**Jim - Honored judge of Brolly Contest at Bude Jazz Festival, England, 1996**

**Jim and Pauline in the hills of Wales.**

CHAPTER 28

# The Millennium

I FINISHED OFF THE 1990's by adding a new place to my playing schedule. They liked my clarinet playing in the United Kingdom. I can understand why because the British loved the New Orleans style of jazz, and that's just the way I enjoyed playing. I looked forward to my UK tour every year because they understood the music and how it should be played. I do not care for some of the ridiculous, amateur and corny so-called Dixieland Jazz bands. There are plenty of great musicians and bands in the US, but there was an overabundance of weekend wonders that were just playing because it was party time and they got to be on stage pretending to be jazz stars. Playing to an audience in the UK was a challenge, because they knew New Orleans jazz and how it was supposed to be played. If you were not playing authentic New Orleans Jazz, you were likely to hear about it on your intermission. I loved it!

I was contacted by the Preservation Jazz Club in Cardiff, Wales asking me if I would be interested in being a guest artist with the Riverside Jazz Band during my 1999 UK tour. This sounded good to me because we had close family friends in Cardiff, Ann and Owen Hext. I had visited them when I was in the UK in 1982. Alan Jones was the coordinator for the jazz club and I told him that I could do it providing he could get me a few more engagements in the area to make the trip to Wales more profitable. He put me in touch with David Griffith from Swansea, Wales who in turn came up with four more jobs and a guest appearance on a Welch television program. We had a deal!

Pauline and I left Portland on August 17th and arrived in Leeds, England airport at 3 p.m. the next day. We were met by our old faithful British agent and friend, Dudley Firth. As usual we stayed in his home and had our fill of roast beef and Yorkshire pudding along with a day of rest. Dudley had a bunch of jobs lined up for me before heading for the Bude Jazz Festival on September 1st.

The first three nights Dudley had me playing with the Annie Hawkins All-Stars at the Bell Hotel in East Yorkshire, a private party the next night and concluding with the Howarth Jazz Festival in West Yorkshire. Annie played the bass and when I met her and listened to her play I wasn't a bit disappointed. She was a middle-aged gal, quite a character, very friendly, and played the old New Orleans style slap bass, similar to Alcide "Slow Drag" Pavageau, with the George Lewis New Orleans Jazz Band. It was a pleasure working with Annie and fortunately I performed with her many times on my later tours.

After a day of rest I went back to the Gildersome Lodge in Leeds to play with Taffy Lloyd's La Harpe Street Jazz band. The owner of the Gildersome, Paul Lawson always had me back to play whenever I was in the UK. He was a nice fellow and a great guy to work for who really loved and promoted traditional jazz. We had a full house that night and it was great to see Paul and all the guys in the band again after playing with them many times before.

The next night we traveled to Rotherham and I worked with Dave Brennan's Jubilee Jazz Band at the Three Horseshoes Pub. Brennan was a banjo player and had a very good band that I would find myself working with in my many future tours. A funny thing happened that night when someone approached me during an intermission and asked me to play

"Stranger on the Shore." I said - of course - and when I got back to the bandstand I relayed the request to Dave Brennan. Dave said, Jim - we don't play that tune - we don't even have the music…that's Acker Bilk's tune! Well, I knew Acker Bilk wrote "Stranger on the Shore," recorded it and made it famous. Back in the early 50s it was number one on the hit parade - it was also Pauline's and my song from Nassau - and the only clarinet player on English soil that played it was Acker Bilk - except that is, for Jim Beatty, who had the music with him and passed it out to the band! When I was playing it you could hear a pin drop and I saw many in the audience with surprised looks on their faces; some of the guys in the band acted like they were committing a major crime. I'm sure they thought I was going to be deported - but the tour went on.

The following evening it was another drive north to Gateshead to play at a jazz club with a band called The Old Glory Jazz Band. Where did they come up with these names? It was a local jazz club that held their events at the local rugby teams bar and club room. Dudley misjudged the distance to the job and we got there way too early, in fact the place was locked up and the band hadn't even arrived yet. Pauline and Dudley were content sitting in the car waiting for the place to open, but I noticed a rugby game going on in the field behind the club and decided to go watch. I was dressed in a blue blazer, white shirt, tie, gray slacks and dark shoes - quite out of place for a rugby match. Nevertheless, I took a seat on the bench and soon became friendly with the rugby players as they came on and off the field, sweaty, bloody and bruised, to get a few swigs of beer out of their keg. It didn't take too long before I was sort of an honorary member of the team and was helping myself to the beer as well. We had a heck of a good time and they said that they would come in and hear me play after the game. The bar finally opened and I went in and met the band and went over the program for the night.

The Old Glory Band didn't disappoint and the crowd was enjoying the music. On our first intermission I had to take a whizz and asked for a men's room. A gentleman pointed way across the room but said if you're really in a hurry there was one right behind the band stand.

So that's where I went and when I opened the door, lo and behold I found myself in the rugby team's shower room. The game was over and here I was standing with a bunch of naked men cleaning themselves up after the big game and still slugging down their beer. I guess they thought we had bonded out on the field and I had to come in to party with them after the game. The team captain made me an honorary member of the team and said -"Glad to have you aboard Mate," I spent the rest of the intermission drinking with my teammates. I'm sure that the band was wondering why their guest star was spending his intermission in the shower room.

For our last day in Yorkshire we stayed at the Bluebell Hotel in Acklam, playing with the Tees Valley Jazz Band. I had worked with these guys before and we got along famously. The next day we drove back to Bradford, Yorkshire, stayed overnight with Dudley and then left for the Bude Jazz Festival. I was starting to feel like a Brit - all I had to do was get used to driving on the wrong side of the road.

The Bude Jazz Festival was bigger and better than ever and this time around they had me playing some different events including what they called the Charity Stomp. There was an extra charge at the door and all the proceeds went to a breast cancer unit at a local hospital. I played a show with my old friends The Chicago Teddy Bears, and another program with the Zenith Hot Stompers. They had me finish the Festival by playing a farewell party on the last night, again with the Zenith Hot Stompers. The next day Pauline and I took a train to Cardiff, Wales into unknown territory.

We visited with Ann and Owen for two days and then checked into the Sandringham Hotel in downtown Cardiff, courtesy of the Jazz

Society. Cardiff seemed to be a pretty wild town with an active nightlife and our room looked out to the main street. I had a feeling that we would not be getting a very good sleep. I was scheduled to play at the Cafe Jazz Room and it was right on the first floor of the hotel, very handy indeed. I just took the elevator down to the lobby and I was on the job. I was the guest artist with the Riverside Jazz Band that night and we had a jam-packed house, because I guess that the Welsh jazz fans had heard about the crazy American clarinet player that had been playing around Britain and Scotland. The Jazz Club and Café Jazz were thrilled with the large crowd and wanted me to commit to come back on my next tour.

The next day I was to play in Swansea, Wales, which was about an hour or so drive from Cardiff. I asked one of the fans at Café Jazz for information regarding bus transportation. He said -no problem - I'll drive you! His name was Paul Dunleavy and was a professional photographer an avid jazz fan. We became very good friends and kept in touch for years to come. Another good friend I met in Wales was Brains Beer! I enjoyed all of the beers in the UK, but this one was in a class all by itself. Even Pauline loved it and she wasn't much of a beer drinker. I could see where Brains was going to make my stay in Wales even better than I had expected.

The rest of the Wales tour had been arranged by jazz writer and promoter, David Griffiths. We checked into the St. Anne's Hotel, graciously provided by Swansea Jazz Promotions. Griffith greeted us at the hotel and filled me in on what was going to happen for the rest of the tour in Wales. He was a character, to say the least, and reminded me somewhat of Woody Allen. He was a very well respected jazz writer, not only in Wales, but the entire UK. He had written an article about me in the local paper that was very flattering and I thought that I better pretty damn well play good that evening. I played with the Gwyn Lewis Band and when I met them they were nervous as hell - they must've read the article. But I calmed them down over a few pints of Brains Beer and we put on a good show for a full house. It was a good band; Gwyn played cornet, and the piano player, Ray Jones, must've enjoyed his Brains Beer, because he looked somewhat like W.C. Fields.

The next day we drove to Carmarthen, Wales where I was scheduled to play at the Four Seasons Hotel with the Welsh Jazz Trio. It was a rather upscale affair and we played to a small crowd that paid big bucks for dinner and show. They put us up overnight and we left the next day for Llangennech, Dyfed, Wales, where we were to do a television appearance.

It turned out that the television show that I was to do was at 6 p.m. and was basically a cooking show that featured a guest visitor they interviewed, which, of course, was me. The show was broadcast in the Welsh language except, for my interview, and then they asked me to play a tune along with the Welsh Jazz Trio. It was a live show and we played "Sweet Georgia Brown" in the key of Ab, that is, everyone except the piano player, who played that tune in the key of F. It was a terrible catastrophe and nothing could be done because we were playing live! I thought of switching to the key of F but then again as soon as I did that I thought the piano player might switch to Ab. I ended the tune quickly and everyone was all smiles like nothing out of the ordinary had happened. Come to find out, that show must not have had much of an audience, because I never heard any bad reports about the music. The people that did tune in must've thought that we were playing modern jazz. We finished out the evening playing at a little jazz club in Stackpole, Wales, and we played "Sweet Georgia Brown," all in the same key of Ab.

For my last show in Wales we played at the Queens Hall Hotel in Narberth, stayed overnight there, and drove back to Cardiff the next day to catch the train to Oxford, England, where I played the last engagement of the tour at The Lamb at Hannay with Dave Moorwood and The Big Bear Stompers. The next day, September 15th, Pauline and I departed from Heathrow airport in London and back to Portland to finish out the year playing with my own band. It was a very successful tour and I was pleased to have added Wales to the itinerary.

Nearing the end of the 90s, Pauline and I were pleased to have an opportunity to reciprocate to some of our friends who had been so good to us on our recent trips to the UK. Jazz promoter, Dudley Firth, who over the years at been so helpful in arranging and scheduling my tours (now officially known as Jim Beatty's UK manager) and his friend, John Ackroyd, vacationed in the US for a month and spent their first two weeks as our house guests. We had a great time showing them the sites, which included various Portland taverns and microbreweries. We even got them up to our summer lake cabin in British Columbia, Canada, and toured Vancouver in my mother-in-law's compact Chrysler convertible - they were two big guys and it was quite a sight to see.

As a special treat for Dudley and John, I put together a jam session in our backyard one Sunday afternoon. Several musician friends showed up, including Ernie Carson, and Dudley prepared his famous curry, which was quite a feat since the temperature gauge never dropped below 80°, while they were here. All our friends loved Dudley and his broad Yorkshire accent; even though I'm sure they never understood a word that he was saying. One afternoon Dudley and my next door neighbor, Kelly Butler, went to the local tavern to drink beer and when they got back home Dudley was quite upset because the bartender had shut him off – saying - she had never seen anyone consume so much beer and she was afraid that he would die of alcohol poisoning. That didn't stop him - he just came back to the house and drank more. Dudley and John left to continue their vacation in California, Arizona, and Nevada. While in Arizona they visited Bob and Stacey. Bob later told me that he made them scrambled eggs for breakfast and they consumed a whole dozen eggs between them.

Shortly after Dudley and John left, our old friends Dave and Zelda Moorwood came over for a visit. I had worked with Dave and his Big Bear Stompers several times at Lains Barn and other sessions and Pauline and I had always been welcomed guests at their home in Wantage, England. We were delighted to have them visit. They rented a car and managed to see a lot the sites in Oregon and Washington in two short weeks.

I couldn't let Dave get rusty while he was here, so I put him to work with my band, playing several casuals as well as the Oregon Automobile Dealers annual get-together on the Oregon coast. That turned out to be a good little band with Dave on banjo, Jim Goodwin playing piano, Jack Dawes on drums, Randy Keller slapping the bass along with myself playing clarinet. We even got some sightseeing in while on the coast, including a visit to Jim Goodwin's farmhouse near Astoria.

Millennium means every 1000 years, but to musicians in 1999 it meant making a killing by hiking their prices by double or triple or more for their New Year's Eve performances. I didn't think too much about it because the Desert Horizons had been more than fair to me and I wasn't about to hold them up for my playing on New Year's Eve. I didn't have to think about it long because early in the year the manager told me that my salary would be doubled for the millennium New Year's Eve celebration. He said he came to that conclusion because that is what the Los Angeles musicians were asking for. It sure sounded more than fair to me and I was completely satisfied with the arrangement. A couple of weeks later the manager came back to me and said, "Jim, I want to talk with you some more about the millennium situation." I thought, "Oh Boy, He's changed his mind about doubling my salary - I knew it was too good to be true." But no, instead he said, "Jim, I've been doing a little more investigating and have found out that the Los Angeles musicians are getting more than double their salary for the millennium New Year, so I'm giving you an extra $250." Gee Whiz - this is getting better all the time, and I haven't even asked for anything.

The Desert Horizons Country Club could well afford to pay me that kind of money because the place oozed wealth. But I was thinking - what about the small nightclubs and restaurants that were struggling along featuring music? They certainly can't afford to be held up by greedy musicians on this one night a year. I know, because I played enough nightclubs in my career and saw how many times it was difficult for them to meet their payroll. Certainly the musicians that they employ will have enough common sense not to demand those ridiculous salaries that some were asking around the country. What happened in many cases was that the nightclubs and restaurants just canceled their New Year's Eve parties for the millennium. Musicians shot themselves in the foot - once again.

The Millennium New Year's Eve celebration at the Desert Horizons Country Club was something out of a fairy tale. The decorations and flowers were absolutely beautiful, along with several ice sculptures. Terry, Dale and I dressed in tuxedos along with the extra musicians that Terry hired for the affair. Hal Brain played the bass and we had an excellent guitar player, Tom Wheat, who was Henry Questa's accompanist from the *Lawrence Welk Show.*

The Desert Horizons had an excellent menu and the food was always good, their steaks, for instance, equaled that of *Ruth's Chris Steakhouse.* Besides steaks, the members were eating prime rib, rack of lamb, chicken Cordon Bleu and lobster, along with flaming dessert dishes. We did our usual three balloon drop for New York, Chicago and finally midnight on the West Coast. We played in the year 2000 with "Auld Lang Syne" - everyone was dancing, hugging, kissing and shaking hands, wishing each other the best for the New Year. As for me, I was starting out the year 2000 with my usual schedule of playing Palm Springs, Phoenix, Portland,

Jamestown, New York, Long Island, the United Kingdom and then back to Portland.

"Should old acquaintance be forgot
And never brought to mind
Should old acquaintance be forgot
In the days of auld lang syne!"

The year 2000 didn't get off to a very good start. It was January 7th when I was at Terry and Dale's house in Palm Springs and received a call from Pauline telling me that my mother had passed away. My mother was 93 and had been living in Norwalk, Ohio, for the past several years with my sister Linda taking care of her until she had to go in to a nursing home. My mother hadn't had an easy life, but she made the best of it by making sure that even though she could not take care of me during the depression that I was well looked after at my grandmother's house in Jamestown.

After talking with Pauline I immediately picked up the phone and called United Airlines. I needed to take a flight out of Palm Springs, continuing to Cleveland, Ohio, in order to get back and help my sister out with the funeral arrangements. Of course, when you book a flight at the last minute, the airlines have you at their mercy and charge you ridiculous airfares. They wanted around $1000 for my trip, but of course in a situation like this, money was no object. I didn't want to deal with the airlines over the phone and decided to go to the Palm Springs Airport myself. When I got there and talked to the United agent she told me there were no flights that left at the last minute and I should check another airline. Just at that moment another agent spotted me, walked over and said, "Aren't you Jim Beatty?" She then asked me to come down to her window. She told me that she and her husband had heard me play many times at the Arizona Jazz Festival and that they loved my music and had several of my recordings. I explained my situation to her and she said - just a moment - and went to her computer and soon produced a round-trip ticket for me for $250. Wow! It sure pays to know people in the right places. It also tells you that the airlines can do most anything for you - if they want to.

Linda and I made the necessary funeral arrangements and drove to Jamestown for the service. We had a viewing and many family and friends stopped by to give us their sympathy. There was a coffee shop across the street from the funeral home and I skipped over for a quick bite to eat. Evidently someone spotted me and alerted the news media and when I got back to the funeral home the funeral director told me I had a phone call. It was Jim Roselli from WJTN asking me for an interview on his radio show. I thought it strange getting a call at the funeral home - but I guess that's what happens when a former Jamestown kid makes good.

After the funeral I went back to Palm Springs and resumed my schedule for the rest of the year. It was basically the same, along with my British tour and playing the Bude Jazz Festival. We did, however, start playing in a new local place, Hayden's Lakefront Grill in Tualatin, Oregon, starting in October. I brought in Pete Pepke for the first guest. It was a big success and we played there for some time to come.

2001 started out very busy. I was driving back and forth on Route 10 between Palm Springs and Phoenix and was grateful that I had a nice big Lincoln Town Car to make the trips more comfortable. I was working my usual jobs with Terry and Dale at the Desert Horizon Country Club and playing with my friends in Phoenix, Cal Abbott, Bob Beck, and Bob Lynn. Beck and Abbott both had extra bedrooms, so there was always a place to stay.

On a sad note, our good friend and UK agent Dudley Firth passed away early in the year. It certainly wasn't a surprise because of the way he treated his body by overeating, smoking heavily, and drinking copious amounts of alcohol. Dudley was a wonderful person and I'm happy that he had the chance to come visit us in Oregon. He did a lot of good things helping musicians, including me. I understand they gave him a big send-off with an authentic New Orleans funeral - jazz bands and all. I'm sure that's just what he wanted.

There was a big change in my playing schedule this year. (2001) because I moved my UK tour to April and May instead of August and September. The reason for this was that I was asked to play at the Liangollen Jazz Festival in Wales in the month of May, and by doing this I could also fit in the Keswick Jazz Festival. This meant, of course, that I would skip the Bude Jazz Festival in September because I had said that I'd never do two tours in a year again. I was also booked in another new club in Pontypool, Wales for two nights.

Pauline and I arrived at Heathrow Airport in London at 11:20 a.m. on April 25, and took a train to Solihull, England, where I was to play with George Huxley at his jazz club located at the Rugby Club. We stayed with George and his wife Ann and it was a pleasure visiting with them. As I said before, George had Sidney Bechet's style down to a science and I loved working with him. We did a crowd-pleasing version of the "Coffee Grinder" that was always fun. Fortunately we would be seeing each other at the Keswick Jazz Festival and we were both looking forward to that.

On April 27th our faithful and dear cousin Judith picked us up at the Huxley's home and we drove to Bradford Upon Avon, where I was to play at their jazz club with the Keith Little Jazz Band and staying at a B & B there. Keith Little was an excellent swinging piano player with equally good side men. We had a great time playing that night and I was happy that I would be playing with Keith and the band again in Cardiff.

The following day we caught a coach to Oxford where I was playing with Dave Moorwood at The Lamb At Hanney. The bus was my favorite means of transportation in the UK because it was reasonable, comfortable, and it took you through all of the little villages and hamlets along the way. Playing with Dave Moorwood and his band was always a pleasure and exciting musically. We spent an extra day with the Moorwoods before leaving to perform with Dennis Armstrong's band in Bristol.

I had known Dennis Armstrong for some time after playing with him at the Bude Jazz Festival several times. He was a happy-go-lucky, lanky Englishmen, who played very good New Orleans Jazz. He had asked me many times to be a guest with his band in Bristol and finally it fit into my schedule. Dennis and his wife, Maureen, met us at the bus terminal and we were invited to spend the night at their house after the evening's performance. We had a big crowd that night and even Acker Bilk was rumored to stop by and see me, although he didn't make it. Dennis was so happy with the unexpected large crowd that he paid me more than what was agreed to. It was totally unnecessary, but it just shows you how nice the British musicians were toward me. This is something that happened many times.

After the job we went back to Armstrong's house and sat around the dining room table eating snacks and drinking lots of good British beer. It was quite late when we went to bed and I was very tired after traveling all day and playing jazz all evening, along with managing to drink many pints of beer. But then the unthinkable happened: I fell into a deep, restful sleep, dreaming of standing at a toilet relieving myself of all that wonderful British beer that I had consumed. I woke up to a warm feeling on my lower body, only to realize that...My God!!!...I've peed the bed! I jumped out of bed with a start, waking Pauline up. She was horrified - as

I was - to say the least. What do I do? What do I say? It will be all over England! "American jazz star, Jim Beatty, wets the bed at cornetist Dennis Armstrong's house." The news will travel across the UK like wildfire! The jazz community has a hotline and musicians are known to be terrible gossips.

Pauline stepped up to the plate and said – "I'll take the blame and say it was me that wet the bed" - Pauline took the bullet for me so that I wouldn't have to suffer the embarrassment with the jazz community. The next morning she told Maureen what had happened and Maureen broke out in a big laugh and said, "Dennis did the same thing last week at a friend's house when he was out on a tour." So the pressure was off and when Dennis heard about it, he had a big laugh as well. The mattress was a thin inexpensive one and they just hosed it off and hung it up to dry. I learned a lesson, that's for sure, and from then on, I empty my bladder before going to bed. And I'm happy to say - it hasn't happened since.

The next morning we boarded a coach and headed for the Sebastopol Social Club in Pontypool, Wales, where I had two nights with the Tom Williams Band. We were met by the jazz club president, Will Harris, and we became very good friends. This was a new venue and a new band for me to work with. It was always stressful for me worrying about the ca-pabilities of the musicians. As it turned out they didn't have a very wide repertoire but we managed to put on a show with what they had, and the important thing was that the crowd loved it. They put us up at a B&B that was also a horse farm that raised horses for foxhunting. Our hosts at the farm were wonderful and amazing cooks. The horses were beautiful and Pauline took advantage of the situation and went riding.

Will Harris was kind enough to drive us to my next engagement in Cardiff. It was familiar territory because we were again staying at the Sandringham Hotel and performing at Café Jazz with the Keith Little Trio.

The crowd was standing room only, partially due to the jazz magazine, *Mississippi Rag*, which had just come out with a full, front page picture of me and an extensive story to go along with it. It was fun being back at Café Jazz and visiting with some old friends, including Paul Dunleavy, who graciously offered us a ride the next morning to Swansea, where I was working with the Gypsy Jazz Trio at the St. James Social Club. Our friend David Griffiths had arranged this job for me and although I wasn't too excited about playing with two guitars and a violin, we made it work, playing swing tunes like "Honeysuckle Rose" and "Lady be Good." They were good musicians and the crowd was happy! They put us up in a wonderful hotel called the Tudor Court Hotel, where we rested up to get ready for our trip to Llangollen, Wales. We had met a lovely couple while playing with Gypsy Jazz, Derrick and Veronica Warren, who graciously offered us a ride to Llangollen because they were going to the Jazz Festival as well. It turns out that they were very active in Welsh jazz circles and promoted concerts themselves. At any rate, Pauline and I were looking forward to the drive across the Welsh countryside.

We arrived at the Llangollen Jazz festival late morning on May 11th and checked into the Hand Hotel. It was a village of about 3000 in North Wales and very picturesque. I looked up the festival's promoter Roy Potts. He was a friendly fellow about my age who played the trumpet and had his own band called Five & a Penny. I worked with his band for a few shows at the Festival and they did a lot of clowning between their numbers. I never did figure out whether they were a jazz band or comedy show. He also wasn't consistent with his music as he had a variety of jazz groups, including a bebop tenor sax player whom I only can describe as Rubeus Hagrid, the half giant, half human, keeper of the keys and grounds of Hogwarts in Harry Potter movies. And horror of horrors, I looked in the program and saw that they had me doing a show with this bebopper. I knew that would not work and went to Roy and told him how ridiculous it was. Roy said – Jim – just don't show up. But of course I did and explained the situation to the modern band and they agreed, so I played half the show and the tenor player played the other half. It was a struggle trying to get through the show with that bebop rhythm section - it was like pulling teeth! Roy jokingly told everyone to keep quiet about his jazz Festival and not tell anybody because the town was too small for a big crowd. He didn't have to worry, I never told a soul - until now.

Following the Festival we went back to England to play with Dave Brennan's Jubilee Jazz Band in Rotherham. We stayed with Val and Dave Brennan for three days because we had three different venues to play; the Rotherham Transportation Club, The Leeds Conservative Club and the Three Horseshoes, Wickersley, Rotherham. Dave is such a pleasant fellow to be around and had a very excellent band that was great to play with. We said our goodbyes to the Brennan's and headed to the Keswick Jazz Festival where we would conclude the UK tour.

The Keswick Festival put us up in the very elegant Royal Oak Hotel. It was like old home week as several of my British musician friends were there, including George Huxley, Dennis Armstrong, Keith Little, Annie Hawkins and several others. There were plenty of late-night jam sessions going and a good time was had by all. I had a rather light schedule myself, mostly doing shows with the Yorkshire Stompers and the George Penman Jazzmen. It was a great tour and it was fun ending up with an appearance at the Keswick Festival, but I decided that I missed playing the Bude Festival in the fall and would like to go back to that again the next year.

We did have a bonus this year. Bob and Stacey were in London because Bob had some political science business in England and it was their 10th wedding anniversary. So we had arranged that before we flew back to the states we would spend two days with them at the Crofton Hotel, Kensington, London. Pauline and Stacey went shopping at Harrods's and Bob and I went to see the Military Museum along with a few British pubs.

Pauline and I departed Heathrow Airport on May 23rd and arrived in Portland the same day at 6:50 p.m. When we got home and opened our luggage we discovered that the jewelry that Pauline had purchased on her shopping trip in London was missing, along with my jewelry (all fake) and a cashmere sweater. Despite all that, we had a great time, playing great music with many great friends.

## CHAPTER 29

# Palm Springs Stars

WITH THE PASSING OF DUDLEY Firth, I was without an agent in the UK. But through all the connections with British musicians and festival promoters I found that I was able to put together my tours via the mail, telephone and computer. Modern day technology was amazing and I could inquire about a date for a show and get an answer within minutes using e-mail.

Such was the case when Bob told us he would be doing a sabbatical at Cambridge University in July 2003. He was planning on his whole family accompanying him on the trip; Stacey, Alec and Keira. Pauline and I got right to work and put a UK tour together for the month of July. It was also our 40ᵗʰ wedding anniversary that year and for a present, Jame, Bob and family put us up at the Kingsway Hotel in London, England. They also gave us tickets to the Phantom of the Opera and a nice dinner out on the town. What a great way to spend an anniversary and to start our month's tour in the UK.

The first night of playing was with Dennis Armstrong and his band at the Horts City Tavern in Bristol. After the job we stayed the night with Dennis and his wife, Maureen, and yes, I emptied my bladder before going to bed. We left by coach early the next morning for my performance with my old buddy Dave Moorwood and his Big Bear Stompers. We played at a new restaurant called The Leather Bottle near Wantage,

Oxfordshire, stayed overnight with the Moorwoods, and caught another early coach the next morning for one night in Bradford-on-Avon playing the local Jazz Club with Spats Langham & the Sporting House Strings. Spats was a great banjo and guitarist, along with being a good entertainer. We had a good crowd and a fun time that night and spent the evening at a very comfortable B&B called The Valley View Inn.

The next day we were in the coach again heading for Cambridge for our visit with Bob, Stacey and the kids. Bob was spending his sabbatical at Cambridge University, a very prestigious university that was founded in 1209 and the second oldest university in the English speaking world. It has a long list of famous alumni that includes Isaac Newton, Charles Darwin and Charles Prince of Wales.

Bob and family met us at the Cambridge bus station and we spent the next three days visiting with them and seeing the sights around that beautiful historical campus. Bob was pretty busy at the University but we had lots of time with Stacey and the grandchildren. Alec was seven years old at the time and was playing pretty good soccer. He had met a few British boys his age and was invited to join a soccer camp there on campus. (he even earned the "most improved player" award at the end of the week). Our visit was short but fortunately we were all going to meet up again later in the month when Bob was finished with his sabbatical.

On the morning of July 15$^{th}$ we boarded the coach for the familiar trip to Cardiff, Wales; staying once again at the Sandringham Hotel and playing at the Café Jazz with the Acme Jazz Band. It was always great to be back in Cardiff and get my yearly supply of Brains Beer. We had our usual full house at Café Jazz and it was fun to be back because we had made so many good friends there.

After two nights at Café Jazz we journeyed the short distance to Swansea to play for the Swansea Jazz Society. This performance was arranged by Derrick Warren and his wife, who we had met two years before in Swansea. They brought in a band that was new for me to work with called The Memphis 7 Jazz Band. The Warren's did a wonderful job in managing their jazz society and consequently we had a huge crowd that I was told equaled Acker Bilk's crowd the month before. However, somehow I didn't believe that and think that they were just trying to flatter me. At any rate, it was a success and they wanted me to come back for future performances. I had two more jobs to play in Wales with the Tom Williams Band for the Torfaen Jazz Club in Pontypool. I had worked with Tom Williams a few times now and things were starting to come together. Our friend Will Harris put this show together for me and we had a great time visiting with him and his family. We stayed at the Ty Shon Horse Farm again and as usual, Agneta and Grahame were great hosts.

David Brennan's Jubilee Jazz Band took advantage of my July availability and featured me as their guest performer for five shows, including a Jazz Festival. The first date with Dave and his band was at Thorsby Hall near Worksop, North Nottinghamshire. It was a local jazz club with a large enthusiastic crowd waiting to hear the band. Stacey Beatty's mom and dad, Sandy and Pete Beak, were visiting Bob and Stacey in Cambridge and they all decided to drive up and hear me play with the Jubilee Jazz Band. It was a family reunion with Pauline, Bob, Stacey, Sandy, Pete, Alec and Keira – an American invasion! The jazz club couldn't have been nicer to my family and even Dave Brennan was having such a good time he got a little buzzed - it was hilarious. Pauline had our grandson Alec helping her sell my recordings and our granddaughter, Keira, joined in the New Orleans parade around the room twirling a small decorated brolly. It turned out to be a great jazz show with Dave and his Jubilee Jazz Band and an extra bonus having the family there. I even played the tourist on a day off and went to Beatrix Potter's home and museum, the children's author of many stories including "The Tail of Peter Rabbit." I went with Pauline, Sandy and Pete Beak, and we stayed overnight.

On July 21st I played the Pickering Jazz Festival with Dave and his band. We were the opening group for the Festival and I must admit we got the Festival off to a great start! Everyone loved the band. We stayed that night at another B&B called the Bridge House and we left by coach early the next morning for Leeds and played the Hanover Arms with Winston's Pennine Jazz Band, then returning the next day to Rotherham to perform with Dave Brennan's band at the Three Horseshoes. The next evening we played the Unwin Road Social Club in Ashfield, North Nottinghamshire. I had one more night to work with Dave and his Jubilee Jazz Band and I hated to see it come to an end. Dave and Val Brennan were such pleasant people to be around and on top of that they were gracious hosts. Dave and his band were easy to work with and everything just seemed to click when I was with them. My last job for this tour was at the Transport Club in Rotherham and of course we wowed them once again. With that we said our goodbyes to the Brennan's, until next time.

Pauline and I had a day to travel to Solihull, England where I was playing with my old buddy George Huxley at the Rugby Club. This was a good way to end the tour because George and his band were on the top of the heap as far as I was concerned. We had a great crowd and a great send off. We said - see you next year! Cousin Judith came to hear the band play at the Rugby Club and drove us to Heathrow Airport for our 1:40 p.m. flight to the United States. The UK was always hard to leave after being around such great music and wonderful people. The nice thing is that we knew we were coming back.

I was asked to play at a jazz club in Hamburg, Germany called The Cotton Club. It was Hamburg's *Jazzkeller* and known throughout Germany for having top rate jazz performers year around. The house band there was also friends of my undertaker buddy Stefan Dabringhaus, and they occasionally played services at Stefan's funeral home in Lübeck - small world. I thought this German appearance was doable by tying it in with my 2004 UK tour and we agreed to tentative dates in early September.

So it was another tour of the UK, this time leaving Vancouver, Canada on Air Canada and arriving at Heathrow, England on the morning of August 23, 2004. The first stop was playing with Dave Moorwood's band for three nights and then one night with Graeme Hewitt's High Society Jazz band at the Fox and Hounds in Theale, Reading. Graeme was a clarinetist and had an excellent band that included Dave Moorwood on banjo. The next morning Pauline and I boarded a coach and headed for the Bude Jazz Festival.

The highlight of my Bude appearance that year was getting together with George Huxley for a three-hour session that they called "Reeds United." They threw in another clarinetist, John Maddocks, and the three of us had a ball playing back and forth for three hours, and the crowd loved it. I also did a show with a band that I had not played with before, John Shillito's Select Six, which turned out to be quite interesting.

Following Bude, it was off to Swansea again, staying at the Devon View Guest House and playing at the Grand Theatre Rooftop with the Memphis Seven Jazz Band. This was the concert put on by our friends Derrick and Veronica Warren and was a huge success with a sellout crowd. I was glad to be back in the land of Brains Beer. I then had a three day jazz Festival in Pontypool, Wales, called The Jazz in the Park Festival. It was an event sponsored by the city and local jazz club. It was mostly out of door concerts, which isn't my favorite situation, however, the weather cooperated fairly well and I think it was a successful festival. We stayed with our friends Will and Sarah Harris who had just acquired a new old home that was very comfortable. Their two boys Joe and Jack were growing like weeds as the years went by.

The next stop was our old familiar home away from home, The Sandringham Hotel in Cardiff, Wales. Pauline and I were on a first name basis with all the employees of the hotel and they were always happy to see us. I played at Café Jazz to a full house of fans that by now were all old familiar faces. Thanking back, I'm still amazed at how wonderfully the people in the UK treated Pauline and I over the years. They made us feel like it was our home.

This finished up the UK tour for the year. I had to shorten it to make room for the trip to Germany. It was getting to the point where I had to make some decisions about less time on the road because things were still busy for me in Portland. That's where my home was and my loyal band members were waiting to get back into the swing of things again.

We flew to Germany out of the Stansted Airport and were met in Hamburg by Stefan Dabringhaus; again presenting us with a beautiful bouquet of red roses that I'm sure were fresh off one of his caskets at the funeral home. We made the short drive from Hamburg to Lübeck, where we stayed with Stefan and Sabine. Stefan had come up in the world and had just opened a brand-new state-of-the-art funeral home in Lübeck. It was beautiful with a comfortable chapel, viewing rooms, casket display room and a preparation room for preparing and embalming bodies. Stefan was a successful businessman and a far cry from the young man I knew years ago that dreamed of being a funeral director.

I played an afternoon show at the Cotton Club in Hamburg and had met with the piano player a few days earlier to agree on the tunes we would play for the performance. It was a Sunday afternoon and the place was jam packed. It was so full, in fact, that Pauline, Stefan and Sabine had to stand for the entire show. I don't know who those Germans thought I was, but they sure turned out in full force to hear me. The owner of the Cotton Club was falling all over me, bringing me all kinds of beers and schnapps. My God, had I drank them all I would not have been able to play. At any rate I enjoyed playing with my German musicians, the crowd loved it and a very good time was had by all. I felt very fortunate because so far in all my travels outside the United States, I hadn't bombed yet! I just kept keeping my fingers crossed.

When I was playing with Terry and Dale at the Desert Horizons Country Club, they would occasionally bring in the male vocalist David Christopher, who had a beautiful voice and a broad knowledge of the great American songbook. He would always be with us every St. Patrick's Day and his version of "Danny Boy" would bring tears to your eyes. For such a big beautiful voice he was quite small in stature, middle aged, and had a long history in show business.

David told me that his grandmother was a Follies dancer and toured with a company called the Dubinsky Brothers. She had a lot of old 78 RPM recordings, including many of vocalist Gene Austin, and that's how he learned to be a tenor from listening to him on his grandmother's windup Victrola. When David was just 13 he sang in country bands in his hometown of Lincoln, Nebraska and later toured with the show *The Music Man* in the Midwest and Eastern states. He also received a scholarship to the University of Kansas for a theater workshop and while there he saw that Mae West was doing a show in Hollywood and he decided to go see her.

Mae West started out in vaudeville and on stage in New York City, later relocating to Hollywood to become a very popular movie star and sex symbol. She made several movies and one of my favorites was the one she did with W. C. Fields called *My Little Chickadee*. David did go see her show and managed to get backstage and meet her. She was so impressed with him and his enthusiasm for her that she offered him a job as one of her assistants and to live in her ocean beach house. David took advantage of this opportunity and worked for her for twelve years until she died in 1980. After her death David began singing in the bands of accordionist Dick Contino and radio and television personality Al Jarvis. He also had a minor acting role in the movie *Myra Breckenridge* and appeared on the television soap opera *The Young and Restless,* and he later worked at a theater production at the Thunderbird Hotel in Las Vegas. He came to Palm Springs and fell in love with the area and performed in the *Fabulous Palm Springs Follies* before producing his own shows in Palm Springs at Lyons English Grill.

That's where I came into the picture. David asked me if I would work in the band backing his shows and also asked if I could put a show together with my own band. This sounded great to me and I went right to work for him and also brought in my own band for four shows. In April 2006 I did a show called "Do You Know What It Means to Miss New Orleans?" and March 2007 we did "The Basin Street Blues." March 2008 we called our show "The Premier Ball" and March 2009 we performed another show called "Back to Basin Street," all with my Portland rhythm section. All shows were sellouts and I was amazed that so many people came from as far away as Phoenix and Los Angeles.

It was a pleasure working with David Christopher because he was such a professional in producing his shows. When I did shows for David with my band I always asked him to come up and sing with us - and the crowd loved it. He had one big show coming up on Memorial Day weekend of 2010 and I wouldn't miss it for the world. It was the one and only "Kay Starr."

When I was a young guy in high school, Kay Starr was one of the most popular singers on the United States pop charts. She covered all the bases and sang all styles from country swing to jazz. Not only that, she was cute and good-looking and the kind of girl that my friends and I would love to have a date with. She was born in Dougherty, Oklahoma in 1922, her father was a full blown Iroquois Indian and her mother was Irish. Kay's family did not make a lot of money but raised chickens at home and every day when Kay got out of school she came home and sang to the chickens. Her parents entered her into a talent contest, she won, and that led to a 15 minute radio show at three dollars a show. They later moved to Memphis, Tennessee and she went into radio there, as well. Jazz violinist Joe Venuti was passing through town with his band and listened to her sing on the radio and offered her a job.

She was only 15 years old and still in school but she sang with Joe and his band in the summertime when school was out. Joe Venuti was very protective of her and on top of that her mother came with her to all her jobs. She was with the Glenn Miller Orchestra for two months before going with Charlie Barnett and his band in 1945. She later went out on her own as a featured singer and in 1956 recorded the number one hit in the United States and England – "The Rock and Roll Waltz." Kay followed that with more smash hits like "Side By Side" and "Wheel of Fortune."

David Christopher had booked Kay Starr, by then 88 years old, into his Lyons English Grille showroom on Memorial Day weekend 2010 and asked me if I'd like to play the show. I was there with bells on. I met Kay Starr in the musician's room so we all could run over the show together. She was wonderful to talk to and surprised that I knew so much about her early life singing jazz with Joe Venuti. We had a packed house that night and Kay sang many of her favorites along with a beautiful rendition of "If You Love Me."

Following the show, Katie (that's what her friends called her), her assistant, along with David and me, sat down and relaxed with some drinks. I noticed that my Scotch and water was disappearing rapidly and I didn't remember even having a sip. What was happening is that Katie was chug-alugging her Scotch and water and switching her glasses with me when I wasn't looking and putting her empty glass in front of me and taking my full one. We later heard from her assistant that Katie loved her Scotch and had to keep an eye on her at all times. Pretty funny!

After we had a few drinks we all decided we were hungry, so David and I went to a restaurant and got some cold sandwiches which we brought back to Katie's hotel room. So there I was, sitting on a bed with Kay Starr, eating a sandwich and drinking a glass of white wine. My childhood dream came true and I was in bed with Kay Starr. The only trouble was that I was 76 years old and Kay was 88, plus we were accompanied by Kay's assistant and David Christopher. Katie hadn't lost her sense of humor and when we opened the sliding door onto the hotel patio to leave - she said, very loudly so everyone could hear – "Thanks for the Business Boys!

The interesting thing I enjoyed about working in Palm Springs was that you never knew what celebrity you might bump into next. One Saint Patrick's night I played at the Desert Horizons along with Terry and Dale and David Christopher on vocals and I spotted the very talented actress and vocalist, Carol Channing, sitting with friends at a table directly in front of the bandstand.

Wow! Carol Channing was like a Kay Starr, only more, because she not only sang but was also an actress, dancer, comedienne and all around entertainer. Born in Seattle in 1921, she got her start on Broadway in 1941 and her career exploded from there to her big performance in the 1961 stage production of *Gentlemen Prefer Blondes* and her hit song "Diamonds Are a Girl's Best Friend."

I think most people remember her from playing the original role of Dolly Gallagher Levi in the 1964 production of *Hello Dolly*. For that she received a Tony award for best actress in a musical. And over the years we would see her on television guesting on shows like *Love Boat, The Muppet Show, Sesame Street* and *The Addams Family.* Probably most people are not aware of the fact that she was the first entertainer to perform at a Super Bowl halftime in 1970 and the only soloist to perform at a Super Bowl more than once, after she did it again in 1972.

Before we started playing that night Terry had asked Carol if she would like to sing a song with the band. She turned him down saying that she was just out with friends for the night and would like to sit back and enjoy herself. On our first intermission I went over to her table and introduced myself, explaining that "Hello Dolly" was one of my favorite tunes to play and I recently had recorded it. She was very charming and I loved listening to her gravel voice and gazing into those big wide open eyes. I repeated Terry's invitation for her to come up and sing a song with us but she said "Thank you Darling, but I'm socializing tonight." And socializing she was, as I noticed she had been belting down quite a few Irish Coffees

We went back to play the last set for the evening and David Christopher charmed the crowd with his tenor voice, singing all the Irish ballads. And then I heard a voice behind me…"Hello Darling." It was Carol Channing and she said to the band…"Hello Dolly" in B Flat! And off we went and she sang the hell out of it. I don't know if she came up because I had asked her to or maybe the Irish coffees had kicked in. The crowd went wild and then she went into "Diamonds Are a Girl's Best Friend." While she was singing she was dancing and kicking her legs high in the air, and by God for a gal in her late 80s they looked pretty good.

I had a nice chat with her after the show and she was very charming to me. I found through the years that most of the great entertainers I had known were just down to earth people that were thankful for their success and the talent they had been given and were grateful to be able to share it with others.

One Hollywood star that I never dreamed in the million years that I would meet was "Cheeta," Tarzan's chimpanzee companion in the popular movie series *Tarzan*. When I was a kid I never missed a Tarzan movie and Cheeta would always steal the show with all his crazy antics.

While I was doing my shows at Lyons English Grill in Palm Springs there was a gentleman, Dan Westfall, that would often attend and I would get to know. Come to find out, Dan ran a home for ex-show business primates and Cheeta was his main tenant. He had elaborate cages in his backyard that were air-conditioned for the hot desert summers and heated in the cool months. He called his home C.H.E.E.T.A. Primate Sanctuary (Creative Habitats and Enrichment for Endangered and Threatened Apes) and it is in a residential section of Palm Springs. I told Dan that I was an old time fan of Cheeta and he invited me to come out and meet him the next afternoon.

When there was a movie featuring an animal, there was usually more than one animal doing the acting, which was the case of Cheeta. He was just one of the original chimpanzees that were in the Tarzan movies of the 30s and 40s. Dan didn't know his age or what Tarzan movies he had been in, but as Dan said, that was a Hollywood mystery, and who doesn't love a Hollywood mystery? Dan got Cheeta from his uncle, Tony Gentry, who was an animal trainer and owned Cheeta. His uncle was getting up in age and Dan promised him that he would give Cheeta a good home for the rest of his life.

It seems that Cheeta had a bit of a love life and his mate gave birth to a baby female chimpanzee, who after reaching adulthood gave birth to a son, Jeeter, named after the main character in *Tobacco Road*. Dan raised Cheeta's grandson like his own and eventually did a show with him, going on the road playing at circuses, nightclubs, television and theaters. Dan did this with Jeeter until 1995 when he retired the act. Dan is still active in show business singing around Palm Springs.

I went to Dan Westfall's house and was amazed at what a wonderful job he had done to make a warm pleasant atmosphere for his primates. Soon after I got there Dan left the room to tell Cheeta that he had company. What a thrill when he walked into the dining room and sat down at the table. He was quite tall and was a perfect gentleman as he sat there drinking a beer and eating a peanut butter sandwich. We made friends easily and he even went over to the piano and played a tune for me. He played some questionable chords, but I didn't complain. When he said his goodbyes he threw me a kiss and we were friends for life. I met his grandson Jeeter too, but he was young, full of hell, and I was happy just to watch him play in his cage.

Dan Westfall and Cheeta were always on my list to visit when in Palm Springs. Dan is such a pleasant guy to be around and he sure has his hands full taking care of the property. Cheeta is always happy to see me and he jumps up and down and squeals with excitement. He seems really happy to see me or maybe he just knows he's going to get a beer and peanut butter sandwich.

On my occasional appearances with Blackburn and Duthie at Hobo's I became acquainted with a nice gentleman who owned a popular gay bar at 10th and Stark Street in downtown Portland. His name was Glen Dugger and he often asked me to stop by and visit his bar someday. I dropped in to see him one evening and he showed me around, and much to my surprise it was a very nice and large establishment with two bars and a light food menu available. The crowd was a friendly one and everybody seemed to know each other. I got the impression that it was more or less like a *Cheer's* bar where the same clique of guys gathered together nightly for their cocktails. Glen named his bar Scandals and it was one of many gay bars in the Stark Street neighborhood.

There was a gay bar next door to Scandals called C. J. Slaughter's, and their big feature was line dancing every night. Across the street from Scandals was a very large bar called The Brig and it had a big jail cell in the middle of the room where everybody danced. A few doors from the Brig there was the Two Sisters Bar and another few doors up the street was the Silverado, a very popular establishment featuring male strippers. And across the street from the Silverado was a scary place called the Eagle where the weirdest of the weird hung out and I was advised never to venture in. So you didn't have to be a nuclear scientist to figure out that Portland had a very large gay population and if you wanted to have a good time you could go out on the town and join in on the fun.

Pauline and I had a couple of hilarious evenings out on the town in gay Portland. Pauline had a girlfriend that she went to school with in Vancouver, whose son had just came out of the closet and told his family that he was gay. She was trying to understand her son and asked Pauline and I if we would take her around to some of the gay life in Portland. First we took her to Darcelle's, an old established female impersonator show. Walter Cole (Darcelle) was an old friend of mine from way back in the late 60s and early 70s at the Hoyt Hotel. He was, and still is, a Portland legend that puts on one hell of a hilarious drag show. So the three of us went to see the female impersonators and then went to Hobo's, where I sat in and played a few tunes with Blackburn and Duthie. Following that we took her up to the Stark Street bars and ended up at the Brig, where Pauline and her friend decided to dance in the cage. They both handed me their purses and off they went! So I am left standing in a very busy gay bar holding two purses! While the girls are dancing the night away, I was standing there with my purses and I had a couple of propositions, so I must have looked pretty cute. That was quite a night and I hope we helped Pauline's girlfriend in her quest to understand her son.

We had another experience at Darcelle's when Johnny Ray was booked to do a show there. Johnny Ray was the number one vocalist in the 1950s and early 60s. He was born in Roseburg, Oregon in 1927 and exploded onto the music scene with his version of "Cry." I remember that he had hit after hit with such tunes as "The Little White Cloud that Cried," "Just Walking in the Rain," and "Walking My Baby Back Home." Johnny Ray was a very close friend of Judy Garland, in fact he was the best man at her wedding. Unfortunately he became an alcoholic and eventually died from liver failure in 1990.

Johnny Ray's show that night was wonderful and he performed all his great hits that everyone remembered him by. A friend of mine at the show told me that Johnny Ray would be going over to Hobo's bar after his performance at Darcelle's, so Pauline and I hurried over to Hobo's after Ray's show. Sure enough he showed up and sat down at the piano and entertained the crowd there for over an hour. Later I was in the boy's room and Johnny Ray happened to walk in. I told him how much I enjoyed his music over the years and he gave me a big kiss on my cheek. Again, I was still cute! That was our night with Johnny Ray in 1985 and it was shortly after that that he passed away.

I had become very good friends with Glen Dugger when, in 2003, he told me that he bought a home in Palm Springs for his future retirement. Glen, being the generous friend that he was, handed me a set of keys for the house and told me it was mine to use any time I wanted. Unbelievable! Now I had a free house in Palm Springs! The house he bought was in a very nice section of Palm Springs just off Highway 111 in the gated community of Deep Well Ranch. There were several tennis courts and three swimming pools to choose from, depending on the temperature you liked. The home was very spacious with two big bedrooms, large dining room, living room, state-of-the-art kitchen and an atrium. It was truly Palm Springs living.

Although I had a place to stay with Terry and Dale, I felt isolated in Palm Desert when I was there. It was okay on the nights that I played with Terry and Dale at the Desert Horizons Country Club but on my nights off I preferred hanging out around Palm Springs because it was much less formal. And now I was doing more work in the city of Palm Springs with promoter David Christopher, so having a house there was perfect timing for me. When I brought the band from Portland down to play, they had a place to stay and hang out; Pauline enjoyed vacationing there with me as well. Pauline and I would often have company and entertain after some of my performances. It was a happy little house for six or seven years until Glen became ill and had to give the house up. All the years that I used his house I only saw him there twice, and both times he was on a big drunken bender. I never had realized that he had a drinking problem - but he did - big time. Sadly he passed away in 2012; Pauline and I lost a great friend and a wonderful person.

My years performing in Palm Springs were memorable ones. People were there to spend the entire winter season or some had just a few days to vacation, but no matter who they were or how long their stay, they were there for a good time and nice sunny weather, and that's what they got. Playing music with Terry and Dale at the Desert Horizons Country Club was a joy and the employees and members couldn't have been nicer to me. And I had the perfect situation for either living with Terry and Dale or staying at my house in Palm Springs. How could I be so lucky?

The little city of Palm Springs had a lot of tales and history to it. It is very gay, of course, dating back to the early days of the movie stars coming to the desert to be themselves out of the limelight of Hollywood. Terry and Dale were good friends with Liberace and filled me in with many of the stories about Liberace's death and the bizarre happenings of his jewelry and costumes after he passed away. I know where they all went, but it's not up to me to discuss it in this book. There were a few little knickknacks from Liberace's house at Terry and Dale's home, but God only knows where they are now, since Terry and Dale are both gone. We'll just put that down to Palm Springs history.

When I had time off I enjoyed just strolling the streets of Palm Springs. Day or night there was always something happening and as I walked down Palm Canyon Drive I would often pass the stars on the sidewalk of the many friends that I had known through the years. Arenas Street was one of the gay bar areas of downtown Palm Springs. There were three popular bars there, Hunters, Street Bar and The Rainbow Cactus, and if I felt like an early dinner I would often take advantage of their nightly "happy hour" free buffet tables. The Rainbow Cactus sometimes would have Rudy de la Mor entertaining at their piano bar. Rudy was an old time lounge-type piano player who also sang. He was discovered by Jimmy Durante as a young man from Chicago and could hold the attention of audiences for hours. He also had the knack of remembering everyone's name in the room. Rudy was one-of-a-kind and unfortunately he died at a rather young age of 73 in 2013.

Like everything else, things change over time, and Palm Springs isn't the same as it used to be for all the years that I performed there. Most of my good musician friends have left the area or passed away and the same with many of the friends that I had met along the way. But the memories remain.

In 2006 Reece Marshburn told me that he had auditioned for a fellow, Tony Starlight, who was opening a new Supper Club and Lounge on Sandy Boulevard in Portland. Reece, of course, got the job and became Tony's piano man and musical director. I remembered the name, Tony Starlight, vaguely, from the 1990s when he was associated with the 1201 Club and Jimmy Mack's in downtown Portland. I never saw him perform because I was touring in those days and when I was in town, too busy to go to hear other performers. But I remember hearing good things about him and especially being a very funny comedian. Tony Starlight was the opening act for comedian Steven Wright when he did his show in Portland and Seattle, as well. In 1999 he moved to Los Angeles and performed there until returning to Portland with his wife Sherry in 2006.

Tony's birth name was Bret Kucera and while working as a line cook at the Virginia Café in downtown Portland he would often be singing Frank Sinatra and Dean Martin type vocals while on the job. Tony told me that a couple of his coworkers were in a little jazz band that played weekends at taverns around Portland and asked Tony to come sit in with them, giving him the name of Tony Starlight. He started singing with the group and one thing led to another and in a matter of a few years he became a popular name in the entertainment industry in Portland. He named his new club Tony Starlight's and when I first walked into his new show room I could dream my way back to the bygone days of the 1920s and 30s nightclubs in the big cities of the United States or of my performing days of the early 1960s in Sparks, Nevada.

Besides being a nightclub owner, Tony is a great entertainer, vocalist and comedian. His impersonation of Neil Diamond is really something to see, along with imitating others like Jimmy Durante, Frank Sinatra, Dean Martin, and many more. I never saw it, but I understand he added a James Bond show to his routine which is said to be out of sight. I will say this - Tony was extremely lucky, and I'm sure he would be the first to admit it, that he had Reece Marshburn with him from the beginning to help put these wonderful shows together. Tony also had a great drummer, Sam Folger, and when I needed a new drummer I borrowed Sam from him. We both shared Reece and Sam between us for a number of years and it worked out perfectly.

After eight years Tony moved out of his Sandy Boulevard showroom and opened a new venture on Madison Street in Portland on August 2014. I did one of the last shows at the Sandy Boulevard location, playing a concert for my 80th birthday celebration. It was a packed house and we had a ball, with Tony coming on stage and joining in on the fun. The new Tony Starlight Showroom became a huge success and it's like being at a big casino in Vegas, minus the gambling tables.

**Jim and Kay Starr, Palm Springs, CA, 2010**

**Terry and Dale, Palm Springs, CA**

**with George Reinmiller Big Band, Portland, OR**

**With Shirley Nanette, Portland, OR**

CHAPTER 30

# Russia

My son Bob, being a political science professor, did a lecture tour of Russia for the US State Department in 2007. Bob thought it would be interesting to include his brother Jame on the tour. Jame, is a stockbroker and at the time also owned three *Buffalo Wild Wings* restaurants in the Portland area and could lecture about the American business world. Bob presented this to the State Department and they invited Jame along on the tour. When Bob toured around the globe he had a habit of passing out one of my CDs as a gift. He gave one such CD to Yulia, Assistant for Education and Culture at the U. S. Consulate in Yekaterinburg, Russia. Fortuitously, the State Department sponsored a Jazz Academy for youth every year and brought in an American musician to play. Yulia told Bob and Jame that she would listen to their father's CD with great interest.

I thought that it would be a wonderful opportunity to travel to Russia but it would be a very slim chance that I would ever hear from the State Department regarding playing and teaching at the Jazz Academy with the hundreds and hundreds of American jazz musicians they had to choose from. However, to my surprise, I got a letter from the Cultural Affairs Department of the State Department requesting another CD and pro-motional material. I didn't get too excited about this because I thought that there were many more American musicians getting the same request. But I was wrong - I got a very nice letter from Yulia telling me that I was awarded a grant to teach at the Jazz Academy for Youth in Yekaterinburg, Russia for the 2009 session. If I accepted, they wanted me to send them my full address, phone number, SSN and my bank and banking account number so they could wire me my grant money, which by the way, was very generous. This is one job that I certainly wouldn't turn down and Pauline and I were looking forward to our Russian adventure.

To start out on the Russian trip, we thought we'd break it up a bit and leave early, spending two days visiting with Dick and Adrienne Henzel in Ossining, New York. We arrived at JFK and I expected Dick to pick us up, but instead, he sent a limo for us. Nice touch! We had a great visit with the Henzels and on September 26th we left JFK for Moscow at 4:20 p.m. and arrived there at 10:10 a.m. the next day, changing planes and arriving in Yekaterinburg at 5:05. While in the Moscow airport, things were very confusing with our luggage change and the Russian airport employees were of very little help. Out of the blue came a cute young Russian girl who spoke perfect English and offered to help us get through the chaos. Her name was Olga, and boy was she a live wire, getting us through the luggage check when they said our luggage was overweight; she simply bribed the checkers! That's one thing I soon found out, you could get anything you wanted in Russia by simply slipping someone a little money on the side. Anyway, Olga lived in Yekaterinburg, and she gave us her phone number and we promised to stay in touch, which we did and she became part of our State Department entourage while we were there.

After arriving in Yekaterinburg we got our luggage, said our goodbyes to Olga, and headed out the gate, only to be greeted by our chauffer from the State Department. I sat in the front seat with him, which I later found out was a no-no, and he drove us to our hotel, The Park Inn. The hotel was very nice and to my surprise it had a well-stocked bar in the lobby along with a buffet table for breakfast, lunch and dinner. It had been a long travel day and we were tired with the jetlag, so after a few drinks and food we called it a night, because the next day was the start of a very busy schedule.

The next morning we were picked up at the hotel by our driver accompanied by Yulia and taken to the US Embassy where we met the U. S. Consul General and other Embassy officials. I was given my schedule for teaching and performing at the Urals Jazz Academy for Youth and was informed that I had two other performances: one at Urals State Estrady (Variety) Theater and the other at the "Ever Jazz" Club (Ben Hall). They had talked to me about these concerts shortly before I left for the trip and I told them that it would be my pleasure. The Theater paid $1000 and the jazz club another $200 and that was over and above my State Department grant. I thought, why not, that would buy me a lot of vodka and caviar.

They had the afternoon all planned for us. First, we had a luncheon at a very nice restaurant and then went to a church in memory of the Russian royal family, the Russian Imperial Romanov family. The church was built on the spot that Tsar Nicholas and Tsamna Alexandra and their five children were shot after the Russian Revolution. It is called "The church of the blood." We then were driven 12 miles outside Yekaterinburg where they were finally buried. After the fall of communism the bodies of the Royal family were exhumed in July 1991 and taken to St. Catherine Chapel of St. Peter and Paul Cathedral in St. Petersburg for their very final resting place, with most of the other monarchs of Russia. President Boris Yeltsin and his wife attended the funeral. Our final tourist attraction for the day was a trip to the Europe/Asian border, where I stood with one foot in Europe and the other in Asia. That was our final day of relaxation and now it was time to get to work.

I found out that the rhythm section I would be working with was composed of an American pianist, Adam Klipple, and a guitar player, a bassist and a drummer, all Russian. Klipple also would be teaching at the Jazz

Academy and had done so in previous years. After rehearsing with him for our concerts, I also found, to my horror, that he was a good musician but a modernist with no intention of trying to conform to my style of jazz. He was a nice enough fellow and I figured somehow or other we would make it work. I was also assigned an interpreter to accompany me wherever I went and boy, did she come in handy. The Jazz Academy building was absolutely beautiful and the music rooms and performing halls were top rate with fantastic acoustics. I could see that this was going to be a wonderful experience. The first day at the Academy started out at 10 a.m. with a press conference composed of me, the U.S. Consul General, Tim Sandusky, Adam Klipple and the College Principal, Victor Pastukhov. This press conference was covered by television, radio and the newspapers. I then realized that this cultural event was very important to the U.S. government and to the Russian government, as well. I also realized that I had better start trying to act important and that included sitting in the back seat of the Embassy's Chrysler sedan.

At noon there was the official opening ceremony, followed by student auditions until 4: 30 in the afternoon. I was one of the judges for the auditions and found that the majority of the students were mostly influenced by modern jazz and had no idea of where jazz came from or its beginnings. Surprisingly, there was one young man who did come out and play some wonderful Scott Joplin Ragtime piano. There was another boy that blew my mind playing Paul Desmond's "Take Five" on his alto saxophone, note for note. Another thing that impressed me, aside from the music, was how well dressed and groomed the children were. The girls had beautiful hairdos and tasteful dresses and the boys had shirts and ties, dress slacks and shiny shoes. Quite a spread from how I saw kids in the US dress for school. I had the boys asking me to autograph their neckties, which I wouldn't do without their parent's permission because they were beautiful ties, but the parents were happy to let me do it and I had a big lineup for necktie autographs.

I also had workshops with the clarinet and saxophone students. I had brought some cute arrangements with me, courtesy of my piano player Reese Marshburn, that the students and I played together. It was fun doing this and it sure kept my interpreter busy. In between all the teaching, Adam, the Russian rhythm section and I got together to rehearse for the theater concert. Because of the huge difference in our styles we decided that I would play half the show with my traditional jazz and let Adam do his modern jazz for the second half.

One of my big assignments was to do a special lecture for all the Jazz Academy students on "The Beginnings of Jazz and The Musicians who Created It." This was something that I started working on back home before we came over to Russia, because it took a lot of preparation. I had to transfer to my iPod many of my early jazz recordings, starting with the Original Dixieland Jazz Band in 1917 and moving on to King Oliver, Jelly Roll Morton, Armstrong, Bechet and many more. Before I went to Russia, the State Department asked me for a copy of my presentation. I thought perhaps they did this because they might want to censor some of its contents. But I was wrong, as usual, because all they wanted to know was the musicians that I would talk about, find their pictures, and project them up on a screen while I was talking about them - talk about modern technology! Pauline sat with a sound engineer and ran my iPod as I was talking about different musicians and bands. My translator was busy doing her job and often had to tell me to stop talking so fast so she could keep up with me. The projectionist did a good job flashing the correct pictures of bands on the screen as I was talking about them. Fantastic!

They held my presentation in the big concert Hall of the Jazz Academy, much to my surprise, because I thought I was doing this just for the students. As it turned out they had advertised it and invited anyone who might be interested to attend. So it seemed like we had a good share of the population of Yekaterinburg there. I was happy with the reaction of all the young students listening to these early jazz records. They couldn't sit still and their feet were tapping along with the beat of all these jazz creators playing their instruments. Oddly enough, some time back in the 1920s Sidney Bechet toured Russia as a young man. So he beat me there by some 70 years.

That evening we played our jazz concert at the Urals Estrady Theater. Our State Department driver ran into heavy traffic and we ended up driving part of the way to the theater on the sidewalk - diplomatic immunity - you know, and I loved it. It wasn't my idea of a theater because it was a large and beautiful concert hall, fantastic acoustics, and had a superb sound system. There were speeches from Russian officials and the US Consul General, and then the musicians were introduced. As planned, I played my half of the show first, starting out with Sweet Georgia Brown and the capacity crowd got right into clapping along with the music. I followed that with Sidney Bechet's *"Petite Fleur,"* and the crowd went absolutely wild with cheers and applause as soon as I started out with the melody. I had no idea that Sidney and his beautiful song were so popular, and in of all places, Russia. The concert went over wonderfully and Adam played his modern jazz the last half of the show with me joining him at the end for the last tune. It was a great show, with a standing ovation. It would've been better if I had a piano player that played my style, but it worked, nevertheless.

The next day was to be a busy day for me because not only was I invited to a dinner reception at the home of Consul General, Tim Sandusky, but I was also scheduled to play at the Ever Jazz Club later in the evening. So after a full day at the Jazz Academy, I returned to the hotel, freshened up, then Pauline and I were picked up and driven to the Consul General's home. It was a large, official residence that was well, but discreetly, guarded. Again, to my surprise, the house was full of Russian city and government officials, radio stations and newspaper reporters. The reception was for The Urals Jazz Academy for Youth and evidently I was the guest of honor, being interviewed on the radio with the help of my interpreter, and talking with newspaper reporters. I was presented with a very large and impressive picture book of the city of Yekaterinburg and its beautiful monuments and buildings. After the presentation I was led to the buffet table that was loaded with a variety of wonderful foods and desserts along with any kind of cocktail you could think of. The Consul General was very considerate and apologized for having his reception on the same night that I was to perform at the jazz club. He led me to his private office where there was a nice sofa and told me that I was welcome to take a nap before going to the jazz club. I took advantage of this, and I'm glad I did because as it turned out I had a long and busy night ahead of me.

When it was time to leave the Consul General's reception Pauline and I got in our State Department car, with our driver, and headed for the Ever Jazz Club, followed by two other State Department sedans, including the Consul General's car. My God, you'd think I was some big time Senator from the United States or something, not just some clarinet player from Oregon. We arrived at the Ever Jazz Cub only to find a full house applauding as Adam Klipple and I walked in with our entourage, including, by the way, our friend Olga that we had met at the airport.

We went immediately to the bandstand and I was happy to see the Russian guitar player, bass player and drummer waiting for me. That made it easy because I could just play selections of tunes that I did with them at the Urals State Estrady concert a few days before. Adam was on piano and we did a half-and-half show with me playing my mainstream jazz for the first set. The audience went wild again when I played Bechet's *"Petite Fleur,"* but this time it was a more intimate setting and I could see many people with tears in their eyes, emotionally touched by the music.

On my break I went to a special table reserved for Pauline and me, along with the State Department entourage that came along for the show. There was plenty of vodka placed in front of me, along with a variety of beers, and I was asked if I would like the specialty of the house – Halibut. I declined because it's hard for me to eat and then play my clarinet. I was served the halibut dinner anyway and I should have known that it is impossible to turn down Russian hospitality when it is offered. I'm glad that they did because it was the best halibut that I ever had... cooked to perfection.

At the end of the evening we said our goodbyes, but getting out of the Ever Jazz Club wasn't as easy as one might think. We had to work our way through a large share of the audience in order to get outside to our waiting car and driver. The jazz fans had their cameras with them and wanted me to pose for pictures with them. They were touching and hugging me like I was some kind of rock star or something. In all my playing in different countries around the world I had never experienced such emotional enthusiasm such as this and certainly not in the United States. It was most gratifying

The next day was the final day of teaching at the Jazz Academy. I got together with the rest of the jury and we went over all the audition results and gave recommendations. I did a master class on playing in an ensemble. After a lunch break we had a creative workshop rehearsing with members of the jury and students for the Gala Session. It ended with an awards ceremony and the Gala jam session with students and teachers. I was presented with bouquets of beautiful flowers along with hugs and kisses. I was sad to see it all end. We had a farewell party in the lobby of our hotel that last evening with a few fans, the State Department entourage, including the Consul General, and of course our friend Olga was right in there having fun with everyone else. And I'll be damned when it was time to go in the morning the same people came back to waive goodbye to Pauline and me as our driver took us to the airport.

Russian jazz critic, Victor Bainov, wrote the following about my performances at the Urals State Estrady Theater and The Ever Jazz Club. To me, he seemed to hit the nail on the head and picked up on the message that I sent with my clarinet playing. After reading this I was satisfied that I did a good job representing the United States in Russia with my music. Again, mission accomplished.

*Jim Beatty* - this is a serious musician who plays only his favorite music. He is not excessively showy. However, to the attentive listener, he is very expressive in his movements and poses. Jim is one of the *Last Mohicans* of jazz. The difference between Beatty and the last of Fenimore Cooper's warrior Mohicans is that the type of jazz musician he exemplifies will never grow old."

Other older, active jazz performers, such as Wayne Shorter, Sonny Rawlins, Ornette Coleman, Ron Carter and Dave Brubeck, are active to this day. Pop music reflects contemporary society, especially the young. But the classics of acoustic jazz are for people of all ages. For example, the whole world danced to Big Band swing, New Orleans Dixieland reflected the joy of the dark-skinned populations of America, and this music is being performed to this day with success." *Viktor Bainov, Yekaterinburg, Russia 2010*

Pauline and I decided to take a few extra days and visit Moscow before we left for home. We were glad we did because it was a wonderful experience to see such a great city, with over 16 million people. Moscow is in western Russia and of course home of the Kremlin where the president lives and all the big government officials have their offices. We visited Lenin's mausoleum and of course the famous St. Basil's Cathedral. Pauline went wild at the Gum Department Store. It's the biggest store that I had ever seen or have ever seen since and I could've left Pauline there and picked her up a few years later. I did notice that the old-time Russians missed communism and they couldn't help but giving Pauline and me a suspicious stare. But the young Russians were very Western and dressed to a "T," with the boys all wearing beautifully polished patent leather shoes. I couldn't resist and bought a pair for myself. Yes, the Russian trip was amazing and one that I'm sure Pauline and I will never forget.

CHAPTER 31

# Fans

I AM A FAN OF the early jazz players, Armstrong, Bechet, Simeon, and others, so I guess that I shouldn't have been surprised when I started to have fans of my own. And, thank goodness, because you needed them to survive in the music business. They talked you up, came to your performances and brought people with them, along with buying all of your recordings as they came out. They could be male or female and anything in-between, with an age range of 9 to 90.

I first started noticing my fans in the 1970's and at first I thought it quite bizarre. Our home in Lake Oswego, Oregon was a large, old, four bedroom house on a considerable amount of property. We had a huge front lawn, which I mowed until the boys were big enough to do it. One beautiful, sunny day I was mowing the lawn and couldn't help but notice a car full of people circling my house. As they were slowly driving back and forth they all stared at me to the point where I started to get self-conscious; did I look ridiculous mowing the lawn with my shirt off? I then became more observant and realized that people were driving by my house at different times, mowing the lawn or not. This went on for some time before it dawned on me that my house was on sort of a drive-by jazz celebrity watch. I figured I had better get used to it or move to a gated community, so I joined the fun and if I happened to be outside during a drive-by, I gave everybody a nice wave.

I would often go to work and find presents waiting for me on the bandstand. They would be from anonymous fans that for whatever reason didn't want me to know where they came from. One such gift was a beautiful engraved piece of wood, about 5 feet long and 2 feet wide, with the words "Jim Beatty Jazz Band" inscribed on it. Probably the strangest gift I had waiting for me when I arrived at work was a large box, and when I opened it I found, staring me in the face, the largest bullfrog I've ever seen in my life. On my way home that night I released it into the wild. Over the years I have also been given a considerable number of cufflinks. The best gift from a fan that I ever received was a beautiful solid gold coin with a long, gold chain attached. It was too big and heavy for me to wear so I gave it to my mother-in-law who wore it for several years. When she passed away I got it back and it sat in my drawer for another few years. I decided it was silly just hiding it away in a drawer, so I took it to a gold dealer and to my surprise received $2000 for it. Now that's the kind of fans I like.

I often traveled to Kennewick, Washington with my band to play for the Tri-Cities Traditional Jazz Society. After one of our appearances, this is what I read in their Jazz newspaper:

> *"Have you ever watched Marian Overturf when Jim Beatty is here? She has very good taste. Yup, she's smitten. I must confess, I am too. I got to talk into the same microphone that he used and he stood next to me when I talked about the generous gift he made of some of his records for our raffle. I really find it hard to talk when he's around."*

Can you believe that?

Another great fan I had was my barber in Lake Oswego, Jack Dick. He started coming to hear the band in the early 80s when we played at the Whaler and he was a dancing fool. Oh, how he loved to dance; in fact, he danced so much that he wore his wife out and he had to go to the other ladies in the room for a swing around the dance floor. Jack and his wife Betty probably came to every public event we played and while they were there Jack was on the dance floor a great deal of the time. Jack and Betty became very good friends, but unfortunately Betty passed away and Jack became a very lonely guy. He continued following the band around but he was heartbroken and drinking quite heavily. One weekend I was quite surprised because we were playing at the Sweetbrier Inn and he never made his usual appearance. A day or two later I went for a haircut and I noticed many bouquets of flowers in front of his barbershop. I found out that had been found dead in his home the night before. I'm sure he died of a broken heart. There were many nights after that when I was playing I could've sworn I saw him in the audience.

Tom Cropper was a fellow that followed my band around quite a bit during the 1980s. He was very enthusiastic about my band and was always coming up with ideas how to promote it. He wrote the lyrics to a song he called "The Jim Beatty Blues," and wanted me to write the music for it. I'm sorry to say that I never got around to writing the music. However, after re-reading the words after all these years I don't think I could write the music to them anyway. Here is "The Jim Beatty Blues," by Tom Cropper:

Jim's the Man
Plays that Horn;
Black Thing
They call the Stick;
Songs He Plays

Sure ain't Corn;
Plays Orleans
Jazz, Songs and Licks

Oh play that Thing
That always Sings
Play the Jim Beatty Blues
Play till Tomorrow, Leave Pain and Sorrow;
Gonna leave my blues away.

Jim sure can give it Gas
Blows his horn like a Blast;
Touch of Chicago, New York and Harlem
Gonna dance those blues Away

Oh play that thing that always Sings;
Play the Jim Beatty blues, play till Tomorrow
Leave pain and Sorrow;
Gonna leave my blues Away.

These are the kind of things Tom Cropper would come up with and he probably spent a lot of time working on it. It's nice to know that there are people around thinking about the music and trying to help you out as much as they can.

While I was playing at the Red Lion Hotel in Portland a very well-dressed middle-aged man, Gregory Mason, came up to me and asked: "Jim...what do you do with your old clarinet reeds when you are done with them"? I told him that I had no more use for them and I threw them away. He then asked me if I would save them and give them to him. I thought that a bit odd, but then again he might have a reed fetish or something. Gregory attended most of our events and every time I saw him if I had a used to reed or two, I would give them to him. Now, Gregory was by no means a nut job. He was well-liked by the followers of my band and would often show up with many of his friends.

Quite some time went by and then one night he approached me and presented me with a framed, lengthy poem – titled – "Reflections in the Reeds." Attached inside the glass frame were two of my clarinet reeds, beautifully mounted. The following are the words he put down on paper.

REFLECTIONS IN THE REEDS
By Gregory R. Mason 2007


THE MUSICIAL ICON STANDS BEFORE US -
WITH A PRESENCE SO CALM AND GENTLE
FILLING OUR SENSES WITH JOYFUL SOUNDS -
FOR WHICH HIS TALENTS ARE INSTRUMENTAL

THERE ARE TIMES WHEN HE SPEAKS TO US -
WITH A LANGUAGE UNIQUE TO ONLY HIM –
AND PASSERBY WILL RECOGNIZE THE DIALECT –
WITHOUT A DOUBT THEY SAY – "IT MUST BE JIM"

THE MUSIC SENDS EACH OF US ON A JOURNEY –
TO A NOSTALGIC TIME AND REMINISCENT PLACE –
WHERE WE CAN RECALL OUR PAST LIFE AND IT'S JOYS –
WHILE PUTTING A SCINTILLATING SMILE ON YOUR FACE.

HE SENDS US ON LIFE CHANGING ADVENTURES –
PENETRATING OUR BODIES AND CARESSING OUR SOULS –
TAKING US ON AN INTROSPECTIVE VOYAGE –
HELPING US TO REGENERATE AND BECOME WHOLE.

THE SOUNDS MAY LIFT US TO THE HEAVEN –
OR PERMIT US TO SAIL ON A SOFT BREEZE –
REWARDING US WITH A PLACE SO SERENE –
ALLOWING OUR FEARS AND ANGST TO BE APPEASED

THE TONES MAY LULL US GENTLY TO SLEEP
OR CREATE WITHIN US A REASSURING SENSE OF PEACE –
THEY MAY INVIGORATE US AND MAKE OUR HEARTS
PULSATE –
OR THEY MAY ALLOW OUR STRESS AND PAIN TO CEASE.

THE MAN HAS A SENSE OF SINCERE COMMONALITY –
WHILE PERPETUALLY EXUDING CLASS AND
SOPHISTICATION –
ALWAYS SHARING HIS PASSION OF LIFE THROUGH HIS
MUSIC –
COMPELLING ALL US TO UTILIZE OUR VAST IMAGINATION.

Wow! So this is why Gregory asked me for my old reeds! I was speechless when he gave this to me. These words he wrote about how I was able to get into his soul through my clarinet playing, just blew my mind. When you're playing New Orleans jazz that's exactly what you're supposed to be doing, reaching people's hearts through your music. Bechet, Simeon, Dodds and Lewis did it to me and now it was my turn. Mission accomplished!

Portland has one loyal jazz fan that shares himself with all the jazz bands and musicians in the area. His name is Larry Cannon and if there's a jazz gathering anywhere you are liable to see him in the front row digging the music. I knew Larry's mom and dad, Maynard and Violet, as they were fans of mine that dated back to 1970s. Violet made umbrellas for the jazz parades and they were absolutely beautiful. Larry travels up and down the West Coast to Jazz Society's and jazz festivals. Everybody knows Larry and Larry knows everybody. If there were more like him, the Portland Jazz scene would be booming.

Probably the most far out, wild and crazy fan that I ever had was a man named John Galbraith, a middle-aged fellow from Vancouver, B. C. He was constantly driving from Canada, down the coast through Oregon and California, and back again in his Volkswagen Camper. The best way that I can describe John Galbraith is that he closely resembled and acted like British actor, Rowan Atkinson's character, Mr. Bean.

The first time I came across John was when I was playing at the Hoyt Hotel in downtown Portland in the early 1970s. I noticed that he would stand in front of the bandstand, listening to us for the longest time and then disappear for a while. While he was listening to the band I also noticed that he never ordered a drink, he just stood there empty handed and enjoyed the music. What I later found out is what he was doing was going out to his Volkswagen camper and having his drinks and not spending his money in the hotel. He found a way to go out for the night and enjoy an evening of music without paying for it.

One intermission John introduced himself to me and we struck up a friendly conversation. Even though he acted strangely and was a bit of an eccentric, I found him quite intelligent and very knowledgeable about jazz. He caught many of the jazz acts when they played in Vancouver and he seemed to know many of them personally, including Billie Holiday. He told me that he enjoyed my playing very much and I'll be damned if he didn't buy one of my albums. I got the impression that he might have been from a well-to-do family and as far as I could figure out, he never seemed to have any kind of occupation. Then again I couldn't see him doing any kind of work. Where he got his money from I never did figure out, but he was on the move all the time in his camper. He would spend a week or two in Portland and then head south and I wouldn't see him again for several weeks when he was on his way back to Vancouver, B.C., where he had an apartment.

On one of John's journeys back to Vancouver he called me at my home and asked a favor. Evidently he purchased a moped in California along with some other things and he was over his limit for bringing things back into Canada. He asked if he could leave the moped at my house until his next trip. Now a Moped is a motorized bicycle that you can also pedal with the motor off. With the engine on it doesn't travel a heck of a lot faster than when you're peddling, however they are a lot of fun to drive. I told John that would be fine and gave him my address to drop it off.

Well, John stopped by the house and Pauline, Jame and Bob met my strange new friend, finding him quite interesting and enjoyable to talk to. After that he became a friend of the family and we would share a number of hilarious adventures with him. He told the boys that they could ride his moped all they wanted and they were thrilled. As it turned out Pauline and I had fun driving around the neighborhood as well.

John Galbraith was a frequent visitor to our house on his trips south. And on the next trip home from California he stopped by the house and left a beautiful little electric organ. Now John did not play music - he just enjoyed listening to it - so whatever had possessed him to buy an organ, I'll never know. We had a piano at our house and the little organ didn't get very much use except when occasionally Jim Goodwin might fool around with it. John was always welcomed to camp in our front driveway in his Volkswagen and use our bathrooms and showers to freshen up in. One year we were painting the house and he even pitched in and helped out. I think he led a very lonely life and somehow felt that he found a family with us.

John always kept a dummy in his camper that went along with him in the passenger seat so that he could use the fast lane on the freeway for two passengers or more. He also purchased two duty free bottles of Scotch before going through each border. He simply told the customs inspector that the other was for his friend that was sleeping in the back of the camper. He was never challenged by the border guards, but perhaps they let him through just to get rid of him. On one trip south he had a bad accident in his pants and found himself with no toilet paper to clean himself up with. He simply went into a supermarket wearing a jacket with shoes and socks. Well, you can imagine what happened in the market and the police were called and he was jailed for indecent exposure. At the trial the next morning the judge released him with the advice to never stop in that part of Washington State again! Coming or going! He was also banned from just about every buffet in Portland after stuffing himself for hours and then filling all of his pockets with fried chicken. Are you starting to see where I'm coming from when I said he reminded me of Mr. Bean?

The band had a rare Sunday off with no jobs during the day or evening and I decided to take advantage of it by having a barbecue at our house for our friends and neighbors. John Galbraith called me from Vancouver and said he was coming down with a lady friend, Elsie, a very elderly lady who lived across the hall from him at his apartment in Vancouver. Evidently, John's mother used to take care of her but his mother had passed away a few months earlier and John had just taken over caring for Elsie. He wanted to come to Portland and take in some music so he made a bed for Elsie in the camper van and was bringing her with him. I told John that we were having a party at the house and to stop by with Elsie and join us. When they arrived we went out to John's camper van and carried Elsie to the backyard and set her down in a chair to enjoy the party along with John and the rest of us. I must say that she sure perked up after a few glasses of white wine and everyone was amused by my strange friend John Galbraith. John and Elsie left the party fairly early to find a motel as they expected to stay around Portland for a week.

During his visit with Elsie, John came out one night to hear me and my band play, leaving Elsie back at the motel. After we finished our performance for the evening I invited John to stop by the house for a visit and nightcap on his way back to his motel and Elsie. It was quite late, or should I say early in the morning, when John and I arrived at my house and sat down for a couple of drinks. Pauline was asleep, but woke up when she heard us talking, and came downstairs to join us. After a few drinks, it was time to call it a night, but it was obvious that John had had too many cocktails to drive back to the motel. We asked him to stay the night, but he said he had to go back to the motel because Elsie was there alone. I was in no condition to drive John to his motel, so Pauline was a good sport and volunteered for the job.

It was a very warm and humid summer night when John and Pauline, dressed in a nightie and skimpy robe, left for the motel. I guess they had quite a time finding it, as it was some distance away in Milwaukie, Oregon. Once getting there, Pauline found it was a small one floor building with 12 units. Pauline got out of the car and went to the door with John to make sure he got in safe and that Elsie was okay. John discovered that he had left the motel key in his camper van back at our house and to make things worse the motel office was closed. They checked the windows and sure enough John had left the window open slightly in the bedroom where Elsie was sleeping. Pauline pulled the window open and crawled through, being very quiet so Elsie didn't wake up while she crept to the front door to let John in. Pauline didn't want to leave until they checked on Elsie, so before she knew it John turned on the lights and Elsie woke up. She took one look at John and Pauline hovering over her bed (Pauline with long blonde hair and wearing a nightgown) and she started ranting and raving at them both - John two-timing her and running around all night with a "f****** tramp." I guess Elsie's language was atrocious as she was yelling at Pauline – "Get out of here you God Damn Tramp!" So, needless to say, Pauline let herself out through the front door and drove home. When she arrived back at our place, I was sound asleep, but believe me I heard all about it the next morning as we drove John's van over to his motel and parked in front of his unit and left.

I wish I could say that this was the end of the story of John and Elsie - but I can't -and it gets worse! A couple of days after Pauline's escapade at the motel, I got a telephone call from John. He was absolutely hysterical and a nervous wreck over the phone. JIM! –He said. Elsie Is Dead! I said John - calm down and tell me what happened. John said that they were planning on driving back to Vancouver that day and when he went to wake Elsie, he discovered that she had passed away sometime during the night. I asked John if he had called the police and he said that he had no intention of involving the United States authorities of her death because it would be too much red tape and they might even accuse him of foul play. I told John that it was a very serious offense not to report a death and if he got caught with a dead body, everyone would think the worst.

John absolutely refused to call the coroner or police and told me he would call me back later and hung up. Ten or fifteen minutes went by when John called again and said – Jim, I got a guy in the next unit of my motel to help me carry Elsie out to the van. I told him that she was very sick and was asleep. So now John had Elsie in his van and planned on driving her back to Canada. John told me that he had carefully hidden her in the back of the van, covering her with blankets and other things. I told John that if the Canadian border guards caught him with a dead body in his vehicle all hell would break loose and he probably would go to jail for the rest of his life! But John wouldn't listen to me - he and Elsie were heading for Vancouver!

Finally, I told John that if he had really made up his mind to go back to Canada that I wanted him to come by my house and have a couple of shots of Scotch to calm down and that I wanted to take a look and see if Elsie was in fact carefully hidden. John said that he would stop by the house and I immediately gathered up Jame and Bob and took them over to a neighbor's house. John arrived and he was a nervous wreck, but I did calm him down with a couple of drinks. Before he left I told him that I would pretend to be a Canadian customs officer and I went out to his van and slid open the sliding door only to have Elsie's head fall out, staring me in the face! Not only that but she was starting to not smell very well. I helped John rearrange Elsie's body in the back of the van, even putting a couple of cereal boxes on top of her to make it look more realistic. Now I was involved in this whole dead body scenario and I was starting to get nervous, and happy to see John and Elsie pull out of the driveway heading north.

I asked John to please call me and let me know when he was safely back in Vancouver, Canada. However, the phone rang only 30 minutes after he left and it was John telling me that he had decided to stop at the VW dealer on the way home for an oil change and lube job. Can you imagine a VW Van up on a hoist with a dead body in it while getting a service job? I told John to please get out of there and get back to Canada before he ended up in jail. Later in the day the phone rang and he was safely back at his apartment in Vancouver. He said he had no problem getting through the border and the border guards never looked in the back. In fact, John stopped at the duty-free and bought two bottles of Scotch - one for him and one for Elsie. As for Elsie - John called a funeral home when he got back to Vancouver and told them that Elsie had died. The funeral director said that they would come over and pick her up - John said - you needn't bother - she's in the van and I'll drop her off. I can't believe that the funeral director didn't call the police after having someone drop off a dead body that had obviously been deceased for a couple of days. But that's Canada!

That was the last time that I saw John Galbraith. A friend of his whom evidently John had told about enjoying my music so much in Portland, called me and told me that John had died from an overdose of alcohol and sleeping pills. I don't think John committed suicide because he was having too much fun just being John Galbraith. I think that he was probably listening to some jazz record, perhaps mine, and had too much scotch along with the sleeping pills - and that was it. I must say this: he was one jazz fan that made my life much more interesting.

Sometime later I got a call from a Vancouver bank asking me if I knew a John Galbraith, and if so - did I have his moped and organ? Evidently he had put them on a credit card and the bank wanted to repossess them for nonpayment. I told the banker that I had them both at the house and to come and get them. They never did.

## CHAPTER 32

# The Partys Over

THE YEARS 2000 - 2010 were busy ones as I was not only traveling as a guest artist but working with my band in the Portland area. There was the usual amount of casuals ranging from weddings, birthday parties and jazz clubs. In the fall of 2002 we started playing the occasional weekend in the lounge of the Sweetbrier Inn, located right off Interstate 5 in Tualatin, Oregon, and only a 10 minute drive from my house...very handy for me. The Sweetbrier was owned by the Nyberg family, had several motel rooms, a restaurant with very good food and several large banquet rooms. They usually had a single entertainer in the lounge during the week and featured bands on the weekend. My band went in as a trio at first but as the crowds increased to standing room only we added a standup string bass in the person of my old friend Dave Duthie from the duo of Blackburn and Duthie at Hobos in downtown Portland.

In addition to Dave, Jim Goodwin played the piano and Jack Dawes was on drums. Management was so happy with the large crowds that they would give me anything I wanted. They had a policy of keeping the TVs on, without sound, during the band's performance. The first thing I did was to insist that as soon as we started playing the TVs were turned off because there's nothing more distracting than a television set during a performance. Our crowd loved to dance, so management bought a portable dance floor and set it up every time we played. We played from 7 p.m. till 11 p.m. so people could have cocktails, dinner and dance the night away.

It was a very casual affair and I think the band had just as much fun as the customers did. Not only that, but the lounge manager, bartenders and waitresses got into the swing of things along with everyone else. It was a happy night every night and sometimes you never knew what might happen. One night, Jack Dawes, who was never late and never missed a job, didn't show up for work. It seems there was a one hour time change forward and he forgot about it. I called his house and said – Jack! Aren't you coming to work tonight? He couldn't believe what he did and said he be there as soon as possible. When he did walk in, everyone in the place was ready to give him the razzamatazz, and he sat down behind the drums that were fortunately set up from the night before and started playing with a paper bag over his head. He was a good sport and the crowd loved him. Another night it was my birthday and of course they had a cake for me, which Jack took and slammed into my face! I had cake and frosting all over my face, down my neck, and on my dark suit. The place went hysterical and people came to see us wondering what was going to happen next.

But there were problems lurking on the horizon and I knew that sooner or later something would have to be done. Jim Goodwin's drinking problem was getting worse by the day. He was such a talented musician and great friend that it broke my heart to watch him steadily go downhill. He couldn't play the cornet anymore because of his teeth, so I put him on piano, which he played wonderfully. However, now he was coming in to work quite intoxicated and playing very badly. I talked and talked with him but there was nothing I could do except replace him.

Good piano players are hard to come by, especially the ones that can play the older style of jazz. There were a couple of piano players around but I thought I could do better by finding someone young and teaching him the ropes. I was thinking about going around to a few of the modern jazz clubs and finding a young piano player who would like to leave the dark side of jazz and come with me and hear the truth! Every once in a while I would play on a sternwheeler that traveled on the Willamette and Columbia Rivers. It was called the *Queen of the West* and I played my clarinet as a substitute with the Pat O'Neil Riverboat Jazz Band. We played an afternoon show and an evening show after dinner. It was following our show that the house band of the ship would start playing for dancing. As a rule the house bands were not very good because they played the old music standards in a very modern style and that just did not work. I therefore got out of the showroom and into the bar as quickly as possible.

The year was 2006 and I will never forget it. As I was exiting the showroom after our performance had ended I passed by the show band playing for dancing and heard a young piano player. I later learned that his name was Reece Marshburn and as I passed him I heard the most beautiful chords coming out of his piano and I immediately stopped dead in my tracks and stood in back of him for the longest time just listening. Reece was around 24 years old at the time and I knew that this was a young man on a mission and going places. The boat docked to let us off in Portland and I didn't get a chance to talk with Reece, but I got his name and phone number from Pat O'Neil and called him the next day. I told Reece that if he ever wanted to leave the show band and come on shore that he had a job with me. He did just that and we have been working together for going on ten years, along with recording many CDs and having a great friendship.

Unfortunately, the Nyberg family sold the Sweetbrier and all the property around it to a company that made them an offer they couldn't refuse. So, in the spring of 2006 it all came to an end when the wrecking ball came sailing through the lounge and the party was over. It's a piece of Oregon's history that is gone and now a huge mall is sitting in its place. I drive by the mall occasionally and sometimes I swear that I can hear the band playing.

Fortunately the Sweetbrier wasn't the only club on the block. There was another restaurant/lounge in Tualatin that also had a hotel attached, called Hayden's Lakefront Grill. We started there by playing special events like Mardi Gras and other such celebrations. Then I got the idea to put on my own shows in their banquet room with my band and hiring a guest performer for each show. My first guest artist was, of course, trombonist Pete Pepke. We added door prizes and a raffle to make things fun. Every concert was sold out with standing room only and everyone was happy; the crowd, the band and particularly Hayden's. In the early days of the Hayden's shows the band consisted of John Bennett, piano, Steve Dickinson, base, Dave Johnson, banjo, Jack Dawes, drums, and me on clarinet and soprano sax.

We held these shows every few months from 2000 - 2010 with a variety of guest musicians, including cornet player Chris Tyle. Chris had worked with me off and on for several years. He had spent a great deal of time playing in New Orleans and touring overseas. Ironically, I worked with his father, Axel, back in 1967 when he was the drummer with the Muddy River Jazz Band. Other guests included my old friend clarinetist Jim Buchmann. Jim had left Portland and moved to Florida working at Disneyland for several years and was also popular around the jazz festival circuit. He decided it was time to move back home and settled in Vancouver, Washington. Pat O'Neil was also a guest along with a couple of great vocalists, Marianne Mayfield and Marilyn Keller. Those were fun times at Hayden's, but it was a lot of work promoting the shows and selling tickets. This fell on Pauline's shoulders and on the night of the show she was at the door taking tickets, seating people, organizing the raffle and door prizes, along with selling my CDs. Pauline probably worked harder than I did on those nights and often she had the welcome help of Jack Dawes's wife Earline. Fortunately, Hayden's never felt the fate of Sweetbrier's wrecking ball and is still there to this day serving good food along with talented entertainment.

Another nice session the Jim Beatty Jazz Band had was at Shenanigans, a restaurant/lounge located in the Red Lion Hotel and operated by Paul Shiva, a longtime Portland restaurateur. I had dealings with Paul when I played for him at another restaurant he owned in downtown Portland a number of years before. I didn't especially care for him then and I was a little hesitant about working for him again at Shenanigans, but I thought that I'd give it a try.

Shenanigan's was in a beautiful setting overlooking the Columbia River and the view was magnificent, especially during the summer months. As it turned out, Paul Shiva wasn't the problem at all, it was his employees. Prior to us playing there on Sundays they had very little business and the bartender and waitresses had a very easy time of it. However, when we started playing we brought our usual large crowds with us and the employees were overwhelmed and completely unprepared. Consequently, the service was terrible. It took forever to get a drink, let alone ordering dinner. The bartenders and waitresses were not very pleasant to the band and we had a hard time getting a drink on our intermissions. I knew that this was not going to work and something had to be done, so I went to Paul and told him that he was losing one hell of a lot of money on Sundays and that he had better come in and do something about it. And that he did. He made a surprise visit the following Sunday and raised hell with the employees, even giving some of them their walking papers. He straightened things out and from then on it was smooth sailing.

As if things in Portland were not busy enough, my annual tour of the UK was still on my schedule…also my yearly jaunt back to Jamestown, New York and the Western Pennsylvania area to play shows along with Pete Pepke.

As of 2001 Dick Henzel retired and he and his wife Adrienne decided to enjoy life with their family and spend the winters in Florida. Therefore he gave up booking the Long Island tours, which worked out fine with me because I could spend that extra time at home with my band. Palm Springs was still busy for me playing with Terry and Dale at the Desert Horizons Country Club and doing shows with David Christopher at Lyons English Grill. And of course I was still burning up Route 10 back and forth, playing the Phoenix, Arizona area.

Sometime during the summer of 2010 I noticed a dull ache in my stomach that wouldn't go away. I went to my doctor and he took x-rays that showed nothing and he just shook his head and couldn't figure it out. Was it an ulcer? Another doctor thought it might be my prostate. Then, while vacationing at our lake home in Canada, I started urinating blood. After we got back to Portland, on September 10th I went to a very good urologist, Dr. Gregory Cost, who I liked and trusted very much. He ordered a CT scan and it was discovered that I had a malignant tumor in my bladder. I mentioned to him that that might be the cause of my stomach pain, but he said no. On October 29th, he successfully removed the malignant tumor and fortunately it was non-invasive. But after I recovered from the operation, I still had that dull pain in my stomach. Hell was around the corner!

Along with my stomach pain, I started to feel weak, generally not well, and I had a strange feeling in my lower body, along with a loss of appetite. We spent Thanksgiving with our son Jame and his family at their winter home in Bend, Oregon. Turkey dinner is one of my favorites and I could hardly force down a bite, there was just no appetite.

To finish out the year, Michael Allen Harrison, a brilliant Portland pianist, asked me to do a few of his Christmas shows with him at the Old

Church in downtown Portland. As I found out, Michael is a wonderful person, a class act and a true professional that I admire to this day. He presents his Christmas shows for most of the month of December every year featuring different types of musicians playing Christmas music to sellout crowds. He scheduled me to play shows on December 6th, 10th, 17th and 18th. I did play those shows and how I got through them I'll never know. Pauline had left for Christmas in Topeka early that year and I was alone. During the Old Church concerts I laid down on a couch as much as I could, but I must say when it came time to perform I somehow got the strength to do it and the shows went over very well. On December 19th I did our annual Christmas concert for the Portland Dixieland Jazz Society with my band and I was exhausted. The next morning I flew to our home in Topeka to join Pauline, Bob, Stacey and the children for the Christmas and New Year's holiday. I was sicker than hell, but I tried not to complain even though the thought of food didn't sound good to me.

We came back to Portland to start out the new year of 2011 and it wasn't good. I was very ill with no appetite and we went to one specialist after another trying to find an answer. The doctors were absolutely without answers to my condition. It wouldn't be too long before I did receive an answer - and it wasn't what I wanted to hear.

In March of 2011 I was admitted to the Legacy Good Samaritan Hospital with a high fever. Pauline had packed me into the car and drove me to the hospital, where she had arranged to have a room waiting for me and bypassing the emergency room red tape. The doctors at the hospital were stymied about what the problem was, until they took a CT scan and found a terrible infection in my intestine that had spread to the liver. All the other doctors that I had gone to were looking at a previous CT scan that had been read wrong so I had been running around with that infection in my system for all those months. I was a patient in the hospital for one month and I ended up getting a colostomy.

The very first day I was in the hospital my door cracked open and a very friendly face poked her head in and said, "Hi, I'm Sallie with Spiritual Care, may I come in?" It was the Reverend Sallie Bowman, an Episcopalian priest from Spiritual Care at the hospital. From then on I could count on her visiting me once or twice a day. If she could not come for one reason or another she would let me know in advance not to expect her that day. She became a great help getting me through all those long difficult days and weeks at the hospital and we became good friends.

She was later to become the Legacy Director of Spiritual Care and also an important part of my future CD, *Old Time Religion*. Sallie was one of the few visitors, other than my family, special friend Cindy Evans, and a few other very close friends, who were permitted to visit me because I needed plenty of rest. Besides that, there wasn't much room for visitors anyway, with all the doctors that were in and out all day; it was like a medical convention.

After being discharged from the hospital I had to wear a bag after having the colostomy operation. On top of that, because I was in bed for a month, I was very weak and needed constant assistance. The doctors wanted me to recuperate at a nursing home, but Pauline would have none of that. She left her part-time job and made me her full-time job. I could never have done it without her. It was a long rehabilitation and it even hurt my lungs when I tried to play my clarinet. But after a few weeks of support from Pauline and many friends I was able to function again. The bag I was wearing was not much fun but not as bad as one might think after you realized that it is part of your life and you had to make the best of it. I was able to start playing jobs again and even played my annual automobile dealers four-day party on the Oregon coast. After six months of living with my bag I was able to have the operation reversed, and following five hours of surgery I was put back together again. This meant starting my rehabilitation all over again, but at least I was rid of my old friend, the bag. I slowly returned to my old activities and even finished a CD recording project I had been working on, *Memories*, recording four songs.

I've had so many places where I loved to visit and perform that it is hard to pick a favorite, but Wales was certainly on the top of the list. Pauline and I always received a wonderful reception there and the Welsh people couldn't have been nicer to us. What was to be my last tour of Wales ended in Swansea, playing for the jazz club there and promoted by our friend, David Griffith. David always had kind words to say about me in his articles in the newspapers, which always helped to bring out a large crowd at my performances.

On the morning of my performance day in Swansea the phone rang and it was David Griffith, asking Pauline and me to join him for lunch at a fish and chips restaurant overlooking the ocean. David said that the cliff side view of the ocean was beautiful and it was known as Worms Head. It was always my routine when I was touring and playing with a new and different band each night to relax in my hotel room, eat in and put together and plan my program for my evening show. Being that it was David Griffith, I decided to change my habit and accept his invitation for lunch; he said he would pick us up at the hotel shortly before noon.

We arrived at Worms Head and David was right; along with a gorgeous sunny day, the view was spectacular. There was a beautiful grassy meadow leading down to a cliff that overlooked a very calm and blue ocean along with several sheep and horses grazing. Before having our lunch, the three of us decided to take the short walk down through the meadow to the cliff to get a better view of the scenery below. We walked down a well- traveled path towards the cliff, when for no reason at all, I broke away from Pauline and David, walking to my left in a different direction.

I strolled along for several yards and glanced over at Pauline and David still walking on their own towards the cliff, not missing me as yet. Then I stopped dead in my tracks when I started to feel a sensation I had never experienced before. It was a feeling of warmth and happiness that started to take over my body to the point where I felt that I was glowing. The only way I can really describe it is to take the best day of your life and magnify it 100 times. I tried to understand what was going on, but whatever it was I didn't want it to stop. I just stood there looking up into the sky and taking in all this wonderful wellness I was feeling.

As I said, it was a bright sunny day at noon time with a few lazy scattered white clouds floating about. It couldn't have been more beautiful, but I was wrong because as I was standing there in this wonderful lovingly warmth, the bright blue sky began to change into an assorted array of swirling and pulsating colors. Every color of the rainbow, and more, sailing through the sky and blending with each other to make more new colors. I was watching a spectacular event in the sky that was absolutely breathtaking. And then I got the feeling that I was weightless and could float up to the heavens at my will. I now realized that I was in the presence of God.

I was obviously being blessed by the Holy Spirit. There was no language spoken, but there was no need for it, just a warm feeling of love and the assurance that all was well. I had the feeling that the Holy Spirit's purpose was to let me know without a shadow of a doubt of his existence. Time seemed to stand still as did everything around me, including the people in the meadow, the horses and sheep grazing. I felt like my body was still aglow and along with the gorgeous, swirling, beautiful pulsating colors in the heavens, I never wanted it to stop

But then, just as quickly as it started, the sky slowly returned to normal, as did the wonderful feeling that I was experiencing in my body. I didn't want this experience to ever end, but I knew it had to. The Holy

Spirit had paid me a visit and let me know of His presence. I'm sure I was like most people who questioned or doubted the existence of God in my life. Now I could put those doubts aside forever and tell anybody willing to listen about my experience that early afternoon on the coast of Wales.

Once I regained my composure, I quickly caught up with Pauline and David. Maybe I wasn't the only one who experienced this holy visit from God; was it a blanket blessing? I asked Pauline if anything out of the ordinary had happened to her and she said, No, what you are talking about. I told Pauline to forget it and I would explain everything back at the hotel. We had a wonderful lunch of fish and chips and mushy peas and returned to our hotel so I could resume putting my show together for the evening performance. I told Pauline the experience that I had and of course she naturally took it all in with great interest. Later, back in the United States, I began to tell a few friends about my encounter and some of the responses I got were – What were you drinking? One relative thought that I was pulling her leg and laughed like hell. So I gave up on telling my story except for those who were really interested. Besides that, it's very difficult for me to tell of my experience with the Holy Spirit, because it's so emotional.

My son Jame often approached me with the idea that I should make a Christian CD. I know now that he was God's messenger. I listened to him because he was the one that insisted that I make a Christmas CD, which I did and it became one of my best sellers. However, the thought of putting together a religious recording sounded like a lot of work, with church choirs and huge arrangements. So I dismissed the idea and went on to record more jazz. Jame did not give up on me and quite often when we met he would again bring up the subject, and I would tell him my arguments against it. So the conversation was tabled temporarily.

On the top shelf of a closet in my office at home, I have a pile of music that has accumulated over the years. It's the music of jazz and dance tunes that I didn't need any more and the music I wanted to keep but had multiple copies of. I was working in my office one afternoon and for no reason at all I decided to purge that pile of music and hopefully get rid of a lot of it that was just gathering dust. So, standing on my tiptoes, I pulled the music down from the shelf and started sorting through it. Mind you, nobody knew about that music in the closet except me. I started sifting through it, slowly discarding music that I would never need again and also doubles of music I wanted to keep. As I got through about half of it I came across a sheet of music that I'd never seen before and it had no reason at all for being there at all. The tune was *"Ava Maria"* by Bach. Puzzled by how it got there in the first place and curious to what it would sound like on the clarinet, I grabbed my horn and started to play it. After I had finished playing the composition, Pauline called up the stairs, "Jim, that was beautiful, what was it?" I told her that it was *"Ava Maria"* and again she told me how beautiful it sounded. And then it hit me like a bolt of lightning! That's it! I don't need a church choir and a big production to play these beautiful holy songs. All I needed was Reece playing his beautiful chords behind me and for the gospel tunes I could use the whole band and vocals. Now it seemed so simple, but it took a long time to wake me up. But where did the music for *"Ava Maria"* come from? As I said, I was the only one that knew of the existence of that stack of music and I sure as hell didn't put it there. The only other person in the house was Pauline, who was unaware of that accumulation of sheet music in my closet. Therefore I came to the conclusion that it came from my newfound friend that I met that afternoon on the coast of Wales and that I was supposed to record a spiritual CD.

When I felt strong enough to tackle another major recording project, I called Reece and told him to hang onto his hat because we were going to record a Christian CD and it would require plenty of research and work. I talked with several of my churchgoing friends and asked them for suggestions of Christian songs that they enjoyed. I listened to many Christian recordings to get more ideas. "*Ava Maria*" was on the top of my list, and I called my old friend, Dick Henzel, who is a very devout Catholic. I told him that he'd be pleased to know that I was going to record "*Ava Maria*" and he said he was excited, but which one are you going to record? I said what do you mean? Which one? Well, it turns out that there are two versions of the composition; one was written by Bach and the other by Shubert. I figured that there was only one way to solve the problem and make everyone happy and that was to record both of them. I did just that and paired them up and recorded one after another. I got together with Reece once or twice with my ideas for the songs and the two of us ran through them. Reece then got to work on the music and sent the musicians involved their parts to play on recording day. We agreed on a recording date in May 2013.

I had asked Reverend Bowman to write the liner notes for *Old Time Religion*. She helped me through those many weeks in the hospital and we became good friends. I couldn't think of a better and more capable person to do it than Sallie, and she was delighted. I should mention that my time in the hospital and two operations left me with a slight tremor in my hands that would come and go. Needless to say, playing the clarinet during the tremors was impossible. I also have a condition called atrial fibrillation, or flutter of the heart. It's a type of abnormal heartbeat. The heart rhythm is fast or irregular or both. The greatest fear when this happens is a stroke.

May 14, 2013 was set for the recording date for *Old Time Religion*. We were to start recording at noon. Reece had one hour set aside for piano and clarinet to record the spiritual songs. At 1 o'clock the other five members of the band were to arrive and we would finish off the rest of the session. When I woke up that morning I could not believe it. I not only had atrial fibrillation but I had a bad case of the hand tremors. All I could do was hope that it would go away. Playing the clarinet with atrial fibrillation can be done but it is very uncomfortable and distracting. But the tremors - forget it - you just cannot play a horn when you have hand tremors. So what to do? I got up and showered, dressed, had a bit of breakfast, put myself and my clarinet into the car and headed downtown to the recording studio. After thinking it all over there was only one thing I could do and that was to cancel the session. I had set aside recording time at the studio and had six musicians coming in to go to work. Reece was waiting for me at the studio and I was going to tell him that it was off and then go ahead and call the rest of the musicians and hopefully catch them before they left the house to come to the studio.

As I was driving down the freeway toward Portland, I decided to say a prayer asking for help of some kind to get me through this terrific problem that I had on my hands. As soon as I said the prayer, within a split second the prayer was answered. My atrial fibrillation was gone and my hands were steady as a rock. I know now that the Holy Spirit decided to follow me through with this project. He certainly gave me enough encouragement to do this recording, including meeting with me on the coast of Wales and sending me many messages and messengers, but I was a bit slow to catch on. The Holy Spirit spent the rest of the afternoon in the recording studio with us. When I arrived Reece was waiting for me and the two of us recorded the spiritual tunes that were scheduled. The rest of the band then showed up and we finished the entire CD in five hours, an almost impossible task for a seven piece band. If you listen to this CD you will come to realize that there was someone else in the studio giving us an extra kick in the rear. The musicians on this recording are the best in their field, but on that afternoon they played just a little bit better.

All good things must eventually come to an end, and as I was growing older I realized that the end of my professional musical career was nearing the finish line. I still had a fairly good command of my horn but physically I noticed I was starting to be unsteady on my feet and it was difficult to get off and on the bandstand without fear of stumbling and falling. On top of that, it was beginning to be quite noticeable that the traditional jazz audience was getting smaller each passing year. Sadly, the diminishing audience was getting older, with few young people becoming interested in the music and joining in the fun, because traditional jazz is happy, foot-tapping music. Not only the audience was growing older but the musicians were as well. So, for the most part, at a traditional jazz function the audience was a sea of white hair listening to six or seven elderly musicians cranking out the music of yesteryear. I was one of those elderly musicians and when I saw pictures of myself, I wasn't too happy about the way I looked. Whatever happened to that young dark-haired musician that I used to know? I was beginning to understand that I had many more days behind me than I had ahead of me.

Through the years I always encouraged younger musicians and hired them in my band as openings occurred. Reece Marshburn, Marianna Thielen and Sam Folger, for instance, were like a breath of fresh air and probably added several years to my musical career because of their contributions to the band. They also became a part of my dream band that I was blessed with the last few years of my career, along with Dave Duthie, Pat O'Neil, and Dave Johnson. This was a group of musicians that played and acted like professionals. They dressed properly, showed up on time, drank sensibly and didn't play any head games with me. This was a dream come true after all the stress I had been through with musicians in my previous bands throughout the years. I thanked God for these wonderful people that I was privileged to work with and it looked like He was still giving me a helping hand.

An age-old problem with musicians is that they shoot themselves in the foot by going out and playing cheaply. This was becoming an epidemic around Portland and I found that even a few musicians in my band were playing jobs for little money. For years one of my band members made a habit of playing at a weekly jam session for free. I would pay him good money one night and the next evening he would be out playing for little or nothing. I didn't like this but I just looked the other way because we live in a free country and it was none of my business what someone did on their own time. Therefore, it started to be very difficult to compete pricewise with the other so-called groups of musicians giving their talents away. It was becoming very discouraging. Sadly, there are several musicians playing weekly club jobs for the same salaries that I paid 25 or 30 years ago. In other words, it was beginning to look more and more like it wasn't possible to make a decent living playing this type of music, and I guess that I was fortunate enough to be in the business at the right time and the right place.

New Orleans jazz, or as many people prefer to call it, traditional jazz, is fun happy music to both listen and dance to. It is very emotional and can give you a big high with its driving swinging beat, and bring you to tears with its haunting, lowdown blues. I helped to preserve this wonderful music by being a part of a group that formed the Oregon City Jazz Society over 45 years ago. Our little club went from meeting at private homes to the Oregon City VFW, Oregon City Elks Club, and finally the Milwaukee Elks Club. Over the years it took the time of hundreds of officers, volunteers and faithful jammers showing up to play one Sunday a month along with a featured musician or band.

The jazz society has had my band play several times. For the past twenty years it became a tradition for the jazz club to feature us at their December Christmas function, because of my albums *Christmas Clarinet* and *Holly Jolly Jazz*. We always look forward to this holiday job and it really puts us into the Christmas spirit by mixing Christmas songs with the regular traditional jazz tunes. It also became the band's annual Christmas party in the offstage band room during intermissions!

In 2014 I started to wrap things up. We had a short run at the Red Lion Hotel in their lounge with my eight piece band that included Marianna Thielen on vocals. The lounge was beautiful, with a wonderful view of the Columbia River and served generous servings of food and drink. We played the first Sunday of every month in the late afternoon and early evening. It could have been the perfect situation but the hotel management was having food and beverage manager and lounge manager problems, to the point where I was tearing my hair out not knowing if we were playing one month to the next. This affected our audience attendance greatly and the whole thing just petered out. If I was younger I would've made this work, but I just didn't have the desire anymore. One of the last jobs we played was my 80th birthday party at Tony Starlight's. It was a blast, a sellout crowd with cake and everything.

The jazz club, now renamed the Portland Dixieland Jazz Society, is still going strong with its dedicated volunteer officers and jam musicians. Trombonist Gary Powell, for instance, shows up early in the morning for every session to set up and run the sound system. And then he has to stay late until everyone is through playing to tear the sound system down and put it away ready for the next show. If you go to one of the meetings you are more than likely to hear reed players Rick Campbell, Tom Dechenne, Barry Benson and Mark Lindau playing away along with trumpet players Warren Dillon, Ron Hayes and Wayne Travillion, trombonist Gary Powell, and Kit Kune. Sharon Swenson, Janet Smith and Dora Gay Pelley are liable to be spanking the ivories on the piano along with banjo players Elwin Keil and Roger Stafford and bass men Jim Foster and John Hutt. Familiar drummers are Gary Smith, Elli Kuni and Bob Chase.

These are just a few of the people that have helped keep traditional jazz alive in the Portland area over the past several years. Although the audience has shrunk considerably, the pilot light is still on and just waiting for the right person or persons to come along and light the flame for the next traditional jazz revival. Who's next?

**Sweetbrier Inn, Tualatin, Oregon, Jim,
Jack Dawes, Reece Marshburn, Dave Duthie**

**Jim and Bill Schonely at Red Lion Hotel**

The Jim Beatty Jazz Band at Red Lion Hotel, Portland,
2015. Pat O'Neal, Reece Marshburn, Marianna Thielen,
Sam Foulger, Jim, Dave Johnson, Dave Duthie

Jim Beatty Jazz Quartet, 2016. Dave Johnson,
Jim, Reece Marshburn, Bill Athens

# EPILOGUE
## THE KING AND I

⁓

It took me just about three years to the day to write this book. It all began on July 4ᵗʰ, 2014 and I wrapped it up on July 3ʳᵈ, 2017. I knew that I would have to write this epilogue, but I wasn't too concerned about it because I was semi-retired from music and didn't have a hell of a lot to talk about other than working on this book for three years. But I was wrong once again.

In the spring of 2017 I got a call from my son Bob. "Hey Dad…I'm taking a sabbatical this summer and plan to visit some of the Balkan countries, including Romania"…want to come?". This is where Transylvania is, home of the famous Dracula vampire. I've always talked about how much I enjoyed going to the spook movies in Jamestown when I was a kid and watching Frankenstein, Dracula and the Wolfman. These movies fascinated me all my life and that spilled on over to both my boys. Boris Karloff, Bela Lugosi and Lon Chaney Jr. were familiar names around our house on Roosevelt Drive. Bob has taken it one step farther and has a mammoth collection of horror movies and books about the horror greats.

This sure was a tempting trip to commit myself to, but on the other hand Transylvania is a long way away. Bob mentioned the trip to his brother, Jame, and he was in 100%. How could I pass up a trip like this accompanied by my two sons? So it was settled; the three of us were off to the land of the vampires.

The date for our trip was set for early June, with Jame and me leaving from Portland on June 9TH; my 83rd birthday. We would fly to Amsterdam, Holland and then to Bucharest, Romania where we would meet up with Bob, who was flying in from London, England. After thinking about our trip I realized that Romania was right next door to Bulgaria. Why not take this opportunity to visit my old friend of 55 years, King Simeon?

I wrote the King and got a quick reply. He indeed would be there and he would love to see me and meet my sons. He said it would be great timing because we would be there for his 80th birthday celebrations on the weekend of June 16th. In my correspondence with the King I also mentioned that I would bring my clarinet along and play a few tunes for him and Queen Margarita like I did some 55 years ago in Nassau. Oh boy - now it looked like I better get busy and start practicing my clarinet. What had started with a funny Dracula tour had turned into a royal recital!

On June 9, Jame and I took our scheduled flight to Amsterdam, Holland and then Romania. We had my birthday party in flight along with drinks, food and a few hours' sleep…business class of course. We made our connections in Amsterdam and arrived in Bucharest, Romania and met up with Bob at our hotel.

We took a 2 ½ hour train ride to Brasov the next day and then a taxi to the *House of Dracula Hotel*, where there was a "Tomb Room" for dining along with a "Torture Room" featuring all sorts of terrible devices on display. Transylvania is mysterious and the natives there truly believe in ghosts and vampires. Our taxi driver told us he never goes to bed at night without putting garlic cloves on his door to protect him from a roving vampire. That night Jame and I stepped out on our balcony with a glass of wine to take in the evening air and found ourselves under attack by vampire bats flying around our heads. Was it safe to go to bed that night? We didn't have any garlic cloves with us but Bob came to the rescue when he took paper and pen and drew crosses and put them on our doors so we would have a safe and peaceful sleep.

The next morning at 9 a.m. the boys arranged for a driver to pick us up and take us on a tour of Transylvania. When I woke up I went to a mirror and checked my neck for vampire bites; all was clear. Our driver took us first to Rasnov Fortress, built originally in 1331. It was high on top of the hill and you had to walk to get up there. It was then I realized that this is something I should've done 20 or 30 years ago…I'm 83 years old for goodness sake! However, I went at my own pace and told Jame and Bob to go ahead and I would catch up. There was so much history there and once I got up into the fortress the view was spectacular.

The next stop was Bran Castle, where in its early days the horrible Vlad (Dracul), known as "The Impaler," was imprisoned. He was a terrible blood-thirsty monster of a man who loved to kill. Many years after Vlad was there the castle was taken over by Queen Maria of Romania in 1920 and in later years it went to her daughter, Princess Ileana. Bran Castle was high up, built on rocks and it was quite a walk uphill to get there…and then an even bigger walk when you got inside. There are legends and beliefs in vampires through-out Transylvania and this castle is what Bram Stoker had in mind when he wrote his novel - *Dracula*.

Our driver then took us to the town of Brasov, where we had dinner and spent the night. The next morning we took a train to Bucharest. It was then we realized that this was the country that John Candy and Eugene Levy must have gotten the idea for their characters of Yosh and Stan Shmenge. *The Shmenge's*, with their high voices and cabbage rolls, were very Romanian. We went out on the town that night to a nightclub with Romanian dancers in traditional costumes along with drinks and cabbage rolls; a perfect way to spend our last night in Romania.

On June 14th we went to the Bucharest train station and boarded our train to Sofia, Bulgaria. We were warned that there was no dining car on this train and we were to bring our own food and drinks. That was no problem because there were plenty of takeout food restaurants at the train station along with stores, so Jame and Bob loaded up with plenty of sandwiches, beer, and wine for the 10 hour journey to Bulgaria. It was a very comfortable train with large windows to look out at the countryside as we rolled along. We had to go through Romanian customs inspection and then after we crossed the Danube River, the Bulgarian customs.

We arrived in Sofia at 10:25 p.m. to a beautiful and modern up-to-date train station and then took a taxi to the Sofia Grand Hotel. After checking in to our rooms we went down to the lobby and enjoyed cocktails before retiring for the night. It had been a long, but enjoyable day traveling through the Romanian and Bulgarian countryside. The next day we had plans for a free day of relaxing and a little sightseeing in Sofia. Little did we know that King Simeon had other plans for us.

The first thing I did the next morning was go down to the front desk of our hotel and inquire as to the distance to King Simeon's Vrana Palace and the availability of taxicabs from the hotel. The hotel clerk immediately turned me over to a Sofia Grand Hotel executive, Kalin Korchev, who explained to me that he was in contact with King Simeon's secretary and that Jame, Bob and I, along with a few other of the King's guests staying at the hotel, were invited for dinner at Vrana Palace that evening. This took me by surprise because all I knew about was a reception at the Palace the next evening at 6 p.m. I said - are you sure? His reply was; "Yes... the King is sending transportation and you and your sons are to be in the lobby at 6 p.m." I was also handed a schedule of events for the celebration of His Majesty King Simeon II's birthday from June 15 – 18, 2017.

I high-tailed it back to our room and told Jame and Bob about the new schedule. We weren't even unpacked yet so we quickly opened our suitcases and checked the condition of our suits after our long journey to Bulgaria. Jame's suit was okay, as was mine, but Bob's was a disaster and full of wrinkles. Fortunately there was a cleaning and pressing service at the hotel and Bob called to have his suit picked up for pressing. Jame and I then became paranoid and had our suits pressed along with our three white shirts. We were all set for a dinner party with the King of Bulgaria at Vrana Palace.

We met in the lobby of the hotel at the appointed time and there were six or eight other guests doing the same. A bus then arrived with the King's royal seal on the front window: "The Royal Shuttle." We boarded the bus and found several other people, mostly couples, already seated as it must've stopped at one or two other hotels before picking us up. The Palace was on the outskirts of Sofia and it was quite a drive through the rush hour traffic. Eventually we turned into a long tree-lined driveway that brought us to the back entrance of the Palace, and standing there was King Simeon waiting to greet us. When we met it seemed like we picked up from where we left off 55 years ago. I introduced Simeon to Jame and Bob and he ushered us in to the Palace and introduced us to his sons, grandsons and granddaughters.

It was a very informal gathering even though we were in this enormous palace full of history. Simeon's wife Queen Margarita was there and immediately came over and greeted me. She wanted to talk about our times in Nassau and even asked me the name of the social hostess there, Auntie Louise Campbell. There were several people already there and sipping on wine when we arrived. There was one very nice friendly lady standing near me who I asked how I could acquire a glass of wine.

She said that's very easy, Mr. Beatty - you just click your fingers and ask for one, and I had a glass of wine immediately. I then asked her how she knew my name and she said that Simeon plays my recordings often when she visits. She then introduced herself as Crown Princess Margareta of Romania and introduced her husband to me - Prince Radu. I told the Princess that Jame, Bob and I had spent a few days in Romania (soft-pedaling the Dracula obsession) and took her over and introduced her to the boys. It was starting to look like this was going to be a fun party when the sliding doors opened to a big room and a beautiful buffet dinner of Bulgarian dishes.

I found Jame and Bob in conversation with a couple that turned out to be Crown Prince Alexander and Crown Princess Katherine of Serbia. As it turned out Bob had planned on visiting Serbia and the Prince and Princess told him they would have a car waiting at the airport and give him and his son, Alec, who was meeting us in Sofia in a couple days, a tour of the Palace. I then realized that all weekend we were to be in the company of King Simeon's Royal inner circle of friends. They were a group of people that couldn't have been nicer. They included, along with King Simeon and Queen Margarita, Queen Sofia of Spain, King Constantine of Greece, Crown Prince Alexander and Crown Princess Katherine of Serbia, Crown Princess Margareta and Prince Radu of Romania, Prince Nikola of Montenegro, Prince Andreas and Princess Stephanie of Saxe-Coburg, Germany, along with Prince Leka and Princess Elia of Albania.

Before we left for the evening Simeon had not forgotten my promise to play my clarinet for him and asked me to do it at the next evening's dinner party. This would follow his reception for 350 people at the palace from 6 p.m. till 8 p.m.

The next morning the Royal bus picked us up and took us to the Cathedral for a celebration of the Kings 80th birthday. The St. Alexander Nevsky Cathedral serves as the cathedral church of the Patriarch of Bulgaria and it is one of the largest Eastern Orthodox cathedrals in the world, as well as one of Sofia's symbols and primary tourist attractions. It was a beautiful ceremony conducted by his Holiness Neophyte, Patriarch of Bulgaria and Metropolitans of the Holy Synod. We then had a tour of the Sofia City Museum and then a five course luncheon at a beautiful restaurant atop of a beautiful Sofia hotel. The security for these events was incredible because of all the royalty and of course the three Beatty boys. There were paparazzi all over the place snapping pictures of the Royal families and probably going crazy trying to figure out who we were. After the luncheon the King told us we didn't have to be back to the Palace until 7 p.m., so we had time to go back to our hotel and rest and freshen up for dinner at Vrana Palace.

Our bus again picked us up at the hotel and when we got on, by this time, we knew everyone and they were all familiar faces. We arrived at the Palace to unbelievable security, including mounted policeman patrolling the woods around the palace grounds. There was a large line of hundreds of people waiting to shake hands and congratulate the King on his 80th birthday. It seemed like everyone who was anybody in Bulgaria was there, and they were dressed to the nines. There was wine served in the front grounds of the Palace for all the guests until 8 p.m. When the reception was over our inner circle once again went into the Palace for a private dinner.

When the dessert was served the King asked me if I would play for Margarita and him. I went to the front of the room and stood in front of the throne and played "Stranger on the Shore," a tune that was popular in 1962 when we were in Nassau. I then played *Petite Fleur* and then went into "Happy Birthday" with everyone joining in and singing along.

Remarkably, throughout the whole day of birthday celebrations, "Happy Birthday" had not been sung to the King, so when I started playing it everyone's face lit up and soon the entire room was singing. All my songs brought back many memories for Simeon and Margarita and the three of us sat down and had a long, friendly, reminiscent conversation when I finished.

We said our goodbyes to the King, Queen Margarita and all our new friends that evening. The next day there was a ride on the Royal train to the Cherepish Monastery and back and then a trip to the Kings Mountain residence. The boys had a bicycle trip planned and I was ready to rest my feet for a while after all the walking in Romania. It was a wonderful fun packed and interesting two days of Royal events and something that I'm sure that Jame, Bob and I will never forget.

**Vrana Palace, Bulgaria. Bob Beatty, King Simeon II, Queen Margarita, Jame Beatty, Jim. June 2017**

**King Simeon II and Jim in Throne Room, Vrana Palace, Bulgaria**

**Jame, Jim and Bob in front of Vrana Palace**

**Jim reminiscing about old times with King Simeon and Queen Margarita**

**Father's Day dinner in Bulgaria. Grandson Alec Beatty,
Grampa Jim, Bob and Jame Beatty. June 2017**

Gregory Porter, jazz singer, was asked if he could ever imagine that he'd be playing for the Queen of England. He said "Well, I couldn't. But my mom said to me, Gregory, your gift will make room for you at the table of Kings." I'm sure that it was the last thing in my father's mind when he gave me my first clarinet that I would be at the table of Kings, but to be fair, who would imagine such a far-out fantasy for little Jimmy Beatty. If my father ever did think about my future he probably thought it would be great if I followed his footsteps and got a good paying job in a factory and play my music on the weekends.

When I got that first clarinet, the first thing I did when I got home was to take it up to my room, open the case, and look at it with awe. I couldn't put it together because my Dad neglected to show me how. I guess he thought my clarinet teacher would take care of that. Nevertheless, it was probably my first valuable possession and it was all mine. Now all I had to do was to make pretty sounds come from it.

I took my clarinet lessons in a little room nestled in an office building in downtown Jamestown. It was quite a walk from where we lived, especially in those horrific Jamestown snowstorms. The first note I learned was - G - and to play that note all you had to do was hold the clarinet, not touch any keys or holes on the instrument, and just blow softly. When I mastered that I slowly added more notes to my memory until I could play enough notes to make a melody. I was so proud when I could play *"Twinkle Twinkle Little Star"* for my mother It wasn't the hardest tune in the world to play but it was a start and I always was thrilled when my mother asked me to play it for company. Everybody would politely clap and I found that I enjoyed having an audience.

My clarinet has taken me on a magical journey all over the world and given me the opportunity to meet interesting people from all walks of life. I found that I enjoyed meeting and talking with people in my musical journey from nightclubs to concert halls. I became friends with doctors, lawyers, politicians, royalty and even people with, shall we say, questionable occupations. It brought me my wonderful wife and family. And, of course I can't forget all the wonderful musician friends I have had over these many years from Wild Bill Davison and Omer Simeon to Pat O'Neal and Reece Marshburn. As time has passed I've lost a good share of my musician friends that I have had along the way, but with all the recordings we made I can bring them back by just putting a record on the turntable or even push a button my phone.

I'm often asked what country I enjoy playing in the most. That's a tough question because every country and people is special in their own way. As far as the jobs I've played in the United States, I do have a favorite: the yearly three-day event put on by the Portland Auto Dealers at the seaside resort of Gearhart, Oregon. It's called the Gearhart Business Seminar, but it's far from being all work and no play because it also includes a very competitive golf tournament. To make it challenging I have my band playing on the first tee while the golfers are taking that very important first swing. We also play the cocktail hour before the nightly dinner. And to get things off to a good start on the first morning of the seminar my band goes from room to room at 6 a.m. waking everybody up and giving out good morning drinks. This affair has been going on since 1925 and 2017 was my 50th anniversary playing the event. So when I say it's my favorite job every year - I really mean it. I've seen so many auto dealers come and go over the years but some of the old dealerships have been passed on to their son's and grandson's, with familiar names such as Wentworth, Lanphere, Meier, Fisher, and Tonkin. One year the Wentworth brothers said to me: "Jim - you would have been fired years ago, but you know too much"!

Looking back, it's hard not to ignore the fact that there was one hell of a lot of drinking going on all around me. This is true because I think I was one of the last of the vanishing breed of wild musicians that spread from the roaring '20s. When I started playing professionally and got into performing nightly in nightclubs, alcohol was part of the job description. And let's face it, hot jazz, cigarettes, whiskey and wild women just go together. If nothing else you had to drink to put up with the customers that were doing those things! However, for the most part I never let the drinking interfere with my work.

I also looked forward to my days off when I would neither smoke nor drink - a welcome relief. Our family vacations at our Sakinaw Lake cottage and camping trips with our trailer were strictly recreational with boating and fishing with the boys. Drinking was strictly a sociable event with family, friends and neighbors. And when the nightclub business came to a screeching halt in the late 1980's and I started touring the world as a featured clarinetist, my drinking became minimal because the spotlight was on me at all times and the last thing I planned to do was to make a fool of myself. Smoking, on the other, hand was impossible for me to stop, especially in the UK, where you had to smoke in self-defense. I eventually gave that up, but not until I was in my 70's! Many doctors have told me that, maybe ironically, my clarinet playing helped keep away lung cancer. I smoked a lot, but I also have been constantly blowing my lungs out for over 70 years. Looking back, I can say, it was fun while it lasted.

The last years of my life have been rather calm, cool, and collected compared to many of the earlier years. That's true because as time went on I got older and so did my musician friends and the audiences that came to hear us perform. Things have changed very drastically in music over the past years to the point where I hesitate to call what many of the bands are playing as music. You hear incredibly loud drums along with screeching, twangy electric guitars accompanied by a noisy tenor sax player spitting out notes that mean absolutely nothing. And we can't forget the smoke machines and the flashing lights along with the musicians flying all over the stage. The musicians very seldom are dressed nicely anymore. A T-shirt, a pair of jeans or shorts along with some dirty sneakers and they all set to go play the job.

But this is all okay because there is room for this type of entertainment and it's quite obvious that people enjoy it. My concern is that for whatever reason bands playing good music with beautiful melodies are hard to come by. New Orleans jazz has always been my favorite way of expressing myself but I also have enjoyed listening to country and bluegrass groups along with taking in the Mexican bands on our vacations in Mexico. They have such a unique way of playing just slightly out of tune on purpose that amazes me. And of course we can't forget the Symphony and listening to Mozart and Beethoven.

I've had the opportunity of lecturing in high schools and colleges around the country and was amazed to find out that the students knew absolutely nothing about early jazz, how it came about, and the names of the musicians who created it. But then again how would they know anything about New Orleans jazz when the high school band directors and college music professors didn't have a clue either. It was the same situation at the Jazz Academy that I taught at in Russia. But once I played records of the early creators like Bechet and Armstrong the student faces lit up and they couldn't sit still tapping their feet to the music. So it's simply a matter of exposure and until that happens things will remain the same.

Things seem to have gone full circle and I find myself in my garage with my old phonograph record player listening to my LP recordings that I bought as a teenager and have followed me in all of my moves. I put myself in a lovely peaceful mood just listening to Sidney Bechet playing "September Song," or George Lewis playing his soulful rendition of "Burgundy Street Blues." If I want to hear something red-hot I play Wild Bill Davison and Sidney Bechet's rendition of "I Found a New Baby." It's probably the hottest jazz record ever made. The music in my garage was a training ground for all the young musicians that joined my band the last few years of my career. In the summertime when the garage door is open the music floats around the neighborhood, beckoning the neighbors to come over for a beer or glass of wine and soak in the sounds.

As for me, if there's still an audience around that would like to hear me play, and I can get my musicians together once again, hell yes! So if you want to have a party and want some music, give me a call. I'm ready!

# ACKNOWLEDGMENTS

WRITING THIS STORY WAS ONE thing but getting it into print was another. To do this my son Bob stepped up to the plate and volunteered to wade through my bad spelling and grammar to be the chief editor. This was an enormous job and for this I can never thank him enough. Also thanks to my son Jame for his help and encouragement.

Thanks also goes to my buddy Mike Bays, who encouraged me to write the book and kept me focused during our weekly Monday morning meetings for the past three years.

I think Starbucks owes us big time!

And, I can't forget my good friend behind the scenes, Kirk McAfee. His help, support and friendship to me and the Jim Beatty Jazz Band has played a big role in our success over the years. He took my hand and led me through the very complicated world of computer knowledge. I am forever grateful and without him this book might have been written in long hand.

Finally, a big thank you to all the fans and friends throughout the world who have shown such appreciation and love for my music. I couldn't have done it without you.

**Jim and Mike Bays**